THE
ADVANCING
WRITER

THE
ADVANCING
WRITER
BOOK 2

PARAGRAPHS AND ESSAYS

■

Karen L. Greenberg

Hunter College

The City University of New York

■

Harvey S. Wiener, Series Editor
Adelphi University

■ HarperCollins*CollegePublishers*

Acquisitions Editor: Mark Paluch
Development Editor: Leslie Taggart
Project Editor: Katharine H. Glynn
Art Director/Design Supervisor: Jill Yutkowitz
Text Design: Circa 86 Inc.
Cover Design: Jill Yutkowitz
Cover Photo: Super Stock Inc.
Production Administrator: Valerie A. Sawyer
Compositor: Ruttle, Shaw & Wetherill
Printer and Binder R. R. Donnelley & Sons Company
Cover Printer: The Lehigh Press, Inc.

The Advancing Writer, Book 2: Paragraphs and Essays

ISBN # 0-06-500302-0

98 99 00 01 02   9 8 7

CONTENTS IN BRIEF

CONTENTS IN DETAIL

FROM THE SERIES EDITOR

The Advancing Writer series addresses the needs of college students who require a course or a series of courses in basic writing skills. Focusing on sentence, paragraph, and essay building as well as essential grammar and usage skills for successful revising and editing, *The Advancing Writer* provides a flexible yet comprehensive program for the beginning student writer at college. Each book in the series is self-contained, student oriented, and course specific; yet the three books together represent an integrated program in written language development. Philosophy, pedagogy, and design features unify the series.

Through this series beginning college writers will learn the power of language in confronting existence and the riches in transforming their private pasts into sensory language. In celebrating personal autobiography as a major force in the basic writing program, *The Advancing Writer* series recognizes that critical thinking begins with examining the self, acknowledging individual history, and thinking about language that connects one's personal reality to the larger worlds of school, work, and society. Yet, even though the writers addressed by these texts may not have fully explored their own linguistic power, they are ripe for challenge to their intellect and creativity. Unlike other basic writing texts, *The Advancing Writer* does not exclude intellectual and creative matters for reflection and analysis by taking a ''remedial'' approach; instead, it provides college-level tasks while showing students how to analyze the decisions they confront as they think and compose.

In each book, students start by examining their own attitudes toward writing and then move on to consider a variety of strategies for prewriting, drafting, revising, and editing. Although drafts of both student and professional writing are provided for discussion of content and analysis of form, students work mainly on their own writing, revisiting earlier drafts as they assimilate new strategies for revising and editing. Students learn to consider the audience for their writing through collaborative reading, writing, and revising activities that give student writers immediate feedback as they think and compose. The series emphasizes that reading and writing are both processes to create meaning, thus promoting a holistic approach to literacy and enabling students to see how writing can help them learn about and understand their academic readings. The practice of syntax, grammar, and usage are merged with genuine rhetorical goals; activities rooted in connected discourse make clear the relations between content and form.

Students and instructors who use the three-tiered program will benefit from the regular reinforcement strategies presented throughout. The books are recursive, building on concepts introduced earlier, or anticipatory, looking ahead to skills to be developed later on, or both. Each text can be used alone; but taken as a whole, *The Advancing Writer* series is a set of interlocking tools for improving students' writing at the beginning level.

Harvey S. Wiener

PREFACE

RATIONALE

The Advancing Writer series was created to meet the diverse linguistic and intellectual needs of today's student writers. Building on related theoretical, pedagogical, and design elements, this series offers instructors and students a systematic and comprehensive approach to writing. The instruction and assignments in the series represent current theory and practice in developmental writing and freshman composition. The instructional material and activities in each book build on each other in a recursive instructional format.

This book, the second in the series, is aimed at helping advancing writers express their ideas clearly and correctly by improving their abilities to develop, revise, and edit academic paragraphs and essays. The text accomplishes this goal by explaining and illustrating the ways in which writers' purposes and strategies and readers' concerns and expectations influence details, syntax, and grammar. Students are encouraged to try a variety of forms and strategies, to examine the relations between their choices and their intentions, and to cast their sentences in correct Academic English syntax and grammar.

Many basic writing textbooks address students as "beginners"—as students who have little experience with writing and who need "remediation." These books condescend to students by oversimplifying the writing process to a "nuts-and-bolts" activity that they can learn by following a fixed set of rules and steps. *The Advancing Writer*, on the other hand, assumes that students are creative and intelligent writers who simply have not had enough experience writing in a variety of roles and registers for a diverse group of concerned readers. Moreover, this book reflects the influence of current philosophies of writing and rhetoric, including social constructivist theory, reader-response theory, and critical thinking pedagogy. All of the activities require students to reflect on their writing processes and to use this self-reflection to improve their writing.

Hundreds of basic writing students have tested the writing activities and assignments in this book. Their responses indicate that these activities helped them examine, expand, and improve their writing processes and paragraphs. This book also affirms students' voices and multilingual heritages. The sample paragraphs and essays reflect the diverse experiences of students who value their own personal and cultural identities.

UNIQUE FEATURES OF THIS TEXT

Clearly the most unique feature of this book is that it is part of an integrated program in written language development. The emphasis throughout the series is on fluency, then clarity, then correctness. Ten other features distinguish this book:

1. *Every chapter emphasizes the importance of writing for personal, academic, and professional development.* The content and organization of the book reflect the belief that writing matters for self-expression, for personal and intellectual reflection and analysis, and for achievement of career goals.

2. *The book illustrates the full complexity of writing as a process that leads to a product.* It explores the entire continuum of the composing process, giving students practice in all stages of it. Detailed help with prewriting, drafting, revising, and editing appears throughout the text. In every chapter, instruction emphasizes that good writing is determined by students' critical analysis of their purpose and their readers' expectations. Moreover, each chapter provides students with opportunities to practice revising their writing for the most important qualities of good writing: focus, development, unity, coherence, and correctness.

3. *Collaborative learning activities help students think and act like writers and demonstrate differences in students' writing processes.* Students work together to read critically, to generate ideas, to respond to drafts, and to edit final revisions. Collaborative activities enable students to see writing as a social activity—to see the effects of their rhetorical and linguistic decisions on their readers. The many peer group activities in the book help students build confidence in their skills as writers and editors in nonthreatening contexts.

4. *The content of the readings, the writing activities, and the exercises comes from the "real" world—from the workplace, the physical and social sciences, and the humanities.* The book acknowledges that experiential description and narration are essential for advancing writers and helps students use their personal experiences to illuminate their academic discourse. The text provides intellectual challenges while simultaneously encouraging students to learn about writing from their own efforts to compose and revise.

5. *The text includes a variety of student and professional readings written by people from diverse ethnic and cultural backgrounds.* These readings serve as stimuli for writing activities, as models of different stages in the writing process, and as realistic examples of the skills students can attain. The readings also address problems that concern today's college

students and ask them to articulate views on issues that will define their
futures.

6. *Every exercise is composed of connected discourse.* The sentences in the
   exercises are logically and rhetorically related, enabling students to
   practice skills within the connected discourse of paragraphs rather than
   in isolated sentences. Writing instructors know how common it is for
   students to complete textbook exercises correctly, only to produce paragraphs full of the very errors that they had just seemed to master in the
   exercises. Part of the reason for this lack of transfer of knowledge is that
   the learning context of disconnected sentences eliminates the relation
   between content and form. In the exercises in this text, the practice of
   skills is merged with genuine rhetorical goals.

7. *Reading and writing are integrated.* Each chapter includes reading and
   writing assignments relevant to the chapter's thematic content and rhetorical strategy. These readings illustrate the various stages of the writing process and serve as models for paragraph and essay development.
   In addition, the readings are preceded by introductions that guide students through the text, and they are followed by "Discussion Questions" that send students back to the text for a variety of analytic purposes. These questions also ask students to bring their own experiences
   and understanding to bear on their interpretations of the readings. Thus,
   this book presents reading as an integral part of students' writing processes.

8. *The book helps each student develop a Writer's Portfolio.* Students practice different strategies and patterns for developing ideas and details,
   and they are encouraged to put drafts and revisions into their portfolios.
   They can read earlier pieces to see how much their writing has improved and to determine what they still need to work on. Indeed, writing
   activities in the portfolio section of the book often ask students to revise
   earlier paragraphs. The portfolio also enables students to reflect on the
   experience of writing different types of paragraphs and essays.

9. *Instruction in academic essay test writing as a writing situation has its
   own unique rhetorical and linguistic demands.* The chapter on essay
   tests and writing competency tests explains how to respond to short-
   answer questions and to essay test prompts. It describes the qualities of
   effective essay test answers and illustrates these qualities with examples
   from various local and state-wide essay tests of writing.

10. *Multiple checklists and visual learning aids help students examine and
    improve their writing.* Students can use the guidelines and questions in
    the checklists to analyze and evaluate their own writing and to help their
    peers improve their writing. The boxes, charts, and illustrations appear-
    ing throughout the book appeal to visual learners. Also included in

every chapter are ''Reminders'': summaries of the major points in each section. In addition, the end-of-chapter ''Points to Remember'' highlight important concepts and skills discussed in the chapter (and in preceding chapters).

OVERVIEW OF THE TEXT

As the organization of this text indicates, advancing writers need to begin from the ''top down'' with large elements (elaboration of ideas and details) and move to smaller elements (features of syntax, grammar, and mechanics). The text asks students to write drafts in the very first chapter, since it is pointless to begin the semester examining the parts of speech if students have not yet done any writing that requires using coherent sentences to communicate their ideas in writing.

Part 1 Principles of Effective Writing

The first chapter helps advancing writers understand the complexity of the writing process (and discourages them from doing the premature revising and editing that research indicates causes so many of the rhetorical and syntactic breakdowns in their writing). Chapter 2 shows students how to plan and write strong paragraphs based on focus, purpose, and audience. Chapter 3 explains the most important qualities of good writing, and Chapter 4 helps students revise and edit their drafts for these qualities.

Part 2 The Writer's Portfolio

The eight chapters in Part 2 are organized by traditional strategies or patterns that student writers can use to develop their ideas and details: description, narration, analysis of processes, comparison and contrast, division and classification, definition, analysis of causes and effects, and argumentation. The strategies are not presented as categories or forms of writing that students must select before they decide how to develop their ideas. Rather, these are the patterns of thinking that we all use to sort out the events and experiences of our daily lives. The portfolio section illustrates the ways in which these patterns overlap and helps students move from one to another as they try to communicate their ideas in writing. In addition, each chapter in this section offers examples of strategies for writing in different content areas and provides students with opportunities to practice writing across the curriculum.

Part 3 Essay Development

This section moves students from the paragraph to the essay. It helps them apply the essential principles of paragraph writing to longer pieces of discourse. It also provides students with a variety of activities for practicing essay introductions, thesis statements, and conclusions. Part 3 also includes a chapter on planning and writing essay tests.

Part 4 The Writer's Handbook

The seven chapters in Part 4 review principles of sentence structure, grammar, usage, vocabulary, spelling, capitalization, and punctuation. Also included is a chapter on sentence variety and style (including sentence-combining activities) and a chapter on academic paper format. This section presents syntax and grammar as a set of choices that depend on the writer's topic and purpose and on the reader's expectations. Punctuation is discussed in terms of its functions (rather than as a series of rules). The aim of the Writer's Handbook is to engage students in using their linguistic resources to expand their ability to write well in a variety of academic and professional contexts.

ACKNOWLEDGMENTS

This is yet another book inspired by my brilliant friend, colleague, and muse—Harvey Wiener. I thank him for sharing his talents and his time with me. He read the many drafts of each chapter of this book with incredible care and attention. I am also grateful to Jane Kinney of HarperCollins for believing in the idea of *The Advancing Writer* series, for making it a reality, and for introducing me to my talented co-authors, Judith Lambert and Peter Rondnione. I thank Leslie Taggart, my development editor, for her patience, energy, and diligence. And I hope that this book pleases my HarperCollins editor, Mark Paluch. He had great faith in the series and provided invaluable guidance in the development of this book. My thanks also go to the other key members of my HarperCollins editorial team: Laurie Likoff, Ann Stypuloski, Thomas R. Farrell, and Katharine H. Glynn.

In addition, particular thanks are due the following reviewers, whose thoughtful comments provided excellent criticisms and helped me improve each draft:

Norman Asmar, Miami Dade Community College
Barbara Beauchamp, County College of Morris
Mark Fink, Cuyahoga Community College
Eddye Gallagher, Tarrant County Junior College
Carin Halper, California State University, Fresno
Jan Hausmann, Southwest State University
Sandra Moore, Mississippi Delta Community College
Mike Orlando, Bergen Community College
Ted Schoenbeck, Cleveland State University

Burton Schweitzer, Manchester Community College
Ernesto Valdes, Miami Dade Community College
Betty Jeane Wallace, Sinclair Community College

I am indebted to the many friends and colleagues whose philosophy and pedagogy served as models for the development of my own writing abilities: Peter Elbow (University of Massachusetts at Amherst), Patrick Hartwell (Indiana University of Pennsylvania), Andrea Lunsford (Ohio State University), Lynn Quitman Troyka (The City University of New York), and Mike Rose (University of California at Los Angeles). I thank them all for their vision and their support. Of course I owe much to the thousands of students with whom I have had the pleasure of working over the past twenty years. And I dedicate this book to the memory of my best teacher—Mina Shaughnessy.

Finally, I must thank James and Sandra Sabella for making sure that I had time to write this book and Marvin A. Miller, reference librarian at the Oceanside Public Library, who found every elusive excerpt I needed. I am also grateful to Allan Brick, Chair of the English Department at Hunter College, for giving me space, time, and endless encouragement. And, as always, I thank my husband Kenneth and our son, Evan, for their patience and their love.

Karen L. Greenberg

THE ADVANCING WRITER SERIES

Editor: **Harvey Wiener** Adelphi University

BOOK 1

SENTENCES AND PARAGRAPHS

ISBN: 0-06-500301-2

Karen L. Greenberg
Hunter College,
City University of New York

Peter Rondinone
La Guardia College,
City University of New York

BOOK 2

PARAGRAPHS AND ESSAYS

ISBN: 0-06-500302-0

Karen L. Greenberg
Hunter College,
City University of New York

BOOK 3

READING AND WRITING ESSAYS

ISBN: 0-06-500303-9

Judith R. Lambert
Richland College

Informed by current theory and research on developmental writing, this exciting new series actively engages students in each stage of the writing process. These comprehensive texts cover all the basics of writing from sentence-level skills to composing the essay while incorporating contemporary teaching strategies, peer collaboration exercises, and grammar in the context of writing. Multicultural readings and student writing are included as bridges from personal to academic writing.

These books were developed as a series right from the start. Instructors can use the one that suits their course level, or all three for consistency across their basic writing program.

from Book 1

Finally, imagine a totally different audience: business people who were considering opening a bookstore in your town or city. What examples should you discuss if you were trying to convince these business people to open their store in your town?

How do the details that you listed to support this topic sentence *differ*

for the three different audiences _____

_____

_____

_____

Here are some questions to consider as you develop ideas and details to support your topic sentence.

QUESTIONS TO ASK YOURSELF ABOUT YOUR PURPOSE AND AUDIENCE _____

Who exactly am I writing for? Who would be interested in reading this paragraph?

- What are these readers like?
- How similar are they to me? Would they react as I do?
- Do I want to share my thoughts and feelings with them?
- Do I want to explain something to them?
- Do I want to persuade my readers to think or to feel or to do something? What? Why?
- How much do my readers already know about my topic?
- What else do they need to know about this topic?

REMINDER: _____

Good writing may have several purposes. When you w
you may also be expressing your feelings and/or trying to
ers to do or to feel or to think something.

from Book 2

Take notes as the person responds. Repeat this activity with several different readers. Then reconsider the focus, purpose, and audience for the draft and decide which of your readers' suggestions you should include in your revision. Revise the paragraph as many times as you need to in order to accomplish your purpose in writing it.

A Revision Springboard: Branching. If you decide that your draft needs additional supporting details, you can try freewriting, brainstorming, and clustering to develop new insights, ideas and details. In addition, you might try doing a form of clustering called branching to evaluate your details and to generate new ideas for your revision. *Branching* is a form of critical thinking that enables writers to analyze the relations among their ideas and details.

BRANCHING A DRAFT TO SEE PROBLEMS IN ITS DEVELOPMENT _____

Analyze the ideas and details in your paragraphs by doing the following:

- Write the topic sentence in a circle in the middle of a sheet of paper.
- Write each of your supporting points in its *own* circle and connect it to the main circle.
- Draw branches out from each supporting point and write in the specific experiences, examples, and reasons you used to develop each supporting point.
- Evaluate each supporting point by asking yourself whether it is clearly related to the topic sentence and is explained in enough specific detail.
- Cross out irrelevant details.
- Develop new details for the circles that do not have enough branches (enough supporting details).

Branching lets you see exactly where you do not have enough supporting details. Here is an example of a student's use of branching to determine whether a draft was developed effectively. The final version of this draft (which appeared on pages – and – in Chapter 2) is printed after the branched analysis.

1st Draft: My First College Registration

My first registration for courses at Valley Central College was a nightmare. I didn't have all the forms I needed. I was very nervous about registering. When I went to registration, the woman behind the desk told

Writing Process Emphasis

This series explores the full **writing process.** Maintaining a focus on the final product, these texts give students detailed help with prewriting, drafting, revising, and editing strategies. Book 1 emphasizes grammar and sentence-level writing. Book 2 concentrates on writing paragraphs.

Book 3 is a rhetorical reader featuring student and professional essays.

`from Book 3`

Responding by Writing

1. Acts of courage come in all sizes. Since the quality of courage is one we all admire, tell a story of personal courage. It may be your own or one you witnessed. It may be physical, mental, or emotional courage. Write for your classmates so they can experience the event as you did, not as disinterested spectators.
2. Tell the story of the bus incident that led to Rosa Parks' arrest from the viewpoint of the bus driver, the white man who didn't have a seat, or another black passenger. How might the event have looked from their eyes? What would they have felt and thought?
3. Create an imaginary dialogue between you and Parks or between Parks and the courageous person you described in question 1. Remember to begin a new paragraph each time the speaker changes and to use quotation marks around each speaker's words.
4. In reporting the story of her research, Ragghianti creates a portrait of her heroine Rosa Parks. Is this an effective portrait of courage? Why or why not? Remember to evaluate the article, not Rosa Parks herself. You might talk about the author's interviews with several people, her selection of Parks' past and present activities, her use of dialogue, the physical description of Parks, her use of historical facts, or anything else that makes this effective or not effective as a portrait of courage.

Momma, the Dentist, and Me

by Maya Angelou

Maya Angelou is best known for her book *I Know Why the Caged Bird Sings,* which is one of four books that make up her autobiography. Her life is the story of joyful triumph over hardship. In this excerpt from *I Know Why the Caged Bird Sings,* Angelou narrates two versions of the same incident with Momma, who is her grandmother.

Thinking Before You Read

Have you ever been treated badly by someone whose service you needed — perhaps a car salesman, personnel in a doctor's office or clinic, a teacher or other personnel in a school, a policeman or other person of authority? Write about that incident in your Idea Bank. Tell what happened

Expanding Your Vocabulary from Reading

excruciating (1) intensely painful
penance (1) payment for a sin, act performed to show sorr

`from Book 3`

Peer Collaboration

Peer collaboration discussions ask students to work together to generate ideas, respond to drafts, and to help edit final revisions.

help you at the current stage of drafting. Your feedback will be only as good as the questions you ask of your readers.

Your questions and concerns about your draft can help a reader look for new possibilities in a draft. First, check your understanding of the assignment (or writing situation, if you are writing for work or personal reasons). Then decide what questions and concerns you have about your draft and inform the reader about them. You should also let your reader know where you are in the writing process. Are you just getting started? Do you know some things you want to write about but can't find a focus or main point? Does the reader see your main point or thesis? Here are some questions whose answers are usually helpful to writers. They are based on the five qualities of good writing and a priority of concerns. Don't overwhelm your reader with too many questions. Choose several whose answers would help you take your draft to the next stage.

Asking for Helpful Feedback

1. Am I on the right track? Am I addressing the assignment?
2. What do you think is my thesis (main point)?
3. Have I written appropriately for my intended audience?
4. What are the strengths of this draft?
5. Is every part well-developed? Are there enough details and examples?
6. Are there any confusing or missing parts?
7. Do all of the parts have a clear connection to the thesis?
8. Is the essay well organized? Is the organization obvious to the reader?
9. What are two or three things I could do to take this draft to the next stage?

Writers are rarely helped by yes and no or right and wrong answers to these questions. If you are giving feedback, write two or three sentences to answer them. Notice that some of them can be answered by paraphrasing parts of the draft or by asking questions or by making suggestions. Even a question seems to call for a yes or no answer, such as "Am I addressing the assignment?" expand on your answer. A description of what you see the writer doing or saying is more helpful than a one-word answer to a question. For example, you have been assigned to write about a lesson you learned as a child and to use examples to explain your thesis. After reading your draft, a reader might write, "You wrote about learning to hide your Hispanic origins because of discrimination. I counted four examples." You could tell from this comment if what is coming through to your reader is what you meant. If it is not, you would know that you need to revise.

In Chapters 1 and 2, you learned how to plan and write discovery drafts of paragraphs. This chapter will show you how to evaluate, revise, and edit your drafts for the most important qualities of good writing. These qualities are described in the chart that follows.

FIVE IMPORTANT QUALITIES OF GOOD WRITING
1. Good writing has a *focus:* Each paragraph has a clear main point or topic sentence.
2. Good writing has adequate *development:* Each paragraph supports the main point with enough specific details.
3. Good writing has *unity:* Each paragraph sticks to its main point.
4. Good writing has *coherence:* Each paragraph is organized logically and flows smoothly.
5. Good writing is *correct:* Each paragraph has complete sentences that are relatively error-free.

Five Qualities of Good Writing

An emphasis on **Five Qualities of Good Writing** in every book helps students remember the important features of good writing: **"Focus," "Development," "Unity," "Coherence,"** and **"Correctness."** Student written samples are included to illustrate effective and ineffective writing.

Begin revising by looking for strengths in your writing—for sentences and words that you really like. Try to figure what you did to achieve these effective parts so that you can improve the weak parts. Here are additional strategies for revising:

- Ask a friend, relative, or classmate to respond to your paper.
- Reread your details: Did you provide enough relevant, specific details to support your main point?
- Add new ideas, details, and descriptive words.
- Cross out ideas, sentences, and words that do not sound logical or interesting or that are not clearly related to your main point.
- Cross out sentences or words that are repetitious.
- Use circles and arrows to indicate how sentences or words should be reorganized.
- Use scissors and tape to cut out sentences or ideas and move them to different places in the draft.

The first strategy—asking for feedback from readers—is the most important one. If you want to see how professional writers use this strategy, get a copy of the film *All the President's Men* (about the Water[...] brought down the Nixon administration). This film profile[...] sional writers work. In one scene, one writer (played by Du[...] ishes a draft of a newspaper story and puts it in a bin for pu[...] writer (played by Robert Redford) walks by the bin, picks u[...] it, and begins making changes in the story. When the Hoffm[...]

Writer's Portfolio

Books 1, 2 and 3 include a **Writer's Portfolio** that covers the rhetorical modes, always with a consideration of the writing situation, audience, and purpose.

For a business course in personal finance, you might be asked to keep a list of your expenditures and create categories for a budget. Division and classification is a way of organizing and simplifying diverse behaviors, information, or ideas.

ORGANIZING DIVISION AND CLASSIFICATION ESSAYS

There are many ways to divide and classify any collection of facts, ideas, items, behaviors, or expenditures. However, the categories should be consistent and exclusive. Consistency means that you decide on one system, or determining principle, for dividing and classifying and stick with it. To classify kinds of desserts, you could use the categories pies, cakes, cookies, but not pies, cakes, and chocolate because "chocolate" is a flavor and the others are not. Exclusivity means categories should not overlap. Each category should be distinct from other categories. To classify kinds of tippers in a restaurant, you could use the categories men and women, but not men, women, and business men because the category "business men" overlaps with the category "men" and excludes business women.

When using categories to make a point, writers usually announce their thinking and organizing pattern with a sentence, such as "Oppressed people deal with their oppression in three characteristic ways." Words such as ways, kinds, types, levels, categories, and groups are signals of classification and division. Writers may announce, for example, that there are "several ways to face oppression," "three kinds of discipline," "several levels of friendship," or "two groups of drivers."

Transitions. Good writers also follow an announcement of the division and classification pattern with clear transition words and phrases as they name and discuss each category. Here are some of the transition words and phrases writers use:

one way	the most	there is
the second way	the next	then there is
the third way	the last	last there is
the fourth way		

Writers may organize their categories from least to most important, from most to least effective, or from largest to smallest. However they order the categories, they help the reader stay on track by using transition phrases and by repeating key words or phrases. Here are sentences from an essay by Martin Luther King, Jr., about the ways of dealing with oppression. Several paragraphs with discussion and examples follow each of the categories in King's essay. The transition phrase if underlined; the repeated key words are in boldface.

Integrated Reading and Writing Approach

In all three books, an integrated reading and writing approach as evidenced in the **Exploring Further** sections encourages students to respond to each other's writing and to the sample readings. In Book 3, critical reading coverage carries this approach one step further.

REMINDER _____
There are many ways to end an essay. A conclusion often echoes something in the introduction–the thesis, a key word, an image, or an incident.

POINTS TO REMEMBER FOR WRITING AN ESSAY _____
• Use your Idea Bank or other discovery strategies to find main point to write about.
• Write a trial thesis and test it.
• Describe your intended audience and purpose.
• Write a discovery draft.

Although you should give your best effort at each step of the writing process, don't overinvest in your discovery draft. Trying to "get it perfect" may create writer's block. Charge through with a draft and be ready for revising.

■ EXPLORING FURTHER

1. Reread "Don't Press Your Luck" on pages 0-0 and the writing you did about peer pressure for Exploring Further in Chapter 1.
2. *Group Work.* Talk about the ideas that emerged in your freewriting or group discussions about peer pressure. What struck each of you as the most important idea about each situation? Take notes about your own and your classmates' ideas.
3. *Writing Activity.* Write a trial thesis for an essay about peer pressure. Use the strategies for writing a trial thesis described in this chapter.
4. *Group Work.* Think about who needs to know what you have written. What audience would benefit and use what you have to say? Parents? Elementary school children? Young teens? College students? Voters? Teachers? Consumers? What do you want them to do or believe?

   Tell your group what your trial thesis is (the main point of your essay), and describe your intended audience and purpose. Help each other test and clarify an appropriate audience and purpose. Write down your group's comments and suggestions about your trial thesis.
5. *Writing Activity.* Write a description of the audience and purpose for your essay on peer pressure.

   Writing Activity. Write a discovery draft of an essay about peer pressure in which you discuss the reasons for peer pressure and give examples. Draw on the ideas and examples of peer pressure you have read, written, and talked about. Name the person or writer whose examples you use.

C H A P T E R

4

READING FOR COMPREHENSION

In Chapters 1 through 3 you have been reading about writing. In Chapters 5 through 13 you will be reading selections from newspapers, magazines, and books. Although this is a writing course, reading, thinking, speaking, and listening are inseparable from writing. Because the communication skills reading, writing, speaking, and listening are interrelated, you can use your stronger ones to help improve your others. For instance, your stronger communication skill may be talking to others. You can use this strength to improve your writing by talking to others as you look for ideas to write about, as you try to find a focus for your writing, and as you revise. Because communications skills are inter-related, good readers are usually good writers and the reverse. Use what you know about writing to help you read better, and use what you know about reading to help you write better.

Reading and writing, as well as the other communication activities, are skills that you can learn and improve by practice, just as you might practice juggling or skateboarding, Like juggling or skateboarding, these communication activities are part mental, part physical, and part emotional. For instance, freewriting is a physical activity that stimulates the mental activity of thinking. Reading is a mental activity that creates physical changes such as in respiration, eye movements, pulse rate, and brain activity. All of these complex activities are affected by your emotional state-how you feel and what you are about.

Earlier you read that negative self-talk creates writer's block for many people, and you looked briefly at your own. You also read how two writers use positive self-talk to create positive feelings that allow them to think and write, and you considered how you can help yourself write. Reading, too, is affected by your feelings, attitudes, and self-talk. Since reading essays is a way of learning to write, let's look at some negative messages that make it harder to read.

Contextualized Grammar Issues

Grammar concepts are discussed in relation to how they affect students' writing. Sentence-level issues are covered both in the writing and grammar chapters.

In Chapter 6, you practiced writing in the "first-person" point of view (*I, we*) and the "third-person" point of view (*he, she, it, they*). Most process analyses are written in a form of the "second-person" (*you*) point of view called the *imperative* ("command"). The subject of an imperative sentence is always you, but the pronoun *you* does not appear; it is "understood." For example, when Group Work activities direct you to "Form a group with two or three other students," you understand that the subject of this command is you ("*You form a group with two or three other students*").

If all the sentences in your process analysis are imperatives, then your paragraphs or essays will sound like monotonous orders. To avoid this, try varying your sentence beginnings so that they don't all start with the verb. Here is an example:

ALL IMPERATIVES:

    To cure insomnia, go to bed at the same time every night, including weekends. Wake up around the same time every morning. Develop a bed-time ritual and use it every night. Drink a glass of mild before retiring, but don't ever drink alcohol, because it disturbs sleep patterns. Finally, stop worrying about your insomnia; that will only make the problem worse. You'll fall asleep way before you die from lack of it.

VARIED SENTENCE BEGINNINGS:

    Here are some tricks for curing insomnia. First, try going to bed at the same time every night and waking up around the same time every morning, including weekends. Since bedtime rituals prepare the mind to relax, develop a bedtime ritual and remember to use it every night. You might drink a glass of milk before retiring, but don't drink any alcohol because it disturbs sleep patterns. Finally, you should try to stop worrying about your insomnia; that will only make the problem worse. You'll fall asleep way before you die from lack of it.

The second version of this paragraph sounds less abrupt and more friendly and interesting than the first one. (For more information on sentence variety, see pages 122-124).

WRITING ACTIVITY 10

Write a "how-to" paragraph about one of the topics below:

    · Choose a college (or a university)

from Book 2

There are two ways to correct missing-verb fragments:

    1. Attach the fragment to the sentence that precedes (You may have to cross out the subject of the frag subject of the sentence to which it is being connec
    2. Add a verb to the fragment.

Here are two fragments, followed by each type of correction

Viruses as deadly as bacteria. Are responsible for many human diseases.

    1. *Attach the fragments to form a sentence:*

        Viruses as deadly as bacteria are responsible for many human diseases.

    2. *Add a verb to each fragment:*

        Viruses are as deadly as bacteria. They are responsible for many human diseases.

Cowpox, a virus that can have painful effects on milk cows. Does not have serious effects on humans.

    1. Cowpox, a virus that can cause painful effects on milk cows, does not have serious effects on humans.
    2. Cowpox is a virus that can have painful effects on milk cows. It does not have serious effects on humans.

from Book 2

WRITING ACTIVITY 3

Underline the fragment in each set of word groups below. Then use one of the two methods noted above to correct each fragment. The first one has been done both ways as an example.

    1. The videotape is a fairly recent invention. *Only about seventy years old.*
    2. The idea of storing information on a magnetic tape first occurred to Valdemar Poulson. A famous Danish scientist.
    3. The videotape that Poulson created. It was a band of stretched plastic.
    4. The plastic covered by a film of magnetic iron oxide.
    5. The iron oxide has tiny particles in it. Particles with the ability to carry an electric current.
    6. A magnetic recording head emits electric signals. These signals, which change the currents in the iron oxide particles.

Grammar Exercises

All exercises are composed of **connected discourse**: sentences (or paragraphs) that are thematically related. This puts grammar skills in the context of rhetorically sound writing. Exercise topics reflect multicultural sensitivity and span the curriculum.

WRITING AND EDITING LOG

Each time your instructor returns a piece of your writing — in your writing course and in every other course—make notes about the piece in this log. You will be able to chart progress and to identify areas that need further improvement.

_____

Date _____ Course _____

Title of Paper _____

Strengths:

Problems and Errors:

Writing Process Log and Teacher Conference Log

These logs provide an easy format for recording the progress of students' writing.

`from Book 2`

WRITING ACTIVITY 9

Brainstorm for five minutes about your favorite place. Write everything down that comes to your mind. If you get stuck, ask yourself the questions on page xx.

GROUP WORK 4

Form a brainstorming group and — together — choose a problem concerning your school (for example, the registration process, placement tests, class size, or student fees). Choose one person to be the group recorder. Then take turns calling out ideas about the problem and solutions for it. Jot down a brief note about every solution that you and your classmates call out. If the group gets stuck, the recorder should read aloud the questions on page xx. When the group finishes, each person should discuss the solution he or she thinks would best solve the problem.

`from Book 1`

WRITING ACTIVITY 10

Write a paragraph or two about the problem that your group discussed in the preceding activity. What is this problem? Why does it cause you (or other students) so much aggravation or trouble? What could the school's administrators, teachers, or students do to solve this problem?

Writing Activities, Writing Assignments, Group Work

These **writing exercises** help students develop and practice their skills and promote peer collaboration. Many are based on the readings and writing samples authored by students and professional writers of different ethnic backgrounds.

that explains the advantages of learning the process. Make sure that you tell readers what materials they will need to accomplish the process; also define any terms that they might not understand. Finally, explain each step of the process in detail and arrange these steps in the order readers must perform them.

`from Book 2`

✔ POINTS TO REMEMBER ABOUT PROCESS ANALYSIS

1. Make sure that your process is narrow enough to explain in a paragraph or an essay.
2. Keep your purpose and your readers in mind as you brainstorm the details for you process analysis. What exactly do you want them to know? What else might they want or need to know?
3. Make your introduction interesting and briefly explain the importance or advantages of the process.
4. Describe any materials or equipment that readers will need to perform the process.
5. Define any terms that readers may not understand.
6. Explain each step in the process clearly and in detail. Also, anticipate readers' confusion or mistakes, and explain what they should *not* do.
7. Use concrete descriptive words and vivid images.
8. Make sure that your details are logically organized— in the order in which they are to be performed—and that you have included transitional words and phrases.
9. Experiment with different conclusions for your narration. Choose the ending that suits your purpose better.
10. Vary your sentence structure so that your process analysis is not a curt set of imperative commands.

Learning Aids

All three books in the series feature learning aids such as **"Points to Remember," "Reminders,"** **checklists, charts,** and **boxes** that reinforce key concepts.

PART 1

Principles of Effective Writing

1

THE WRITING PROCESS

Writing well is a real challenge. Student writers often get discouraged with writing because it is so nerve-racking for them. They often don't realize that writing is hard work and that even professional writers find writing tough and frustrating. The novelist Gene Fowler wrote, "Writing is easy. All you have to do is sit down at a typewriter and wait for drops of blood to form on your forehead."

Many people not only find writing to be a painful experience but also believe they lack the skill to write well. However, good writing is as much a matter of attitude and process as it is of skill. Do you think that if you can just perfect your grammar skills, you will enjoy writing more and write better? If you do, consider the fact that a person can master all the rules of grammar and sentence structure and still dislike writing and feel that his or her writing is not very good.

This chapter will help you master the rules and skills of writing well. It will help you confront any negative attitudes you might have toward writing or your misperceptions of the writing process. Then it will help you feel more confident about your writing ability by showing you how to solve writing problems such as the ones below:

> I don't have anything to say.
> I have some ideas, but I can't get started.
> I can tell you my ideas, but I just can't write them.
> I know what I want to write, but I don't know how to organize my
>   ideas.

GETTING STARTED

Good writing does not flow magically from the pens of successful writers. Usually it is a product of extensive planning, organizing, drafting, and revising. Some successful writers spend hours thinking about a topic before they write a word. Others write a sentence or a paragraph over five or six times until they are satisfied with it. Writing will become easier for you if you think of every assignment as a series of overlapping activities:

- Thinking and reading about the topic
- Talking to others about your ideas
- Jotting down ideas and notes
- Using prewriting strategies (described in this chapter)
- Discovering what you know and think about the topic through the process of writing a draft about it
- Rethinking and rewriting the draft several times
- Editing and proofreading the final version

You already have all the skills necessary to accomplish these activities. Now you have to work consciously on improving them. Here are some suggestions for doing this.

Think and Behave Like a Writer. If you want to be a better writer, you have to sharpen your eyes—those on your face and the one in your mind. Good writers are always looking for interesting sights, behaviors, and problems and recording their reactions to them. In addition, good writers are always writing, especially to themselves. They set aside time every day to write in a journal, or an *Idea Bank.*

> **REMINDER**
> A journal, or an Idea Bank, is a notebook in which writers record their observations, thoughts, and feelings.

Start behaving like a writer today. Buy a notebook to serve as your Idea Bank and keep it with you at all times so that it is handy when you see, hear, or read something that intrigues or upsets you. Pay close attention to the world around you and record in your Idea Bank what you see, hear, smell, taste, and feel. When you face a problem, take out your Idea Bank and write down how you feel. Write about what the problem is, the causes of the problem, or some possibilities for solving it. If you see an unusual picture or read an interesting essay, story, or poem, copy it or cut it out and paste it into your Idea Bank. Then write down your reactions to the picture or the story.

Here is a sample from a student's Idea Bank. Note that the writer did not correct her grammar or sentence structure errors.

I read a great quote today - "all knowledge is born of doubt". Boy is that true. Kids and teenagers learn by doubting their parents and teachers. And by experimenting. I think science begins with people doubting each other and things. I doubt myself alot. I doubt others alot. What can I learn from this? What can I learn from my doubt?

Think of your Idea Bank as a journal in which you should write every day. Get into the habit of writing regularly so that the physical act of getting words onto paper (or computer screen) becomes normal and routine for you. Use your Idea Bank to loosen up your hand and mind and to understand that it is okay to write down your thoughts and feelings without knowing exactly what it is you are writing about. Recognize that your best ideas will probably occur to you *as you write.*

IDEAS FOR WRITING IN YOUR IDEA BANK ——————
Here are some suggestions for your Idea Bank:

- A memory and what it means to you now
- A significant event that occurred today and your reactions to it
- An unusual sight, sound, or conversation
- A person whom you care about deeply
- Something a friend did that surprised you
- A current fear, anger, joy, suspicion, or trouble
- An interesting poster that you saw recently
- A picture or photograph in a book, newspaper, or magazine and your reactions to it

(Continued)

- A quotation from a book, newspaper, or magazine and your reactions to it
- A comment made by one of your teachers
- A problem or an issue raised in a television program
- A poem and your responses to it
- A favorite meal or recipe
- A feeling about writing
- Something that you want to change about yourself
- A wish, dream, goal, or hope

WRITING ACTIVITY 1

Start an Idea Bank: Carry around a small notebook for recording your ideas whenever they occur to your. Write at least three entries in your Idea Bank today.

WRITING ACTIVITY 2

Choose two of the topics from the list on pages 5 and 6 and write at least one page about each topic in your Idea Bank.

Stop Criticizing Your Writing. Criticism is appropriate for the final stage of the writing process, when you have finished revising your draft and are ready to find and correct any errors. However, you will never get to this stage if you criticize your ideas, notes, and early drafts. Indeed, the best way to make sure that your writing *never* improves is to criticize it continuously and convince yourself that you can't write well.

Here is an excerpt from a student's Idea Bank that shows how self-criticism can sabotage good writing.

Man, I am so grossed out by the bathrooms in this school. Everything is covered in graffitti. Big red words like fresh blood. Red, yellow and green swirls ~~sto~~ melting together like candy canes. Is graffitti art?

Forget about it! Graffitti stinks even if its pretty, its vandalism. How ~~about~~ would these so-called artists feel if someone came into their homes and drew florescent green graffitti on their walls. What if someone wrote their name in neon blue blobs on their doors. Why do people do graffitti anyway? Are they that ~~des~~ desperate for attention, is that the only way they get recognition? I don't know. This idea is dumb. And my writing stinks.

This excerpt contains several ideas that the student writer could develop into interesting paragraphs and essays. Moreover, this student is behaving like a writer—noting her thoughts and feelings in words and using writing to make sense of them and the world. But she has a serious attitude problem. Instead of giving herself credit for her sophisticated thinking and analyzing, she criticizes herself: "Dumb." "My writing stinks."

Do you criticize your ideas and drafts? If so, you are hurting your writing process. By censoring and criticizing your ideas, you are setting yourself up to fail. Instead of criticizing your thoughts, concentrate on relaxing. Allow yourself to write whatever comes into your mind. Do *not* evaluate your thoughts—just get them onto the pages of your Idea Bank before they slip away.

WRITING ACTIVITY 3

What attitudes and habits are holding you back from becoming a better writer? Below are statements describing attitudes and habits that cause problems for many writers. Which ones do you recognize?

I don't write very well.
I get nervous and worried when I have to write.

I know what I want to say, but I just can't get it out on paper.

I can't become a better writer because I don't have a ''gift'' for writing.

I don't like to reread or rewrite what I've written.

I'm embarrassed to put my ideas on paper because I always make grammar and spelling mistakes.

I almost never show my writing to anyone but my teacher.

Do you have any of the feelings or habits in this list? What other negative attitudes toward writing do you have? How might they be interfering in your attempts to improve your writing?

Write a letter to yourself describing your writing attitudes and habits. Discuss how your attitudes or habits might be holding you back from becoming a better writer. Suggest changes in your attitudes and habits that might make writing more pleasurable. The next time you write something, try out your suggestions.

Try Out Different Strategies for Discovering Ideas. No one is born with a special talent for creating good ideas and sentences. Successful writers work hard at finding interesting ideas. They devote much time to listening and observing carefully. They keep Idea Banks so that they always have thoughts and feelings available to write about. They think about the minutes and hours of their lives, and they find quiet time to close their eyes, to reflect on events, and to listen to their inner voices.

One way to improve your creative ability to generate interesting ideas and details is to write in your Idea Bank as often as possible. To build the habit of describing sights, sounds, thoughts, and conversations in your Idea Bank, write in it for at least ten minutes every day. Choose a time and a place for writing and do it every day until it becomes automatic. This will help you feel more comfortable with writing and will provide you with a permanent record of your ideas and observations, a record that is always available to you when you need a topic or some ideas for an essay or another writing assignment.

WRITING ACTIVITY 4

Write in your Idea Bank for at least ten minutes about the word *writing*. Write everything that comes to your mind when you think about *writing*. Do *not* reject any of your thoughts. Do not worry about sentence structure or grammar.

In the preceding Writing Activity, you wrote continuously for ten minutes about anything that came to your mind. This kind of prewriting or limbering-up activity is called *freewriting*. It is a wonderful strategy for discovering what you are thinking or feeling and for exploring your ideas about an assigned topic. It involves writing without stopping: Your pen or pencil never leaves the page. Since you do not have to show your freewriting to anyone, you don't have to worry about correctness or neatness.

Freewriting is a particularly useful strategy for writers who fear writing or have a mental block about it. By writing without stopping (even if all you write is ''I hate writing'' over and over again), eventually other ideas will begin to flow from your mind to your page. The professor who developed this technique, Peter Elbow, noted the following about it:

> Freewriting is the easiest way to get words on paper and the best all-around practice in writing that I know. To do a freewriting exercise, simply force yourself to write without stopping for ten minutes. Sometimes you will produce good writing, but that's not the goal. Sometimes you will produce garbage, but that's not the goal either. You may stay on one topic, you may flip repeatedly from one to another: it doesn't matter. Sometimes you will produce a good record of your stream of consciousness, but often you can't keep up. Speed is not the goal, though sometimes the process revs you up. If you can't think of anything to write, write about how that feels or repeat over and over 'I have nothing to write' or 'Nonsense' or 'No.' If you get stuck in the middle of a sentence or thought, just repeat the last word or phrase till something comes along. The only point is to keep writing.

WRITING ACTIVITY 5

Freewrite for five minutes about the topic ''love.'' Write continuously about everything that comes to your mind when you think of the word *love*. Do not lift your pen or pencil from the paper (or your fingers from the keyboard) until the time is up. If you run out of things to say, write about how you feel about the experience of running out of things to say. The objective is to fill a page with words, impressions, thoughts, ideas—anything that comes to mind.

GROUP WORK 1

Form a group of three or four. Spend three minutes silently freewriting everything you can think of about the word *friendship*. Write your ideas in ''list'' format. When the time is up, each group member should read three words or sentences from his or her list. Your classmates' ideas will probably stimulate you to think of totally new ideas about friendship. Add these new ideas to your list.

WRITING ACTIVITY 6

Examine the notes that you wrote for the preceding Group Work activity. Circle the words or phrases that seem most important and draw lines between circles that seem related in some way. Then look at these circles and select any two or three that interest you. Use the material in these circles to write a paragraph about friendship.

Brainstorming is another strategy for discovering and developing ideas. Created by businesspeople to solve problems, brainstorming is usually done in groups. You begin by thinking about the problem or the topic that is your focus. Then each person tosses out an idea (and writes it down), and no one is allowed to criticize any of the ideas. The goal is to get as many ideas as possible down on paper, no matter how unreasonable or silly they might seem. If you are brainstorming alone, begin by writing down the topic that you have chosen or have been assigned to write about. Then list everything that comes to mind about it. If you get stuck, ask yourself the Reporter's Questions below.

> ### REPORTER'S QUESTIONS TO
> ### HELP YOU BRAINSTORM ━━━━━━━━━━━━━━━━━━━
> If you get stuck when you are brainstorming about a topic, ask yourself the following questions and write down your answers.
>
> - What do I know about this topic?
> - Who? What? When? Where? Why? How?
> - How does this topic make me feel? Why?
> - What are the effects of this topic on me or my friends?
> - What interests me about this topic?
> - What is my point of view about the topic?
> - What is this topic similar to and how is it similar?
> - What is it different from and how is it different?

Here is a sample of a student's brainstorming about the topic "the person you admire most." Note that when the writer got stuck, he wrote a few questions about the topic and his responses to these questions.

Magic Johnson

Brave and couragous idol

Admitted he's HIV positive   *Why?*

He'll be a teacher - a fighter against AIDS

What else?

Role model for ~~Black and~~ all teenagers
   (especially Black teens)

How??
   Preach about safe sex
   Put out booklets about AIDS

What else?
   Great athlete. Greatest living basketball
   Inspirational role model.   player.

How?
   Caring, loving husband and father

What else?
   He's larger than life - so famous
   Big, strong, smart. talented
   Humanitarien - helps everyone.

This student jotted down many thoughtful details. Which of these details do you think could serve as the basis of a descriptive composition? Why? What other details would you add?

_____

_____

_____

_____

_____

WRITING ACTIVITY 7

Brainstorm for five minutes about the person whom you admire most. Write everything down that comes to your mind. If you get stuck, ask yourself the reporter's questions on page 10.

GROUP WORK 2

Form a brainstorming group and—together—choose a bothersome problem concerning your school (for example, the registration process, placement tests, class size, or student fees). Choose one person to be the group recorder. Then take turns calling out ideas about the problem and solutions for it. Jot down a brief note about every solution that you and your classmates call out. If the group gets stuck, the recorder should read aloud the questions on page 10. When the group finishes, each person should discuss the solution he or she thinks would best solve the problem.

WRITING ACTIVITY 8

Brainstorm for five minutes about a problem that you once had—or are currently having—with money. When you finish brainstorming, circle the best ideas.

Another popular strategy for creating and organizing ideas is *outlining*—listing ideas by headings and indented subheadings. Making an informal or "scratch" outline of your freewriting or brainstorming can help you select and organize your ideas and make sense out of your seemingly chaotic notes. Outlining is different from freewriting or brainstorming: Writing an outline requires that you know, in some detail, what you want to write about and how you want to organize your ideas. For example, here is the outline prepared by the student who wrote the brainstorming list on page 11 of this chapter.

Magic Johnson
1. Couragous Idol
 A. Admitted he's HIV positive
 B. Will teach us about AIDS
 C. Will fight against AIDS

2. Role Model
 A. Will encourage minority teenagers to practice safe sex
 B. Will continue to work for charities
 C. Will continue to be a great husband and father

3. Larger than Life Hero
 A. Great athlete
 B. Best living basketball play
 C. Caring, giving person
 D. Dedicated humanitarien

Note that in order to develop the outline above, the student had to decide which items in his list to include and which to omit. Preparing this informal outline helped the writer plan and organize his details. Some writers find this process of turning notes into an outline very useful. It enables them to divide up their ideas and sequence them into a logical order.

However, other writers find outlining to be a frustrating task because they haven't generated enough details to begin thinking about sequence and order. Also, outlining gets some writers in trouble because they feel that once they have prepared an outline, they must stick to it and ignore any new ideas that occur to them as they begin to write a draft. These writers should not outline because it stops them from discovering what they want to say about a topic *as* they are writing about it.

Instead of outlining, you might want to try another helpful prewriting strategy called *clustering*. Clustering is a visual technique that helps you record ideas as they occur to you and relate these ideas in a logical way. Begin clustering by writing your topic in one word or phrase in the middle of a piece of paper and drawing a circle around it. Then do the following:

- Think about the circled word or phrase. What related ideas does it bring to mind?
- Write down a word or phrase to summarize each related idea.
- Draw a circle around each word or phrase and connect each circle back to the circle that inspired the new idea.

Here is a sample of a student's cluster:

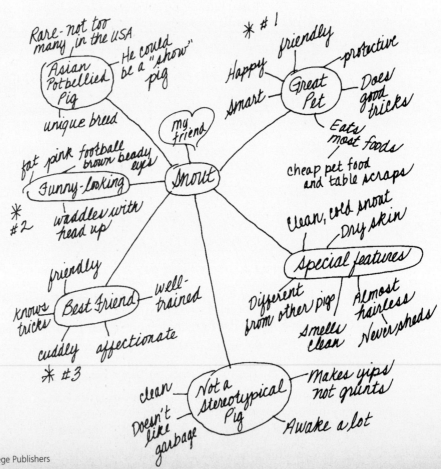

Clustering is a powerful tool for generating and developing details because it shows you the places where you need to add examples and illustrations to each circled idea. When you get stuck, you can return to the original circled word—or to any of the clusters—and begin a new cluster. Because clustering relies on visual prompts—circles and lines as well as words—it can help you see the interrelations among your ideas and details.

In the cluster on page 14, the student starred the three clusters that seemed most important to him, and he numbered them in the order in which he wanted to discuss them in his composition. Clustering also helped this writer identify the places where he needed to generate additional details to illustrate his ideas. When the writer examined clusters #2 and #3, he realized that they had fewer details than the other clusters, so he decided to add additional details to them.

WRITING ACTIVITY 9

Do some clustering about *one* of the following topics: "music," "trust," "sports," "teenagers," or "drugs." As ideas occur to you, write them down, circle them, and connect them to the ideas that inspired them. When you finish, put a check mark next to the cluster (or clusters) of circles that you might want to write about.

The circles that you check or star in your clusters are potential ideas for you to write about in your Idea Bank or in a classroom writing assignment. For example, here is the paragraph that the writer developed from the cluster on page 14:

Snout

After years of birds, fish, cats, and dogs, I have finally found the perfect pet—pigs. My Southeast Asian potbellied pig Snout is the best friend I have ever had, and I've had many animal friends. Snout is everything you could want in a pet. He's happy, smart, friendly, and protective. And contrary to what everyone assumes about pigs, he is NOT dirty. He doesn't root around in the garbage or roll in the mud. Instead, he waddles down the sidewalk like a proper little pet, head up, snout forward, and body swaying like a pink football. And Snout is very smart. He responds to commands better than other animals do, and you can teach him more tricks than you can teach a dog. Unlike other pets,

Snout knows exactly what he is and is not allowed to do. In fact, he is better trained than my kid brother. Also, Snout is quiet and calm and he's very loving. All in all, he's a terrific pet.

What did you like best about this paragraph?

_____

_____

_____

_____

_____

Reread this student's cluster on page 14. Which circles did the writer include in this paragraph? Why do you think he chose these?

_____

_____

_____

_____

Should the writer have included details from other circles in his cluster on page 14? Why or why not?

_____

_____

_____

_____

_____

_____

WRITING ACTIVITY 10

Do some clustering about the word *freedom*. When you finish, put a check next to the cluster (or clusters) of circles that challenge you most. Number them in the order that you might discuss them if you were going to write a paragraph based on this cluster.

REMINDER ——————————————————————

Effective writing begins with careful observation and listening. It also requires a willingness to discover what you have to say through writing in an Idea Bank, freewriting, brainstorming, and clustering.

Another strategy for generating ideas for writing is asking yourself *"What if"* questions: "What if computers could think?" "What if people never died?" "What if we could read each other's minds?" "What if the telephone was never invented?" "What if every American could have free health care?" Asking and answering "What if" questions develops your imagination and creativity. As you ponder the answers to your questions and visualize the consequences, novel ideas may pop into your mind. Jot down these ideas in your Idea Bank as possible topics for future pieces of writing.

Asking "What if" questions can also help you develop ideas for a topic that you have been assigned to write about. For example, below is a sample of a student's efforts to generate details about an assignment that asked her to discuss the dropout problem at her college:

What if I dropped out now?
    ↳ job (money)
        probably minimum wage
        never get a profession

What if my best friend dropped out?
        money? feeling like a failure (she
        already feels like she can't succeed.
        She isn't doing well.)

What if everyone dropped out?
Teachers would teach each other!

What if we didn't need college for a profession?
Everyone would have similar jobs.

GROUP WORK 3

Work with a partner or two classmates on this exercise. Together, write at least five "What if" questions for each of the following topics: (1) language, (2) aging, and (3) forms of transportation. Here is an example of a "What if" question on "language":

What if everyone in the world spoke the same language?

When you finish writing your questions, share them. Then discuss possible answers to these questions.

COMPOSING A DISCOVERY DRAFT

A *discovery draft* is a writer's first attempt at developing an idea in paragraph or essay form. You have already written discovery drafts in some of the Writing Activities in this chapter. As its name implies, a discovery draft is a rough copy in which writers discover what they know about a topic and what they want to say about it *as* they write about it. A discovery draft can be disorganized and messy because it is merely a first draft. Ronald Lunsford, a writer and English professor, writes this about his discovery drafts:

> I have learned that regardless of what I know about a subject, I often—most times—produce bad writing about that subject before I produce good writing. But I can work through this bad writing and do the necessary preliminary work when I have confidence that the "bad" writing is going to help me find what I want to say.

Is your writing process similar to Lunsford's? Do you produce "bad" writing as you struggle to figure out exactly what you want to say in a draft? If you do, keep reminding yourself that this is okay. First you need to discover your ideas before you can shape them into "good" writing.

Before you write a discovery draft, do some freewriting, brainstorming, or clustering about your topic. Then begin composing the draft by identifying the most important or interesting main point of your notes or clusters. Choose the notes or clusters that seem to illustrate or support this main point and rewrite them into your draft in complete sentences.

As you do this, you will probably think of new ideas and sentences to add to your notes. Don't be afraid to cross out sentences and write in new ones. Add details in the margins and connect them to sentences with lines, loops, or arrows. (Just make sure that you can read your own writing!) If you get stuck, read what you have written—from the beginning—and figure out what you still need to say about your topic. Do some additional freewriting about the last idea that you wrote about in your draft. Or stop writing and try to tell your ideas to a thoughtful person whom you trust. Sometimes talking about the ideas in a draft helps writers see them more clearly.

When you write a discovery draft, you are building and shaping your ideas and details. Harry Brent, also a writer and English professor, compares this process to sculpting:

> I tend to see my approach to writing as like a potter's approach to making something out of clay. I begin with the material, and then try to coax it into various forms. If one form does not seem to be taking shape correctly, I may try a different form. Or I may add new materials and let the project take another direction. Never do I start out to "develop an idea." I always build material into an idea. . . . I like to wander and let the point of the journey emerge.

 ## WRITING ACTIVITY 11

For Harry Brent, writing a draft is like shaping a piece of clay. What is writing like for you? Baking a cake? Picking a scab? Practicing a new sport? Write a paragraph that begins with this opening: "For me, writing a draft is like . . ."

QUESTIONS TO CONSIDER AS YOU
COMPOSE A DISCOVERY DRAFT _____

You might find it useful to ask yourself the questions below and jot down your answers. Use the answers to help you continue drafting.

1. What do I want my readers to know about this topic?
2. What point (or points) do I want to make about it?
3. Who am I writing for?
4. What do these readers already know about this topic?

(Continued)

5. What might they need or want to know about it?
6. What do I want to make my readers think or feel or do about this topic?

Remember that a discovery draft can be messy and filled with mistakes. Just concentrate on getting your ideas onto the page in a way that makes sense. Don't worry about a particular sentence or word or about your grammar, spelling, or punctuation.

Here is a discovery draft that a student wrote about the topic "a favorite place and what it means to you." Note that the writer did not stop to correct any errors in this draft.

My husband is a football nut. Every morning he grabs the newspapers and skims threw the sports pages. checking out the scores of the games he somehow missed watching. Then he reads the fine print. He reads the fine print about every football player and team. He can recite the names of every important player in the NFL and AFL. And he memorizes most of their playing statistic too. He watches every football game he can. Even the college games. We never go out on a Sunday afternoon or talk on a Monday night when the big games are on TV, when he watches these games he gets so involved that he screams and roars at the TV. Sometimes he curses the coach so loud that I expect the coach to turn around and tell off my husband.

I think my husband is adicted to football; he even talks about it in his sleep! And I am a football widow.

WRITING ACTIVITY 12

Write a discovery draft of a paragraph about one of the entries in your Idea Bank. If you can't make any progress, or ask yourself the questions on page 19.

WRITING ACTIVITY 13

Write a discovery draft based on the clustering that you did for Writing Activity 10 on page 17.

WRITING ACTIVITY 14

Write a discovery draft based on the brainstorming that you did for Writing Activity 8 on page 12 or the clustering you did for Writing Activity 9 on page 15.

WRITING ACTIVITY 15

Write a discovery draft on the problem and its solution that you brainstormed about for Group Work 2 on page 12.

REVISING AND EDITING

The more that writers revise their work, the better their writing will be. All successful writers know this. In fact, the novelist James Michener—whose books have sold millions of copies—once said, "I'm probably the world's worst writer. But I'm the world's best rewriter."

How do experienced writers shape a draft into a finished, polished piece? They reread the draft over and over, each time focusing on a different problem. In their first revision, they might look for ways of clarifying their main points and adding or improving supporting details. Then they might work on deleting details or words that are confusing or irrelevant to their point. In the next draft, they might concentrate on the organization of the paper, looking for ways to make the connections among their ideas and sentences more logical and clear. Finally, they check for errors in sentence structure, grammar, vocabulary, spelling, and punctuation, and they proofread for handwriting or typing errors.

This process of revising and editing is time consuming and difficult. But it often results in writing that communicates what you want to say clearly, forcefully, and correctly. Obviously, not every piece of writing that you do will have to be revised three or four times. However, any writing that matters to you deserves your attention and your effort at each stage of its planning, drafting, revising, and editing.

WRITING ACTIVITY 16

What are your reactions to what you just read about revising and editing a draft over and over? How can revising and editing your drafts help you improve your writing? Write down your responses in your Idea Bank or on a separate piece of paper.

SUGGESTIONS FOR REVISING A DISCOVERY DRAFT —————

First look for the strengths in your writing—the sentences and words that you really like. Try to figure out what you did to achieve those effective parts so that you can improve the weak parts. Here are some strategies for revising:

- Reread your draft several times, looking for strengths and weaknesses in your ideas and organization.
- Reread your draft aloud to hear the way you arranged sentences and used words.
- Ask a friend, relative, or classmate to respond to your draft.
- Reread your details: Did you provide enough relevant, specific details to support your main point?
- Add new ideas, details, and descriptive words.
- Cross out or delete ideas, sentences, and words that do not sound logical, relevant, or interesting.
- Cross out or delete sentences or words that are repetitious.

- Use circles and arrows to indicate how sentences or words should be reorganized or block and move them on your computer.
- Use scissors and tape to cut out sentences or ideas and move them to different places in the draft if you are working from hard copy.

The next few pages illustrate a student's attempt to write a paragraph about the topic "a terrifying experience." As you read this student's notes and drafts, look for the changes that the writer made. What did he add, delete, or rearrange?

Cluster

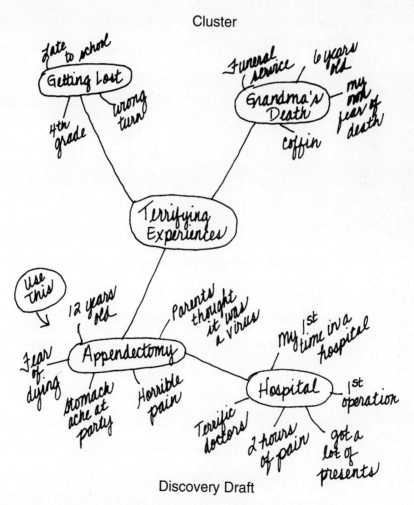

Discovery Draft

The first time I was in the hospital ~~happened~~
was when I was 12 and I had to have an appendectomy.

I was sick the day before but I really wanted
to go to Jenny Sciara's party. When I got home
~~I went to~~ my mom gave me ~~food~~ ^{biscuits} to calm my
stomach. In the middle of the night ~~I awoke~~
woke up screaming in pain. I went to the
hospital but they couldn't operate. I had to
lay on a ~~bed~~ stretcher for two hours. The
pain was intense, ~~I felt like~~ I really hurt.
Finally they gave me anesthesia and I finally
felt the pain ~~go away~~ subside. I start
sweating whenever I think about ~~the pain~~
it today.

First Revision

(Including a Classmate's Questions)

necessary?

The most terrifying experience of my life was (when I was in the
hospital) to have an appendectomy when I was twelve years old. ~~What an experience!~~ The day before it happened, I (was sick) with a slight *How?*

what else?

stomachache, but I really wanted to go to ~~Jenny Sciara's~~ *a friend's* party with my
can you describe it?

friends. By the time I got home, however, the pain in my lower abdomen

I think you need quotes here

was horrible. My parents said it was a virus and to calm down. My mom
gave me some tea and biscuits to "settle my stomach" and I went to sleep.
Describe it

But at 2:00 I woke up screaming with hot pain throughout my stomach. *Who?*

Either explain this or cross it out.

An ambulance took me to the nearest hospital but (they) couldn't operate
because the food that I had eaten the night before was still in my
digestive system. (I got sicker and sicker.) I had to shake in pain like a
snake on the stretcher for two whole hours. Finally, (they) said it was okay
Who?

How? to put me under and as the anesthesia started to (go in) my brain, I finally

only today? felt the pain subside. When I woke up it was gone. ~~It was amazing. The~~ ~~pain was gone.~~ But I will never forget it. (Today) I start shaking and

where? sweating whenever I think about that two-hour wait in the stretcher in that hospital.

I think this needs more descriptive words.

Final Version

The most terrifying experience of my life was the emergency appendectomy I had when I was twelve years old. The day before it happened, I had a slight stomachache and felt a bit queasy, but that didn't stop me from going to a party with my friends. By the time I returned home, however, the ache had grown into a throbbing pain in my lower abdomen. My parents dismissed it as a virus, and my mom gave me tea and biscuits to settle my stomach. I went to sleep, but I woke up at 2:00 in the morning with a knife of hot pain slicing through my stomach. My dad called an ambulance, which sped us to the nearest hospital. All I wanted was relief from the agony that banged like a hammer in my stomach, but the doctors could not operate until the food I had eaten the night before passed through my digestive system. For two hours I writhed in pain like a dying snake. Finally the doctor said it was okay to put me under. As the black fog of anesthesia started to cloud my brain, I finally felt the pain subside. It was gone when I woke up. However, I will never forget it. Every time I think about that two-hour wait in the stretcher outside the operating room, I start to shake and sweat as if it was happening again.

■ EXPLORING FURTHER

Here is an essay by Barbara Abercrombie, the author of two novels and several books for children and teenagers. In this piece, she discusses the importance of keeping a journal.

Keeping a Journal

For my thirteenth birthday my parents gave me a five-year diary. The pages were dated, so I always felt guilty if I skipped a day, or frustrated when I had a lot to report and not enough space to write it all down. For the most part, I filled it with descriptions of teenage boys—what they looked like and things they said and did—followed by rows of exclamation points. I gave up on the diary when I was about sixteen. Years later in a creative writing class I began keeping a journal, which sounded more serious than writing a diary.

Whether you call yours a diary, a journal, or simply a notebook, this daily record can be one of your most important tools as a writer. It's your camera, a place to record raw material for future fiction, poems, or articles: details of daily life, overheard dialogue, descriptions of landscapes, rooms, faces, weather, behavior. It can be as personal or as impersonal as you want it to be. There are no rules to keeping a journal.

If you've just begun to write, keeping a journal can be a way to establish the habit of writing regularly, though the words ''habit'' and ''regularly'' may seem contradictory to anything creative. When you're inspired, you create, and inspiration, as we all know, has no regular habits. Inspiration is the spark, the pressure to give form to chaos, and to put experience or dreams into words. Unless you're a saint or a genius, it's rare to wake up every day feeling inspired. However, when you force yourself to write in a journal regularly, even fifteen minutes a day, the act of writing can lead to inspiration.

Keeping a journal can help you learn about yourself, find out what you think and feel. Use it to discover what you really want and need to write about and the pattern of your highs and lows.

Your journal is a place to find your voice and tone, the true rhythm of your writing. When we begin writing, most of us sound self-consciously literary and stiff, or chatty and sometimes a bit hysterical, with exclamation points and capitalized or underlined words. Your journal can be a place to experiment. Try writing an entry in the third person, using the present tense, or from the point of view of your dog or cat. A journal is a private place to take risks.

In *A Writer's Diary* Virginia Woolf asks herself what kind of a diary she'd like to write and answers: ''I should like it to resemble some deep old desk, or capacious hold-all, in which one flings a mass of odds and ends without looking them through.'' *Without looking them through*—that's important. Try not to censor yourself. Fill your journal with odds and ends, quotes, a running list of the books you read, a record of anything that reflects your inner life and thoughts. Include pictures and clippings that spark your imagination, poems and song lyrics that move you. Write letters in it that you never mail.

There are no rules, but follow this advice: Guard your journal's privacy. Don't let anyone read it. If you want to share a journal entry, copy it out first. Otherwise you may find yourself censoring what you put in it or writing for an audience. Three-ring lined notebooks of about one hundred pages make ideal journals; undated pages give you a greater sense of freedom.

If you feel stuck or overwhelmed when you look at all those blank pages, here is an exercise to get you started: Think about the instant you woke up this morning. Did an alarm clock wake you? Music from a clock radio, another person, your own internal clock? What was your immediate thought or feeling? A dream you'd just had, a physical sensation, joy, dread, a gray blur? Whatever it was, begin writing about it on the first page. Write down *anything* that comes into your head, and continue to write for five minutes. Don't let your pen or pencil stop moving. Memories may surface, maybe something that has nothing to do with waking up this morning. This is called automatic writing (also free writing, stream-of-consciousness, and right-brain writing). It's a useful exercise whenever you're stuck or can't get started.

Now, taking your time about it, write about the first thirty minutes of your morning. Record all your sensory impressions. Did you hear voices, TV music, traffic, birds, or an appliance running? Did you touch skin, water, a pet, something soft, or something rough? Did you taste toothpaste, a cigarette, medicine, food, coffee? Did you smell soap, bacon cooking, smog, perfume? Did you look out your window? What does the wall opposite your bed look like? Describe the way your sheets and blankets look in the morning. Include just the details without commenting on your observations.

In Thornton Wilder's classic play, *Our Town,* there's a powerful and moving moment at the end when Emily returns from the dead to say good-bye to the things she'd taken for granted when she was alive: clocks ticking, her mother's sunflowers, freshly ironed dresses, food and coffee. "Do any human beings ever realize life while they live it?—every, every minute?" she asks.

Realizing life is what writing is all about. Good writing comes from paying attention. Tomorrow in your journal try writing again about the first thirty minutes of your day, but this time make a conscious effort from the moment you wake up to pay attention. Pretend you're Emily returning from the dead for one more look at your life. Pretend you're five years old. Pretend you're from Mars. Pretend whatever is necessary to help you see your own life with fresh eyes and take nothing for granted. The emotional impact of Emily's speech is based on specific and ordinary details of daily life.

May Sarton's published journals about her struggle to grow as a writer and human being weave their spell in part by her faithful rendering of daily life: the seasons, the quirks of an old house, beloved pets, working in a garden, preparing meals. See how simply she begins *Journal of a Solitude:* "September 15th. Begin here. It is raining. I look out on the maple, where a few leaves have turned yellow, and listen to Punch, the parrot, talking to himself and to the rain ticking gently against the windows." In her journals you also find the raw material that she later transforms into her fiction and poems.

To make or break a habit, it's been said, takes twenty-one days. Here are twenty-one suggestions to get you started writing in your journal every day until doing so becomes a habit:

1. What three things in life sustain you emotionally and spiritually?
2. Using all five senses, describe the place you're writing in.
3. How do you feel today? If you come up with a word that can describe food it's not a feeling. How does this emotion make your body feel?
4. What ten things give you joy?
5. List five things you want. List five things you need.
6. Describe yourself in the third person.
7. What's the best thing that's happened this week? The worst?
8. What is the weather like today? The color of the sky? Is there wind? How does the weather smell? Taste?
9. Write a letter to someone famous, alive or dead.
10. Write a letter to someone you love. Include a request, a regret, and an appreciation.
11. Find a quotation that moves you and copy it down in your journal. Why does it move you?
12. Write a memory from your childhood. Begin with the words, I remember . . .
13. What three goals do you have for the coming year?
14. What do you want to be doing next year at this time? In five years?
15. What's keeping you from doing it right now?
16. Have an imaginary conservation with someone or something that's troubling you.
17. If you could change one thing about yourself, what would it be?
18. Describe a recent dream. If you can't remember one, make one up.
19. Describe something beautiful you saw yesterday. Something ugly.
20. Write about the best meal you had this week. The worst.
21. What are you wearing right now? Describe your clothes in detail to someone from another century.

WRITING ASSIGNMENT

Choose one of the statements or questions on Abercrombie's list. Do some freewriting, brainstorming, and clustering to generate ideas about the suggested topic. Write a one-paragraph discovery draft. The audience for this draft is classmates who want to get to know you better. Then improve the clarity and revise the organization of the draft.

✔ POINTS TO REMEMBER ABOUT THE WRITING PROCESS

1. Good writing results from a series of overlapping activities, including thinking, planning, noting, drafting, revising, editing, and proofreading. Be willing to devote time and effort to each part of the process.
2. Behave like a writer: Observe what goes on around you, read newspapers and magazines, and listen to other people's ideas. Every day, use your Idea Bank to record interesting or puzzling things that you have seen, read, or heard and to describe your reactions to them.
3. Stop criticizing your ideas, notes, and drafts. Instead, concentrate on what is particularly good about your writing.
4. Try out different strategies for generating ideas and details. Experiment with freewriting, brainstorming, and clustering or use them all in combination.
5. Write discovery drafts in which you explore what you know and feel about your topic. Determine what you still need to find out about it.
6. Revise, edit, and proofread your discovery drafts.

PLANNING AND WRITING STRONG PARAGRAPHS

In Chapter 1, you learned about the writing process and about how to develop ideas for writing. This chapter will help you shape your notes and ideas into effective paragraphs.

Most paragraphs are part of a longer piece of writing. Some are quite short, some are long, and some stand alone as a complete composition. Regardless of their length or purpose, a paragraph is a group of sentences that develops one main point. A strong paragraph often begins with this main point. The rest of the paragraph gives illustrations of the point or evidence for it. Here are three basic strategies for writing strong paragraphs:

1. Make a single point clearly and completely.
2. Develop or support this point with specific details.
3. Organize these details logically.

MAKING A POINT CLEARLY: THE TOPIC SENTENCE

How do you decide the main point of your paragraph? Sometimes a teacher will tell you the focus of your writing assignments. Other times, you will have to choose a topic to write about. To select a topic, use the strategies that you learned in Chapter 1—freewriting, brainstorming, and clustering—to discover what you might want to write about. Your Idea Bank can also supply you with dozens of topics for writing.

An appropriate main point for a paragraph can be a feeling or an experience that you want to describe to your readers:

I'm really enjoying this writing course.
This past semester has been the worst one in my academic career.

It can also be an idea that you want to explain or to prove:

> The fear of getting bad grades stops many students from working together on class projects.
> The drinking age should be raised to twenty-three.

The main point of a paragraph is called its controlling idea, or *topic sentence*. Like a title, the topic sentence lets readers know what the paragraph is about; however, there is a difference between a paragraph's title and its topic sentence. A title is usually a fragment, or part, of a sentence. A topic sentence is always a complete sentence. A fragment—such as "a gifted teacher" or "the best course I have ever taken"—might be an effective title, but it is not a topic sentence. A topic sentence is a complete thought that limits the paragraph to a single point:

> Humanities 101 is the most difficult course I have ever taken.
> My English 100 instructor is a gifted teacher.

If you examine paragraphs in books and newspapers, you will see that sometimes the topic sentence occurs in the middle or at the end of the paragraph. Some paragraphs don't even have a topic sentence. Often, though, the topic sentence of a paragraph appears as the first or second sentence. If you begin paragraphs with a topic sentence, it will remind you of your main point and let readers know immediately what the paragraph is going to be about.

WRITING ACTIVITY 1

This Writing Activity will help you identify the differences between titles and topic sentences. In the space next to each set of words below, write *T* if the words would make an effective title or write *TS* if they would make an effective topic sentence for a paragraph.

1. __T__ Learning how to drive a car.

2. _____ The best parent in the world.

3. _____ My mother has always been my best teacher.

4. _____ The complexity of college registration procedures.

5. _____ Registering for college courses is complicated.

6. _____ Being single has many advantages.

7. _____ The importance of regular exercise.

8. _____ The need to conserve energy in America today.

After you have finished labeling the ideas above, rewrite each one that you labeled as a *T* (a title) to turn it into a topic sentence for a paragraph. Here is an example:

_____*T*_____ Learning how to drive a car~~x~~ *can be dangerous.*

The topic sentence of a paragraph serves as a helpful guide for readers and writers. In addition to letting readers know what to expect from the rest of the paragraph, a clear topic sentence helps the writer decide what kinds of details to include in the rest of the paragraph. The paragraph below, written by sportswriter Roger Kahn, illustrates this point.

> For two decades Mickey Charles Mantle of Commerce, Oklahoma, Yankee Stadium, New York, and Dallas, Texas, bestrode [straddled or ruled] the world of baseball. He could throw and he could run down fly balls. Someone with a stopwatch timed him from the batter's box to first base in 3.1 seconds. No ball player has yet matched that speed. He drove in home runs for shattering distances: 450 feet, 500, 565. With any swing he could make a ball park seem too small. Sometimes when Mantle connected, the big number 7 stirring as he whipped his bat around, it seemed that a grown man was playing in a park designed for Little Leaguers.

The topic sentence—that Mickey Mantle "bestrode," or ruled, the world of baseball for two decades—is stated in the first sentence. The rest of the sentences in the paragraph provide specific details to support this idea.

Note that an effective topic sentence has two parts: (1) a topic and (2) key words that limit the topic and express the opinion or point you want to make about this topic. Here are examples:

A. My Math 101 teacher is one of the most intelligent people I know.
B. For two decades Mickey Mantle bestrode the world of baseball.
C. Raul Julia is a wonderful role model for Puerto Rican children.

The topic of sentence *A* is "My Math 101 teacher," and the key words that limit the topic are "one of the most intelligent people." Given this topic sentence, both the writer and readers know what to expect from the paragraph that will follow it: details showing how and why the teacher is so intelligent. Thus, the key words *limit* what the writer can say about the topic—they focus the writer and readers on only one aspect of the topic. In developing this topic sentence, the writer cannot describe the teacher's looks or personality or teaching style. She must focus only on the teacher's intelligence.

Compare sentences *A, B,* and *C* to statements that do not have key words expressing an opinion or a reaction to the topic:

> D. My Math 101 teacher assigns homework every day.
> E. For two decades Mickey Mantle played baseball.
> F. Raul Julia is a Puerto Rican actor.

Each of these three sentences expresses a fact, but none of them has any key words to convey the writer's opinion or point about the fact. They are merely facts. If a writer were to use any of these sentences as the topic sentence for a paragraph, he or she would have difficulty finding much to say about these statements.

Here are possible revisions of sentences *D, E,* and *F* above. Each revision uses key words to express a point that could be developed in a paragraph. Note that the key words in each sentence are underlined.

> G. The homework that my Math 101 teacher assigns every day is <u>very challenging</u>.
> H. For two decades Mickey Mantle <u>was the best player in professional baseball</u>.
> I. Raul Julia is a <u>multitalented</u> Puerto Rican actor.

Sentences *G, H,* and *I* illustrate how the key words in a topic sentence limit a paragraph's focus. For example, the key words in sentence *G* help the writer see that she has to provide examples of her Math 101 homework and reasons why it is so challenging. The writer of sentence *H* must provide details illustrating the point that Mantle was the best player of his time. And the key word in sentence *I* helps the writer focus on examples of Raul Julia's many talents as an actor.

Thus, the key words in a topic sentence have two important purposes:

- They remind the writer what the paragraph is about and what it is *not* about.
- They provide a focus for the writer to develop in the remainder of the paragraph.

WRITING ACTIVITY 2

Some writers do not write a topic sentence for a paragraph until *after* they have generated details for it. This Writing Activity lets you try out that process. Read each set of details on pages 34 and 35, and then write a topic sentence for them. The first one has been done as an example.

1. *Being an "older" college student is an enjoyable experience.*

Most of my college classmates are younger than I am, by at least ten years. However, they always make me feel comfortable and welcome, and I've become very friendly with several of them. Also, several students have told me that they have learned a great deal from the experiences I have described in class and from my comments and point of view.

2. _____

_____

When people watch television in the dark, they cannot see the picture clearly. This occurs because our eyes function best when viewing white light, so a light background makes the picture clearer. In addition, a television screen in a totally dark room creates a glare that is unpleasant and that causes eye fatigue.

3. _____

_____

One type is Karma Yoga, which teaches people how to separate themselves from their attachments to material things. Karma Yoga also emphasizes the separation of the soul and the body. Another form of yoga, Hatha Yoga, teaches people how to live longer and keep their bodies healthy. It focuses on physical exercises. Bhakti Yoga is different from both of these, in that it emphasizes love for God. It teaches people how to control themselves so that they can show their love for God.

4. _____

_____

Children between the ages of six and eleven watch an average of twenty–three hours of television a week. Often they put off other activities, such as reading or playing sports, in order to sit in front of the TV, mesmerized by its blinking image. Even worse, the only time most children willingly move away from the TV is during commercials in order to get something to eat. So not only are they sitting passively for hours, but they are also eating more and gaining too much weight.

5. _____

_____

For example, some video-game players talk about "cranking through" (finishing a game easily), "sky surfing" (disappearing at the top of the screen), and "total shredding" (maneuvering very quickly). Another term that many players obsess about is "going ballistic" or suddenly improving their skills greatly. Finally, no one who plays Nintendo or Sega ever wants to "die" or "get slammed" (lose the game).

REMINDER
A topic sentence includes a topic and key words that limit the topic and convey the point that the writer wants to make about the topic or the writer's opinion of it. When you write a topic sentence for a paragraph, choose precise key words to express your idea or opinion about the topic. Avoid vague, "all-purpose" words such as *good, nice, great,* and *bad.*

The paragraph below is a draft by a student about her mother. Does it have a clear topic sentence?

Draft Paragraph

I love my mother very much. She is a special person. She acts like a mom and a best friend and a teacher. I am an only child, and my mom and I do a lot of things together. She helps set goals for me to reach, and she always helps me think through ways of achieving these goals. She is also very wise and patient, and she helps me learn new things and new skills. She does many things, and she does them all well. When I make mistakes (which I usually do), she asks questions that help me understand where I went wrong. My mom also makes me feel good about myself. She is beautiful inside and out. I always enjoy being around my mom.

This draft lacks a clear topic sentence. Is the writer's main point "I love my mother" or "my mother is a special person"? Because she did not have a clear topic sentence, the writer did not stick to a single main point. Instead she wrote many seemingly unrelated details. For example, what does the fact that the writer "does a lot of things with her mom" have to do with her statement that her mother "is beautiful inside and out"?

WRITING ACTIVITY 3

Read the following paragraph, which is the revision of the preceding student draft. What are some differences between the revision and the draft?

Revised Paragraph

I've had many teachers in my life, but my mother has always been the best one. All through my life, my mom and I have always discussed goals for me to reach and she has always helped me think through ways of achieving these goals. In addition, when she helps me learn a new skill, she is incredibly patient and she answers all my questions calmly and honestly. Her explanations of problems are clear and precise. If I make mistakes (which I usually do), she tries different ways of showing me how to learn the skill or handle the problem or she asks questions that help me understand where I went wrong. My mom also makes me feel good about my accomplishments, and her praise really matters to me. I wish that all my *real* teachers would be as good as she is.

Does the revision have a topic sentence? If so, what is it? What are the key words in it?

_____

_____

_____

Why is the revised paragraph stronger than the draft on page 35?

_____

_____

_____

_____

The topic sentence of the revision (''I've had many teachers in my life, but my mother has always been the best one'') helps the writer stay focused on her main point.

One of your first challenges as an advancing writer is to learn how to develop a topic sentence that is neither too general nor too narrow for your paragraph. For example, examine the statements below, *none* of which is an effective topic sentence for a paragraph.

- a. Vacations are beneficial. [This is too general. It would taken an entire essay—or book—to explain the benefits of vacations.]
- b. Students can learn the steps necessary to succeed in college. [This is also too general. These steps would take much more than one paragraph to develop in detail.]
- c. Most of the buildings at Middletown Community College are built of stone. [This is too narrow. It is a statement of fact that needs no development.]
- d. My bedroom is done in primary colors. [This is also too narrow. It is a fact that needs no support.]

Here are revisions of these statements.

- a. A holiday vacation at a dude ranch is very beneficial for people of all ages.
- b. Any student can learn the steps necessary to study for a test in accounting.
- c. The stone buildings at Middletown Community College make the place seem like a medieval fortress.
- d. My bedroom looks like a circus ring.

REMINDER ⎯⎯⎯⎯⎯⎯⎯⎯⎯⎯⎯⎯⎯⎯⎯⎯⎯⎯⎯
An effective topic sentence is a complete sentence that states the single main point of the paragraph. This idea should not be too general or too narrow.

GROUP WORK 1

Form a group with two other students. Choose one person to write the group's responses on a separate piece of paper. Below are several statements. Decide if each one would make a good topic sentence for a paragraph. If not, explain why not and revise it to make it into an effective topic sentence. The first one has been done as an example.

1. My family has always been very supportive of me. *Too broad*

   My parents have always helped me learn from my mistakes.

2. The field of psychology offers many career possibilities.

3. A pediatric nurse takes care of sick infants and children.

4. Racism is a problem in American society.

5. My kitchen is the place where my family often gets together.

6. My house is unique.

7. Computers are changing our lives.

8. Being a parent is difficult.

WRITING ACTIVITY 4

In the spaces below, write a topic sentence that you might want to make if you were asked to write a paragraph about each of these topics. Do not write a paragraph; just write an appropriate topic sentence. Make sure that each topic sentence is a complete sentence.

1. a parent

   _____

   _____

   _____

2. a sport

_____

_____

_____

3. a current problem in your life

_____

_____

_____

_____

 GROUP WORK 2

Form a group with two other students. Take turns reading aloud one of the topic sentences that you wrote for the preceding Writing Activity. When it is your turn to listen, write down your classmate's topic sentence. Then list the ideas and details that you would expect to follow this topic sentence if the student were to write a paragraph based on it. When everyone has finished reading the ideas aloud, discuss the supporting details that you listed. If you had difficulty listing any supporting details for your classmates' topic sentences, explain why these topic sentences might not be effective.

KNOWING YOUR PURPOSE AND AUDIENCE

How might you begin developing details for a paragraph? The first step is to consider your purpose—that is, why you are writing—and your audience—your intended readers. Often, beginning writers feel that their only purpose in writing is to please their teacher. They don't realize that they must also have their own purpose for writing a particular paragraph or essay. Strong writing achieves a clear purpose. Here are three common purposes for writing:

- To *express* something important to ourselves or to others.
- To *explain* something or share information with readers.
- To *persuade* readers to think or feel or do something.

Your purpose governs the length of each paragraph that you write, and it influences the details you select to develop the topic sentence. For example, suppose a writer wanted to develop a paragraph about the following topic sentence:

Coaching my town's league baseball team has given me much satisfaction.

If the writer's purpose is to express his feelings, he could tell a story that shows how coaching made him happy. If he wanted to explain how being a coach has been a satisfying experience, he might present examples that illustrate his point. Or if the writer wanted to convince readers of his point, he could provide facts and reasons about coaching to support his assertion.

In addition to considering their purpose, successful writers also think about their audience—the readers for whom they are writing. Keeping the intended audience in mind helps writers figure out how much their readers already know about the topic and what their attitudes are toward it. This helps the writer select appropriate details to develop the topic sentence—details that the reader will understand and not be offended by.

For instance, suppose you decided to develop a paragraph that supports the following topic sentence:

My neighborhood is a wonderful place to raise a family.

Your purpose is to convince readers of this assertion. What examples or reasons would you provide if your intended audience for this paragraph is friends who live in the neighborhood?

_____

_____

_____

_____

What examples would you provide if you were writing for a potential home or apartment buyer who had never visited your town?

_____

_____

_____

_____

_____

What examples would you provide if you were writing for a business-person considering opening a children's toy store in your town?

_____

_____

_____

_____

How are the details that you listed to support this topic sentence *different* for the three different audiences?

_____

_____

_____

_____

QUESTIONS TO ASK YOURSELF
ABOUT YOUR PURPOSE AND AUDIENCE _____

Here are some questions to consider when you are writing a topic sentence and supporting details.

- Who exactly am I writing for? Who would be interested in reading this paragraph?
- What are these readers like?
- How similar are they to me? Would they react as I do?
- Do I want to share my thoughts and feelings with them?

(Continued)

- Do I want to explain something to them?
- Do I want to persuade my readers to think or to feel or to do something? What? Why?
- How much do my readers already know about my topic?
- What else do they need to know about this topic?

WRITING ACTIVITY 5

Below are several topics and two potential audiences for each topic. In the space next to each topic, write a topic sentence about it. Then list the kinds of details that you might include if you were developing a paragraph about this topic sentence for each of the audiences. The first one has been done as an example.

1. discipline *Discipline doesn't have to involve punishment.*

Audience #1: Parents of young children

Put child on bed or in a corner

Ask her to explain what she did wrong

Discuss other people's feelings

Reward child for good behavior

Audience #2: Parents of teenagers

Discuss family values and rules

Discuss consequences of hurtful behavior

Provide independence with structure

Praise good behavior

2. your college's registration procedures _____

_____

Audience #1: Students who plan to attend your college

_____

_____

_____

_____

Audience #2: Your college's administrators

_____

_____

_____

_____

3. smoking _____

_____

Audience #1: Teenagers who smoke

_____

_____

_____

Audience #2: Scientists who study smoking

_____

_____

_____

4. a favorite meal _____

_____

Audience #1: Your friends

_____

_____

_____

Audience #2: A chef at a restaurant

_____

_____

_____

_____

DEVELOPING A POINT WITH RELEVANT DETAILS

Strong paragraphs are built from supporting details—examples, facts, stories, and reasons that enable readers to understand the writer's point. All of these details must be *relevant:* they must relate clearly and logically to the topic sentence of the paragraph. Furthermore, a writer must provide enough details to support fully the point he or she is making in a paragraph. How do you decide how many details are "enough" to support your topic sentence? You make this decision by reconsidering your purpose and your audience.

QUESTIONS TO ASK YOURSELF ABOUT PARAGRAPH DEVELOPMENT

- How familiar is my reader with me and with my topic?
- What kinds of details should I include in the paragraph to develop or to prove my main point to this reader?
- How many details will I need to include to develop or support my point adequately for this reader?
- How specific should these details be to help my reader understand exactly what I mean?

WRITING ACTIVITY 6

After you read each of the student paragraphs below, write answers to the questions below it.

Paragraph #1: A Best Friend

My friend, Lydia Carbello, has all the qualities one could want in a best friend. She is loyal and true. Lydia and I have been close friends for almost nine years, and we share a special friendship. I can always turn to her with my problems. That is what best friends are for. I can share anything with her. Once we even shared a boyfriend! His name was Doug and we both went out on dates with him at the same time. That was one of the funniest experiences in our friendship. Lydia is really a wonderful person. That is why I consider her my best friend.

Underline the topic sentence of this paragraph (if it has one).

1. What do you think was the writer's purpose?

   _____

   _____

   _____

2. What audience do you think the writer was writing for?

   _____

   _____

   _____

3. Did the writer accomplish her purpose (for this audience)? Why or why not?

   _____

_____

_____

_____

_____

_____

4. Did the writer provide enough specific details to convince you of the truth of her topic sentence? If not, what other details should (or could) be included? Where?

_____

_____

_____

_____

_____

_____

Paragraph #2: My First College Registration

My first registration for courses at Valley Central College was a nightmare. To begin with, the college did not send me all of the forms that I needed to select courses nor did it send me a time schedule. Even worse, I didn't realize that I was missing these forms until I stepped up to the registration counter after waiting on line for an hour. The woman behind the desk smiled sweetly and told me to go to the registrar's office to get the rest of the required forms and then to return and wait in line again. I was fuming, but there was nothing I could do but follow her directions. Of course I got lost on the way to the administration building, and when I finally got there, no one was around to show me where the registrar was. When I finally found the office, I was sickened to see that I had another hour-long wait. At this point, I was ready to leave and take the semester off from school, but I waited, got the forms, and returned to the registration counter. Yet another hour later, my registration was processed and I was relieved. However, this relief dissolved into terror when I got home and realized that the computer had made an error and I would have to return and repeat the whole procedure the following day.

Underline the topic sentence of this paragraph (if it has one) and circle the key words that express the writer's opinion.

1. What do you think was the writer's purpose?

   _____

   _____

2. What audience do you think the writer was writing for?

   _____

   _____

   _____

3. Did the writer accomplish his purpose (for this audience)? Why or why not?

   _____

   _____

   _____

   _____

4. Did the writer provide enough specific details to convince you of the truth of his topic sentence? If not, what other details should (or could) be included? Where?

_____

_____

_____

_____

WRITING ACTIVITY 7

Write several sentences that develop or support each of the following topic sentences.

1. My favorite place in the world is _____.
(fill in)

Audience: Your classmates.
Purpose: To describe this place in such a way that readers can experience it from your perspective.

Details: _____

_____

_____

_____

_____

_____

_____

_____

2. The best way to study for a test is _____.
                                              (fill in)

Audience: Readers who do not know you.
Purpose: To convince readers that your way of studying is an effective method.

Details: _____

_____

_____

_____

_____

_____

_____

3. Drinking and driving is _____.
                                 (fill in)

Audience: High school students who do not know you.
Purpose: To convince readers not to drive after they have drunk any alcohol.

Details: _____

_____

_____

_____

_____

_____

_____

_____

_____

GROUP WORK 3

Form a group with two classmates and exchange the sentences that you wrote for the preceding Writing Activity. Take notes on each classmate's details and when it is your turn to read be prepared to explain to him or her whether, in your opinion, these details (1) were relevant to the topic sentence and (2) were adequate to accomplish the purpose.

REMINDER _____
Support the topic sentence of each paragraph with enough relevant details and examples to achieve your purpose.

WRITING ACTIVITY 8

Choose one of the topics below and do five minutes of brainstorming and clustering about it. Examine your notes and develop a topic sentence that you want to make about this topic. Write down the topic sentence, think about your purpose and audience, and then do five minutes of brainstorming and clustering about your idea, your purpose, and your audience. Use your notes to write a discovery draft of a paragraph that develops or supports your topic sentence. (Refer to ''Questions to Consider as You Compose a Discovery Draft'' on pages 19 and 20 of Chapter 1.) Then revise this paragraph using the ''Suggestions for Revising a Discovery Draft'' on pages 22 and 23 of Chapter 1.

- a special relative
- a problem with money
- a favorite place
- a problem in school
- a major responsibility at home
- a movie that you particularly liked

- a problem in your neighborhood
- a proud moment

USING SPECIFIC LANGUAGE

When you write a paragraph, how general or specific should your details and your language be? The answer depends on your topic, your purpose, and your readers. Here is a cartoon that illustrates this point:

For Better or For Worse®   **by Lynn Johnston**

The teenager in the cartoon feels that he has been forced to be too specific about his evening activities. How do you think his mother feels?

As you develop details for your paragraphs, you need to think about what your readers know about your topic and what they know about you. For example, suppose you wrote the following sentence. How do you determine whether it is specific enough?

The surgery I had several years ago was a frightening experience.

If this sentence were part of a letter to your family or close friends, its vague language ("the surgery," "several years ago") would be perfectly acceptable. Family and friends would know exactly what you were referring to. However, if the sentence were part of a college essay, readers would find it very vague: What kind of surgery? When exactly did it happen? For these readers, the writer might use more specific language:

The appendectomy I had when I was twelve years old was the most frightening experience of my life.

The sentence could be revised to be even more specific:

> The most frightening experience of my life was the emergency appendectomy I had at Bay Memorial Hospital on July 5, 1986, when I was twelve years old.

Can you think of a reader who might need or want to know the extra information given by the very specific details in the last version?

In general, your topic, purpose, and readers determine how specific your details should be. But remember that specific words communicate more information than vague, general ones. For example, how much information is communicated by the word *car*? Close your eyes and think of a car. Can you visualize it in your mind? Probably not, because the word is so general. Now try to visualize a more specific version of a car—a Ford Taurus. What does this car look like? Here is a more specific substitute: a "gleaming new black Ford Taurus with dove gray leather seats." Can you close your eyes and see this car now?

WRITING ACTIVITY 9

Rewrite each group of words in *general-to-specific* order in the space below. The first group has been done as an example.

1. dog, collie, animal, pet

   animal, pet, dog, collie

2. left fielder, athlete, baseball player, person

   _____

3. citrus fruit, food, lemon, plant

   _____

4. school, Idaho Institute of Technology, institution, university

   _____

5. soda, liquid, cola, Diet Coke

   _____

Strong paragraphs have details that are *concrete* and *sensory*. A concrete word or phrase refers to something that is real; sensory refers to something that appeals to one of our five senses: sight, hearing, smell, taste, and touch. For example, a book is a concrete object, but knowledge is not. "Knowledge" is an abstract term—a concept that we cannot see or touch. A "worn-out old book with a cover the color of ashes" is a sensory image that helps a reader see the object from the writer's perspective. Concrete, sensory language communicates ideas more clearly than do abstract words because it enables readers to understand exactly what the writer means.

For example, let's say a writer wants to make the following point to develop the topic sentence "The garbage dump in my town is hazardous to people's health":

The dump's odors are dangerous.

Does this detail give you a clear impression of the dump's smell? Do you know what the writer means by "dangerous"? Here is a revision that includes concrete, sensory language:

Smoky, sulfurous fumes smelling like rotting eggs seep out from the dump into our homes and our lungs.

Here is another example of the difference between general, abstract words and specific, concrete language:

My roommate often looks messy and dirty.

My roommate's clothes hang off him in wrinkled rolls. His rumpled, greasy shirt looks as if he hasn't changed it in a week, and his ragged denim pants have ink spots and food blotches all over them.

The details in the last example create a clearer picture of the roommate than do the vague words in the first.

HOW TO MAKE YOUR DETAILS MORE SPECIFIC ⎯⎯⎯⎯⎯

Here are some strategies for making the details in your paragraphs more effective:

- Refer to people or objects by their exact names. (For example, rather than writing *a famous Native American writer,* use the person's name: *William Least Heat-Moon.*)
- Use specific words rather than general ones. (For instance, instead of writing *The executive drove a nice car,* use concrete words: *Leora Suarez, the president of Suarez Real Estate, drove a new Mercedes 300 SL.*)

(Continued)

> • Use sensory words that illustrate sights, sounds, smells, tastes, textures, and feelings. (Rather than describing a pie as *a lemon pie*, use words that enable readers to see and taste it: *a fiery-yellow lemon pie tasting so tart that it made my lips pucker.*)
> • Use precise verbs to express emotions and actions. (For example, instead of writing that someone *walked* across a room, use an expressive verb, such as *rambled, strutted, strolled,* or *sauntered.*)

Chapter 4, on revising and editing paragraphs, will help you improve the specificity of your details. Chapter 5, on description, will provide you with opportunities to practice writing sensory language.

WRITING ACTIVITY 10

Rewrite each vague detail in the sentences below. Add concrete, sensory words and phrases to create distinct images for a reader. The first sentence has been done as an example.

1. The rain made a loud noise.

   The steady plink, plink, plink of the rain sounded like a ticking clock.

2. The meal was sickening.

   _____

   _____

3. The room is a disaster.

   _____

   _____

4. The animal was gross.

   _____

   _____

5. The woman is gorgeous.

_____

_____

6. The movie was awesome.

_____

_____

7. The teacher is terrific.

_____

_____

 GROUP WORK 4

Form a group of three students and choose one person to record the group's notes. Read the paragraph below. Then, as a group, decide which details are too vague and abstract. Brainstorm together to create more specific concrete, sensory substitutes for these vague words and phrases. Make sure the recorder gets the substitute language down on paper to share with the rest of the class.

The forest behind my home is mysteriously beautiful. There are lots of interesting trees, covered with amazing leaves of all different shapes and colors. When the leaves get full, they shade the ground and it gets dark. The darkness is a bit scary, but it is also quite pretty. You can sit beneath the trees and see many lovely sights. The noises of the different animals are fascinating. This forest is truly an awe-inspiring place.

As you compose the supporting details of your paragraphs, include descriptive details about specific sights, sounds, textures, sensations, feelings, odors, and tastes. Here is an example of a paragraph developed with sensory details. As you read it, try to imagine this place in your mind's eye.

I spent the autumn months with my family at our summer cottage, on a mountain about fourteen miles from Tuscumbia. It was called Fern Quarry, because near it was a limestone quarry, long since abandoned. Three frolicsome little streams ran through it from springs in the rocks above, leaping here and tumbling there in laughing cascades wherever the rocks tried to bar their way. The opening was filled with ferns which completely covered the beds of limestone and in places hid the stream. The rest of the mountain was thickly wooded. Here were great oaks and splendid evergreens with trunks like mossy pillars, from the branches of which hung garlands of ivy and mistletoe, and persimmon trees, the odour of which pervaded every nook and corner of the wood—an illusive fragrant something that made the heart glad. In places the wild muscadine and scuppernong vines stretched from tree to tree, making arbours which were always full of butterflies and buzzing insects. It was delightful to lose ourselves in the green hollows of that tangled wood in the late afternoon, and to smell the cool delicious odours that came up from the earth at the close of day.

—Helen Keller

The sensory details in this paragraph create vivid images that are especially amazing when you realize that the author, Helen Keller, was blind and deaf from two years of age on.

WRITING ACTIVITY 11

Choose a place that has made a strong impression on you and write a paragraph describing it for readers who have never been there. First compose a topic sentence that states your main impression of the place. Then develop and select details that clarify and support this impression. Make sure to use concrete, sensory language to make the place come alive for readers. Revise your paragraph using the "Suggestions for Revising a Discovery Draft" on pages 22 and 23 of Chapter 1.

ORGANIZING DETAILS LOGICALLY

Paragraph development and organization are interrelated. The order that you select for arranging your ideas depends on the kinds of details you have generated to support the topic sentence. Below you will read about three common patterns of paragraph organization. Chapters 5 through 12 will help you learn more specialized methods of organizing details in paragraphs.

Details Can Be Arranged Chronologically (in Time Order). Chronological order is an effective organizational strategy if your details tell a story, describe a process, or describe a series of actions that take place one after another. Keep the sequence of events clear and don't leave out any steps that the reader needs to understand your story or process. Here is a student paragraph that illustrates the use of chronological order to relate a story.

Every time I hear about someone having an operation, I remember the absolute terror I felt the first time I had surgery. I was eleven years old and I broke my arm on a diving slide to home base that won the baseball game for my Little League team. The surgeon who was going to operate on my shattered arm bone was delayed in an earlier surgery and I had to wait outside the operating room alone for an hour. I was so nervous that I had to go to the bathroom four times, and each time, the nurse had to unwind the rugged green straps that held my arm rigid on the stretcher. As she moved my arm to release the tapes, the pain slashing through it felt like a burning scalpel. Finally my doctor showed up and said, "Let's get the show on the road." Some show! The orderly moved me into the operating room, which was so white and shiny, I was temporarily blinded. I panicked and started screaming until the doctor threatened to tape my mouth shut. Worried about suffocating, I shut up, but then I started to shake and couldn't stop. The nurses piled blankets on me but I wasn't cold, just scared. I was shivering so much that the doctor couldn't get the IV needle into my arm and four nurses had to hold it down. Next, the doctor started the drip into my arm and told me that I would get a little sleepy. As my brain clouded, I felt like I was dying and I started to scream again. That's the last thing I remember about the operation, but I will never forget the panic and horror of the two hours that preceded it.

WRITING ACTIVITY 12

Write a discovery draft of a paragraph based on one of the topics below. Use chronological order to organize your details.

- an experience I will never forget
- my proudest moment
- a frightening experience
- losing my wallet (or pocketbook or bookbag)
- my first experience driving a car (or truck)
- my first day on a new job
- the time I met my best friend
- my first day at college
- the birth of my child
- becoming a grandparent
- the happiest moment of my life

Details Can Be Arranged Spatially (in Order of Location). When you describe a person, a place, or an object, you can arrange your details according to the way they are arranged in space. Pretend you are a video camera panning the object being described: Move from top to bottom, left to right, far to near, inside to outside, or vice versa. Make sure that your reader can follow the logic of your spatial order. Here is an example of a paragraph in which the details have been arranged by order of their location in a room.

The kitchen held our lives together. My mother worked in it all day long, we ate in it almost all meals except the Passover *seder*. I did my homework and first writing at the kitchen table, and in winter I often had a bed made up for me on three kitchen chairs near the stove. On the wall just over the table hung a long horizontal mirror that sloped to a ship's prow at each end and was lined in cherry wood. It took up the whole wall and drew every object in the kitchen to itself. The walls were a fiercely stippled whitewash, so often re-whitened by my father in slack seasons that the paint looked as if it had been squeezed and cracked into the walls. A large electric bulb hung down the center of the kitchen at the end of a chain that had been hooked into the ceiling; the old gas ring and key still jutted out of the wall like antlers. In the corner next to the toilet was the sink at which we washed, and the square tub in which my mother did our clothes. Above it, tacked to the shelf on which pleasantly ranged square, blue bordered white sugar and spice jars, hung calendars from the Public National Bank on Pitkin Avenue and the Minsker Progressive Branch of the Workman's Circle; receipts for the payment of insurance premiums and household bills on a spindle; two little boxes engraved with Hebrew letters. One of these was for the poor, the other to buy back the Land of Israel.

—Alfred Kazin

WRITING ACTIVITY 13

Look through your Idea Bank or the freewriting, brainstorming, and clustering that you did for Chapter 1 or for this chapter. Select a topic that could be developed with descriptive details that are organized spatially. If you cannot find an idea you want to develop, think about a special place or room and what it means to you. Write a discovery draft of a paragraph describing this topic or place. Organize your details spatially.

Details Can Be Arranged Emphatically (in Order of Importance). Most types of details can be arranged from least important to most important. When you use this organization, you build your details logically, saving the most interesting or important points for the end of the paragraph. Because this order emphasizes the last detail, it is called "emphatic." This type of organization is appropriate for any paragraph composed of facts, examples, and reasons. Here is a student example.

Marijuana should be legalized and available for people dying of cancer or AIDS. Although the public often associates marijuana with hard-core drug users, this drug has many properties that can help terminal patients. For example, concentrated marijuana tablets, which are available from medical laboratories, induce relaxation in people who take these pills. Cancer and AIDS patients need this chance to relax and feel better because it will help them stay stronger physically and psychologically. In addition, concentrated marijuana causes people to feel giddy and giggly, and several researchers have shown that laughter helps terminal patients feel better and stronger. Finally, high doses of marijuana can relieve pain for as long as five or six hours. Research has also shown that patients' immune systems improve when they are relieved of intense pain. Clearly, people struggling with the agonies of cancer and AIDS deserve pain-free periods when they can relax and laugh. They deserve medically supervised access to marijuana.

ENDING A PARAGRAPH WITH A "CLINCHER" SENTENCE

A paragraph that stands alone or a long paragraph within an essay should conclude with a sentence that restates or comments on the main point. This concluding sentence is often called a "clincher" sentence because it summarizes the paragraph, pulling together its details. Without a clincher ending, a paragraph often sounds like the writer simply got tired and stopped writing. The following paragraph illustrates the use of a clincher sentence to sum up its points. Like the paragraph on page 32, it was written by Roger Kahn about Mickey Mantle.

> He is thirty-nine now and so enormously powerful that he can drive a golf ball 400 yards. But baseball begins with a man's legs, and Mickey Mantle's right knee is grotesque. Four injuries and two operations have left the joint without supportive structure. It flexes outward as well as in, bone grinding on bone, and there is nothing more that surgery can do. "A flail knee," doctors say, and make analogies to a floppy rag doll. So, still sandy-haired, still young, but no longer able to play ball, Mantle sits in Dallas, living hard, dabbling at business, working at golf, cheerful to be sure, but missing major league baseball more than he ever thought he would.

WRITING ACTIVITY 14

Write a discovery draft of a paragraph based on one of the topics below. Use emphatic order to organize your details.

- an important problem that many teenagers have
- an important problem that many parents have
- reasons you enjoy a particular sport or hobby
- the benefits of knowing more than one language
- reasons you do or do not smoke cigarettes

GROUP WORK 5

Select one of the discovery drafts that you developed for a Writing Activity in this chapter. Exchange drafts with one or two classmates. Answer the following questions about your classmate's paragraph (on a separate piece of paper).

1. What did you like best about this paragraph? Why?
2. What did you think was the writer's purpose?
3. Did he or she accomplish this purpose? Why or why not?
4. Which details helped you understand the writer's main point?
5. Where might the writer add more details to help you understand his or her point better?

GETTING READERS' RESPONSES

Use the checklist below to help you identify problems in your discovery drafts and to get readers' responses to them. Ask family, friends, and classmates to answer the questions below honestly and fully.

DISCOVERY DRAFT CHECKLIST

1. Does the paragraph have a clear topic sentence that expresses the writer's main point or opinion?
2. Is the topic sentence appropriate for the paragraph or is it too general or too narrow?
3. Are the details appropriate for the writer's purpose and audience?
4. Are there enough details for the writer to accomplish his or her purpose?
5. Are there any details or sentences that do not illustrate or explain the topic sentence?
6. Which details include sensory, concrete language? Which details are too vague or abstract?
7. Can you follow the order in which the details are developed? Is there a more appropriate way of organizing these details?
8. Does the paragraph have an effective clincher sentence?
9. What suggestions do you have for improving this draft?

■ EXPLORING FURTHER

This essay was written by Sue Lorch, an English profesor at the University of South Carolina at Aiken. In this essay, she explains her attitudes toward writing and her development as a writer.

Confessions of a Former Sailor

I do not like to write. Most people to whom I reveal this small, personal truth find it exceedingly odd, suggesting by their expressions that I ought either to repair my attitude or develop the discretion necessary not to go around telling people about it. Apparently these people hear my confession as an admission of fraud. Because my professional life centers on the written word— on producing it, interpreting it, teaching it, and teaching others to teach it, people assume that I should enjoy writing. Not at all. I inevitably view the prospect of writing with a mental set more commonly reserved for root canals and amputations: If it must be done, it must be done, but for God's sake, let us put it off as long as possible.

It has not always been thus. It has, in fact, been very much un-thus. While I will not claim ever to have written eagerly, I once wrote willingly, putting pen to paper, if not with glee, certainly with aplomb. From elementary school on, I launched myself into writing assignment after writing assignment without blushing or blanching. While my classmates bit pencils, twisted hair, chewed lips, and despaired, I sailed smoothly down the page, serene and sure. I wrote of Dick, Jane, and Sally, of Spot and Puff. I wrote of my summer vacation and my favorite places. And as the years passed and the pencils changed from fat and red to thin and yellow, I wrote of Ionic columns, *Julius Caesar,* the Kennedy assassination (Jack), and Chaucer's *Prologue.* Number two pencils gave way to blobbing ball-points and I rolled on, writing of reproduction in single-cell organisms, the Kennedy assassination (Bobby), Vietnam, and *Othello.* Whatever the subject, I sailed forth on an endless sea of words, undaunted, unafraid. And my classmates bit pencils, twisted hair, chewed lips, and despaired.

Now as I sit here gnawing my pen, twisting my hair, chewing my lip, and despairing of ever getting this essay done to my satisfaction, I look back on those days with a faint nostalgia. I no longer write with ease. The words do not flow, and I have lost my capacity for sailing down a page. I have left the smooth waters of confidence for the rough roads of doubt, but I have become a better writer thereby.

The good ship *Easy Writer* did not go down until my senior year in college. My arctic iceberg appeared on the horizon in the person of one Maurice Hatch, professor of English, destroyer of dreams. Had I known what was to follow, I feel sure I would not have pled so ardently to be admitted to his already closed advanced composition course. But I had no spyglass into the future, and with all the eloquence I could muster and only a fleeting regard for the truth, I begged to be allowed in the class. I cited the imminence of my impending graduation (true), the sterling reputation of the professor (true) and the course (true), my dedication to scholarship and learning (hmmm), and my sharp desire to hone my writing skills to a scalpel's edge in preparation for the rigors of graduate school (hah).

This last was an outright lie. I did have plans for graduate school, although not within the instant, which is what I implied. I did not, however, even for a nanosecond believe that my writing skills needed a keener edge put on them. What could be improved? I had sixteen years of almost solid A's on written work, and the smattering of B's I had received came, I firmly held, from my own inattention or disdain for the task at hand or from the ignorance or animosity of the benighted individual assigning the grade. How could one improve upon perfection? My true reasons for wanting in the class were three: It met at a time that fit my schedule; it was required for the teaching certification that I had decided to pick up as a practical complement to my lovely but increasingly unsaleable B.A. in English; and, most important, it would be an easy A. Or so I thought.

Today, after having myself turned a deaf ear to many similar pleas, I'm unsure why Professor Hatch admitted me to that class. At the time I was certain that he made an exception for me because he perceived my astonishing abilities. He knew that he would not have to take time and trouble teaching me to write, that my papers would not require laborious marking, extensive commentary. I did not make mistakes. Hadn't Miss Ruth, who was my twelfth-grade English teacher as she was my daddy's before me, always spoken highly of my command of The Rules (a command I gained cheaply, having heard the language correctly used from the cradle)? Hadn't my high-school friends turned to me for additional help in penetrating the mysteries of who and whom? Didn't my college suitemates seek me out for the answer to that great imponderable: "Do I need a new paragraph here?" That Professor Hatch could know none of this never occurred to me. I had grown up, or more accurately, had spent my first seventeen years in a very small town, one whose population was a fraction of the university's I now attended, and I still expected everything about me, good or ill, to be public knowledge.

Today, I would guess I gained my seat either because the student who left his office as I entered it had just dropped or because Professor Hatch felt sufficient obligation to his profession—I had announced my intention eventually to join it—to save it from an insufferably arrogant sort who couldn't perceive that the wind filling her sails was only so much hot air.

Had I listened carefully on my way into the Fine Arts building, there to knock out with grace, alacrity, and ease my first paper, I might have heard the soft strains of "Nearer My God to Thee." I was about to go under. Deaf with confidence, I heard nothing. I was concentrating on spotting the buoy signaling the location of the painting I was to describe, and sure enough, there it was—a tight knot of pencil gnawers. My classmates. I sailed up, sat down, and let the words flow. What could be so difficult about describing an oil on canvas depicting a few cows standing in a field surrounded by trees, I wondered. As I left some thirty minutes later, my one-draft, sure-fire A paper stowed in my knapsack, I hope I refrained from smiling smugly at the gnawers, twisters, and chewers. I doubt that I did. Arrogance has a way of turning the milk of human kindness to clabber, particularly in someone twenty-one. Near-rer tooo Theeeee.

When the papers were returned a scant two days later, I opened mine confidently in class, my eyes searching the pages for the familiar letter acknowledging my prowess of pen. In the world according to Lorch, only the timid, unsure, iffy writers, the gnawers, twisters, and chewers, waited until they reached the privacy of their homes before checking their grades. I had nothing to fear, and sure enough on the last of three pages there was my . . . no, wait, this can't be right. There's a side missing from my A; it looks like an, it is . . . oh, no. I quickly decided that the few words following the F didn't require reading until I got back to the privacy of the dorm. To say that I was shocked is to mince the matter exceedingly fine. I could not have been more stunned had the paper I held metamorphosed into a mule and kicked me in the face.

It took me quite a while to garner the strength to reopen that paper and peruse the unthinkable, but I did so with a fierce determination to go and sin no more. I would take the good professor's remonstrances to heart, look up whatever rules of good writing I had inadvertently violated, observe them, like Horatio, with the very comment of my soul, and then get back into my boat, steering forever a more carefully charted course. I suspected a problem with semicolons, or perhaps my who's and whom's were slipping. These matters had been the bane of many of my classmates in freshman composition (a course wherein we had discussed two books—*Franny and Zooey* and Cassirer's *An Essay on Man*—and no one had ever said a single word about writing except that we were to do it). But no, the comment scratched there said my paper was boing. Boing. BOING? Now what did that mean? I was puzzled but rather relieved, actually, to discover that my paper was boing. I was not committing crass errors; this was something I had never heard of, a violation of a rule that perhaps even Miss Ruth didn't know. Then the fog lifted. That word wasn't boing; it was *boring*. My paper was boring.

During the painful process of revising that paper—the words following *boing* indicated that I must do just that—I became an uncertain writer, a slow writer, the hair-twisting, lip-chewing concentration of concern that I remain today. Every time I set down a sentence, a phrase, a word, there rose before me the specter of Professor Hatch, bored and baleful. I tried to imagine what would interest him—an effective use of colons perhaps, more adjectives, maybe an allusion to classical myth. What was the name of that cow Jove courted in the form of a bull? Crumpled wads of yellow paper soon littered the floor around my desk. I saw no need to return to the Fine Arts building to view the painting again as I had the most complete, albeit boring, description of it that anyone could wish. I had described it in meticulous detail, top to bottom, left to right, down to counting the spots on the cows. What did Hatch want?

Not for life, love, or sacred honor (a concept intimately tied in my mind with the need to make A's) could I conceive of the means whereby I could make my description more interesting. The painting wasn't interesting; it was, after all, of a bunch of cows standing in a nondescript field, and images of pastoral perfection and bucolic bliss did not accord with my view of the world in 1968. As the pile of yellow paper at my feet grew deeper, my mood grew darker. I was going to have to take myself to see that so-called art again, through the rain this time, and I didn't want to. I was bored into a near coma by the thing the first time I saw it, and the second time could only be. . . . Whoa. Wait. What had I just said? Could it be that my paper was boring because I had been bored? Had something of *me* inadvertently crept into a paper about a picture? Now I was in deep trouble. Not only did I have to go look at it, I was going to have to become interested in it. Professor Hatch may have been Scylla, but apparently I had served as my own Charybdis. I began to conceive of writing as something of a tricky business.

Standing again in front of Bossy, Elsie, and the rest of the lowing herd, I felt a faint but nagging guilt. I feared I might be cheating; I was fairly sure I was skirting the edges of the unethical; I knew I was violating the laws of the sea. On my way across campus I had devised a radical plan: I would abandon ship. Not only had my paper failed to pass muster, my trusty sit-right-down-and-write-myself-an-essay technique had failed along with it. I intended to give up both, at least temporarily, whatever the cost to my sense of personal integrity or to my vision of what the composing process of a competent English major should be. The captain was not going down with the *Easy Writer*. It was now my firm intention not to rewrite the essay I had, but to start over, and to start over not by writing, but by staring, staring with the fixed purpose of discovering something of sufficient interest about that painting to convey to Professor Hatch.

Planted squarely in front of the canvas without pad and pen and viewing it *in toto,* I immediately noticed something that had escaped my attention during my initial inch-by-inch, left-to-right, top-to-bottom, pen-to-paper tour. One of those cows, the one center canvas and (presumably) closest to artist and viewer, had rather an odd look about her. While her sisters placidly chewed cud and cropped grass, their expressions registering blank, bovine contentment, this old girl stared straight out, eying the observer with a look that suggested you were quite close enough, thank you, and if you ventured another step, she was prepared to take action. This painting didn't promote an image of the world as pastorally perfect or bucolically blissful; it suggested the tenuousness, the fragility of such tranquillity and peace. With a deft stroke of the brush, a single line above a cow's eye, this unknown artist had managed to convey the old Virgilian truth: *Et in Arcadia Ego.* Nothing perfect endures. That, I thought, was interesting. That I could write about. Land, ho.

My sailing days were over, but my travails were not. Back at my desk I soon found that, on land anyway, discovering one's destination and figuring out how to get there are two very different things indeed. Finding the subtle irony of that painting had given me direction and purpose. I knew where I wanted my paper to go. How, though, was I to get there? By what route? By which conveyance? My all-purpose sea chart for getting through a description—begin at the upper left of whatever and move clockwise until you come round again to the starting point—was not going to get me where I needed to be. Should I begin with the cow? Her eye? The herd? The field? Should I focus first on what the painting initially seems to be or on what it actually is? It was not that I could not find a path, but that I could see so many of them. Which was most direct? Which would require detours? Where were the dead ends?

My problems were complicated by my constant awareness of someone following me—Professor Hatch. It was his arrival, after all, that would signal the success of the trip. I must lead him to the prospect from which he could best see the painting as I saw it; we had to reach the same destination. To lose him along the way would surely be worse than boring him. That complicated the matter further. In addition to deciding the route at every crossroads, apparently I was also responsible for leaving a trail of crumbs for those coming behind to follow. This business of land travel was burdensome, but it seemed the only way to travel. Eventually, I earned my A.

In the doing and the redoing of that paper I learned more about the writing process than I had in the previous sixteen years of my education. At the time I lacked both the vocabulary and the theoretical basis for understanding precisely *what* it was that I had learned. Not until several years later, after I had read Kinneavy, and Winterowd and Emig and Moffett, woud I have the terms to analyze my own experience and discoveries. In 1968 words and phrases such as *rhetorical situation, audience, communication triangle, prewriting,* and *editing* were not a part of my lexicon. I had, however, at last become aware at an intuitive level of the concepts those terms represent, and I knew that, for me at least, writing would always be hard work. Correctness, conformity to rules is a simple matter; communicating effectively to another human being is not.

I travel down the page today in the style I developed that semester after my sleek little sloop went under. My progress is now that of a '39 Ford negotiating hard terrain, a Ford operated by a slightly dim twelve-year-old child lacking entirely any experience with a stick shift. I have trouble getting started. I move by fits and starts. I lurch. I shudder. I come to screeching halts only to leap forward again. I bump; I scrape; I rattle. Sometimes I get lost. Other times, I get where I'm going only to discover I'm not where I want to be. Occasionally I arrive—only occasionally. And when I do it's so awfully nice to be there that I decide to stay put, postponing further road trips until sheer necessity forces me out again.

I do not like to write; it is an always slow, frequently difficult, and sometimes painful process. Few things, however, offer the satisfaction of having written.

Discussion Questions

1. What do you think Lorch's main point is?
2. What do you think was her purpose in writing this essay?
3. Whom do you think she envisioned as her readers?
4. What might be another title for this essay?
5. Which details describe concrete things? Which ones describe specific sights and sounds?
6. What did Lorch mean when she wrote, ''The good ship *Easy Writer* did not go down until my senior year in college'' (the first sentence of the fourth paragraph)?
7. How are the details in this essay arranged?
8. What did you like or not like about this piece of writing?
9. In what ways are Lorch's experiences with and attitudes about writing similar to yours? In what ways do they differ?

WRITING ASSIGNMENT 1

Write a paragraph about a special moment in your life, an experience that you will never forget. It might be a moment of great triumph or great tragedy for you. Think about what you learned from this experience—about yourself or about other people or things. Do some freewriting, brainstorming, or clustering about the questions Who? What? Where? When? How? and Why? Develop details that make the moment come alive for your readers. Organize these details chronologically.

WRITING ASSIGNMENT 2

Write a paragraph describing one of the topics below. Use spatial order to organize your details.

- a person whose looks are very striking
- my grandmother's or grandfather's face

- my child's room
- my English classroom
- my car
- my favorite restaurant
- my favorite meal

WRITING ASSIGNMENT 3

Examine the advertisement below, which lists some reasons why students chose to go to Manhattan College. Write a paragraph explaining why you decided to go to the school that you are currently attending. Think about what you will need to explain to your readers about yourself and your school. Do some freewriting, brainstorming, or clustering to develop examples and reasons that support your topic sentence. Organize these details in emphatic order.

"The professors know me as a student, not as a number."

Why did you choose Manhattan College? **❝** I looked at some colleges that had 200 or 300 kids in a class, looking at a TV screen to listen to a lecture. Manhattan has an average of 20 to 30 kids in a class. **❞** What do you think of the professors? **❝** The professors knew our names by the second week of school. And they tell us to call anytime if we have a problem. **❞**

MANHATTAN COLLEGE
GETTING THE EDGE ON EDUCATION.
RIVERDALE, NEW YORK 10471 (212) 920-0200

✔ POINTS TO REMEMBER ABOUT PLANNING AND WRITING STRONG PARAGRAPHS

1. Use the prewriting skills that you learned in Chapter 1 (freewriting, brainstorming, and clustering) to decide what you want to say about your topic.
2. Choose one main point that you want to describe or support in the paragraph.
3. Write a topic sentence about this main point—a complete sentence that is clear and specific and that is not too general or too narrow for a paragraph.
4. Think about your purpose and about your readers' expectations.
5. Use freewriting, brainstorming, or clustering to develop appropriate stories, facts, examples, or reasons to support your topic sentence.
6. Select supporting details that are relevant to your topic sentence.
7. Make sure that you have provided a sufficient number of details to accomplish your purpose, given the audience for whom you are writing.
8. Use specific, concrete language and descriptive words that appeal to readers' five senses.
9. Make sure that your details are organized logically in an order that readers will be able to follow.
10. End with a clincher sentence that sums up the paragraph or that restates the topic sentence in different words.

3

FIVE QUALITIES OF
A GOOD PARAGRAPH

Before you can revise your paragraphs, you need to evaluate their strengths and weaknesses. In order to do this, you have to develop criteria for what you value in good writing. What is your definition of ''good'' writing? In the space below, write down the qualities that you think make a piece of writing good.

_____

_____

_____

_____

_____

   Many students think that good writing is writing without any mistakes. But writing can be neat and correct and also illogical, unclear, or boring. Good writing expresses a writer's ideas clearly and strongly in language that is appropriate to the concerns and expectations of the intended readers. Effective writing has a clear focus, logical development, unity, coherence, and correct sentence structure and grammar.
   In Chapter 2, you learned how to plan and write discovery drafts of paragraphs. This chapter will show you how to evaluate your drafts for the most important qualities of good writing.

FIVE IMPORTANT QUALITIES OF GOOD WRITING

Writing should have a **focus**:	Each paragraph has a clear main point or topic sentence.
Writing should have adequate **development**:	Each sentence supports the main point with specific details.
Writing should have **unity**:	Each paragraph sticks to its main point.
Writing should have **coherence**:	Each paragraph is organized logically and flows smoothly.
Writing should have **correctness**:	Each paragraph has complete sentences that are relatively error-free.

FOCUS

Good writing has a *focus*—it makes a clear point. It says something worth saying, something that the writer believes is important to communicate. In order to shape your notes and drafts into an effective piece of writing, you must clarify your focus and develop it into an effective topic sentence.

A paragraph without a clearly focused topic sentence can be very confusing. For example, here is a paragraph in which a student writer responded to the assignment ''Describe your impression of a room in your home so that classmates who have never seen this room will understand what it means to you.'' The paragraph below has many interesting details, but it lacks a clear focus.

My Attic (Draft)

My attic is at the very top of the house, high above my bedroom. The door to the attic is in my closet. I climb through this door at least once a week. It is incredibly quiet in the attic. The thick white pads of insulation prevent voices or sounds from coming in. It is also quite dark. There is only one light bulb up in the wooden rafters and it sends down a thin beam of yellow light. However, this is enough light for me to read my sports books or write in my journal. Often I just sit back and inhale the musty smell of the dust and mold on the walls and floors. The dust is so thick that I can almost taste it. There is one window in the attic, but it is so covered with grime and thick dust that hardly any light seeps in from outside. Even though I am at the highest point in the house, my attic feels like a cave. Like a bear, I'm glad I have my own cave.

The writer did not accomplish his purpose; he did not communicate his main impression of this room. The writer mentioned three potential focuses: The attic is ''quiet,'' it is ''dusty,'' and it is ''cavelike.'' However, his details didn't support any of these focuses. When the writer's classmates pointed this out to him, he selected one focus and revised his paragraph to support it.

My Attic (Revision)

My attic is my hideaway cave. At least once a week, I climb up into this quiet private space at the top of the house. Like a cave, the attic is silent and dark. The thick white pads of insulation prevent voices or sounds from coming in. They also keep out the light. Sitting in my attic, I feel like a bear that is hibernating. Nobody and nothing can bother me up there. If I want to do something, I can switch on the single light bulb up in the wooden rafters and it sends down a thin beam of yellow light. Usually, however, I just sit back and inhale the musty smell of the dust and mold on the walls and floors. The dust is so thick that I can almost taste it. I feel warm, peaceful, and safe. Like a bear, I'm glad I have my own private cave.

The revision is better than the draft because every detail illustrates a single focus: ''My attic is like a cave.''

Below is another's writer's response to the same assignment. Note that this writer began by considering several possible focuses.

My Mother's Powder Room

Possible Focuses:

1. This room is very feminine. It reminds me of when I used to dress up like my mom and other pretty women.
2. This room is light and bright and makes me feel happy.
3. The room is like a little girl's room. It reminds me of when I was an innocent child.

When I have children and a home of my own, I hope to have a powder room just like my mother's. If I don't, I will keep returning to my mother's because it reminds me of my childhood happiness and innocence. When I close the door inside this white and pink world, I feel like a young girl again. The tall walls still tower over me, making me feel little. The puffs of pink in the snow-white wallpaper still seem like cotton candy and I remember when I tried to lick one because it looked so sugary sweet. The floor is covered in soft rose carpeting that feels as comforting as a baby's quilt. Above this plush floor stands the long, straight mirror. Dozens of tiny lights dance brightly around the mirror like circus strobes and they radiate a glowing warmth. Soft music flows from the white Mickey Mouse radio on the sink. I curl up on the fat pad of the chair and play with the shiny white jars of makeup. The pressures from school and job melt away and I am safe and secure once again.

1. What is the focus (the topic sentence) of this paragraph?

   _____

   _____

   _____

2. The writer's purpose was to convince you of her main impression of this room. Did she accomplish her purpose? Why or why not?

_____

_____

_____

_____

WRITING ACTIVITY 1

Choose one of the paragraphs that you wrote for Writing Assignments 1, 2, or 3 on pages 67 and 68 of Chapter 2. Reread it and decide whether it has a clear focus. Does the paragraph have a single topic sentence? If so, what is it? What are the key words in this topic sentence that limit the focus? Is every sentence clearly related to these key words? If not, revise the paragraph so that it focuses on one main point.

DEVELOPMENT

Effective writing develops a topic sentence with specific details. Writers who give examples of exactly what they mean enable readers to share their thoughts. Vague or inadequately developed writing is often unconvincing. Chapter 2 provided an introduction to concrete, sensory language. The remainder of this book will help you make your writing "come alive" by teaching you how to develop your points with abundant specific details—stories, facts, examples, and reasons.

Effective development consists of details that "tell" and "show." When you "tell" about a topic, you are summarizing what you know and what you feel about it. When you "show" a topic, you are describing exactly what the object or person looks like, sounds like, feels like, and so forth. Here are two descriptions that illustrate this difference. The second paragraph is a revision of the first.

DR DOS (Digital Research's Disk Operating System) is going to revolutionize IBM computers and their clones. It is installed differently than other systems. Also, it has many excellent features that make it easier to use and superior to the current standard, Microsoft's MS-DOS.

The writer's purpose was to convince readers of the benefits of this new computer operating system. Did her draft convince you? Why or why not?

_____

_____

_____

Here is the writer's revision.

    DR DOS (Digital Research's Disk Operating System) is going to revolutionize IBM computers and their clones. Unlike all other operating systems, DR DOS is installed on a ROM card or chip, so it takes up less memory and it boots up instantaneously. No longer do users have to grind their teeth waiting for the disk to grind up the DOS; now it appears in the blink of an eye. DR DOS also has many superior features, including a full-screen editor for users to write commands directly into text, built-in directories, and password protection. These features make it easier to use and superior to the current standard, Microsoft's MS-DOS. DR DOS is the fastest, most powerful operating system there is.

How did the writer's revisions help her accomplish her purpose?

_____

_____

_____

The revision is more effective than the draft because it gives many examples of the benefits of the new system. By spelling out the specific "superior features" of DR DOS, the writer "shows" specific details to illustrate and support her topic sentence.

> **REMINDER** ——————————————————————
> Effectively written paragraphs have clearly focused topic sentences that
> the writer supports with specific details and development.

Often writers "tell" about rather than "show" an observation or experience because they assume that their reader has a similar point of view and
will intuitively understand what they mean. For example, here is a description
in which a student writer "tells" about a movie she saw but does not provide
any specific details. Does the paragraph describe how and why the movie
scared the writer?

Draft

Terminator 2 is a scary movie. The violence was so intense that it

was terrifying. In addition, the movie's futuristic special effects were even

more fearful than the violence. The scenes of agony and violence left me

sick with fear.

If you did not see the movie, could you visualize it from this description?
You probably couldn't because the writer did not provide any details. Although
she stated her main impression (that the movie was very scary), she did not
develop this impression in any detail. Instead, she assumed that everyone
would understand what she meant by terms such as *violent, scary,* and *futuristic.*

Below is a revision in which the writer concentrated on "showing" what
she saw, heard, and felt. Evaluate this revision for adequate development by
answering the questions that follow it.

Revision

Terminator 2 is a scary movie. Almost every frame is violent and

bloody. People and robots get stabbed in the head or the eyes, gunned

down in a rain of bullets, or smashed up by cars and trucks. This violence

is particularly scary because you never know when it is going to happen.

For example, the Terminator 2 seems to be a gentle and quiet man and

then suddenly his arm turns into a gleaming spike that slices through a woman's head. Also, the movie's special effects are very frightening, especially its futuristic images of a nuclear bomb. As the bomb explodes into a swelling orange mushroom, it turns all the houses and trees into smoke. It melts people's skin, sizzles their muscles, and burns their skeletons to ashes. These scenes of agony and violence left me sick with fear.

Does the revision convince you that this movie scared the writer? Why or why not?

_____

_____

_____

Which details in the revision were the most convincing?

_____

_____

_____

_____

GUIDELINES FOR EVALUATING FOCUS AND DEVELOPMENT ———
Evaluate the focus and development of your paragraphs by asking yourself the following questions:

- Does the paragraph have a clear topic sentence? If so, what is it? If not, what should you focus on?
- What is your purpose for writing this paragraph?
- What kinds of readers do you have in mind?
- Given your purpose and your audience, are there enough details, examples, and reasons to develop and support this topic sentence?

(Continued)

- Where do you need to do more "showing" and less "telling"?
- Have you used specific language so that readers will understand exactly what you mean?

 WRITING ACTIVITY 2

Practice what you have learned by evaluating the following student paragraph for effective focus and development.

A Special Person

Last year, while clicking through the channels on my new cable television hookup, I accidentally discovered an entertainer who changed my life, Paul Rodriguez. I had never heard a Latino comedian before, especially one who cared so deeply about poor minority children and adults. And I had never heard a television entertainer perform so proudly in Spanish. Listening to Rodriguez do his comedy routine in Spanish and English really knocked me out. Also he was very funny but he showed respect for Hispanic people and culture. His desire to help Hispanic kids was obvious. Rodriguez is obviously very special. Since that day, I have tried to watch every Rodriguez routine on television. And every time I see Rodriguez perform, I become even more inspired. I too want to be a Latino comedian and help others.

1. Does the paragraph have a topic sentence? If so, what is it? If not, write a sentence that sums up the paragraph's main point.

   _____

   _____

   _____

2. Did the writer provide enough details, examples, and reasons to develop and support his ideas? If not, at what points in the para-

graph are more specific details necessary? What do you need to know?

_____

_____

_____

_____

_____

3. Did you understand exactly what the writer meant? If not, which words or sentences were too vague?

_____

_____

_____

4. If the writer were your classmate, what would you tell him about this paragraph? What revising suggestions might you offer him?

_____

_____

_____

_____

_____

 WRITING ACTIVITY 3

Think about a movie or a television program that you saw recently and that made an impression on you. What is the name of the movie or program? If you had to summarize your main impression of this movie or television program in one word, what would that word be? Do five minutes of brainstorming or clustering about this main impression. Jot down details that "show" exactly what you saw, heard, and felt when you watched the movie or program. Also note how this movie or program made you feel and why it elicited this response from you.

WRITING ACTIVITY 4

Reread your notes for Writing Activity 3. Turn these notes into a discovery draft about your main impression of the movie or program. Develop this impression in specific details that will enable your classmates and teacher to see what you saw, hear what you heard, and feel what you felt. Keep the focus on your main impression and select only those details that illustrate it. Revise this draft using the "Discovery Draft Checklist" and the "Points to Remember" on pages 61 and 69 in Chapter 2 and the "Guidelines for Evaluating Focus and Development" on pages 77 and 78 of this chapter.

PROVIDING PEER FEEDBACK

For many of the activities in this book, you will be working with a partner or a group, reading each other's work and providing evaluative feedback. This process reflects the way most professional writers work: They share their drafts with friends, colleagues, and editors, who help identify strengths and problems in the drafts. For example, read the acknowledgments on page xxi of this book to see the names of all the colleagues and editors who helped me improve this text.

Some students worry that they are not good enough writers to be able to offer helpful feedback about their peers' writing. However, providing feedback does *not* mean judging a piece of writing; it means sharing one's reactions. You don't have to be a great writer to tell classmates what you liked best about their paragraph or to point out places where you had trouble understanding their ideas. Here are some guidelines for providing helpful feedback to your partners.

PEER EVALUATION GUIDELINES

1. Listen carefully to what the writer has to say about the piece of writing. Find out what his or her purpose and intentions are.
2. Look for strengths as you read your classmate's piece for the first time. Your goal is to let the writer know what he or she did particularly well. What did you like best about the writing?

3. Unless the writer asks you to find spelling and punctuation errors, ignore them. Read the paper a second time, looking for problems in meaning: Look for places where you don't get the writer's point and sentences that you don't understand.

4. When you identify a confusing or illogical part, be sensitive. Ask the writer what he or she meant, and explain why you did not get that meaning from his or her sentences or words.

5. Use "I" statements to share your responses ("I'm not really sure what your point is in these two sentences") rather than critical statements ("These two sentences are really unclear"). (Other examples of "I" statements are "I understand what you wanted to show, but I think you need more examples and more sensory words" and "I'm a little confused about how these two sentences are related. They don't seem connected to me.") "I" statements are less threatening than critical comments.

6. Remember that your goal is to help one another. Treat your partners—and their writing—with respect.

GROUP WORK 1

Form a group with two other students. Take out one of the paragraphs that you wrote for Writing Assignment 1, 2, or 3 on pages 67 and 68 of Chapter 2. Trade paragraphs with your classmates and use the guidelines above to evaluate the focus and development of your classmates' paragraphs.

GROUP WORK 2

Form a group with three or four classmates. Evaluate the focus and development of the following draft of a student paragraph by answering the questions below the paragraph. Choose one person to record the group's responses (on separate paper).

Draft: My Brother

My brother Hui Ling is a wonderful person. He can be the most charming person in the world. Sometimes, however, he can be extremely confusing. He's like an absentminded professor. When he focuses on you, he is a delight to be with. When he is daydreaming, he loses track of what you are saying and his responses don't make much sense. Hui Ling is six years older than I am and I have always looked up to him. He is a very kind person. My brother is smart, caring, and thoughtful and because of these qualities, many people really enjoy talking with him. He can be confusing and in a world of his own and that drives some people crazy. Our parents died and we have no other brothers or sisters. That's one reason why I try to get along well with my brother. My brother can be annoying. I have learned to put up with his dreaminess and his strange behavior. I love him very much.

1. Does the paragraph have a clear main point? If so, what is it? If not, what do you think the writer should focus on?
2. If you were revising this paragraph, what would you write as a topic sentence for it?
3. Has the writer provided enough specific details to support his or her points? If not, where are examples, reasons, and other details needed to help you understand the writer's idea?

UNITY

Another important quality of good writing is *unity,* or singleness of purpose and development. In a unified paragraph or essay, all the sentences work together to support and develop the central focus. Effective writers help readers follow their ideas by ensuring that every detail sticks to the main point.

Let's look at how the lack of unity in a paragraph can confuse readers. The paragraph below is a student's response to a report titled "Women at Thirtysomething" issued by the U.S. Department of Education in 1991. Underline the details that do not seem relevant to the main point of the paragraph.

Draft

(1) A college degree may not benefit women as much as it benefits men. (2) Recently, the U.S. Department of Education published a report about this. (3) It seems that employers are not rewarding female workers

who have college degrees. (4) Male college graduates get better positions and earn more money than do better-qualified female graduates. (5) This report tells the findings of a recent study. (6) Male and female college graduates who took the same kinds of college courses and who worked in the same job for the same number of years make different salaries. (7) The researcher who did this report is a senior research associate in the Department's Office of Research. (8) He has done many important studies. (9) This study showed that male graduates earn 15 percent to 60 percent more than female graduates for their effort and qualifications. (10) Many female graduates have changed their careers recently. (11) This report shows that women cannot assume that their college degrees will earn them good jobs and salaries.

This paragraph is not unified. Sentence numbers 5, 7, 8, and 10 do not relate clearly to the main point stated in sentence 1. By breaking up the unity of the paragraph, these irrelevant details confuse readers. Here is the writer's revision.

Revision

A college degree may not benefit women as much as it benefits men. According to the U.S. Department of Education, male college graduates get better positions and earn more money than do better-qualified female graduates. Researchers found that male and female college graduates who took the same kinds of college courses and who worked in the same jobs for the same number of years make different salaries. Their study showed that male graduates earn 15 percent to 60 percent more than female graduates for their effort and qualifications. In addition, the women graduates had more unemployment than the men did. This report shows that women cannot assume that their college degrees will earn them good jobs and salaries.

This revision is more effective than the draft because every sentence develops the paragraph's main point. It has unity.

Practice your ability to evaluate unity by examining the paragraph below.

(1) Although I look very different from my adoptive parents, I am incredibly similar to them in terms of temperament and values. (2) I am quiet and shy like my mother, and I share her love of learning and books. (3) My mom is a housewife, and she does volunteer work at the local hospital, reading to elderly patients. (4) My mom and I even share fictional tastes: We both like mysteries and spy novels. (5) I hope to become an English teacher one day. (6) I am Mexican and my parents are Anglos. (7) Although my personality is similar to my mother's, I also share many of my father's traits. (8) He and I believe that athletic competition helps people become stronger and feel better about themselves. (9) Like my dad, I excel in basketball, football, and tennis and I love watching sports on television. (10) My father was once a U.S. Tennis Association ranked player and he is still a great player. (11) Both of my parents have always shown me how important it is to respect and care for other people. (12) When I was a child, they took turns spending time with me and helping me understand the importance of fair play and of helping others. (13) Today, these values are still with me and I am active in many charitable organizations that assist the poor. (14) I am particularly concerned about homelessness. (15) In conclusion, although my genes and my looks differ from my parents', I share their concerns, their favorite activities, and their values.

1. Which sentence expresses the topic sentence? _____

2. Which sentences do not seem relevant to this topic sentence?

_____

3. How can the writer improve this paragraph?

_____

_____

_____

_____

 WRITING ACTIVITY 5

Evaluate the unity of the paragraph below by answering the questions that follow it.

Children of divorce often suffer a lot of pain and guilt. My parents got divorced when I was four, and I spent most of my childhood thinking that their divorce was my fault. Neither of my parents ever discussed the divorce openly with me, and I was sure that they split up because I had driven them crazy. After the divorce, my mother went back to work. Throughout the years, I never gave up trying to get them back together again. Every time I failed at this, I felt doubly guilty. When I finally realized how much my mother and father hated each other, I died inside. But I wouldn't dare discuss my pain with them. I am never going to get married. The only times I did let my pain and anger out were when they tried to use me as a middleman. Almost every time I went to one of their homes, they would say things like, "Tell your father that he can't see you next week if he doesn't send me a check immediately." There were other things that made me want to yell. I would scream back, "Tell him yourself!" I couldn't wait for the day that I could get my own apartment and never have to shuttle back and forth between them again.

1. What is the focus or topic sentence of this paragraph?

_____

_____

2. Which supporting details did you think were most effective in illustrating the writer's main idea?

_____

_____

_____

_____

3. Is this paragraph unified? If so, why? If not, which sentences should be crossed out?

_____

_____

GROUP WORK 3

Form a group of three. Take out the final version of the paragraph that you wrote for Writing Activity 4 on page 80 of this chapter (about a movie or television program that made an impression on you). Exchange paragraphs with a classmate. Evaluate the unity of your classmate's paragraph by answering the following questions (on a separate piece of paper).

1. What is the focus or the topic sentence of this paragraph?
2. Is each sentence related to this focus?
3. Who do you think the writer's audience is?
4. What do you think the writer's purpose is?
5. Is this purpose accomplished with the details in the paragraph?
6. Does any sentence seem unrelated to the focus of this para-

graph? If so, which one(s)? Should the writer omit or revise these sentences?

7. How can this paragraph be made more unified?

COHERENCE

Well-constructed paragraphs and essays also have *coherence:* Each idea is clearly and logically related to the one that comes before it and to the one that follows it. Coherence means "sticking together," and the details and sentences in coherent writing stick together in an order that flows smoothly.

How is coherence different from unity? Imagine that a paragraph is a brick wall of a house. If all the bricks in the wall are similar in shape, size, color, and pattern, then the wall is unified. Now look at the wall closely in your mind. The cement or mortar that connects the bricks to one another is what makes the wall coherent. Like the bricks in the wall, the sentences in your paragraphs need to be cemented together in a logical way.

In Chapter 2, you learned how to achieve coherence in your writing by organizing details in a logical order. As you develop examples and reasons to support your main idea, you should be thinking about an appropriate order for presenting these details. You can arrange your ideas chronologically, spatially, or emphatically. The decision depends on the kinds of details that you have composed and on your focus, your purpose, and your readers.

Another way to achieve paragraph coherence is to use *transitions*—words and phrases that signal the relation among your ideas and details. *Trans* means "across," and transitions reach across sentences to show the connections between ideas in the same sentence, between details in different sentences, and between ideas in different paragraphs. In the box that follows, some common transitions are arranged according to the type of signal they provide readers.

TRANSITIONAL WORDS AND PHRASES FOR ACHIEVING COHERENCE

- **To signal the time relation of the next detail:** *first, second, third, next, then, after, before, during, as, now, meanwhile, at last, immediately, finally*
- **To signal that the next detail is similar or is an additional example or reason:** *also, in addition, furthermore, moreover, similarly, first, next, last, finally*

(Continued)

- **To signal that the next detail is an example:** *for example, for instance, thus, in other words, in particular*
- **To signal that the next detail is different:** *on the other hand, however, nevertheless, still, but, although, even though, in contrast, on the contrary*
- **To signal that the next detail is a consequence:** *as a result, consequently, hence, so, therefore, thus*
- **To signal that the next detail is a conclusion:** *in conclusion, in summary, on the whole, therefore, thus*

Let's look at a paragraph that does not have coherence. As you read the paragraph below, circle each sentence that seems choppy or that doesn't seem logically related to the sentence that precedes it.

I adore my five-year-old daughter, Serena. She drives me crazy. This morning she dumped her breakfast of hot oatmeal on the cat. She tried to wash it off him by pouring her glass of water on him. I started yelling at her. Serena didn't stop making a mess. She stared defiantly at me and smashed a chocolate cookie all over the table. I spanked her. I told Serena to go get dressed. I cleaned the kitchen. I went to see how she was doing. I got angry all over again because Serena had tied her sneakers together and was hopping all around knocking things over. I started to scream. She looked up at me and said, "Please don't be mad Mommy. I'm only a little girl." I melted. She is really a little devil, not a little girl. She's my devil and I love her.

This paragraph has excellent details, but they don't make sense next to each other because the writer did not use any transitions. For example, the first and second sentences do not have any clear relation to each other.
Now read the revised version of this paragraph:

Although I adore my five-year-old daughter, Serena, she drives me crazy. For instance, this morning she dumped her breakfast of hot oatmeal on the cat. Then she tried to wash it off him by pouring her glass of water on him. <u>Even though</u> I started yelling at her, Serena didn't stop making a mess. <u>In fact</u>, she stared defiantly at me and smashed a chocolate cookie all over the table, <u>so</u> I spanked her. <u>After that</u>, I told Serena to go get dressed <u>while</u> I cleaned the kitchen. <u>When</u> I went to see how she was doing, I got angry all over again <u>because</u> Serena had tied her sneakers together and was hopping all around knocking things over. I started to scream, <u>but then</u> she looked up at me and said, "Please don't be mad Mommy. I'm only a little girl." I melted. She is really a little devil, not a little girl. <u>Nevertheless</u>, she's my devil and I love her.

The transitions make the relations between the sentences clear. The details in this revision are logically arranged and they stick together—they cohere.

Notice that you do not need to put a transition at the beginning of every sentence in order to make your paragraphs coherent. You will have to decide which sentences are clear and effective without transitions and which ones need transitions to signal their relations to other ideas in the paragraph.

WRITING ACTIVITY 6

Improve the coherence of the paragraph below by writing in appropriate transitional words and phrases to show the relationships between the ideas. Choose transitions from the list on pages 87 and 88, and try to vary the transitions that you select.

There are several different types of hearing aids available to help people who are hard of hearing. I was born with a severe hearing loss, and I've been wearing aids since I was a year old. _____ I wore a body-assisted hearing aid, which was a microphone that fit behind my ears and an amplifier that strapped to my chest. _____ this device helped me hear, it annoyed me and I kept pulling off the amplifier. _____ the microphones irritated my ears. _____ I was fitted with another type of aid, the in-the-ear kind. I liked these hearing aids because they were more comfortable. _____ they were hidden inside my ears, so kids didn't notice them as much as they noticed the body-assisted aids. _____ the in-the-ear kind weren't strong enough to help me hear low- or high-pitched sounds. I could't hear my friends when they giggled, screamed, or whispered, _____ I started to feel left out and sad. _____ my parents took me to get a third kind of aid called cochlear implants. These were surgically inserted into my inner ears, _____ no one can see them and they can't annoy me. To me, this is the best type of aid because it is invisible and it has helped me tune back into the world.

Practice your skill at evaluating coherence by examining the following discovery draft by a student. Is it coherent?

Discovery Draft

(1) The day I baby-sat for my twin nephews was the most frustrating experience I have had in a long time. (2) They decided to chase my cat around the living room, turning it into a disaster area. (3) They knocked over the chairs. (4) They climbed onto my new oak table. (5) They scrambled off the table and accidentally scattered all my important papers and reports. (6) They broke the buzzer on my apartment door. (7) I grabbed them and told them to go to the bedroom and watch television. (8) That turned out to be a bad idea. (9) I found them sitting in a pile of feathers that had come loose during their pillow fight on my bed. (10) They caught the cat and tried to strangle her. (11) Lunch deteriorated into a food fight, and soon the twins were covered in ketchup. (12) I told them that if they made another mess, they would never be allowed back in my

home. (13) I was thinking of tying them up, but my sister arrived. (14) Instead of being sorry, they yelled "Who cares! We don't even want to be here now." (15) She asked me if I could baby-sit the following Saturday. (16) I had a fit and pushed her and her family out the door.

Here is the student's revision of this draft. Circle the transitions that the writer added to clarify the relations among his details.

Revision

(1) The day I baby-sat for my twin nephews was the most frustrating experience I have had in a long time. (2) First, the twins broke the buzzer on my apartment door. (3) Next they decided to chase my cat around the living room, turning it into a disaster area. (4) After the boys knocked over the chairs, they climbed onto my new oak table. (5) Then the little monsters scrambled off the table and accidentally scattered all my important papers and reports that I had been working on before their arrival. (6) When they finally caught the cat and tried to strangle her, I grabbed them and told them to go to the bedroom and watch television. (7) That turned out to be a bad idea. (8) When I went to see how the boys were doing, I found them sitting in a pile of feathers that had come loose during their pillow fight on my bed. (9) After I finished screaming at them and cleaning up the mess, I took them into the kitchen to eat. (10) Of course, lunch deteriorated into a food fight and soon the two devils were covered in ketchup. (11) After cleaning them up, I told them that if they made another mess, they would never be allowed back in my home. (12) Instead of being sorry, the boys yelled, "Who cares! We don't even want to be here now." (13) At this point I was thinking of tying them up, but then my sister arrived. (14) When she asked me if I could baby-sit the following Saturday, I had a fit and pushed her and her family out the door.

Which sentences did the writer switch to make the revision more coherent than the draft? (Write the sentence numbers below.)

_____

_____

How did the transitions make the revision more coherent than the draft?

_____

_____

_____

_____

Remember that when you write a discovery draft, you shouldn't worry about unity and coherence because your goal is to generate as many ideas as possible and to get them all down on paper (or up on screen). When you revise your discovery draft, however, you need to impose order on your ideas. Reread every draft from the perspective of an unknown reader and look for places where information is missing and where sentences and details do not seem logically related to one another. Chapter 4 will teach you additional strategies for improving the unity and coherence of your writing.

REMINDER ―――――――――――――――――――――――――
Effective writing is unified and coherent. When you finish writing a draft, check every sentence to make sure that it clearly develops or supports your topic sentence and that it is logically related to the sentences that precede and follow it.

GUIDELINES FOR EVALUATING
UNITY AND COHERENCE ―――――――――――――――――
Evaluate the unity and coherence of your writing by asking yourself the following questions:

- Does the paragraph have a clearly focused topic sentence?
- Does every sentence develop or support this topic sentence?
- Is every sentence logically related to the ones that precede and follow it?

• Is the paragraph logically organized and developed?
• Are there appropriate transitions to signal the relations among the details in the paragraph?

GROUP WORK 4

Form a group of four. Select one person to read aloud the student paragraph below. It is a revision of the paragraph that you read for Group Work 2 on pages 81 and 82 of this chapter. Evaluate this paragraph for unity and coherence by answering the questions that follow it. Choose one person to record the group's responses.

Revision: My Brother

My brother Hui Ling is like an absentminded professor. When he focuses on you, he is attentive and charming and a delight to be with. However, when he is daydreaming , he loses track of what you are saying and his responses don't make much sense. Like a teacher, Hui Ling is extremely smart. In fact, he has an IQ of 155. He is a genius and he gets so involved thinking about an idea that he literally doesn't hear people speaking to him. Often he is in a world of his own, and his confusing responses drive some people crazy. Yet when Hui Ling focuses on you, he is caring and kind. If you ask him to help you with a problem, he will teach you how to solve it. He is endlessly patient and he rarely gets angry, even when he has to explain something three times. Thus, although Hui Ling's dreaminess can be annoying, I have learned to put up with his strange behavior. And I love him very much.

1. Reread the draft on pages 81 and 82. What changes has the writer made to improve the unity and coherence of this paragraph?
2. Does this revised paragraph have a clear main point? If so, what is it?

3. In this revision, has the writer provided enough specific details to support his or her points? Why or why not?
4. Is this paragraph unified? Why or why not?
5. Is this paragraph coherent? Why or why not?

CORRECTNESS

The fifth quality of good writing is correctness. Academic and professional writing should conform to the *conventions of correctness* agreed upon by teachers and experts in the field. In writing, these conventions are the ones that are used by authors of books, articles in newspapers, and essays in magazines and journals. They include correct sentence structure, grammar, spelling, punctuation, and capitalization. Writing that has many mistakes or unconventional forms is unclear and difficult to read. Errors interfere with a reader's interpretation of the writer's meaning, and they are annoying and distracting to most readers. For instance, what is your reaction to the student paragraph below?

All bicycle riders should wear bike helmets. Because these can save lives and prevent terrable injuries. Every day someone dies in a biking accident, every hour a person suffers a crippeling head injury on a bike. These statistics became reel for me last summer. When I saw both of these awful thing happen. Me and five friends went on a twenty mile bike trip. I was the only one wearing a bike helmet and it save my life. At one point in the trip we hit a wet patch of road and we all started skidding like sleds on ice. Me and two of my friends could'nt control our bikes and we crashed into an on-coming cars. One friend was killed instantly, the other is still in a comma. And I am still morning them both. Wishing that they had been force to wear helmets. If they had they would still be cycling with me today.

The details and the organization of this paragraph are fine, but the errors in sentence structure, grammar, and spelling are not what we expect to see in academic writing. In addition, the errors convey the impression that the writer doesn't care enough about the reader or the topic to edit and proofread his work. If you care about your topic and reader, you will edit your writing.

You can find strategies for editing and proofreading your paragraphs in Part 4 of this book, "The Writer's Handbook." Chapters 15 though 21 will provide you with instruction and practice in identifying and correcting common errors in academic English conventions. Below is a chart of these errors. Note that each error is preceded by the correction symbol that your teachers may use when they mark your writing. Also note that each error is followed by the number of the page in this book where the error is discussed.

CHART OF COMMON ERRORS AND CORRECTION SYMBOLS

agr   error in agreement of subject and verb (pp. 487–496)

cap   letter should be capitalized (pp. 556–562)

cs   comma splice (p. 426)

dm   dangling modifier (pp. 431–432)

frag   fragment (pp. 411–424)

mm   misplaced modifier (pp. 431–432)

¶   indent for a new paragraph

//   parallelism error (pp. 434–437)

pl   error in a plural noun or ending (p. 507)

poss   error in a possessive pronoun or ending (pp. 581–582)

pron   pronoun reference error (pp. 504–505)

∧   add the omitted punctuation mark

sp   spelling error (pp. 545–547)

vb   verb error (pp. 472–487)

ww   wrong word (p. 520)

GETTING READERS' RESPONSES

Use the checklist below to help you evaluate your drafts and those of your classmates. You can also ask family, friends, and classmates to read your writing and to answer the questions below.

CHECKLIST FOR EVALUATING THE FIVE QUALITIES OF A GOOD PARAGRAPH ———————

Focus

1. Does the paragraph have a single clear topic sentence? If so, what is it? If not, what might it be?
2. Does the paragraph stick to this focus and purpose?

Development

3. Given the writer's purpose and audience, are there enough examples and reasons to develop and support this topic sentence?
4. Are all the details appropriate for the writer's purpose and audience?

Unity

5. Does every sentence support and develop the topic sentence?
6. Does the paragraph stick to its main point?

Coherence

7. Is every sentence logically related to the ones that precede and follow it?
8. Has the writer used appropriate transitions to signal the relations among the details in the paragraph?
9. Is the paragraph organized clearly and logically?

Correctness

10. Does the paragraph have complete sentences that are relatively free of errors in grammar, spelling, punctuation, and capitalization?

■ EXPLORING FURTHER

This chapter helped you learn how to evaluate a paragraph for five important qualities of good writing. The reading and writing activity that follows will enable you to practice and improve your ability to evaluate these qualities.

Below is an essay that a student wrote for his university's test of minimum writing competency. Use the "Checklist for Evaluating the Five Qualities of a Good Paragraph" on page 96 to help you evaluate each of the paragraphs in this essay, one at a time. Use a separate piece of paper to write your answers to the questions in the checklist.

Essay 3B

(1) I agree that television does have an harmful effect on young people. (2) The young people will watch television then to do home work or prepare themselves for a test. (3) They will make up excuses for not doing the homework or prepare themselves for the test, the excuse might be one of the following: it doesn't matter if I fail the test I will still pass the class, it's only one homework assignment I will be missing, or the teacher shouldn't fail me because I missed one or failed one test. (4) This is how the young people feel, they would watch television before they would read a book. (5) I know they feel that way because all my friends are like that and I use to be like that. (6) I use to watch television then to read a book or do homework until I realized how important an education was. (7) Watching television wouldn't get me a job.

(8) Television changes some peoples life styles they try to be like the person on the television. (9) After the program is over they might say I want to be like him or her. (10) They don't realize that is a person playing the role of a character. (11) If the character does something the young person might think that it is done like that in real life. (12) The young person could get hurt doing something that they might seen on television. (13) Then they wouldn't understand why it don't happen the same way for them. (14) Until someone explains to them that certain this on television only happens on television.

When you finish evaluating this essay, turn to page 98 at the end of this chapter to see what the test evaluators said about it.

✔ POINTS TO REMEMBER ABOUT GOOD WRITING

1. Each paragraph should have a focus, or topic sentence—a complete sentence that is clear and specific and that is not too general or too narrow for a paragraph.
2. The focus of the paragraph should be developed by appropriate stories, facts, examples, or reasons.
3. Every supporting detail in the paragraph should be relevant to the topic sentence.
4. The details should include specific, concrete language and descriptive words that appeal to readers' five senses.

5. The details should be organized logically in an order that readers can follow.
6. Each sentence should be logically related to the ones that precede and follow it.
7. Appropriate transitions should be used to signal the relations among the ideas.
8. Every paragraph should have complete sentences that are relatively free of errors in grammar, spelling, punctuation, and capitalization.

The test essay on page 97 was scored by two teachers. The scale that they used was developed by a universitywide committee of college composition teachers. Its scores range from 1 (lowest) to 6 (highest). A passing score is 4 or higher. Essays that receive a score of 3 or lower fail. Here is what the essay test evaluators had to say about this essay, which they both scored a 3.

Comment on Essay 3B

This essay has been given a score of 3 largely because of problems in development and grammar. Within each paragraph the writer's efforts to develop ideas tend to lead him off the track (sentence 3) or to offer other arguments that he does not express clearly or develop well (sentences 7, 11–14). In addition, the writer has recurrent grammatical problems, especially inaccurate sentence boundaries (sentences 3, 4, 5, 7, and 8), subject-verb agreement (sentence 13), and verb forms (sentences 5, 6, and 12). Finally, his vocabulary is often limited and becomes repetitious (sentences 4–7).

This essay is a 3 and not a 2 primarily because the writer uses language with relative ease. He begins by responding to the topic and he offers two separate arguments to support his position. Some of the sentences are relatively clear (sentences 1 and 5).

CHAPTER

4

REVISING AND EDITING PARAGRAPHS

In the preceding chapters, you learned how to plan and write strong paragraphs and how to evaluate them for five important qualities of effective writing. Now you're ready for the most important step in improving your writing: revising. As the author Elaine Maimon noted, "Good essays aren't written; they're rewritten." However, revising means much more than copying a paper over in neater handwriting. Revising means "re-seeing," rereading a piece of writing, evaluating its strengths and weaknesses, and using feedback from readers to add, delete, and rearrange words and sentences. Here are the five revision strategies that you can practice in this chapter:

Step 1:   Revising the topic sentence for a clearer focus
Step 2:   Revising details for your purpose and audience
Step 3:   Revising for more logical organization
Step 4:   Revising for greater unity and coherence
Step 5:   Revising and editing for clarity and correctness

ANALYZING YOUR REVISING PROCESSES

Experienced writers agree that all good writing always involves revising. Rarely do skilled writers produce clear, fully developed pieces on their first attempt. Instead, they treat their drafts as experiments. Experienced writers know that they will have to clarify, cut, rearrange, and rewrite each piece several times. However, readers usually see only the final, polished version, and most writers do not talk about all their revisions. Thus, some readers believe that good writing flows magically from the pens of skilled writers. For inexperienced writers, this belief is particularly discouraging because they

99

don't possess any magic pens. They have to learn the crucial role that revision plays in producing a successful piece of writing.

Here is the "truth" about writing and revising, stated eloquently by the novelist and teacher Maya Angelou:

> It costs so much to write well. It is said that easy reading is damned hard writing, and of course that's the other way around, too—easy writing is awfully hard going to read. But to make a poem or an article, a piece of journalism, sing—so that the reader is not even aware that he or she is reading—means that one goes to the work constantly: polishing it, cleaning it up, editing, cutting out, and then finally developing it into a piece that hopefully sings. And then one shows it to an audience and a critic says, "She's a natural writer." There's nothing natural about it. It costs a lot. . . . Hard work. It's hard work.

Do you have misconceptions about revising? Are you revising your work effectively? Evaluate your revising processes by answering the questions below as honestly as possible.

1. If you are assigned a piece of writing, when do you begin doing it?

   _____

   _____

2. How many drafts do you usually write when doing a paper for one of your classes?

   _____

   _____

3. If you do revise your papers, what do you try to improve in each of the versions?

   _____

   _____

4. Are you willing to add new details and to reorganize your paper to make it clearer and more logical? Why or why not?

   _____

If you typically begin a writing assignment a day or two before it is due, then you aren't allowing yourself enough time to reread, rethink, and improve your writing. Similarly, if you write only a single version of an assigned paper, you are depriving yourself of the opportunity to clarify and correct it. Also, if you think that revising means only correcting obvious errors, you are missing the chance to craft a paper that you and your readers will find worth reading.

Remember, revising is the way to succeed in writing, not a sign that you have failed. Follow the advice of two famous novelists: Isaac Bashevis Singer, who noted that "the wastepaper basket is a writer's best friend," and Vladimir Nabokov, who wrote "I have rewritten—often several times—every word I have ever published. My pencils outlast their erasers." Revise your paragraphs until they "sing."

WRITING ACTIVITY 1

Think about your answers to the four questions about revising on page 100. Write a letter to yourself describing how you could make your revising processes more effective. Describe what you think you should do to allow yourself more time to write and to revise. Also describe the kinds of revisions you might make in your drafts to improve their clarity and organization.

Most writers find it difficult to revise a draft that they have just written. The writing is too fresh in their minds, and it is difficult to see places where the details and connections are missing or are confusing. Before you revise your writing, you need to get some distance from it so that you will be able to analyze it from the perspective of your intended readers. Here are some techniques for gaining this distance.

TECHNIQUES FOR GAINING DISTANCE ON YOUR DRAFTS

- Put the draft away for several hours so that you forget what you were thinking when you wrote it. This makes it easier for you to read and evaluate what is actually on the page, rather than what was in your mind as you wrote.

(Continued)

- Adopt an imagined reader's perspective. Imagine your reader's personality, concerns, interests, values. Consider how he or she will respond to your writing.
- Pretend to be the reader for whom you are writing. Reread your draft from this reader's perspective to see if the reader would be confused by any parts.
- Read the draft aloud so that you can hear where it sounds strong and effective and where it is confusing and unclear, or ask a friend or relative to read it aloud, and as you listen to the draft take notes on problems in it.

STEP 1: REVISING YOUR TOPIC SENTENCE FOR FOCUS

The first thing you did when you composed your drafts was to develop a topic sentence that fit your purpose for writing and your intended audience. You can begin revising your paragraph by checking this main idea. Ask yourself the following questions:

1. Is my topic sentence a complete sentence?
2. Does it have key words that limit the topic—that express my opinion or the point I want to make about the topic?
3. Is my topic sentence too narrow or too broad?
4. Will readers understand my purpose for writing this paragraph?

If your answer to any of these questions is ''No'' or ''I'm not sure,'' then rewrite your topic sentence.

Here is an example of a student's attempt to revise the topic sentence of a descriptive paragraph he had written for a school assignment.

Missouri offers many things to many people. The area that I live in, the Ozark Mountain region, is a good example. People who are interested in pioneer life can visit Silver Dollar City and Joplin City and experience life in the 1880 Ozark mining towns. They can also tour the Shepherd of the Hills Homestead and learn about life on the Western frontier. Or they can go to the Mansfield Homestead, which is the place where Laura Ingalls Wilder wrote all her Little House on the Prairie books. The Ozark Mountain region also has dozens of monuments to our country's past. For instance, the George Washington Carver Monument in Diamond explains all about Carver and his accomplishments, and the Civil War Monument in Carthage describes many war battles. It seems that wherever you go in the Ozarks, there are sites that will help you relive the past.

Does this paragraph support its topic sentence, "Missouri offers many things to many people"? Here are the notes that the writer's classmates wrote to him as they answered this question:

Joe, you should make the second sentence into your controlling idea. Ellen

Missouri offers many things to many people. The area that I live in, the Ozark Mountain region, is a good example. People who are interested in pioneer life can visit Silver Dollar City and Joplin City and experience life in 1880 Ozark mining towns. They can also tour the Shepherd of the Hills Homestead and learn about life on the Western frontier. Or they can go to the Mansfield Homestead, which is the place where Laura Ingalls Wilder wrote all her Little House on the Prairie books. The Ozark Mountain region also has dozens of monuments to our country's past. For instance, the George Washington Carver Monument in Diamond explains all about Carver and his accomplishments, and the Civil War Monument in Carthage describes many war battles. It seems that wherever you go in the Ozarks, there are sites that will help you relive the past.

Joe, These details are only about the Ozarks not about all of Missouri. Sue-Ann

Dear Joe, Your controlling idea is real general and vague. Why don't you change it to fit your details about Ozark region and the Western past. Tom T.

Here is the writer's revised topic sentence:

Missouri's Ozark Mountain region offers many opportunities to experience what life was like on the Western frontier.

This topic sentence is more narrow and focused than the original, and it lets readers know what to expect from the remainder of the paragraph.

GROUP WORK 1

Form a group with two or three students and work together to revise the topic sentence of the following student paragraph.

Studying for Tests

Studying for tests can be fun. One way to study for a test is to reread your textbook and your notes several times, highlighting key points with a yellow marker. When you study this way, you are memorizing important facts and details that you might have to discuss on the test. An even better way to study is to take notes on the material being tested. The act of writing down key ideas and information kind of imprints the material in your brain because you are summarizing it in your own words. However, I think the most effective method of studying for a test is to study with a group of three or four classmates. Together you can discuss what might be on the test and quiz each other about ideas and information. Your classmates can help you analyze and learn important ideas that you might not have studied if you were alone. Using one or more of these study techniques can help you do better on any test.

1. What is this writer's purpose?

2. Which key word in her topic sentence focuses and limits the details that can be used to develop the paragraph?

3. Is this key word appropriate for the details that the writer discusses in her paragraph? If not, revise the topic sentence so that it focuses on the details that the rest of the paragraph develops.

WRITING ACTIVITY 2

Take out a paragraph that you wrote for one of the Writing Activities or Writing Assignments in the preceding chapters. As you reread the paragraph's topic sentence, ask yourself the four revising questions on page 102. Revise your topic sentence to make it more focused and more specific.

STEP 2: REVISING DETAILS FOR YOUR PURPOSE AND AUDIENCE

The next step in revising a paragraph is determining whether your details support the topic sentence clearly and adequately. To do this, you will need to read and think critically about your draft.

Reading and Thinking Critically. Reading and thinking critically does not mean tearing a piece of writing apart, looking for errors. Rather it means analyzing the paragraph or essay and questioning its effectiveness. (Indeed, the word *critical* comes from the Greek word for "question.") When we read and think critically, we examine our writing to see if it makes sense, if it is believable, and if it is logically developed.

Revising

Unless you are writing for yourself, the best way to read and think critically about the details in your writing is to reread it from the perspective of your intended readers. Here are some questions for you to consider about your purpose and audience.

QUESTIONS FOR CRITICAL READING AND THINKING

1. Was my purpose to express my feelings or to share something important with my readers? If so, will they find my story or my examples believable and interesting?

2. Was my purpose to explain something to readers? If so, will they understand my examples and reasons? Will they find them logical?

(Continued)

3. Was my purpose to persuade readers to think or feel or do something? If so, will they be convinced by my reasons?
4. If I become the intended reader and look for strengths in the draft, which details are very specific and convincing? Which images are clear and concrete? How can I build on these strengths to improve the weak parts of the draft?
5. Are there places in the draft where the reader might respond by saying, ''Huh? What do you mean?'' ''Give me an example,'' or ''So? So what's your point?'' What kinds of facts, examples, and reasons should I add?

Most writers underestimate readers' needs for concrete details and for specific examples and reasons. If you suspect that your draft does not have enough specific supporting details to achieve your purpose, then do some more freewriting, brainstorming, and clustering to develop new experiences, examples, and reasons. In addition, if your draft has details that are not clearly and logically related to the topic sentence, either cross them out or add words that explain how they are related to your main idea. Read and think critically: If a detail doesn't make sense or isn't relevant, cross it out. No matter how hard you worked to develop your details, if they don't clearly support your topic sentence, they don't belong in the paragraph.

Here is an example of how a student evaluated and revised his draft for focus and development. Note the marginal comments that this writer wrote to himself as he reread his draft. Examine the changes that he made on the draft and then read the final revision (which follows the draft).

1st Draft: Dinosaurs

Purpose: To explain why I think meat-eating dinosaurs are so

   fascinating.

Audience: Classmates who might not know too much about

   dinosaurs.

Rearrange?

Better word?

Ever since I was four years old, I've (thought) that meat-eating

dinosaurs were the most interesting things that ever lived. These~~giant~~ *carnivores roamed?*

~~meat-eaters~~ (lived) on the earth millions of years ago. ~~They were called carnivores because they ate meat. Many other dinosaurs lived at the~~

Maybe put in details about their teeth?

~~same time. They were called herbivores or plant-eaters.~~ The carnivores ate the herbivores. The first giant carnivore to appear was Allosaurus. He

How large?

was [extremely large] and weighed ~~a couple~~ of tons. Most

about four

Why is its weight important?

allosauruses lived in North America and Africa. The largest carnivore was Tyrannosaurus rex. All the other dinosaurs feared him. (He was

which

Why?

(descended from Allosaurus.) When I was a child, I used to have

nightmares about (him.) Now, I wish I could have been there to see (him)

that I am older

rule the earth.

use another word?

Final Revision: My Favorite Dinosaurs

Ever since I was four years old, I've been fascinated by dinosaurs, particularly the meat-eating ones. These giant carnivores roamed the earth about 200 million years ago. They had teeth as big and sharp as daggers that they used to chomp the flesh off the plant-eating dinosaurs. The first giant carnivore to appear was Allosaurus. It stood about fifteen feet tall and weighed about four tons. Even with all that weight, it could move quickly to catch its prey. The largest carnivore was Tyrannosaurus rex, which was descended from Allosaurus and looked like a larger version of it. T-rex was a fierce hunter and all the other dinosaurs feared it. When I was a child, I used to have nightmares about T-rex's huge, razor-sharp teeth crunching my bones. Now that I am older, I wish I could have been around to see this great beast rule the earth.

This example illustrates the importance of revision. By rereading and rewriting this paragraph several times, the writer clarified and tightened his ideas. The topic sentence of the revision is more focused, and the supporting details are more specific and descriptive. In addition, the writer eliminated the irrelevant details and reorganized his details more logically. For example, note that the writer deleted the irrelevant details about herbivorous dinosaurs and replaced them with specific information about and images of the teeth of carnivorous dinosaurs. By taking out irrelevant information and adding more specific facts, images, and reasons, this writer greatly improved his draft. The revision is more tightly focused and more convincing than the draft.

REMINDER ⎯⎯⎯⎯⎯⎯⎯⎯⎯⎯⎯⎯⎯⎯⎯⎯⎯⎯⎯⎯⎯⎯⎯⎯⎯⎯⎯⎯⎯⎯⎯⎯⎯

Examine your draft's supporting details to see if they are concrete and specific and if they clearly and directly support the topic sentence. Decide whether you have enough supporting details to accomplish your purpose in writing the paragraph.

WRITING ACTIVITY 3

Take out the writing that you did for one of the Writing Activities in Chapter 2. Write a paragraph based on *one* of these sets of details. When you finish writing, put away your draft for several hours. Then reread it and ask yourself the Critical Thinking questions on pages 105 and 106. If you haven't accomplished your purpose through your examples or reasons, do some prewriting to develop additional supporting details. Revise the paragraph until you think your intended reader would find it clear and effective.

WRITING ACTIVITY 4

Evaluate the effectiveness of the topic sentence and supporting details in the paragraph below by answering the four questions that follow it. Then revise the paragraph and rewrite it on a separate piece of paper.

Draft: Quitting Smoking

Quitting smoking takes a lot of time and effort. It took me a year and a half to stop smoking, and every day was painful. I smoked for many years, and I really wanted to stop. I began by keeping a list and figuring out when I smoked. I tried to cut down the number of times I smoked. I tried visualizing how awful smoking was for me. Also, I thought about trying to cut down on my drinking, which was not good for me either. When that didn't work, I read reports about the bad effects of smoking. I learned that people should work hard to break this awful habit because smoking is really bad for you. In addition, smoking can lead to early death. Even worse, the smoke that smokers breathe out can harm other people. I psyched myself up to smoke less. I was able to do it, and now I haven't smoked for over a year.

1. What do you think was the writer's purpose?
2. What is the topic sentence in this paragraph?
3. Does each experience, example, and reason support this main idea? If not, cross it out.
4. Does the paragraph accomplish the writer's purpose? If not, where does it need additional or different details?
5. Are the details specific enough? Do they contain sensory images that enable readers to experience the details from the writer's perspective? If not, circle the places where more specific or sensory details are needed.

WRITING ACTIVITY 5

You probably know that smoking is dangerous and can lead to fatal lung cancer. Write a paragraph about why teenagers should not smoke. Develop a purpose for writing, an audience for whom you are writing, and a topic sentence. Support this idea with personal experiences, examples, and/or reasons. When you finish writing, put the draft away for a few hours. Then revise it using the strategies that you have learned so far in this chapter.

WRITING ACTIVITY 6

Who is your favorite celebrity? For five minutes, close your eyes and become this person. Imagine yourself doing something that this person does very well. What are you doing? What are you thinking? What do you see, hear, touch, smell, and taste? How do you feel? Write a draft of a paragraph describing your imagined experience being this celebrity.

WRITING ACTIVITY 7

Take out the draft that you wrote for Writing Activity 6 above. Choose a person you think is a competent *reader* to help you revise this paragraph. Ask him or her to answer these four questions:

1. What do you think was my purpose in this paragraph?
2. Does each experience, example, and reason support the main idea of the paragraph? Which ones do not?
3. In your opinion, does the paragraph accomplish my purpose? If not, where does it need additional or different details?
4. Are the details specific enough? Do they contain sensory images that enable you to experience details from my perspective? If not, where are more specific or sensory details needed?

Take notes as the person responds. Repeat this activity with several different readers. Then reconsider the focus, purpose, and audience for the draft and decide which of your readers' suggestions you should include in your revision. Revise the paragraph as many times as you need to in order to accomplish your purpose in writing it.

A Revision Springboard: Branching. If you decide that your draft needs additional supporting details, you can try freewriting, brainstorming, and clustering to develop new insights, ideas, and details. In addition, you might try doing a form of clustering called *branching* to evaluate your details and to generate new ideas for your revision. Branching is a form of critical thinking that enables writers to analyze the relations among their ideas and details.

> **BRANCHING A DRAFT TO SEE PROBLEMS**
> **IN ITS DEVELOPMENT** _____
> Analyze the ideas and details in your paragraphs by doing the following:
>
> - Write the topic sentence in a circle in the middle of a sheet of paper.
> - Write each of your supporting points in its *own* circle and connect it to the main circle.
> - Draw branches out from each supporting point and write in the specific experiences, examples, and reasons you used to develop each supporting point.
> - Evaluate each supporting point by asking yourself whether it is clearly related to the topic sentence and is explained in enough specific detail.
> - Cross out irrelevant details.
> - Develop new details for the circles that do not have enough branches (enough supporting details).

Branching lets you see exactly where you do not have enough supporting details. Here is an example of a student's use of branching to determine whether a draft was developed effectively. The final version of this draft (which appeared on pages 46 and 47 in Chapter 2) is printed after the branched analysis.

1st Draft: My First College Registration

My first registration for courses at Valley Central College was a nightmare. I didn't have all the forms I needed. I was very nervous about registering. When I went to registration, the woman behind the desk told me to go to the registrar's office to get the right forms and then come back. I was really annoyed at the tone of her voice. You could tell she enjoyed torturing new students! Anyway, I went to get the forms, but of course I got lost. When I finally got there, I had to wait an hour. I met a person who went to my high school, we talked the whole time we were on line. I finally got the forms and returned to the registration counter. One hour later, my registration was processed and I was relieved, but I got really crazed when I got home and realized the computer made an error and I had to do the whole thing all over again.

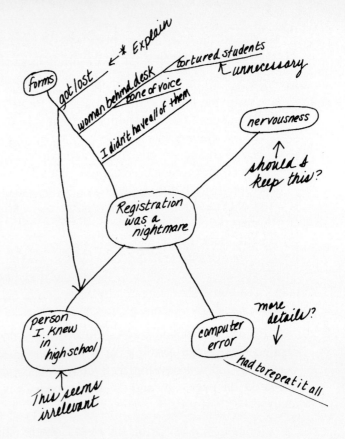

Final Version: My First College Registration

My first registration for courses at Valley Central College was a nightmare. To begin with, the college did not send me all of the forms that I needed to select courses nor did it send me a time schedule. Even worse, I didn't realize that I was missing these forms until I stepped up to the registration counter after waiting on line for an hour. The woman behind the desk smiled sweetly as if she felt sorry for me. In a motherly voice, she told me to go to the registrar's office to get the rest of the required forms and then to return and wait in line again. I was fuming, but there was nothing I could do but follow her directions. Of course I got lost on the way to the administration building, and when I finally got there, no one was around to show me where the registrar was. When I finally found the office, I was sickened to see that I had another hour-long wait. Students clustered together in an unruly line, biding their time smoking, mumbling to each other, and staring off into the space of their private dreams. At this point, I was ready to leave and take the semester off from school, but I waited, got the forms, and returned to the registration counter. Yet another hour later, my registration was processed and I was relieved. However, this relief dissolved into terror when I got home and realized that the computer made an error and I would have to return to repeat the whole procedure the following day.

WRITING ACTIVITY 8

Practice your ability to identify problems in development by branching the student draft below. Follow the guidelines for branching a draft on page 111. Your goal is to identify each statement in the draft that needs additional supporting details or that needs to be made more specific.

The registration process at my college seems like a big test to separate out students who are going to succeed from those who will not. If you can figure out how to register, you can handle every other assignment in college. The first problem is interpreting the directions in the registration letter. Next students have to calculate the number of "real" credits and "full-time equivalent" credits they need to take in order to qualify for their financial aid. If they manage to do this, they get to request a program in the computer maze (if the computers are working!). Then students have to figure out what to do when most of the courses that they wanted to take are already closed. The whole procedure makes many students feel like dropping out of college before they even begin.

WRITING ACTIVITY 9

Plan and write a paragraph about your first college registration. Develop a purpose for writing: Do you want to entertain your readers with stories about this experience? Do you want to describe your first registration and explain your reactions to it? Or do you want to persuade readers to believe something based on your first registration experience?

After you finish writing your draft, branch it to identify places where you need additional supporting details. Then use all the techniques that you learned in this chapter to determine which parts need to be revised. Finally, revise the paragraph to make it clearer, more logical, and more specific.

If you reread your revision and decide that it still needs more details to support or to prove your topic sentence, you might experiment with adding some facts and statistics. Facts and statistics are similar in that both can be verified as being true. For example, if you state the date of an event or the size of an object, readers can determine whether it is true or false. Both facts and statistics (figures, percentages, and measurements) are effective details for explaining or supporting a topic sentence. For example, which detail in each pair below communicates the writer's point more effectively?

A. *Allosaurus* dinosaurs had good teeth for eating meat.
B. *Allosaurus* dinosaurs had sharp, pointed teeth with half-inch, knifelike notches on one side to tear meat.

C. *Diplodocus* was an extremely long dinosaur.
D. *Diplodocus* was 90 feet long, or the length of three city buses in a row.

Another type of supporting detail that you might want to include in your revision is *testimony*. Testimony consists of statements by people whom you know or by experts whom you have heard—at lectures, on the radio, or on television. Testimony also includes summaries or quotations of information you find in books, newspapers, journals, magazines, and class notes. Here is an example of the use of expert testimony to support a point:

E. According to Paul Serano of the American Museum of Natural History in New York City, a dinosaur is any one of a large group of reptiles that lived from about 200 million years ago to about 65 million years ago (personal interview, June 14, 1992).

As you can tell from examples *B, D,* and *E* above, facts, statistics, and testimony are all effective material for developing and supporting the main points of paragraphs. Below is a student paragraph illustrating the use of facts and statistics to support a topic sentence:

Women and the "Glass Ceiling"

Women who hold jobs in state and local governments face a "glass ceiling," or hidden bias, that stops them from getting promoted to senior or manager positions. According to a recent report in *Newsday* (1/2/92), there are many women in federal, state, and local government jobs, but they are not doing too well at the top. Women make up only 31.3% of top managers, while women in lower levels of public service constitute 56.5% of these workers. In comparison, men hold 68.7% of the senior positions and 43.5% of the lower-paying jobs. Antifemale bias is even more damaging to minority women, who hold only 3.1% of the top management jobs. These figures show that despite all the advances working women have achieved, they still are denied entry to the most senior and best-paying positions in government.

GROUP WORK 2

Form a group with two other students and choose one person to record the group's answers to the following questions about the preceding paragraph.

1. What is the writer's topic sentence and purpose?

2. Which facts or statistics are most convincing in supporting this topic sentence?

3. What source does the writer cite for these facts and statistics?

4. Is this source reliable? Why or why not?

5. The preceding paragraph is a draft. What suggestions do you have for revision?

**GUIDELINES FOR USING
STATISTICS AS SUPPORTING DETAILS** ─────────────

1. Select your statistics from reliable sources and tell readers exactly what sources you used.
2. Make sure you understand what your numbers mean.
3. Use statistics sparingly and explain their importance. (Don't pile them up in your paragraph and leave it to your readers to interpret them.)
4. Use numbers and the symbol for percent unless the percent is the first word in the sentence: "*Forty percent* of the students and *29%* of the teachers in my college are minorities."
5. Hyphenate fractions: "Almost *two-fifths* of the students are Asian."
6. Spell out (and hyphenate) numbers under 100: "*Eighty-five* of the *610* freshmen are Latino." If a sentence begins with a number, spell it out even if it is higher than 100: "*Two hundred fifty-six* of these students have a grade-point average of 3.5 or higher."

How readers respond to facts, statistics, and expert testimony depends on the reliability of your sources. When you use someone else's ideas or opinions to support yours, you must make sure that the person is telling the truth and is *not* omitting information that doesn't fit his or her belief.

If you are using testimony from notes that you took at an interview or about a talk show, make sure you noted the source's credentials. Check whether the source is an acknowledged expert in the field that he or she is discussing. Finally, make sure that you write down the source's name, title, and affiliation (school or business name) as accurately as possible. Here is an example of the effective use of expert testimony:

Some writing teachers think that revising is not a separate writing activity but is merely the repeated drafting of a paper. For example, Donald Murray has pointed out that revision "is not another step in the process, it is the process repeated as many times as is necessary to produce a text worthy of editing. I no longer see revision as a separate part of the process, but merely as a repetition of the process until a draft is ready for editing" (56–57). I agree with Murray. When I compose and revise my paragraphs, I am doing the same thing: I am trying to clarify my ideas and make them more vital and more believable for my readers. Thinking of revision in this way has helped me become less anxious about following the correct steps to produce a good piece of writing.

The writer felt that Donald Murray's words expressed exactly what she wanted to say about revision, so she quoted them as a supporting detail in her paragraph. If the writer had included Murray's words without citing him and without enclosing his words in quotations, she would be guilty of *plagiarism.* Plagiarism is a serious offense. Never borrow someone else's words or ideas and incorporate them in your writing as if they were your own thoughts.

There are two ways to integrate testimony into your writing. First, you can *quote* the material directly from the book, magazine, or report in which you found it. Quoting involves (1) copying the material exactly as it appears in the original, (2) enclosing it in quotation marks, and (3) identifying the source. (See Chapter 21 on how to use quotation marks correctly.)

If you want to summarize an important idea or detail that you have read or heard, you can *paraphrase* it, using your own words. You don't need to enclose a paraphrase in quotation marks, but you do need to identify the source of the ideas. Here is how the writer of the paragraph above revised her work so that she paraphrased the source instead of quoting it:

Some writing teachers think that revising is not a separate writing activity but is merely the repeated drafting of a paper. For example, Donald Murray has pointed out that revision is actually the process of drafting a piece over and over until it is ready to be proofread and corrected (56–57). I agree with Murray. When I compose and revise my paragraphs, I am doing the same thing: I am trying to clarify my ideas and make them more interesting and more believable for my readers. Thinking of revision in this way has helped me become less anxious about following the correct steps to produce a good piece of writing.

GUIDELINES FOR USING TESTIMONY AS A SUPPORTING DETAIL ————

1. Copy down the source's (the interviewee's or the author's) words exactly as they were said or written.
2. Check that this source is an expert on the topic.
3. When you quote or paraphrase a source in your paper, cite the author's last name and the relevant page number(s). Put parentheses around the author's last name and the page number(s), but don't write "page" or "p." and don't precede the page number with any punctuation mark:

   "Always revise" (Murray 58).

4. Use quotation marks correctly. (See Chapter 21.)
5. Academic disciplines have different guidelines for citing the sources of the paraphrases and quotations that you include in your research papers. If your teacher does not tell you how to cite your sources and how to write a list of the works that you cited, use the guidelines described in the 1984 edition of the *MLA Handbook for Writers of Research Papers,* published by the Modern Language Association.
6. Interpret or evaluate the testimony you use so that readers will understand why you think it was important enough to include in your paper.
7. Use quotations and paraphrases sparingly.

WRITING ACTIVITY 10

Reread your paragraph on teenagers and smoking that you wrote for Writing Activity 5 on page 109. Then read the following excerpt from an essay titled "Teenagers and Tobacco Use." This essay was written by the California Medical Association and published on page 1 of their newsletter *HealthTips* (April 1990).

After you read the excerpt, revise your paragraph, incorporating any statistics and testimony from the excerpt that you think might make your paragraph stronger.

Teenagers and Tobacco Use

Cigarette smoking is a major public health problem, associated with an excess rise of cancer, chronic lung disease and cardiovascular (heart and blood vessel) diseases. An estimated 390,000 deaths per year are linked to smoking cigarettes—tobacco use is responsible for one of every six deaths in the United States. Approximately 20% of the teenagers in the United States are regular cigarette smokers. Smoking among teenagers is of particular concern because the earlier one starts to smoke, the more difficult it is to quit. Those who start to smoke at a young age have longer cumulative smoking time and thus face a higher risk of disease. Unfortunately, many teenagers are either not aware of or do not consider the health consequences of this habit.

The health problems related to smoking are numerous. Scientific studies have linked smoking to deaths from lung cancer, emphysema, chronic bronchitis and coronary artery disease. Cigarette smoking is the major single cause of cancer death in the United States and a major cause of heart disease. About 1000 different substances have been identified in tobacco smoke—including known cancer-causing substances found in the tar of the cigarette. Each time smokers inhale smoke from a cigarette they expose their mouth, throat, lungs and bloodstream to a mixture of nicotine, poisonous gases and tars. Nicotine, similar to heroin and cocaine as an addictive substance, causes increased stress on the heart. Poisonous gases like carbon monoxide increase the effects of coronary artery disease. Since smoking interferes with the lung's natural cleaning system, the habit makes smokers more vulnerable to infection. Smoking also causes cough, shortness of breath, respiratory infections, dental and gum disease and wrinkled skin.

In addition to causing illnesses, smoking is expensive. Someone smoking a pack of cigarettes per day may spend over $600 a year on their habit. Smoking is also a form of personal pollution. It is not glamorous like the advertisements may lead one to believe; it causes bad breath and tobacco-stained hands and teeth, soiled clothing and burns in personal belongings. Smoking not only hurts the smoker but may also be a hazard to their nonsmoking friends, and may later affect their children. Friends and children are ''passive'' smokers and are affected by the side-stream smoke of the cigarette.

Teenagers frequently view developing cancer or any other chronic fatal health problems as remote and unimportant possibilities. Many believe that smoking just a few cigarettes won't hurt because they can stop whenever they want. Few realize just how addictive the nicotine in cigarettes is—and how difficult it is to quit smoking. Cigarette ads have a strong impact on people between the ages of 12 and 18 years. Advertisements which insinuate that smoking is ''in'' "fashionable" and "sexy" are targeted at teenagers. Teens should realize that it is all part of a ploy to get them addicted to the nicotine, and that health and attractiveness are increased by not smoking.

GROUP WORK 3

Form a group with two other students. Exchange the paragraph that you revised for the preceding Writing Activity. Write answers to the following questions about your classmates' paragraphs.

1. What is the writer's topic sentence and purpose?

2. Has the writer provided enough relevant details to support his or her opinion? If not, where does he or she need to add additional details?

3. Which statistics, quotations, or paraphrases are most convincing in supporting the topic sentence?

4. Did the writer cite his or her source correctly?

5. What suggestions do you have for revision?

REMINDER ――――――――――――――――――――――
A strong paragraph has enough relevant experiences, examples, and reasons to develop and support its topic sentence and to achieve the writer's purpose. If the paragraph includes facts, statistics, and testimony as supporting details, the writer must paraphrase or quote them accurately and cite their sources correctly.

STEP 3: REVISING FOR LOGICAL ORGANIZATION

As you add new supporting details to your paragraphs, make sure that they fit together logically in an order that readers can follow. Some writers revise their organization by drawing circles around words or sentences and using arrows to indicate the places where these should be moved. Other writers prefer "cutting and pasting"—scissoring out sentences and taping them together in a new order. Writers who use computerized word-processing programs have it easy: The program enables them to add and move sentences around almost magically.

Here are some critical reading and thinking questions for you to consider as you evaluate the organization of your drafts and revisions:

1. *If I used chronological (time) order,* did I arrange my details in the order in which they actually occurred? Did I leave out any points or steps?
2. *If I used spatial order,* did I organize my details in a way that will enable readers to visualize what I am describing?
3. *If I used emphatic order (order of importance),* did I arrange my details from least to most important?
4. Did I include appropriate *transitions* to help readers see the connections among my details?

Read the following draft of a student paragraph. Are the reasons logically organized? Can you tell how they are related to one another?

Most of my friends are parents, and as far as I can tell, many of them had children for the wrong reasons. Several of my friends became parents to have someone that would give them unconditional love. Parents are supposed to love and nurture a child, not the other way around. Some friends gave birth to babies that they weren't ready to raise because their boyfriends or husbands really wanted a child to prove how macho they are. To me, making babies to prove one's manliness seems absurd and very unfair to the child. Children cannot take care of their parents' emotional needs and problems. Some friends had children to strengthen a shaky marriage. They assumed that a baby would make them and their husbands closer and would help them stop fighting. It didn't. People should have children because they love them and they are ready to provide them with an emotionally and financially stable life.

The topic sentence of this paragraph is that many of the writer's friends had children for the wrong reasons. In order to persuade her readers to believe her assertion, the writer provides three examples of these "wrong reasons" (to get unconditional love, to satisfy their boyfriends or husbands, and to strengthen a shaky marriage). These reasons are convincing, but they are not logically organized. Why is the need for unconditional love discussed first?

And how is this reason related to the one about macho boyfriends and husbands that follows?

After hearing these questions from classmates, the writer attempted to revise her organization. Here is a copy of the revisions she made on her draft.

Most of my friends are parents, and as far as I can tell, many of them had children for the wrong reasons. ~~Several of my friends became~~ *The main reason* parents to have someone that would give them unconditional love. *I think this is a terrible reason* ∧

move down (maybe save for ending)

Parents are supposed to love and nurture a child, not the other way around. Children cannot take care of their parents' emotional needs and problems. Some friends gave birth to babies that they weren't ready to raise because their boyfriends or husbands really wanted a child to prove how macho they are. To me, making babies to prove one's manliness seems absurd and very unfair to the child. *An even worse reason* ~~Some friends had~~

move up (first)

for having   was to   Several friends
∧ children ~~to~~ strengthen a shaky marriage. ~~They~~ assumed that a baby would make them and their husbands closer and would help them stop
This was irrational.
fighting, ~~It didn't.~~ People should have children because they love them and they are ready to provide them with an emotionally and financially stable life.

add why

Here is the writer's final version of this paragraph:

Most of my friends are parents, and as far as I can tell, many of them had children for the wrong reasons. One reason some of these women gave birth to babies that they weren't ready to raise was because their boyfriends or husbands really wanted a child to prove how macho they are. To me, making babies to prove one's manliness seems absurd and very unfair to the child. An even worse reason for having children was to strengthen a shaky marriage. Several of my friends assumed that a baby would make them and their husbands closer and would help them stop fighting. This was another irrational reason. In fact, the added emotional and financial pressures of caring for an infant increased the intensity of their battles. However, the main reason several of my friends became parents was to have someone that would give them unconditional love. I think that is the worst reason of all to have a child. Parents are supposed to love and nurture a child, not the other way around. Children cannot take care of their parents' emotional needs and problems and they should never be expected to. People should have children because they love them and because they are ready to provide them with an emotionally and financially stable life.

The final version is clearer and more convincing than the draft because the examples have been rearranged to improve the paragraph's organization. Now readers can understand the order of importance of these details to the writer.

WRITING ACTIVITY 11

This activity will help you improve your ability to identify and revise problems in logical development. The seven sentences below are not developed in a logical order. Rearrange them by numbering each (1, 2, 3, and so on). Then rewrite the sentences (on separate paper), using your new order to form a coherent paragraph.

_____ Finally, some students drop out because they become so involved with alcohol or drugs that they can no longer function in school.

_____ They simply do not have enough money to pay tuition and to support themselves or their families.

_____ Either they lack the academic skills necessary to succeed or they lack the motivation to do all of the required work.

_____ Whatever their reason for leaving, college dropouts are depriving themselves of the opportunity to have fulfilling and rewarding future careers.

_____ The major reason most of the dropouts I know left school was because they needed to work full-time.

_____ Students drop out of college for several reasons.

_____ Another reason people leave school is because they are unable to make good grades.

WRITING ACTIVITY 12

Do you have children or are you planning to have children one day? Plan and write a paragraph about why you wanted or may want to become a parent *or* about why you do not want to have children. (Or plan and write a paragraph about the reasons people should or should not have children.) When you finish your draft, put it away for a while. Then revise it, using the strategies that you have learned in this chapter. Finally, evaluate your paragraph using the checklist on page 96 in Chapter 3 and revise the paragraph again.

STEP 4: REVISING FOR GREATER UNITY AND COHERENCE

In Chapter 3, you learned how to evaluate your paragraphs for unity and coherence. As you add, delete, and rearrange details in your drafts, the relations among your ideas may become blurred. Thus, you may need to revise your paragraph again to make it more unified and coherent. You can do this by answering the following questions:

1. Does my entire paragraph stick to one main point? If not, where does it go off on a tangent?
2. Does every sentence develop or support the topic sentence? If not, which sentences should I cross out?
3. Is every sentence logically related to the one that precedes it and to the one that follows it? If not, which sentences should I cross out, rearrange, or rewrite?
4. Which sentences need transitions to show their relation to the preceding sentences?

GROUP WORK 4

Get into a group of three students. Examine a paragraph that you wrote for one of the Writing Activities in this chapter. Exchange paragraphs with another student and read your classmate's paragraph. Write answers to the four questions above. When you get your classmate's comments back, revise your paragraph in light of his or her answers.

In addition to using transitions to signal the connections among ideas, there are two other strategies for improving the unity and coherence of your paragraphs. One is *repeating the key words* that limit the focus of the topic sentence. The other is *using pronouns and synonyms* to keep your main point echoing throughout the paragraph. Pronouns are words that take the place of nouns (for example, *he, she, it, his, their, that, some, most, another*). Synonyms are words with almost the same meaning.

Below is an example of the use of repetition, pronouns, and synonyms to make writing more coherent. Note that (1) key words and their synonyms are in bold type, (2) references to "firecrackers" or synonyms for firecrackers are underlined, and (3) pronouns referring to the brother are circled.

Children don't understand how **dangerous firecrackers can be.** My younger brother now knows the **damages that these <u>explosive devices</u> can inflict.** (He) has a permanent souvenir from (his) attempt to light <u>a firecracker</u> last July Fourth. As (he) watched (his) friends detonate <u>fiery missiles</u> into the night sky, (he) decided (he) wanted to light one too. However, (his) <u>Fire Candle</u> wouldn't explode. It sputtered and coughed but it would not ignite. So my brother held it up to (his) face to see what was wrong with it. As (he) did, it rocketed out, blasting rainbow sparks around (his) head and completely shattering (his) left cheek. After six surgeries, my brother's face is now close to normal. But the ugly red scars on (his) cheek remind everyone **how hazardous <u>firecrackers</u> really are.**

In the preceding paragraph, the writer used repetition, synonyms, and pronouns to point readers' attention back to the key words in her topic sentence.

WRITING ACTIVITY 13

Read the paragraph below, which you worked on for Writing Activity 6 in Chapter 3. Note that this version includes transitional words and expressions the writer added. As you read this paragraph, do three things:

- *Underline* the words *aid* or *aids* every time they are repeated.
- *Underline* the synonyms for these words.
- *Circle* the pronouns that refer back to them.

Hearing Aids

There are several different types of hearing aids available to help people who are hard of hearing. I was born with a severe hearing loss, and I've been wearing aids since I was a year old. First, I wore a body-assisted aid, which was a microphone that fit behind my ears and an amplifier that strapped to my chest. Although this device helped me hear, it annoyed me and I kept pulling off the amplifier. In addition, the microphones irritated my ears. Next I was fitted with another type of aid, the in-the-ear kind. I liked these hearing aids because they were more comfortable. Also they were hidden inside my ears, so kids didn't notice them as much as they noticed the body-assisted ones. Unfortunately, however, the in-the-ear kind weren't strong enough to help me hear low- or high-pitched sounds. I couldn't hear my friends when they giggled, screamed, or whispered, and I started to feel left out and sad. Finally, my parents took me to get a third kind of aid called cochlear implants. These were surgically inserted into my ears, so no one can see them and they can't annoy me. To me, this is the best type of aid because it is invisible and it has helped me tune back into the world.

REMINDER _____
Signal the connections between your ideas by repeating the key words in your topic sentence, by using transitions, and by using pronouns and synonyms that refer back to the main point of your topic sentence.

WRITING ACTIVITY 14

Plan and write a paragraph about one of the topics below. (The key words in each topic are underlined.) When you revise your paragraph, use repetition, synonyms, and pronouns to refer back to your key word (or words).

- My favorite neighbor
- How to break a bad habit
- What success means to me
- The benefits of exercising
- The worst job I ever had

- The qualities of a good wife/husband
- Similarities between two sports
- Differences between high school and college
- Reasons people lie
- Reasons people don't vote

STEP 5: REVISING AND EDITING FOR CLARITY AND CORRECTNESS

At a certain point in the revision process, writers decide "Enough!" Either they are finally pleased with their work or they have run out of time and motivation. In either case, they are *not* yet done with their paragraphs. Now they must edit them for clarity and correctness. Editing is the process of identifying and correcting errors and unconventional forms in a piece of writing. Here are some strategies you can use to edit and proofread your paragraphs.

EDITING AND PROOFREADING STRATEGIES

When you finish revising a paragraph, do the following:

- Read each sentence aloud slowly, looking for missing or misused words.
- Read each sentence aloud slowly again, looking for errors in sentence structure, grammar, punctuation, spelling, and capitalization.
- Put a ruler or a sheet of paper under each sentence to force yourself to check one line of writing at a time.
- Look up every word that you are not sure you have spelled correctly.
- Reread your paragraph for the errors that you know you frequently make.
- Type your paragraph and examine it for errors. It is much easier to identify mistakes in typed copy than in handwriting.

Before you edit your paragraphs, follow the techniques for gaining distance on your drafts described on pages 101 and 102 of this chapter. Then examine every word in your revision for two types of errors: (1) careless mistakes and (2) errors that you tend to make every time you write. Many writers find it helpful to develop their own checklists of typical errors that they can refer to every time they edit their writing. Here is an example of a checklist that you might want to copy. Every time you receive a paper back from a teacher, you can use this checklist to help you keep track of your common errors and to correct them.

Checklist of My Typical Writing Problems and Errors

Problem or Error	Cause	Correction

The most difficult part of editing is reading what actually is on the page, not what was in your mind as you wrote or what you assume readers will understand about the words on the page. Read your writing aloud to identify missing words. Check every word to make sure it is the right word for the sentence in which you have used it. Also examine each word to see if it has the correct ending and is spelled correctly. Finally, don't hesitate to ask family, friends, classmates, and tutors to help you revise and edit your writing. Experienced writers know the value of getting feedback from friends and colleagues. Every essay, article, and book that is published—including this one—is critiqued by numerous reviewers and editors who help the authors find, revise, and correct problems and errors in their writing. Act like a professional writer: Get feedback and help from people you trust.

> **REMINDER**
> Evaluate your drafts for the five qualities of good writing: focus, development, unity, coherence, and correctness. Revise and edit every draft over and over until you feel that it is complete, clear, logical, and correct.

Below and on the pages that follow are samples of a student's attempt to revise and edit a paragraph about being learning disabled. As you read each version, think about the changes that you would advise the writer to make in it in order to improve its clarity and development.

Draft: My Dyslexia

Some people think of a learning disability as a curse. I think of a learning disability as an oportunity. My dyslexia has given me the oportunity to prove that I can be sucessful. It helped me work hard and suceed. I was diagnosed as a dyslexic in the second grade. My teecher knew that something was wrong with the way I was sounding out letters and trying to make them into words. She sent me to a speshalist who said I had dyslexia. I just assumed that I was different from other children. I didn't think I had a defect, I just thought i was different. My parents and tutors helped me. I did well in high school. Now I am in college. I have new goals. And I know that I can prove that I can suceed.

Revision: My Dyslexia

Some people think of a learning disability as a curse but I think of a learning disability as a speshal oportunity. My dyslexia has given me the oportunity to show how strong I am and how determined I am to suceed. It has force me to work harder than other student, also it motivated me to strive for excellance and sucess. I have never thought of being disabled as having a defect or a deficientcy. In fact, I was diagnosed as a dyslexic in second grade. My teechers told me that I was speshal, I had a unique way of learning to read and learn. Later, when I realize that I could not read letters and words easy, I just assumed that I was different from other children, not deficent just different. With the help of my parents and tutors. I learned how to compinsate for my specific reading problems. I also learned how to organize my time, to plan my academic task, and how to do well on tests. I worked very hard to overcome my dificulties, I made honor role the last three years in high school. Now I am in college. And I know that I will acheeve my goals again, I have another oportunity. I'll prove to everyone that learning disabled students can suceed.

Final Version: My Dyslexia

Some people think of a learning disability as a curse, but I think of it as a special opportunity. My dyslexia has given me the opportunity to show how strong I am and how determined I am to succeed. It has forced me to work harder than other students do and it has motivated me to strive for excellence and success. I have never thought of being disabled as having a defect or a deficiency. In fact, when I was diagnosed as a dyslexic in second grade, my teachers told me that I was special. I had a unique way of learning and reading. Later, when I realized that I could not read letters and words easily, I just assumed that I was different from other children. Not deficient just different. With the help of my parents and tutors, I learned how to compensate for my specific reading problems. I also learned how to organize my time, how to plan my academic tasks, and how to do well on tests. I worked very hard to overcome my difficulties and I made honor role the last three years in high school. Now I am in college, and I have another opportunity to achieve my goals again. I will prove to everyone that learning-disabled students can succeed.

With the help of his classmates, his tutor, and his teacher, this writer has produced a final version that is far clearer and more powerful than the original draft. The writer is already achieving his goal!

GETTING READERS' RESPONSES

Use the checklist below to help you identify problems in your paragraphs and to get readers' responses to them.

REVISING AND EDITING CHECKLIST _____

1. Is the topic sentence appropriate for the paragraph?
2. Does the paragraph have enough relevant, specific details to illustrate or support the topic sentence?
3. Where does the paragraph need additional experiences, examples, reasons, facts, statistics, or testimony?
4. Where does the paragraph need more specific words and sensory images?

(Continued)

5. How can the organization of the paragraph be made more logical or more effective?
6. Which sentences should be omitted or rearranged to improve the unity of the paragraph?
7. Where does the paragraph need transitions, repetition, pronouns, and synonyms to make it more coherent?
8. Does the paragraph have any fragments or run-ons?
9. Which sentences are incomplete or have errors in grammar, punctuation, spelling, or capitalization?
10. What suggestions do you have for further revision?

■ EXPLORING FURTHER

Before you read the excerpts in this section, please do Writing Assignment 1 and Writing Assignment 2.

WRITING ASSIGNMENT 1

Write a paragraph describing and explaining your opinion of television. Begin by doing freewriting, brainstorming, or clustering to generate details about television. Here are some suggestions for prewriting. Feel free to ignore them; they are simply suggestions to get you started:

- What comes to your mind when you think about watching television?
- How much television do you watch? Why?
- How does television influence your life or the lives of your family or friends?
- Is watching television good or bad for the American public? Why?
- Do children watch too much television?

Use the strategies that you have learned in this book to plan and write a topic sentence and a paragraph about television.

WRITING ASSIGNMENT 2

Take out the draft that you wrote for Writing Assignment 1 above. Use the ''Discovery Draft Checklist'' on page 61 of Chapter 2 to analyze and revise this draft. Then use the guidelines for branching a draft on page 111 of this chapter to help you identify places in the draft that are unclear or unconvincing. Think about your intended reader and what this reader already knows about television and how he or she might feel about it.

Then develop additional experiences, examples, and reasons to include in your revision.

Below is a table called "TV by the Numbers," from an article compiled by Valerie Fahey, and an excerpt titled "Tuning the Kids In," by Deborah Franklin. They appeared in a 1992 issue of *In Health* magazine. The table provides data about television watching in the United States. The second is an essay about children and television. What is your opinion about the influence of television on children and teenagers? Keep an open mind as you read these excerpts. They might cause you to reconsider your beliefs.

*TV by the Numbers**

93 million
Total number of television sets in the United States

2.25
Average number of sets per home

14
Percentage of homes with four or more sets

84
Percentage of households with a TV in the bedroom

78
Percentage of homes with TV remote controls

66
Percentage of people who "graze" or "channel surf," using a remote control to watch two or more programs at once

47
Number of hours the TV stays on in the average home, per week

75
Percentage of homes with a VCR

2
Average hours' worth of programs recorded daily to watch later

6 million
Average number of videos rented daily

3 million
Average number of public library items checked out daily

24
Percentage of adults who rate TV as their favorite way to spend an evening

15
Percentage who rate reading as their favorite evening activity

65
Percentage of viewers who think TV has a positive effect on their lives

* Valerie Fahey, "TV by the Numbers," *In Health,* Vol. 5, No. 7, January 1992, page 35.

Average amount of time people watch TV weekly:
Children 2 to 5 years: 22 hours
Children 6 to 11: 23 hours
Girls 12 to 17: 25 hours
Boys 12 to 17: 24 hours
Women 18 to 34: 25 hours
Men 18 to 34: 22 hours
Women 35 to 54: 29 hours
Men 35 to 54: 25 hours
Women 55 and over: 37 hours
Men 55 and over: 33 hours

42
Percentage who say they watch too much TV

13
Percentage who consider themselves addicted

62
Percentage who say they unwind by watching TV

1
Percentage who say they unwind by having sex

Tuning the Kids In

Until recently, warnings to parents about TV have been long on vitriol and short on practical advice. What exactly is a parent supposed to say that doesn't boil down to "Turn it off" and "No"?

Jay F. Davis, an education specialist for the Los Angeles–based Center for Media and Values, has some alternatives. The two-year-old nonprofit organization is dedicated to teaching children as well as adults to be media literate—active, critical thinkers about what they watch, hear, and read. In kid language, the lessons are these:

YOU'RE SMARTER THAN YOUR TV

"Neither adults nor children do everything or believe everything they see on TV," Davis says. "If we did, our lives would be dominated by gunfights, drug deals, and quickly resolved living room arguments." Still, it takes time and practice to acquire discriminating thinking skills; parents can encourage independent thinking in children by teaching them to notice how a TV character's behavior and reactions are similar to or different from the way the youngsters themselves might have acted or reacted in the same situation.

TV'S WORLD IS NOT REAL

Although they may not believe everything they see in a sitcom, adults as well as kids often assume when watching the news, a documentary, or a political debate that what's being presented is unadulterated reality. It's important to point out to kids that several people—including reporters, producers, and editors—made decisions about which pictures and which sound bites to use. That sort of selection process, of course, is true of newspaper and magazine stories as well, but Davis suggests that TV may be a bit more misleading because seeing something "with your own eyes" tends to lend the televised moment veracity.

According to child psychologists, kids under seven are especially vulnerable to the illusion that even entertainment shows and commercials portray real events. Without preaching or needlessly taking the fun out of fantasy, parents can help young people discern fact from fiction in both ads and programming by occasionally pointing out inconsistencies: "How come Theo (a teenager on 'The Cosby Show') seldom studies? Do you think he has as much homework as you do?" or "Have *you* ever seen a raisin dance?"

TV MAKES IT SEEM AS THOUGH SOME PEOPLE ARE MORE IMPORTANT THAN OTHERS

This gets at the idea that there are values implicit in every televised (or spoken or written) message, values that a viewer may not agree with. For example, Davis points out, "On the whole, TV presents a generally male and white perspective on the world—everyone else is less important and much more likely to get killed."

His solution is to invite discussion with the kids whenever you notice something you think is biased in whatever direction, and to encourage them to watch for stereotypes.

TV USES TRICKS TO PUSH YOUR EMOTIONAL BUTTONS

Laugh tracks, scary music, and romantic candlelight are all timeworn television techniques that tell us what we're meant to feel when. A woman whose head is tilted looks seductive, a man who grasps objects tightly seems more virile— advertisers and directors know these tricks, Davis says, and if you and your kids recognize them, too, you are less likely to be emotionally manipulated.

To get the point across to young kids, suggest they help you count the canned laughter sequences in an episode of their favorite show, or analyze what happens in the plot each time the music changes. Before long, everybody will notice patterns. Such scrutiny, Davis says, goes a long way toward demystifying TV without removing its magic.

SOMEBODY'S ALWAYS TRYING TO MAKE MONEY WITH TV

"I'd like to be able to control the Ninja Turtle/Strawberry Shortcake mania that infects my children and their friends," Davis says. He suggests that similarly frustrated parents teach even young kids to be savvy consumers. You can begin by reminding children that most of what they see on TV is, to varying degrees, designed to get somebody to buy something. To illustrate the point, you might look critically together at the different kinds of advertisers that sponsor your family's favorite shows.

On a sitcom about single mothers, for example, commercials are more likely to plug products that advertisers believe appeal to women—personal hygiene products, underwear, or household items—while an action-adventure show is more likely to feature beer commercials, or ads for razors or pickup trucks. You can make a game with the kids out of that kind of analysis—first predicting the sorts of commercials that will air, then checking to see if you're right, and discussing the findings.

Discussion Questions

1. Do you ever use a remote control device to watch two or more programs at the same time? What was your reaction to the author's terms for this activity—"grazing" or "channel surfing"? Can you create a better term?
2. Which statistic in "TV by the Numbers" most surprised you? Why?
3. The Franklin essay quotes Jay F. Davis's exact words as follows: "Davis points out, 'On the whole, TV presents a generally male and white perspective on the world—everyone else is less important and much more likely to get killed.' " (Note that a quotation within another quotation is enclosed in single quotation marks.) What does Davis mean by this? Do you agree?
4. What might be a more appropriate title for this essay?
5. Which statements in the essay did you think were most interesting or most important? Why?

WRITING ASSIGNMENT 3

Revise again the revision that you wrote for Writing Assignment 2: Choose statistics or testimony that you read in the preceding excerpts to add to your revision. Select the statistic (or statistics) *or* the testimony that most affected or interested you. Revise your topic sentence in light of this statistic or testimony. (If your opinion has changed after reading these excerpts, write a new topic sentence.) Apply the guidelines for using statistics on pages 115 and 116 of this chapter or the guidelines for using testimony on pages 117 and 118 to help you integrate the information into your revision. When you finish revising your draft, edit and proofread it using the checklist on page 127.

 POINTS TO REMEMBER ABOUT REVISING AND EDITING

1. Use the techniques described on pages 101 and 102 of this chapter to gain some distance from your drafts.
2. Examine each paragraph's topic sentence. Make sure that it is a clear, specific, complete sentence.

3. Reread every supporting detail and make sure that it is relevant to the topic sentence. If it isn't, cross it out.

4. Make sure every detail includes specific, concrete language and descriptive words that appeal to readers' senses.

5. Branch each paragraph to see where it needs additional supporting details.

6. Use prewriting strategies to develop new experiences, examples, and reasons to illustrate your topic sentence.

7. Include facts, statistics, and testimony to clarify or support your topic sentence.

8. Check to make sure that your revised details are organized logically in an order that readers can follow.

9. Make sure that each sentence is logically related to the ones that precede and follow it.

10. Edit every paragraph to make it relatively free of errors in sentence structure, grammar, punctuation, spelling, and capitalization. (If you are writing with a word-processing program, use the ''spell-checker'' and the ''grammar-checker.'')

P A R T

2

The Writer's Portfolio

THE WRITER'S PORTFOLIO

What do you do with your drafts and notes, your revisions, and the final versions of your paragraphs and essays? Do you keep your essays after your instructor evaluates or grades them? You should. In fact, you should keep all your writing in a big folder, and periodically, you should read earlier pieces to see how much your writing has improved and to determine what you still need to work on. You can learn how to improve your writing by thinking about the pieces that you have already written *and* by reflecting on the experience of writing different types of paragraphs and essays.

A writing folder is often called a *portfolio,* a term used to describe an artist's collection of his or her best works. A student's writing portfolio, however, is simply a collection of writing over an extended time period. It includes drafts and polished pieces. It may also contain brainstorming notes, outlines, discovery drafts, revisions, peer responses, unfinished drafts, and drafts that were abandoned (accompanied by explanations of why the writer felt they were not worth revising). If you keep a writing portfolio, you will have a detailed portrait of your development as a writer.

If you have never kept a writing portfolio, start now. The eight chapters in Part 2 include many opportunities to develop paragraphs and essays for your portfolio. The chapters are organized by strategies or patterns that you can use to develop your ideas and details: description, narration, analysis of processes, comparison and contrast, division and classification, definition, analysis of causes and effects, and argumentation. These strategies are not categories or forms of writing that you must select before you decide how to develop your ideas. They are simply the patterns of thinking that we all use to sort out the events and experiences of our daily lives. Since these patterns overlap, it is easy to move from one to another as you try to communicate your points in writing.

Depending on your purpose and your audience, you might use only one of these strategies or several of them in a paragraph or essay. For example, imagine that you are composing a draft on the topic "the benefits of exercise" for an audience of classmates who do not exercise regularly. Here are some ways in which you could use these strategies or patterns to develop your ideas:

Description: Use sensory details to illustrate the positive feelings, improved health, and firmer bodies that people get from exercising.

Narration: Relate experiences and events that show how you or someone you know benefited from exercising.

Analysis of a process: Explain the sequence of steps required to start a regular program of exercising.

Comparison and contrast: Explain the ways in which different forms of exercising have similar benefits and (or) different benefits.

Division and classification: Categorize the different ways in which people can exercise regularly and (or) the different types and benefits of each exercise.

Definition: Explain what you mean by "regular exercise" and explain exactly what you mean by the health-related benefits that you think exercise provides people.

Analysis of causes and effects: Explain how and why exercising makes people feel better mentally and physically.

Argumentation: Offer examples and reasons to convince readers that they should begin a program of regular exercise immediately.

Do you see how these strategies overlap and how the last one, argumentation, often is a combination of the others?

In the chapters that follow, you will learn how to use these strategies to shape your thoughts for different aims and readers. As you respond to the assignments in this section of the book, put your notes, drafts, revisions, and final versions into your portfolio. At least once a week, reread some of the pieces in your portfolio and ask yourself questions that will help you evaluate your writing. Here are some questions to consider:

Do my notes contain interesting ideas for new essays?

Do I have any drafts that I should revise again?

Which drafts did I abandon? Why?

Is there a type of writing that I dislike doing? Why?

Is there a type of writing that I do well? Why?

What did I learn about writing from my work on a particular draft or revision?

Have my peers' responses to my drafts helped me improve these
   drafts? If so, how? If not, why not?
Have my teachers' responses to my drafts helped me improve these
   drafts? If so, how? If not, why not?
What do I like best about my writing now?
Where do I still need help as a writer?
How do my most recent pieces compare with my earlier ones?
What do the drafts and revisions in my portfolio reveal about my pro-
   gress as a writer?

Answering these questions will help you understand your growth as a
writer and will help you celebrate your writing strengths.

DESCRIPTION

Description is the most powerful tool in a writer's craft. It requires the writer to see the world in a new way and it enables readers to share the writer's experiences and perceptions. By describing an object or an issue in detail, you show readers what it means to you and convey your understanding of it. Thus, much of the writing that you do at school and at work will include descriptive details.

In Chapter 3, you learned about the five qualities of good writing: a clear focus, logical development and organization, unity, coherence, and correctness. Effective description also has two other features:

1. Good description has an abundance of specific details that paint vivid pictures for readers.
2. Good description also has many words and images that appeal to readers' senses (sight, hearing, smell, taste, and touch).

This chapter, and the ones that follow, will give you many opportunities to practice writing description and to use the composing and revising skills that you learned in the preceding chapters.

UNDERSTANDING THE IMPORTANCE OF DESCRIPTIVE DETAILS

Almost all the writing that you will do in school and in your profession requires description. You may be asked to describe a person, a place, or an object so that your reader will be able to experience it the way that you do. Or you may be asked to describe an idea, a problem, or a solution in a way that will enable your reader to understand things from your perspective. Almost every college writing assignment calls for some description. For example, here is an assignment that does not include the word *describe* but that must be answered with description:

> Compare the Islamic Center of Greater Toledo to traditional Muslim centers in the Middle East. Then explain why conservative Muslims might object to some of the practices in the Toledo center.

In order for students to "compare" these two types of Muslim communities, they would have to *describe* each and *describe* the ways in which they are similar and different. Similarly, students' responses to the second task would require them to *describe* the practices that conservative Muslims might object to.

Description is creating pictures with words. The better you are at conveying your thoughts and impressions in specific language and sensory images, the better your readers will understand your perceptions and point of view.

Here is an example of a brief descriptive paragraph. As you read it, consider whether you can envision the animals in your mind's eye:

> Newts are a type of salamander. They are born as green larvae and then they turn red. Eventually, they grow feet and turn green. Mature newts leave the water to stay in the forest. They have a highly developed sense of smell. They are excellent creatures.

This description is too vague; it does not convey exactly what the writer saw. Here is the actual description of these animals, as written by the novelist Annie Dillard.

> Newts are the most common of salamanders. Their skin is a light green, like water in a sunlit pond, and rows of very bright red dots line their back. They have gills as larvae; as they grow they turn a luminescent red, lose their gills, and walk out of the water to spend a few years padding about in damp places in the forest floor. Their feet look like fingered baby hands, and they walk in the same leg patterns as all four-footed creatures—dogs, mules, and for that matter, lesser pandas. When they mature fully, they turn green again and stream to the water in droves. A newt can scent its way home from as far as eight miles away. They are altogether excellent creatures, if somewhat moist, but no one pays the least attention to them, except children.

Dillard mixes scientific facts and sensory details to help readers understand her perception of newts. Note that Dillard's paragraph is longer than the summary preceding it. As you revise your paragraphs by adding specific descriptive details, they will become longer and better developed.

OBSERVING AND NOTE-TAKING

The best discovery technique for drafting a description is careful observation. Ideally the person, place, or thing that you are describing is available for you to examine closely. If not, shut your eyes and examine it in your mind. Pay close attention to the smallest details and then start taking notes. Exactly what do you see, hear, smell, taste, and feel? If you get stuck, try some freewriting, brainstorming, or clustering.

As you try to describe your impressions of the person or thing, remember to use specific, sensory language. In the preceding chapters, you learned the importance of being specific and of writing details that appeal to readers' senses. Effective description requires concrete, sensory language to make details "come alive." For example, compare the two brief descriptions below. Which one is more effective? Why?

Original

brodterm

Yesterday I ate at Pizza Palace. The meal was so (disgusting that I couldn't even eat it.

Revision

Last night I ate dinner at Pizza Palace. I knew I was in trouble when I bit into my pepperoni pizza and heard a snapping crunch. I felt like I was munching on dried-up shoe leather shavings. After I spit out the ancient pepperoni, I noticed that the pizza sauce was the color of curdled old blood. Blobs of grayish cheese were sliding across the sauce, giving off an odor of foot sweat. I gagged, dumped the mush back on my plate, and staggered to the bathroom.

The revision lets you know exactly what this writer means by a "disgusting" meal. The revised details are so clear that they might make you nauseous!

WRITING ACTIVITY 1

Circle every sensory image in the revised description of the "disgusting" meal. Then list each in the appropriate space below:

Sights   *Sounds*   *Odors*

Tastes   *Textures*   *Feelings*

Which image did you like best? Why?

_____

_____

_____

Inexperienced writers often use vague words that don't communicate clear sensory images to their readers. For example, let's look at some notes written by a student in preparation for a paragraph about her favorite room. How effective are these notes below in letting you "experience" her room?

beautiful quilt on the bed   old desk

comfortable mattress   many stuffed animals

strange-looking lamp   good smell

new computer   pictures on wall

thick red carpet   white bedposts

Do these notes help you to experience what her room is like? Why or why not?

_____

_____

_____

_____

Here are additional notes that this writer took after she did some brainstorming about her room. How do these differ from the ones above?

2 creamy white bedposts

a fat red ball on top of each post

red balls have brown spots (slightly rotten apples)

beautiful old quilt—pink and peach swirls

looks like melted peach melba ice cream

each puff of the quilt feels like a tiny pillow

quilt—smooth satin, shiny and worn in places

lamp looks like a swollen goose with a long neck

shiny new Apple computer has a big green blinking eye

Because the writer has now specified exactly what she sees and feels, her additional notes paint a clearer picture of some of the things in her room. As you take notes for your descriptions, include words that show exactly what you see, hear, taste, smell, and feel.

> **REMINDER**
> Effective description uses concrete, sensory details to convey the writer's impression of people, places, objects, events, or issues.

BUILDING VIVID IMAGES

Writers build images from specific sensory details. For example, the writer of the notes above began by using the word *beautiful* to describe the quilt on her bed. Realizing that this word was too vague, she substituted words that appeal to readers' senses: colors (''pink and peach''), shapes (''swirls''), and textures (''melted peach melba ice cream'').

An effective method for collecting and organizing sensory details is to list your notes in a *Sensory Chart* similar to the one in Writing Activity 1. To make a Sensory Chart, draw six columns, one for each of the five senses and one for the feelings or emotions that the thing or place evokes in you. Then examine the subject of your description carefully and write down your observations on the chart. Remember to use all of your senses. Here is an example of a Sensory Chart about the room in which I do most of my writing.

Sensory Chart

Sights	*Sounds*	*Odors*
mountains of messy books	click-clacking computer keys	rotten potato chip smell
papers strewn like garbage at a landfill	whispery whir of the computer fan	damp, musty wood odor
dozens of computer disks stacked upon each other like square plates	creaking of my steel chair sounds like a broken tuba	sour smell of wood oil I used to clean my desk

Tastes	*Textures*	*Feelings*
salty chips with rancid flavor of stale oil	soft, dry dust tiny sharp pebbles of dried-up chips	peace, calm dark, quiet secure cave

WRITING ACTIVITY 2

Here are two paragraphs from a student essay that was recently published in a book of prizewinning student writing. The author, Bruce Adams, describes an experience he had working as an emergency medical technician. Circle every sensory image that the writer used and list each one in the Sensory Chart that follows.

By looking out the window of the ambulance, I can see we are getting close to the hospital. As we speed by familiar buildings, the flashing emergency lights turn them into hundreds of freeze-frame photographs. The strobe lights turn everything that their light falls on a monotone hue of either red or blue. The siren's only rival is the screaming of my patient, which pierces the air like an explosion in the night. I struggle for balance while crouched on the floor as the vehicle makes a sharp turn into the parking lot.

As I stand up, I feel the warm sensation of liquid running down my pant leg into my shoe. For the first time I realize that I am covered with warm, sticky blood. We wheel the patient from the ambulance onto the ambulance loading dock. The heat lamps overhead radiate a soothing warmth against the cool, humid night air. The calloused police officers look on casually at the action passing before them. They have seen all this too many times to be shocked or even curious.

Sensory Chart

Sights	*Sounds*	*Odors*
Tastes	*Textures*	*Feelings*

DEVELOPING A TOPIC SENTENCE AND DESCRIPTIVE DETAILS

Remember that a strong paragraph focuses on a single topic sentence. The main focus of a descriptive paragraph should be your dominant or overall impression of the person, object, or place being described. The key words in the topic sentence should limit this impression. Here are some examples:

The *ugliest creature* I have ever seen is my pet toad.
My English classroom is *extremely depressing*.
Our Thanksgiving dinner is always a *joyful celebration*.
My dad's workroom is filled with *unpleasant odors*.

As you examine or think about the place or object that you are describing, jot down notes on your dominant impression of it: If you had to sum it up in one word or a phrase, what would that word or phrase be? If you are trying to describe a person in one paragraph, you should focus on your dominant impression of the person—the particular feature or quality that you find most striking about the person. Think about your purpose and your intended readers in order to shape your dominant impression into a topic sentence.

In the description below, note how the writer selected details that supported and illustrated his dominant impression of his grandmother as a woman "of great inner strength."

I close my eyes and see my grandmother standing proudly at the door of our kitchen, a woman of great inner strength. Despite her crippling arthritis, she stands straight and still like a drill sergeant inspecting her troops. She holds her head up as if a spike ran from her grizzled black hair to the base of her spine. The brittle brown skin of her face has been softened by age and hard work, but the chin that she juts out is shiny and unlined. Her clothes are grey and worn but they are so stiff with starch that they could stand by themselves. She seems rigid, but then a tiny smile catches at the corners of her mouth, signaling her love and pride.

Here is another description of a grandmother. Notice how the novelist, Marilynne Robinson, also developed details that illustrate her dominant impression of her grandmother.

My grandmother was not a woman given to excesses of any kind, and so her aging, as it became advanced, was rather astonishing. True, she was straight and brisk and bright when most of her friends had bobbling heads or blurred speech or had sunk into wheelchairs or beds. But in the last years she continued to settle and began to shrink. Her mouth bowed forward and her brow sloped back, and her skull shone pink and speckled within a mere haze of hair, which hovered above her head like the remembered shape of an altered thing. Tendrils grew from her eyebrows and coarse white hairs sprouted on her lip and chin. When she put on an old dress the bosom hung empty and the hem swept the floor.

And here is one more description of a grandmother, a poem by the writer Ray A. Young Bear.

grandmother

if I were to see
her shape from a mile away
i'd know so quickly
that it would be her.
the purple scarf
and the plastic
shopping bag.
if i felt
hands on my head
i'd know that those

were her hands
warm and damp
with the smell
of roots.
if i heard
a voice
coming from
a rock
i'd know
and her words
would flow inside me
like the light
of someone
stirring ashes
from a sleeping fire
at night.

All of these grandmothers come alive in the writers' vivid images.

Here are some suggestions for creating a topic sentence and specific sensory details for your descriptive paragraphs.

DEVELOPING A TOPIC SENTENCE AND SUPPORTING DETAILS FOR A DESCRIPTION OF A PLACE OR AN OBJECT ─────────
Write down answers to the following questions:

1. What is most striking about this place or this object? What is my dominant impression of it?
2. What are its outstanding sights, colors, sizes, and shapes?
3. What are its outstanding sounds, smells, tastes, and textures?
4. What factual and sensory details will help my readers see, imagine, or experience what this place or object is like?

 WRITING ACTIVITY 3

Choose a place or an object that you would like to describe and make a Sensory Chart for it. List as many details as you can under each heading. Examine your chart for a focus and develop a topic sentence about this place or object. Circle all the details that are related to your topic sentence. Do some freewriting, brainstorming, or clustering to develop additional details about the topic sentence. Then use these details to write a brief description of the place or object.

DEVELOPING A TOPIC SENTENCE AND SUPPORTING DETAILS FOR A DESCRIPTION OF A PERSON _____

Write down answers to the following questions:

1. Exactly who is this person? What is your relationship to him or her?
2. What is most striking about this person? What is your single dominant impression of him or her?
3. What physical characteristics of the person contribute to your dominant impression of him or her? For example, do his or her looks, clothing, or voice contribute to your dominant impression?
4. What characteristic behaviors or gestures contribute to your dominant impression?
5. What else about this person's character, personality, or use of language contributes to your dominant impression of him or her?

WRITING ACTIVITY 4

Write a paragraph about a person whom you know well. Begin by developing a Sensory Chart about this person. Then do some freewriting, brainstorming, or clustering about him or her. Decide on your dominant impression of the person: Ask yourself what word best describes this person. Then develop details that illustrate this impression and write a unified and coherent paragraph. Use sensory words and images to enable your readers to see and hear this person.

GROUP WORK 1

Here are nine questions for you and one or two partners to use to help you improve your descriptive paragraphs. Take out a paragraph that you wrote for one of the Writing Activities in this chapter. Exchange descriptions with a partner, and answer the following questions on a separate piece of paper.

1. What do you think was the writer's purpose in this description?

2. Does the paragraph have a topic sentence? If so, what is it?

3. Which supporting details were most effective in conveying the writer's impression of the object, place, or person?

4. Which words helped you see, hear, and sense what this object, place, or person is like?

5. Where does the writer need to add more specific sensory words and images?

6. Are any details or sentences unrelated to the topic sentence? If so, which ones?

7. Does the organization and development of this paragraph seem logical to you? If not, which parts are confusing or do not seem logically related to each other?

8. How can the writer make the paragraph more unified and coherent?

9. What suggestions do you have for improving this paragraph?

In Chapters 3 and 4, you learned how to revise a draft to make it clearer and stronger. Here is a student's descriptive composition that illustrates this process. Her notes for this description appeared on page 146 of this chapter. The handwritten comments in the margin were written by classmates with whom the writer shared her draft.

Luisa,
These are first-rate details but they don't seem to focus on one main idea. I'm not sure about your focus.
Lee-Ann

Luisa's Uncorrected Discovery Draft

My room is the place where I dream. At the center of the room is my bed, which is made of old white oak. At the head of the bed is two white bedposts. The posts at the foot of the bed are little stumps. On top of the bedposts at the head is a fat red ball. These balls are probably made of brass but somebody painted them dark red and the paint chipped away leaving brown spots that make them look like rotten apples. My bed has a beautiful old quilt on it that my grandmother made for my mother and she gave me. Each puff of the quilt feels like a tiny satin pillow. It is pink with peach swirls in it. The swirls look like melted peach melba ice cream. My antique dolls sit on top of the quilt. Next to the bed is an old-fashioned brown table. It has a lamp on it that looks like a swollen goose with a long skinny neck. And next to the lamp is the big green blinking eye of my computer. I spend a lot of time in my room.

> Luisa – This makes me see your room. But I don't get the connection between some of your details. For example, what does the computer or the lamp have to do with your bed? – Tony

After talking with the classmates who responded to her draft, Luisa wrote a new topic sentence: "Like me, my room is a bit old-fashioned." Focusing on this new main idea helped Luisa select and sharpen details for her revision.

Luisa's Revision

Like me, my room is a bit old-fashioned. At the center of the room is my bed, which is framed in white Victorian oak. The front of the bed is guarded by tall, creamy-white bedposts. The posts at the foot of the bed are little white stumps. On top of each bedpost is an oversized red ball. The posts are so old that the paint has chipped away, leaving brown brass spots that make the balls look like rotten apples. My grandmother's wedding quilt drapes over the bed like a blanket of melted peach melba ice cream. It is made of dozens of tiny satin pillows that have become shiny with age. Sitting high up on the puffs of the quilt are my antique dolls, my prize possessions. They too shine with age and love. Each one looks like a princess on her throne. My bed is their castle.

This revision is more focused, unified, and coherent than the original draft.

Figurative Language. In her revision, Luisa used comparisons to help readers understand her perceptions of her bed and the feelings it evoked in her. A comparison that uses the words *like* or *as* is called a *simile*, and it can help readers see things the way you do. For instance, how does the simile in the second sentence below enable the writer to communicate her vision more clearly than she did in the first sentence?

1. His face was very white.
2. His face was *as white as the underside of a fish that had died several days ago.*

Below is another example of how an effective simile can sharpen description:

1. She holds her head up high.
2. She holds her head up *as if a spike ran from her grizzed black hair to the base of her spine.*

Why is the second sentence more effective than the first?

A comparison that leaves out the word *like* or *as* is called a *metaphor:* "He is the calm at the center of my storm." A metaphor implies that the two things being compared are actually the *same* thing. They don't merely resemble each other; one is the other. By conjuring up a vivid image in a few words, metaphors add sparkle to your descriptions and help readers perceive things from your viewpoint. In the paragraph below, notice how the writer Alfred Kazin uses comparisons to help you understand how he felt about the kitchen in his boyhood home.

> The kitchen was the great machine that set our lives running; it whirred down a little only on Saturdays and holy days. From my mother's kitchen I gained my first picture of life as a white, overheated, starkly lit workshop redolent with Jewish cooking, crowded with women in house-dresses, strewn with fashion magazines, patterns, dress material, spools of thread—and at whose center, so lashed to her machine that bolts of energy seemed to dance out of her hands and feet as she worked, my mother stamped the treadle hard against the floor, hard, hard, and silently, grimly at war, beating out the first rhythm of the world for me.

The comparisons that Kazin wrote help you to see his kitchen as a "machine" that "whirred down" on certain days. They also help you see his mother at work as he saw her—"lashed to her machine" and "grimly at war."

WRITING ACTIVITY 5

As you read the student paragraph below, circle every comparison (every simile and metaphor).

The local bus station is a filthy mess. It looks like a massive

black hole. You can hardly see the rough gray paint on the walls because they are covered with ragged yellow posters that are peeling off like scabs. Big green and purple whirls of graffiti have been smeared across the paint and posters, and they drip down to the brown puddles on the floor. The gray-green tiles on the floor are covered with patches of dark mud and dirt. An awful odor rises up from these patches, which smells like a mixture of sweat and old food. The heavy, still air feels like a dirty blanket. I cannot wait to get outside into the clean, sunny street.

On a separate piece of paper, note the comparisons that you liked best in this description and explain why you found them particularly effective.

WRITING ACTIVITY 6

Pick an object to describe. Examine it closely; then touch it, roll it around, sniff it, and taste it. Next, write the following phrase on a piece of paper: "This object is like _____." Spend at least five minutes writing down all the things that the object is similar to or that it reminds you of. Stretch your imagination: Be as absurd as possible and do not censor any of your comparisons. When you are finished brainstorming, select the simile or metaphor that you like best and expand it into a paragraph about the object. Use additional similes and metaphors to describe specific features of the object.

WRITING ACTIVITY 7

Write a paragraph describing the best teacher you ever had (now *or* in the past). Imagine that you are writing to students who are considering taking a course with this teacher. Don't "tell" about your teacher; instead use words that show what he or she looks like and how he or she behaves. Make the person come alive for your readers. Use similes and metaphors to describe your teacher's personality, attitudes, and behavior.

WRITING OBJECTIVE AND SUBJECTIVE DESCRIPTIONS

The details that you compose and select for your descriptive compositions depend on your purpose and your intended readers. Reread the description of the bus station on pages 154 and 155, and think about the writer's purpose and intended audience. Whom do you think the writer envisioned as his readers? How can you tell?

This description of a bus station is a *subjective* one—it conveys the writer's impressions and feelings through vivid images and metaphors. Consider whether the writer would have used the same details if he were working for the Department of Sanitation and was writing a report about the conditions of this particular station. For this purpose and audience, the writer would have had to write an *objective* description—one that provides factual details. For example, in describing the floor he might have used facts and numbers: "One hundred ten of the 140 ceramic floor tiles are all or partially covered with a mudlike substance."

TYPES OF DESCRIPTION

Here are some differences between objective and subjective description.

Objective	Subjective
Focus is on the object.	Focus is on the writer's impression of the object.
Writer includes details about the object.	Writer includes personal responses (thoughts and feelings).
Writer describes observable, measurable facts.	Writer uses similes and metaphors.
Writing style is serious and matter-of-fact.	Writing style can be informal and emotional.

Effective description often includes a mix of objective and subjective details. Only you can decide whether to use subjective details, objective details, or both in your writing. As with most choices in writing, this decision must be based on your topic, purpose, readers, and style (how you like to write).

GROUP WORK 2

Work together in a group of three or four. Read the two descriptions below, each of which describes the rainfall in Texas. Then choose one person to record the group's responses to the questions that follow the descriptions.

Description #1

Texas rainfall varies mostly from east to west rather than north to south, though north-central Texas does get a few more inches of rain than south Texas each year. The driest part of Texas is the Trans-Pecos region between Big Bend and El Paso, where the average annual precipitation is nine to twelve inches. The Davis Mountains of the Trans-Pecos get a bit more, up to eighteen inches a year. The wettest places are in east Texas, ranging from fifty-two inches a year in the Houston area to fifty-six inches a year on the lower Louisiana border. In areas between far west Texas and far east Texas, rainfalls average twenty-five to twenty-eight inches a year.

Description #2

In a country with an average rainfall of twelve inches, a rancher can get his full allotment overnight. He is quite likely to get his rain not in slow, life-giving patters over the growing period, but in a few violent surges measured in inches. Then, of course, the dry, hard ground throws off the water, refuses to absorb and store it against future need and use, sends it hurtling down into the gullies and on to the draws and to the river and finally to the sea, of no use to any man. The water comes with such force that it erodes new paths and leaves the hills marked and torn. It forms veritable streams in its rush to the draws, hurtling over land that was dry that morning, and it catches the cattle and bowls them off their feet and rolls them bawling toward the draw until they drown; and their bodies fetch up eighty miles away when the water falls. And then it may not rain

again for a year.

1. In what ways do these two descriptions differ?

2. What do you think was the writer's purpose in the first description? Who was the intended audience?

3. What do you think was the writer's purpose in the second description? Who was the intended audience?

4. Which description can you visualize in your mind more easily? Why?

WRITING ACTIVITY 8

On page 159 is a picture of Terry Fox, a runner who lost his leg to cancer and who attempted to run across North America to raise money for cancer research. Carefully examine the picture and then write two separate descriptions of it. Your first description should be an *objective* one. Write exactly what you see in the picture, as if you were describing it to someone who cannot see it. The second description should be *subjective:* Explain how the picture makes you feel and describe the details that evoke this emotional response. When you are done writing, revising, and editing your two descriptions, be prepared to discuss the ways in which they are similar and different.

ORGANIZING DESCRIPTIVE DETAILS

Part of planning a description is deciding how to arrange your details in a way that makes sense to readers. One way to organize a description of a place or an object is spatially: left to right, top to bottom, outside to inside, or near to far. Another way of building a descriptive impression is to move from the most important feature to less striking features (or you can move from the least significant feature to the most important one).

Below is a description of a bedroom by the writer M. F. K. Fisher. As you read it, see if you can picture the room in your mind's eye. What order did Fisher use to arrange her details?

At the very top of the stairway on the third floor at the back of the house, in the attic of the house really, were the rooms that Madame

Ollangier had for rent. There were two tiny rooms, long and narrow, with the most hideous wallpaper I have ever seen. There was a big window in each room, looking down into the hard gray little court.

The entrance was at the top of the stairs, and in the back of them were a sort of storage attic and two miserable servants' rooms. The bedroom of the rooms for rent was papered in mustard and black stripes, about eight inches wide, with a band of American Beauty roses around the attic ceiling. It looked like marble—brown and mottled, orange and mustard—to tie the whole thing together, to make it look elegant. And there was a pair of mustard-colored old tiered velvet curtains across the window, with a little brown radiator underneath that made a terrible crashing and banging and hissing every morning, and since it sat right under the window the heat went right up and out the window.

What order did Fisher use to organize her details?

_____

Which details enabled you to experience the bedroom as Fisher did?

_____

_____

_____

_____

Fisher organized her details spatially, in the order in which she saw them as she looked around the room. She used transitions such as ''at the very top'' to help you follow the order of her details. Below are some transitions that are frequently used in spatial descriptions.

TRANSITIONS THAT INDICATE
SPATIAL ORDER ━━━━━━━━━━━━━━━━━━━━━━━
Here are some transitional words and phrases that signal the spatial relations among details in a physical description.

> *at the top, on top, above, beneath, below, on the bottom, next to, beside, left, right, center, front, back, middle, between, under, closest, furthest, near, far, up, down*

WRITING ACTIVITY 9

Reread the student description of the bus station in Writing Activity 5 on pages 154 and 155. On a separate piece of paper, write answers to the following questions about the description.

1. How did the writer organize the descriptive details in this paragraph?

2. Is the writer's order logical? Why or why not?

3. How else could the writer have organized these details?

WRITING ACTIVITY 10

Write a one-paragraph description of a room or an object to which you feel a strong attachment. Use words and details that show your readers why this room or object is so special. When you revise your paragraph, make sure that it conveys your dominant impression of the room or object. Also make sure that every detail supports that dominant impression. Add additional concrete, sensory images and similes and metaphors. Then check to see that you have developed your details in a logical order that will make sense to your readers.

GROUP WORK 3

Get into a group of three or four students. Choose an object that the entire group can observe and take notes on for five minutes. After the time limit is up, select one group member to be the recorder for the description that the group will write. Together the group should create a topic sentence that reveals their dominant impression of the object. Then each person should volunteer one or more descriptive details that support this impression. When the group feels that the paragraph is complete, they should revise it together.

WRITING ACTIVITY 11

Choose an object to observe over a short period (a week or ten days). Select something that changes, like a piece of food or a plant. Every other day, observe it closely and record your impression of it and your observations of the way it looks, sounds, smells, tastes, and feels. Take notes on every change that you notice and describe the way these changes alter the overall appearance of the object that you are observing. On the last day, write a description of the way this object changed over time.

WRITING ACTIVITY 12

This activity will help you practice your skill in writing objective, scientific description. Choose an animal to observe and describe. Imagine that you are planning a paragraph for a science course. To do this, you will have to take notes that describe the animal in accurate factual detail. You may also want to consult a book about the animal to find out additional information for your description. If you do, refer to pages 115 through 118 in Chapter 4 about paraphrasing someone else's words and about using statistics.

Descriptive Summaries. A summary is itself a type of descriptive writing—it is a brief description of the main idea and key supporting points of a reading selection. A summary restates only the most important points in a piece of writing. Thus, writing a summary differs from writing a paraphrase, in which you must restate all the ideas of a piece of writing in your own words. (See pages 117–118 in Chapter 4 for guidelines on paraphrasing.)

Summarizing is an excellent way of learning because it requires you to think critically about the material that you have read. In writing a summary, you must decide the most important ideas that are in a piece of writing and present these parts in your own words.

> ## GUIDELINES FOR WRITING
> ## A DESCRIPTIVE SUMMARY ————————————
>
> 1. Take notes on the main ideas and the most important details.
> 2. Ask yourself, "What is the main thing that the author wanted me to learn from this?" Your answer can be the opening sentence of your summary.
> 3. In your own words, briefly state the key ideas and the most important details.
> 4. Present these ideas and details in the order in which they occurred in the material that you are summarizing; do *not* rearrange the organization of the details.
> 5. Revise your summary for unity, coherence, and correctness.

WRITING ACTIVITY 13

Write a summary of the essay by Sue Lorch on pages 62 through 67 of Chapter 2.

GETTING READERS' RESPONSES

Use the checklist below to help you revise the drafts of your descriptive paragraphs. Ask family, friends, and classmates to answer the questions below honestly and fully.

DESCRIPTION CHECKLIST ————————————————————

1. Does the description have a clear, focused topic sentence that is neither too narrow nor too broad? If so, what is this idea? If not, what might it be?
2. Where does the writer need to add more details to develop and illustrate the topic sentence or the dominant impression of the draft?
3. What is the writer's purpose and audience?
4. Are the details appropriate for this purpose and audience? If so, why? If not, why not?
5. Which details are irrelevant to the main idea? Why?
6. Which sensory images are particularly striking and effective? Which details need additional concrete, sensory images?
7. How are the details organized? Is there a more appropriate or logical way of organizing the details?
8. How can the writer improve the unity and coherence of this draft? Where are additional transitions needed?
9. Which sentences have errors in them?
10. What suggestions do you have for improving this description?

■ EXPLORING FURTHER

The reading that follows incorporates the kinds of descriptive paragraphs that you have practiced writing in this chapter. This student essay, titled "Emergency Room," is the one from which the two paragraphs in Writing Activity 2 on pages 147 and 148 were excerpted.

By looking out the window of the ambulance, I can see we are getting close to the hospital. As we speed by the familiar buildings, the flashing emergency lights turn them into hundreds of freeze-frame photographs. The strobe lights turn everything that their light falls on a monotone hue of either red or blue. The siren's only rival is the screaming of my patient, which pierces the air like an explosion in the night. I struggle for balance while crouched on the floor as the vehicle makes a sharp turn into the parking lot. Finally, the ambulance jerks to a stop. I know that we have arrived at our destination, the emergency department.

The pain in my hands grows worse as the time goes by. The amount of pressure I have had to put on the subclavian artery to stop the bleeding is causing my hands to cramp. Suddenly, my mind is diverted from the pain as the rear doors fly open and the cool night air rushes in, chilling the sweat on my face. The doctor looks at me. I shake my head. This patient is probably going to die no matter what we do. Most of his life-sustaining blood lies in the parking lot of an east-side bar where he was shot. With the swiftness of a cobra strike, his assailant struck the fatal blow with a sawed-off shotgun. Where once were an arm and chest wall there are now grotesque fragments of human form.

As I stand up, I feel the warm sensation of liquid running down my pant leg into my shoe. For the first time I realize that I am covered with warm, sticky blood. We wheel the patient from the ambulance onto the ambulance loading dock. The heat lamps overhead radiate a soothing warmth against the cool, humid night air. The calloused police officers look on casually at the action passing before them. They have seen all this too many times to be shocked or even curious.

My adrenaline is peaking as we hit the malfunctioning electric doors with a crash. As the three of us enter the emergency department, we turn sharply into room two: the crisis room. The humming white lights are almost blinding after the darkness of the night. The room is lined with people in statue-like poses in anticipation of our arrival. As we position the patient onto the hard table, I notice that the once screaming man is now silent and motionless.

A crash shatters the silence as an over-eager intern knocks over a mayo stand, scattering the once-sterile surgical instruments onto the floor. The charge nurse just rolls her eyes as she bends over to begin picking up the instruments. The body is quickly enveloped by a group of surgeons. A sterile and gloved surgeon signals to me and simultaneously I withdraw my paralyzed hand as he reapplies pressure to the damaged artery. The once-quiet room is now a flurry of activity with blood pressure cuffs squeezing, electrocardiogram indicators beeping, and oxygen outlets hissing. The attending emergency room physician stands with his arms folded watching the orchestration of activity. He gives his nod of approval to the chief surgeon as he walks toward the head of the table.

The chief resident of thoracic surgery is now standing directly beside the table. He carefully surveys the damage done by the shotgun. He quickly turns toward the mayo stand and grabs a bottle of betadine solution and pours it over the entire chest. The betadine turns the flesh orange as the excess spills onto the floor, staining the surgeon's tennis shoes. The charge nurse adjusts the overhead light which illuminates the surgical field. The surgeon squints as he looks at the skin in the reflection of the overhead light. He turns to the mayo stand and carefully picks up the shining stainless steel scalpel. With his left hand he palpates the chest wall. Precisely but quickly, he cuts the skin between the protruding ribs. As the blade slices through the skin, the skin separates without help. The normally yellow fat globules, turned orange by the betadine, balloon from the incision. With his second pass of the blade, a popping sound is made as he enters the pleura of the inner chest wall. Blood spurts out with a forceful gush, covering the surgeon's gown and gloves as he separates the two sections of the rib cage. The charge nurse hands him the rib spreaders with a slap.

He deftly inserts the apparatus into the separation between the two ribs. He manipulates the spreaders with machine-like precision. The cartilage of the ribs pops like the knuckles of a boastful schoolboy as they are spread to form an unnatural opening into the man's chest. The surgeon reaches his gloved hand into the cavernous opening and works his way past the ribs, clotted blood, and lung tissue to the heart. He carefully palpates the organ. It is flaccid and void of life's blood. He shakes his head as he examines the heart further. He grimaces as he feels the large puncture wound in the posterior aspect of the left ventricle. He instinctively reaches for the cardiac patches and sutures but stops short as he realizes the damage is too extensive for repair. He looks at the emergency room attending physician as if to ask a question. The attending just shrugs his shoulders and sighs. There is a moment of stillness as the surgeon removes his hand from the man's chest and pronounces the time of death.

The feeling is just coming back to my hands as I attempt to write my trip report. My clothes are wet with blood and smell like a slaughter house. My legs are beginning to itch from the combination of dried sweat and blood. My mind drifts as I think of how much we can do for some patients and how little we can do for others. I ask the unanswerable question of why some people die as others live. All we can do as paramedics is give each patient our all.

I look toward the emergency room doors to see my partner coming toward me. He calls my name and motions toward the ambulance. He says we have another call waiting for us. ''The natives must be restless tonight,'' he says. ''We have another shooting.''

Discussion Questions

1. Did the writer convey a dominant impression of his experience in working as an emergency room medical technician? If so, what was it?
2. What might be another title for this essay?
3. What was the writer's purpose in writing this essay? What did he want to show or convince his readers of?
4. Which details were most effective in enabling you to experience the ambulance ride? Why were these details so powerful?
5. Which details were most effective in enabling you to experience the emergency room? Why were they so powerful?
6. Did the objective details and the medical terminology that the writer included help or hinder your understanding of his description? Why?
7. How did the writer achieve unity and coherence?

WRITING ASSIGNMENT 1

Write a description of an unforgettable experience that you had. Like the author of "Emergency Room" did, focus on a dominant impression and use sensory details to develop and illustrate that impression.

WRITING ASSIGNMENT 2

Write a composition describing yourself. You might want to begin by thinking of the one word that best describes you at this point in your life. Or you might want to imagine that you are writing for a specific person and purpose. For example, you could write a description that will convince a person whom you find attractive to go out on a date with you. Or write a description that will convince a potential employer to hire you. Or write a description that will convince a school to which you might want to transfer to accept your application.

 POINTS TO REMEMBER ABOUT DESCRIPTION

1. Use all your senses to observe the person, place, object, or event you are describing. What exactly does it look, sound, smell, taste, and feel like?
2. Take notes as you observe and use specific, concrete words and phrases to create sharp, vivid images.
3. Limit your description to one dominant impression and make sure that you state it clearly.
4. Make comparisons and use similes and metaphors.
5. Decide on an appropriate balance of objective and subjective details.
6. Provide enough details for your reader to experience the person, place, object, or event in the way that you did.
7. Make sure that your details are logically organized.

C H A P T E R

6

NARRATION

Narration is storytelling, and we are all expert storytellers. Every time someone asks us, "What happened?" we narrate a sequence of events, selecting the facts that seem most important at that given moment. When we put these narratives down on paper, we can reflect on their meaning, reorganizing them according to our purpose and our focus. Writing about the events in our lives helps us understand them better and learn from them. Thus, much of the writing you do will be narrative in nature, based on your experiences and your reflections on the meaning of these experiences. For instance, you may be asked to describe an important event in your life so that you can understand it more fully or examine its impact on your behavior and your beliefs. Or you might be asked to state a point or a theory and to relate a story that supports this point or theory.

Effective narration has qualities similar to those of good description:

- A clear focus and purpose
- Abundant details that enable readers to visualize exactly what happened
- A clear description of the writer's thoughts and feelings about the experience so readers can share the writer's perspective and reactions
- A logical organization

FINDING IDEAS FOR NARRATIVES

Your memory is filled with narratives, experiences that shaped your personality and perceptions. Have you been writing down any of these in your journal, or Idea Bank? (See pages 4–5 in Chapter 1 about keeping an Idea Bank.)

If you are writing in an Idea Bank on a regular basis, you will have dozens of ideas for stories about yourself and the world around you. Your Idea Bank is the place to describe your memories, to record the events that are taking place in your life each day, and to describe your responses to these events. Writing about your daily experiences enables you to think more fully about them and to make sense of them. The more frequently you write in your Idea Bank, the more material you will have for narrative paragraphs and essays.

Below is an Idea Bank entry made by a writing student for a narrative assignment. As you read it, consider whether it is ready to be shared with others. If not, why not?

I miss Dad a lot today. I keep thinking about that killer basketball game I played with him. God, was he tough. Much bigger and better than me. He killed me but I fought back. And I realized what he was trying to show me. Wow! What an unbelievable experience!

Since the writer is remembering an event in her life, the plot, characters, and setting are all clear to her. If the writer wanted to turn this entry into a paragraph, she would have to flesh it out with descriptive details. But first, she would have to decide on her reason for sharing this experience with readers: What did she learn from it? What point does it illustrate?

DECIDING ON A FOCUS AND PURPOSE

A narrative should have an essential point or a topic sentence. In order to write a good narration, you must decide on your focus and your purpose. You might want to tell a story in order to share an interesting or important experience you had, to explain why you hold a particular belief, or to support a theory or a point of view.

Here is the paragraph that the writer of the preceding Idea Bank Entry developed for her writing course. As you read it, think about the student's purpose in narrating this story.

The toughest basketball game I ever played was my first one-on-one game against my father. At six-foot two and 194 pounds, my father towered over me like a giant. I was big for a ten-year-old, five-foot one and 100 pounds, but I was no match for a huge bear of a man. He could cross the court in six thundering steps, leaving me running behind him trying to catch up. "Come on," I thought to myself. "You're quicker. You can beat him." Darting and dodging around him, I kept grabbing the ball and jumping for a slam dunk. But he was always there, pushing me down and grabbing the ball from my slippery hands. He was like a black cloud looming above me, raining down tiny drops of sweat. His voice sounded like thunder as he bellowed at me, "What's the matter? Can't keep up?" My insides churned as I realized he was cheating, purposely playing me unfairly. His huge leathery hands kept pinning me down and pushing me away as he flew up to the basket and scored point after point. Suddenly I felt my white-hot anger current switch on, and I started to fight back. I banged him in his skinny shins, and as he was yowling, I slammed in three points. I ran him down till he was shaking and yelling, "Enough." Bitter anger poured out of my mouth like vomit. When I was done, he smiled at me and whispered, "But you didn't quit. It wasn't fair, but you didn't quit." And that was when I realized what he was doing. He was showing me that if I wanted to play in the professional female basketball leagues, I had to know early on that life wasn't going to be fair. I was going to get pushed around like dirt, but I couldn't ever quit. And I haven't.

What was the writer's topic sentence?

_____

_____

Did her narrative convince you of this point? Why or why not?

_____

_____

_____

_____

Which details and images did you like best? Why?

_____

_____

_____

_____

Note that the writer of the preceding paragraph chose to describe a specific event that occurred within a limited time span. She could have described other games that she played with her father or other events that occurred on that day, but this approach might have blurred her point. One way to create effective narration is to focus on a single incident that you can recall clearly and describe sharply with concrete images and vivid metaphors.

PURPOSES FOR WRITING NARRATIVES _____
You might choose to include narrative paragraphs in academic essays for many reasons, including the following:

- To share an important experience or incident that was special to you or that continues to bother you
- To relate an experience that reveals something about you or about someone else
- To summarize an event that you saw or read about in order to explain its significance
- To describe an experience that illustrates a point or a position

---

Appropriate details for narrative paragraphs depend on the writer's focus and purpose. For example, read the following notes that a student wrote in preparation for an essay. Each purpose (described below) might lead to a different essay.

ASSIGNMENT: Write an essay for my classmates about my

experience losing the final race of the 100-yard dash at the

Alameda County Fair, a race that I had been practicing for

daily for about two years.

Possible Purpose 1 (Expressive): To share this experience and explore why it was important to my sense of myself and of the person I wanted to be.

Possible Purpose 2 (Explanatory): To describe this experience and explain how it showed me that trying one's best can be as gratifying as winning.

Possible Purpose 3 (Persuasive): To use this experience to illustrate the point that people can fail at their most important goal and still go on to achieve success.

WRITING ACTIVITY 1

Reread your Idea Bank, or journal, and put a check next to an entry that describes a memorable event. Search your memory and try to recall everything you can about this event. Do some freewriting, brainstorming, or clustering about the event. Write down notes about what you saw, heard, felt, and experienced. You might want to make a Sensory Chart (like the ones you wrote for Chapter 5). Next, figure out the main point that you want to make about this event and a purpose for writing. Then write a topic sentence. Turn your notes into a paragraph describing why this event still stands out so sharply in your mind.

Narrating a personal experience is an effective strategy for supporting a point or for suggesting a truth about life. For example, here is an excerpt from a book by Ryan White, the hemophiliac teenager who died of AIDS-related illnesses in 1991. In the paragraphs below, White narrates an experience that shows how the fear of AIDS makes people do senseless, cruel things:

Then came Easter Sunday. Normally, at our church, the whole congregation says "Happy Easter!" to each other this way: Our minister steps forward to the front pew, shakes a few parishioners' hands, and says "Peace be with you." Then those people turn to their neighbors and shake *their* hands, and so on, all the way to the back of the church, where we were sitting.

The family in the pew in front of me turned around. I held my hand out—to empty air. Other people's hands were moving every which way, in all directions away from me. No one in the whole church wanted to shake my hand and wish me peace on Easter.

My family and I filed out of church in silence. "Maybe I should run after a few people and grab their hands, just to shake them up," I said to Mom. You could tell nothing was going to make Grandma feel better. She looked devastated, like she was going to burst into tears any minute. Grandpa said grimly, "I'm never going back." And he didn't.

CONSIDERING YOUR READER'S NEEDS

The key to good narration is attention to detail. The more specific details you include, the richer and more interesting your description and narration will be. However, as with all writing, the details that you select and develop to support your points depend on your purpose and your readers' needs. How much do your readers already know about you and about the event you are recounting? If they know very little, then you have to include details that answer the "Reporter's Questions":

Who? What? Where? When? How? Why?

Your answers to these questions will help readers understand what happened and why it was important to you.

As you freewrite or brainstorm to create notes for narrative paragraphs, remember to include details that appeal to all five senses. Think about the people and the places that you are describing: What do (or did) they look like and sound like? What smells remind you of them? If you are narrating an experience that occurred in the past, close your eyes and replay the events in your mind as many times as you need to in order to remember specific details.

In addition, don't forget to include details about your responses and reactions to the experience that you are relating. How did you feel when it occurred? Why? How do you feel about it now? Why? Let your emotions and your voice come through so that readers can understand the significance of the experience for you. Developing a draft of a narrative may help you understand the events or experiences more clearly. Share your reflections with readers: Explain why the experience was so meaningful, or how it changed you, or what it taught you.

WRITING ACTIVITY 2

Write a narrative about an unforgettable moment or experience in your life. Imagine that the reader is someone who does not know you at all. What will this reader need to know about you in order to understand your narrative and your point of view? Use the Reporter's Questions, above, to help you generate details. Your paragraph (or paragraphs) should enable readers to understand (1) exactly what happened, (2) how you felt about it, and (3) why this event made such a lasting impression on you.

In addition to needing specific sensory details, readers need logical development. The basic structure for narrative writing is *chronological*—the order in which events occurred in time. Arranging details chronologically helps readers understand the relations among the events in your narration.

Below is a brief student essay that is not logically organized. Can you follow the sequence of events?

What surprised me most when I got to college was how easy high school really was—that I could have done much better than I did. The scholarships. In high school, they told us about them, but you really didn't know what you needed to do, as far as activities and how good your grades had to be. I mean college is much harder and I can do it. We had counselors. But they just said, "Do good. Do good." But why? They always told us, "Do your best. Do your best." And we'd do the work and pass and all that.

Something that really surprised me my senior year was class rank. I know I could have been more than I was. Everyone goes around saying, "You're smart. You're smart. But I wasn't that much into books. I was the one who talked and talked. The one with common sense. I was surprised at my rank—it was worse than I thought. There was so much I didn't know until it was too late in my senior year. Maybe I would have gone to Harvard or something. Now I realize that I could have knocked it out in high school.

Because the events discussed in the preceding paragraphs are not written in the order of their occurrence, they are difficult to understand. Compare the paragraphs above to those below, in which the details are discussed in the order in which they happened. The paragraphs below were published in a national newspaper article.

After a year of college . . .

At the end of their first year of college, we talked with Earnestine ''Dee-Dee'' Harley, 19, Jeff Lawrence, 19, Nanette Salas, 18, Melissa Dugan, 19, and Anna Sepanic, 19, at the Camden campus of Rutgers University in New Jersey. We asked what had surprised them most when they got there and why they were going to college.

Dee-Dee: What surprised me most when I got to college was how easy high school really was—that I could have done much better than I did. I mean, college is much harder, and I can do it. I wish I'd done better then. There was so much I didn't know until it was too late in my senior year.

The scholarships. In high school, they told us about them, but you didn't really know what you needed to do, as far as activities and how good your grades had to be. We had counselors. But they just said, "Do good. Do good." But why? They always told us, "Do your best. Do your best." And we'd do the work and pass and all that. But when it was time to go to college, we found out then. I mean, you know you need good grades, but how good?

Something that really surprised me my senior year was class rank. I didn't know how it worked. I was surprised at my rank—it was worse than I thought. Everyone goes around saying, "You're smart. You're smart." But I wasn't that much into the books. I was the one who talked and talked. The one with common sense. But the ranking has to do with book-wise and grade-wise. My grades were good, but they could have been better. Now I realize that I could have knocked it out in high school. I know I could have been more than I was. Maybe I would have gone to Harvard or something.[1]

WRITING ACTIVITY 3

Write one or two narrative paragraphs about what surprised you most during your first semester at your current school. Imagine that the reader is someone who does not know you. Think about what this reader will need to know about you in order to understand your narrative and your point of view. Use the Reporter's Questions on page 172 to help you generate details for this narrative. Your paragraph (or paragraphs) should (1) describe the event or experience that most surprised you, (2) explain how you felt about it, and (3) explain how you feel about it now or what you learned from it.

GROUP WORK 1

Get into a group of three or four students. Together, do some brainstorming about the picture on page 175. Who might these people be? What

---

1. "Dee-Dee," from FRESH VOICES® by Lynn Minton, PARADE, August 2, 1992. Reprinted with permission from Parade. Copyright © 1992.

might have happened? Where? When? How? Why? Choose one person to write down the group's responses. Then together the group should create a narrative about the events in this picture or about the events leading up to the picture.

 WRITING ACTIVITY 4

In the paragraph below, Gordon Parks, the famous photographer, film director, and writer, explains what happened to him when he heard the news about the assassination of Martin Luther King, Jr. As you read this paragraph, think about the information that Parks left out. What did he assume his readers knew?

On a peaceful April afternoon in 1968, terrible news flashed over my car radio as I drove through Los Angeles. ''Martin Luther King has just been shot by an unknown gunman . . .'' I braked the car to a stop, stunned. The announcer's words kept spilling into the car with details—until finally they turned into a commercial expounding the merits of some dog food. The tone of his voice had lost all urgency, fallen back into a jargon of ordinariness. What was done would stay done seemed to be the essence of his manner. I sat by the curb, feeling suddenly isolated as traffic kept whizzing by. Why hadn't all the other drivers stopped as I had stopped? Didn't they hear? Didn't they contemplate the tragedy? Surely now the entire country would be caught up in the most hostile quaking of the black revolution. Despite all those other cars rushing past, there was for me a sound of silence; a crushing, respectful silence for the most revered of our civil rights leaders who had been gunned down. For a man who loved peace so much, no fate could have been worse. Throughout America a lot of black people would be praying; but some would probably be buying guns. This I was thinking as I finally drove off.

1. What was Parks's main point?
2. What did he assume that readers already knew about the incident he describes in this paragraph?
3. What did Parks mean when he wrote, ''For a man who loved peace so much, no fate could have been worse''?
4. How did Parks organize the details in this narrative?
5. Which details did you like best? Why?

 ## WRITING ACTIVITY 5

Write a paragraph about an upsetting or a terrible experience. Your final version should describe exactly what happened, why it happened, and how you felt and reacted. You might also want to explain what you learned from this experience.

If you are having difficulty developing details for narrative paragraphs, use the questions at the top of page 177 to generate new information.

NARRATIVE QUESTIONS ───────────────────

Here are some questions about the experience that you are narrating that you should consider:

1. Exactly what happened?
2. Where and when did it happen?
3. How did it happen?
4. Who was involved, and what did they do and say?
5. What *exactly* did you see, hear, smell, and feel?
6. What were your reactions to the people and events?
7. How did this experience affect you (and/or others)?
8. Now that time has passed, what meaning does this experience hold for you? Can you interpret it in different ways? (Does it hold more than one meaning for you?)
9. What did you learn from this experience?
10. What would you do differently if this experience happened again?

USING VIVID AND CONCRETE DETAILS AND IMAGES

Narration and description work together. Readers can't experience the events you are relating unless you use sensory details and vivid images to describe exactly what you saw, heard, and felt. Like description, narration relies on interesting similes and metaphors (which you practiced writing in Chapter 5). For instance, consider the two sentences below. Which one paints a clearer picture of the writer's feelings?

A. The rope was tight, and my arms started to hurt.
B. The rope was a vise, and my arms started to pulse as if they were exploding.

What is the simile in the second sentence? What is the metaphor? (See pages 153–155 for a reminder about how similes and metaphors work.) How do both help you feel what the writer was feeling?

Below is a student paragraph that integrates sensory details and vivid imagery into narration.

I learned about religion on my eighth birthday. On that day, I was strolling home from school with a group of friends. As usual, we were telling jokes and fooling around, and we didn't notice the four boys silently following us. Soon, however, we all heard them. They seemed to be moaning some kind of menacing chant. Although we couldn't make out their words, the low rumble was terrifying. Suddenly, one of the boys grabbed me and started screeching words that would stay in my head forever—"Christ-killer, Christ-killer!" He pulled out a filthy rope and wound it around my arms, screaming, "You little kike. I'm gonna kill you like you killed Christ." I couldn't believe it. They were going to kill me because I was Jewish. The rope was a vise, and my arms started to pulse as if they were exploding. Feeling faint, I sobbed out an answer that I thought would make them stop: "Stop! Think about it—Christ *was* a Jew!" The face of the boy who was strangling my arms turned tomato red with anger. Then he shouted that I was a liar and that all Jews had to suffer for killing Jesus Christ. Just as my arms were tingling into numbness, my father came running down the block with my brother and they chased the boys away. Later that afternoon, we found out the ringleader's name, and my father and I went to his house to see his father. The man politely denied that his son was involved in the incident. But as we walked down the path from his house, we heard him call to someone inside, "That was the Christ-killers. They just left."

This powerful narration makes its point about how people "learn about religion" through specific, concrete details. Instead of "telling" us what happened, this writer "shows" us. We hear the crowd moan and see the tormenter's face turn red with rage. We experience the writer's terror and his shock.

The writer of this paragraph organized his details chronologically, using transitions such as "soon," "suddenly," "then," and "later" to help readers follow the order of his details. Below are some transitions that are frequently used in narration.

TRANSITIONS THAT INDICATE CHRONOLOGICAL ORDER

Here are some transitional words and phrases that signal the time relations among details in narrations.

first	immediately	eventually	later
in the	then	suddenly	last
beginning	during	gradually	finally
second	while	now	afterward
next	after		

WRITING ACTIVITY 6

Here is another narrative paragraph, an excerpt from Richard Rodriguez's autobiography, *Hunger of Memory*. Like the preceding writer, Rodriguez makes his narrative come alive with vivid sensory images and metaphors.

> It was unsettling to hear my parents struggle with English. Hearing them, I'd grow nervous, my clutching trust in their protection and power weakened. There were many times like the night at a brightly lit gasoline station (a blaring white memory) when I stood uneasily, hearing my father. He was talking to a teenaged attendant. I do not recall what they were saying, but I cannot forget the sounds my father made as he spoke. At one point his words slid together to form one word—sounds as confused as the threads of blue and green oil in the puddle next to my shoes. His voice rushed through what he had to say. And, toward the end, reached falsetto notes, appealing to his listener's understanding. I looked away to the lights of passing automobiles. I tried not to hear anymore. But I heard only too well the calm, easy tones in the attendant's reply. Shortly afterward, walking toward home with my father, I shivered when he put his hand on my shoulder.

Answer the following questions on a separate piece of paper.

1. What was the writer's point?

2. Which "who, what, where, when, how, and why" questions did the writer answer?

3. Which descriptive details enabled you to understand what the writer experienced?

4. What order was used to develop this paragraph?

5. What did you like or dislike about the paragraph?

Below is another sample of narrative writing that uses vivid descriptive detail to make a point. It comes from a report by journalist Melinda Liu about the food served in rural China.

Pass a Snake, Hold the Rat

A guide to Chinese food you can't get in takeout

According to a Chinese proverb, people will "eat anything with four legs, except for the furniture." Restaurants throughout China, particularly in the south, are proving it. Newsweek's Melinda Liu has toured several of China's more exotic culinary establishments and tasted a few offerings guaranteed not to be on the menu of your favorite takeout place. Dishes are rated on a scale of zero to four chopsticks:

Bear (One Chopstick)

I love imperial-style banquets. But I find one of China's most famous dishes, braised bear paw, overrated. Connoisseurs insist on left paws, softer and more succulent because bears lick them more frequently than right paws. Boned and simmered, the padded cushions are sliced wafer thin and served with small game birds. The taste is lackluster, and the thought of how it's butchered hard to stomach. Still, this Manchurian delicacy is so popular some restaurants keep wild bears in cages out back for last-minute feasts.

Snake (Four Chopsticks)

One of China's most seductive dishes is snake soup sprinkled with aromatic wisps of chrysanthemum petal. For a spicier treat, there is snake meat stir-fried with civet cat (looks like an elongated raccoon) and a little red chili; it's called "The Dragon Battling the Tiger." When the Chinese say snake is "hot," they're talking folk medicine, not temperature. Superstition has it that it's better to partake of snake during cold weather. As Confucius once said: "A great person eats nothing out of season."

Scorpion (Three Chopsticks)

Speaking of Confucius, I found several subtle specialties in his hometown of Qufu in eastern China. Deep-fried scorpion is the star on the menu of the Confucius family mansion, which has been transformed into a hotel. The arachnids arrive crisp and golden on a pristine white platter, with their tiny gossamer talons outstretched. They have virtually no flavor, but the crunchy texture is sensational. Eat just a few; scorpion is supposed to have cancer-preventing qualities but it's risky in large doses. Not so admirable was an earthier-tasting banquet chaser: fried cicada grubs.

Pangolin (Thumbs-Down)

Avoid pangolin stew, which is a big disappointment not only for its musty taste but because the animal is an endangered species. Some restauranteurs sell pangolin, which looks like an armadillo with pointy scales, only under the table. They worry about Chinese authorities who have declared it a protected animal. Seldom do I turn down an adventurous dish, but you have to draw the line somewhere. While you're at it, call the World Wildlife Fund.

Dog (One Chopstick)

Man's best friend finds its way into woks in many parts of China. When I sampled the dog meat at an open-air market in Yunnan province recently, however, I was disappointed. A good dog should taste like tender veal. But I found this meat cold, greasy and the flavor obscure. This made the normal qualms about consuming a household companion even harder to swallow. The service also left something to be desired— that is, unless you enjoy seeing a cook heedlessly attack the hindquarters of a roast dog with a cleaver.

Rat (Two Chopsticks)

After exploring the Chinese back roads for more than a decade, I thought I'd eaten everything. Then I stopped by Zhang Guoxun's restaurant, a delightful—and trendy—establishment in downtown Guangzhou. Proprietor Zhang's specialty is free-range field vole—better known as rat. Zhang insists these are healthy rodents caught by rural peasants more than 40 miles outside the city and raised on roots and berries, but they looked like any old sewer rats. Besides Vietnamese-style rat hot pot, he also serves rat kebab, crisp-fried rat with lemon and ''German style'' peppered rat. Aficionados say the piquant flavor is a cross between dog and frog. Unfortunately, the restaurant's recent popularity led to demand's outstripping supply. It was fresh out of rat. Only during my last hours in Guangzhou did Zhang receive a new cage of plump, hissing rodents. He prepared them by dunking the creatures, weighing up to a pound and squealing and struggling, into a pail of boiling water to be defurred. One even escaped from the bucket and ran across my shoe. I was all set to sample a rat kebab, then suddenly I glanced at my watch. Rats: I was late for the train to Hong Kong, and would just have to take a pass.

Which descriptive details make this narrative particularly interesting to read?

_____

_____

_____

_____

 ### WRITING ACTIVITY 7

Describe a memorable meal or food that you once ate. When and where did you eat this meal or food? How did it look, smell, taste, and feel? Why did it make such an impression on you?

> **REMINDER** ━━━━━━━━━━━━━━━━━━━━━━━━━━━━━━━━
> Effective narration relies on concrete, sensory details and vivid images and metaphors to tell a story that supports a point or lesson.

WRITING DIALOGUE

Several of the narrative paragraphs that you have read in this chapter included *dialogue*—the actual words that people said. Dialogue is a powerful narrative tool because it enables readers to enter your experience and hear exactly what you did. For example, which of the following sentences has more impact on your emotions? Why?

The boy shouted that I killed Christ.
The boy shouted, "Christ-killer, Christ-killer!"

Inexperienced writers often neglect to use dialogue because they don't know how to punctuate it. Here is a brief summary of the rules for punctuating dialogue. Don't try to memorize all these rules. Instead, use this as a reference guide the next time you are editing a narrative with dialogue in it.

**GUIDELINES FOR
PUNCTUATING DIALOGUE** _____

1. Make sure that you are actually using the words that were spoken—a *direct quotation*. If you are simply summarizing someone's spoken words, this constitutes an *indirect quotation,* which should *not* be enclosed in quotation marks:

   Bill said, ''Maria has always loved me.''
   Bill said that Maria has always loved him.

2. The spoken words are enclosed in quotation marks, and the first of the spoken words is always capitalized:

   Carlos responded, ''Maria has always loved *me.*''

3. If the spoken words are followed by a statement of who was speaking, put a comma at the end of the spoken words, *before* the final quotation marks:

   ''She has always loved me,'' asserted Bill.

4. If the spoken words are a question followed by a statement of who was speaking, put a question mark *before* the final quotation marks:

   ''Has she always loved me?'' wondered Bill.

5. If the statement of who was speaking comes before the spoken words, put a comma at the end of the statement and put a period at the end of the spoken words, *before* the final quotation marks:

   Bill announced, ''She has always loved me.''

6. If the statement of who was speaking comes before the spoken words and the spoken words are a question, put a question mark *before* the final quotation marks (and do *not* put any other final punctuation after the quotation):

   Bill worried, ''Has she always loved me?''

7. When the spoken words are not a question but a part of a larger sentence that is a question, put the question mark *after* the final quotation marks:

   Is it really true that Bill said, ''She has always loved me''?

GROUP WORK 2

Form a group with two classmates. Choose one person to record the group's answers. Below is a series of indirect quotations. Together, re-write each as a direct quotation. The first one has been done as an example.

1. Jared returned from school and announced that he was so hungry, he could eat an ox.

   Jared returned from school and announced, "I am so hungry, I could eat an ox."

2. When his parents did not respond, he asked them what they were making for dinner.

3. His mother was busy typing a report and told him to make himself something to eat.

4. Jared didn't want to eat alone, so he asked his father to make something, but his father replied that he had already eaten dinner.

5. His father added that he hadn't known when Jared was coming home, so he had made himself a microwave pizza.

6. Jared became annoyed and told his parents that he was angry they had not waited to eat dinner with him.

7. His mother looked at him and answered that it was unfair of him to expect them to wait to eat with him because he had not wanted to eat dinner at home for the past four nights.

8. His father said that he felt Jared was being selfish.

9. His mother added that if Jared wanted to eat dinner with them, he ought to let them know in advance.

10. Jared thought about what his parents said and then told them that he realized they were right.

WRITING ACTIVITY 8

Think about the most embarrassing moment you ever experienced. Why was it so embarrassing? What did you learn from it? Write a paragraph narrating what happened. Develop a purpose for this paragraph, and write a clear topic sentence about the experience. Then write specific details about where, when, and why this event occurred and about who was involved. Also include the dialogue—the words everyone said—as you remember it. (If you don't remember the exact words, make them up.) When you finish writing the paragraph, edit the punctuation of the dialogue, using the guidelines on page 183.

WRITING ACTIVITY 9

Write a paragraph about *one* of the topics below:

• an incident or experience that you will never forget
• an experience that taught you a lesson about the opposite sex
• an experience that proved you could take care of yourself
• an experience of winning a desired prize or achieving an important goal

   Begin by doing some prewriting (freewriting, brainstorming, or clustering). Then decide on a purpose for writing, and write a topic sentence about the main point that you want to make in this narrative. Use sensory details to make the participants and the experience come alive for your readers. Also use dialogue so that readers can hear exactly what the participants said. Edit the dialogue using the guidelines on page 183. When you finish writing, reread your paragraph from the point of view of an unknown reader: Will your details enable this reader to relive your experience and understand its meaning for you? If not, revise your details or add new ones.

GROUP WORK 3

Work with two or three classmates on this assignment. Read the following discovery draft of a student paragraph about an unforgettable experience. As you read it, put a check next to any sentence that seems vague, unclear, or confusing. When you finish reading, write answers to the following questions (on a separate piece of paper):

1. What did you like about the paragraph?
2. What part was confusing or difficult to understand? Why?
3. What suggestions do you have for improving the paragraph? (For example, where does it need additional details? What kinds of details? Should the writer add dialogue? If so, where and why?)

Choose one person to record the group's comments and suggestions.

My Worst Day

I remember seeing my son in the hospital after his accident and worrying that he was going to die before I could tell him I was sorry and tell him I loved him. Before the accident, we had a fight and we didn't make up. Then he was in intensive care and all I could think was that he was going to die hating me. He was a mess. I didn't know what to do. He eventually woke up. That hour was the longest one of my life. But we made up and everything was okay. I learned not to stay in a fight with my kids.

WRITING A THIRD-PERSON NARRATIVE

Most of the writing that you have done here has been in the first person (*I, we*) about your experiences. However, if you were asked to write about someone else's experiences, then you would use the third-person point of view (*he, she, it, they*). Here is a student essay, written in the third person, that was a response to the assignment, "What living person do you admire most?" As you read the essay, notice how the student uses narration to explain why she admires the person she has chosen.

Wilma Mankiller is a symbol of the strength and wisdom of Native American women. The more I learn about her, the more I want to model my life on hers. Mankiller is the first woman chief of the Cherokee Nation, and she has struggled for years to make her life and her people successful. She and her ten sisters and brothers were born on a small Oklahoma "reservation" that did not have running water or electricity.

When she was twelve, the government forced her family to move to a crime-ridden housing project in San Francisco. This was part of a government effort to integrate Native Americans into the culture of modern cities, but it failed with Mankiller. She and her family never gave up their tribal traditions and culture. "I am Cherokee born and bred and so shall my children's children be," she once said. In 1977, Mankiller returned to Oklahoma to work for the Cherokee Nation, but in 1979 she was crushed in a car accident that almost killed her. Mankiller had several surgeries and fought her way back to recovery. Then she started working full-time to get basic health and educational services for her people. She accomplished so much that she became famous for her efforts. She was elected chief in 1979, and she is still the chief and a beloved leader today.

By briefly detailing the events of Mankiller's life, this narration achieves the writer's purpose of convincing us that "Mankiller is a symbol of the strength and wisdom of Native American women."

WRITING ACTIVITY 10

Write a paragraph or two about the person you most admire. Use the descriptive techniques that you practiced in Chapter 5 to make this person come alive for the reader. Use narration to illustrate why this person is so special to you.

Much of your writing for college courses will call on your ability to produce third-person narration. For instance, here is a reading from a social history course that uses narrative to make its point:

Fidel Castro was born in 1927, the son of a successful Spanish immigrant family. While studying in Havana, Castro became involved in student politics, became a radical, and turned against the Batista regime. Arrested and then released from jail, he fled to Mexico in

1955. In December 1956, he returned to Cuba with a small band of followers. For two years, Castro led a guerrilla war from a remote mountain hideout. Batista reacted with a policy of repression so intense he lost public support. On New Year's Eve, 1958, Batista fled into exile, and a week later, Castro and his forces entered Havana in triumph.

After the revolution, Castro promised free elections, democratic government, and far-reaching social and economic reforms. At first, Castro had the support of the United States. However, he lost this support when, in an attempt to consolidate his power, he failed to hold free elections, seized properties belonging to U.S. citizens, banned criticism of the Cuban government, and jailed and executed opponents. Thousands of refugees, mostly members of Cuba's middle class, escaped to the United States and other nations.

Here the writer uses narration to make the point that Castro became a more authoritarian dictator than the leader he defeated. These narrative paragraphs use facts rather than sensory images to illustrate the writer's point.

History is not the only subject that requires effective factual narration. Many social science and natural science teachers ask students to write *case studies* and *laboratory reports,* both of which describe and interpret behavior and procedures over a specific time period. In order to write an effective case study or lab report, the writer must record the details of events in exactly the order that they occur. For example, here are a medical student's lab notes for a report on the components of blood.

The first step in determining the components of blood was to examine a small sample of blood that had been drawn from a group of healthy college students during their routine physical exams. I placed the tube of blood into a centrifuge. After the tube had spun for three minutes in the centrifuge, I removed it. Then I examined the blood in the tube. Approximately 60% of the blood had formed a clear layer made of a straw-colored, watery liquid. Next, I examined this part of the blood under a light microscope and identified it as plasma, which is mostly water with some proteins and cell wastes in it. The other 40% of the blood, a dark, reddish-colored, opaque liquid, had settled to the bottom of the tube. When I examined this part under the microscope, I saw red and white blood cells. The red blood cells looked like scarlet disks. They contained hemoglobin, which carries oxygen. The white blood cells looked like yellow powder puffs. Then I noticed that there were many fewer white blood cells than red ones.

What was the writer's purpose in this narration?

_____

_____

How did the writer organize this report?

_____

_____

_____

Which transitions helped you understand the sequence of events?

_____

_____

 GROUP WORK 4

Go to the library with two classmates. Each of you should look up a different book in the card or computer catalog, find this book, and check it out. Then you should meet and discuss all the steps that you had to follow to find and check out the book. Take notes as you and your classmates talk. Together develop a short essay that narrates the steps required to find and take out books at your school's library. Begin the essay with a statement that all of you agree on—for example, ''Taking out books at the Clemson Library is easy'' (or difficult, or complicated, or whatever adjective best describes the procedure).

WRITING ACTIVITY 11

Here is the discovery draft from page 186 of this chapter. On it are comments made by this student's classmates. Compare these comments to the suggestions that you and your group made for the Group Work 3 activity on pages 185 and 186. Following these comments is the student's revision.

When did this happen?

Discovery Draft

What's your main point?

What happened to him? What did you feel and think?

I remember seeing my son in the hospital after his accident and worrying that he was going to die before I could tell him I was sorry and tell him I loved him. Before the accident, we had a fight and we didn't make up. Then he was in intensive care and all I could think was that he was going to die hating me. He was a mess. I didn't know what to do. He eventually woke up. That hour was the longest one of my life. But we made up and everything was okay. I learned not to stay in a fight with my kids.

What do you mean?

Anna — Could you add more details about exactly what happened and why?

Final Revision

Five years ago, I learned something that forever changed me and my relationships with my children. On that fateful day, I had a typical screaming fight with my thirteen-year-old son, Bobby. I have long forgotten what it was that we fought about, but I will never forget how angry he was when he left the house. He slammed the door, screaming, "You hate me! You're mean and unfair and I can't take it anymore." I was upset, but I remember thinking that he would calm down and be home in time for dinner, as he always was after a fight. But dinnertime came and went and there was no Bobby. When the phone rang, I knew something was really wrong.

The police who drove me to the hospital told me that Bobby had been running down Main Street when he was hit by a car whose driver didn't see him. I was frozen with fear. When I finally saw Bobby, all I could see were the tubes covering his still body. I sat by his side for an hour. I didn't hear any of the nurses and doctors who tried to talk to me. All I heard was Bobby's voice echoing inside my brain: "You hate me!" "I can't take it anymore!" My son was going to die before I could tell him I was sorry and tell him how much I loved him.

Bobby finally woke up from his coma and eventually he recovered fully. Because of this incident, I vowed never to let him or my other kids walk out in anger. To this day, we always resolve our fights before any of us leaves the house. It helps us remember how much we love and value each other.

Answer the questions below on a separate piece of paper.

1. What details in the revision helped you understand what this writer experienced?
2. Why do you think the writer divided the revision into three paragraphs? What is the point of each paragraph?
3. How did the author change the organization of the draft?
4. What did you like best about the revision?

GETTING READERS' RESPONSES

Use the following checklist to help you identify problems in your narrative paragraphs and to get readers' responses to them.

NARRATION CHECKLIST

1. Does the narration focus on a main point, an assertion, or a theory? If so, what is it?
2. Are there enough details to enable readers to visualize who was involved in the event and where and when it took place? If not, where are more details needed?
3. Are there enough details to enable readers to understand exactly what happened, how it happened, and why it happened? If not, where are more details needed?
4. Are any details irrelevant to the point of the narrative or repetitious? If so, which ones?
5. Is the dialogue appropriate? Is it correctly punctuated? Is additional dialogue needed elsewhere in the narrative to make it more interesting or convincing? If so, where?
6. Will the reader understand the writer's thoughts and feelings during the experience being narrated?
7. Is the time sequence clear and are the details organized logically?
8. Is the narration unified and coherent?
9. Are the sentences clear and correct?
10. What suggestions do you have for improving this narration?

■ EXPLORING FURTHER

The following narrative, "A Question of Language," was written by Gloria Naylor, an award-winning novelist. In this narrative, Naylor describes an experience that had a great impact on her life.

A Question of Language

Language is the subject. It is the written form with which I've managed to keep the wolf away from the door and, in diaries, to keep my sanity. In spite of this, I consider the written word inferior to the spoken, and much of the frustration experienced by novelists is the awareness that whatever we manage to capture in even the most transcendent passages falls far short of the richness of life. Dialogue achieves its power in the dynamics of a fleeting moment of sight, sound, smell, and touch.

I'm not going to enter the debate here about whether it is language that shapes reality or vice versa. That battle is doomed to be waged whenever we seek intermittent reprieve from the chicken and egg dispute. I will simply take the position that the spoken word, like the written word, amounts to a nonsensical arrangement of sounds or letters without a consensus that assigns "meaning." And building from the meanings of what we hear, we order reality. Words themselves are innocuous; it is the consensus that gives them true power.

I remember the first time I heard the word *nigger*. In my third-grade class, our math tests were being passed down the rows, and as I handed the papers to a little boy in back of me, I remarked that once again he had received a much lower mark than I did. He snatched his test from me and spit out that word. Had he called me a nymphomaniac or a necrophiliac, I couldn't have been more puzzled. I didn't know what a nigger was, but I knew that whatever it meant, it was something he shouldn't have called me. This was verified when I raised my hand, and in a loud voice repeated what he had said and watched the teacher scold him for using a "bad" word. I was later to go home and ask the inevitable question that every black parent must face—"Mommy, what does 'nigger' mean?"

And what exactly did it mean? Thinking back, I realize that this could not have been the first time the word was used in my presence. I was part of a large extended family that had migrated from the rural South after World War II and formed a close-knit network that gravitated around my maternal grandparents. Their ground-floor apartment in one of the buildings they owned in Harlem was a weekend mecca for my immediate family, along with countless aunts, uncles, and cousins who brought along assorted friends. It was a bustling and open house with assorted neighbors and tenants popping in and out to exchange bits of gossip, pick up an old quarrel or referee the ongoing checkers game in which my grandmother cheated shamelessly. They were all there to let down their hair and put up their feet after a week of labor in the factories, laundries, and shipyards of New York.

Amid the clamor, which could reach deafening proportions—two or three conversations going on simultaneously, punctuated by the sound of a baby's crying somewhere in the back rooms or out on the street—there was still a rigid set of rules about what was said and how. Older children were sent out of the living room when it was time to get into the juicy details about "you-know-who" up on the third floor who had gone and gotten herself "p-r-e-g-n-a-n-t!" But my parents, knowing that I could spell well beyond my years, always demanded that I follow the others out to play. Beyond sexual misconduct and death, everything else was considered harmless for our young ears. And so among the anecdotes of the triumphs and disappointments in the various workings of their lives, the word *nigger* was used in my presence, but it was set within contexts and inflections that caused it to register in my mind as something else.

In the singular, the word was always applied to a man who had distinguished himself in some situation that brought their approval for his strength, intelligence, or drive:

"Did Johnny really do that?"

"I'm telling you, that nigger pulled in $6,000 of overtime last year. Said he got enough for a down payment on a house."

When used with a possessive adjective by a woman—"my nigger"—it became a term of endearment for husband or boyfriend. But it could be more than just a term applied to a man. In their mouths it became the pure essence of manhood—a disembodied force that channeled their past history of struggle and present survival against the odds into a victorious statement of being: "Yeah, that old foreman found out quick enough—you don't mess with a nigger."

In the plural, it became a description of some group within the community that had overstepped the bounds of decency as my family defined it: Parents who neglected their children, a drunken couple who fought in public, people who simply refused to look for work, those with excessively dirty mouths or unkempt households were all "trifling niggers." This particular circle could forgive hard times, unemployment, the occasional bout of depression—they had gone through all of that themselves—but the unforgivable sin was lack of self-respect.

A woman could never be a *nigger* in the singular, with its connotation of confirming worth. The noun *girl* was its closest equivalent in that sense, but only used in direct address and regardless of the gender doing the addressing. *Girl* was a token of respect for a woman. The one-syllable word was drawn out to sound like three in recognition of the extra ounce of wit, nerve or daring that the woman had shown in the situation under discussion.

"G-i-r-l, stop. You mean you said that to his face?"

But if the word was used in a third-person reference or shortened so that it almost snapped out of the mouth, it always involved some element of communal disapproval. And age became an important factor in these exchanges. It was only between individuals of the same generation, or from an older person to a younger (but never the other way around), that "girl" would be considered a compliment.

I don't agree with the argument that use of the word *nigger* at this social stratum of the black community was an internalization of racism. The dynamics were the exact opposite: the people in my grandmother's living room took a word that whites used to signify worthlessness or degradation and rendered it impotent. Gathering there together, they transformed *nigger* to signify the varied and complex human beings they knew themselves to be. If the word was to disappear totally from the mouths of even the most liberal of white society, no one in that room was naïve enough to believe it would disappear from white minds. Meeting the word head-on, they proved it had absolutely nothing to do with the way they were determined to live their lives.

So there must have been dozens of times that the word *nigger* was spoken in front of me before I reached the third grade. But I didn't "hear" it until it was said by a small pair of lips that had already learned it could be a way to humiliate me. That was the word I went home and asked my mother about. And since she knew that I had to grow up in America, she took me in her lap and explained.

Discussion Questions

1. Which sentence begins the actual narration? How do you know?
2. What might be another title for this narrative?
3. What point is Naylor using this narrative to illustrate?
4. What did Naylor mean by her comment that although she heard the word "nigger" dozens of times, she didn't really "hear" it until the third-grade boy called her one?
5. Was Naylor's use of dialogue effective? Why or why not?
6. Which details were most effective in enabling you to experience this event in the way that Naylor did?
7. How did Naylor organize this narrative?
8. What made this narrative unified and coherent?

WRITING ASSIGNMENT 1

Write a composition about an event that changed your life or your perception of people (or one person). Explain what your view or perception was *before* the event and how the event caused the change in your view or perception. Provide enough details so that readers who do not know you will understand exactly what happened to you and how it changed you.

WRITING ASSIGNMENT 2

Write a composition describing the most memorable job experience or job interview that you ever had. Make sure that your readers will understand why this experience or interview stands out in your memories.

WRITING ASSIGNMENT 3

Narrate an account of the most difficult problem you ever had to solve. Make sure your readers will understand why this problem was so difficult, how you solved or dealt with it, and how you felt about dealing with it.

When you finish writing these assignments, use the Narration Checklist on page 192 to help you improve your drafts.

✔ POINTS TO REMEMBER ABOUT NARRATION

1. Make sure that your narration states or implies a specific point.
2. Keep reminding yourself of your purpose in writing the narration so that you don't go off on irrelevant tangents.
3. Limit your narration to the description of one event or a series of brief, closely related events.
4. Select and emphasize details that are appropriate to your purpose and to your readers' needs. Consider exactly what information your readers will need to understand your perspective on the events you are relating.
5. Use your senses to describe the event or events. What exactly did you see, hear, smell, and feel? How did the people look and behave?
6. Use concrete, descriptive words and vivid images.
7. Use similes and metaphors to make your writing come alive.
8. Make sure that your details are logically organized and that you have included transitional words and phrases.
9. Include dialogue that reveals the thoughts and emotions of the people involved and follow the guidelines for punctuating dialogue correctly.
10. Experiment with different conclusions for your narration. Try ending with the final event. Then write an ending that summarizes the entire experience's significance. Choose the ending that suits your purpose better.

PROCESS ANALYSIS

When we analyze processes, events, or objects, we try to figure out the important characteristics that make these things what they are. Analyzing requires us to break something down into its essential steps, parts, or features. One of the most common forms of analysis that we do is *process analysis*—explaining how to do or make something, how something works, or how something happens. You have already learned the two writing skills needed to write a process analysis—describing and narrating. In order to explain how and why something works or occurs, you can *describe* its parts in clear, precise language. To explain how to do or to make something, you can *narrate* a series of steps or instructions in a logical sequence.

In school and at work, you will have to write many analyses of processes, ranging from simple instructions for making or preparing something ("How to Mix Your Own Paints" or "Six Steps for Preparing a Good Science Lab Report") to comprehensive explanations of complex processes ("How Congress Turns a Bill into a Law" or "How to Build a Linear Mathematical Model of an Oxygen Molecule"). An effective process analysis explains each step clearly and completely, and it shows the reader why this process is important. In addition, it exhibits the other qualities that you have been developing in your writing, including a clear focus, concrete and sensory language, unity, coherence, and correctness.

DETERMINING THE TOPIC AND THE PURPOSE
OF A PROCESS ANALYSIS

The first step in developing a ''how-to'' analysis is choosing a suitable topic. Often teachers do this step for students by assigning a topic: ''Explain the procedure for registering for courses at our college.'' ''Describe the process by which people register to vote.'' ''Explain how to control or eliminate agricultural insects with 'natural' insecticides.'' If your teacher does not assign a topic, then you have to decide on your own what process or skill to explain. One strategy for doing this is to ask yourself questions:

- What process or skill do I know how to do well and enjoy doing?
- Who is my reader, and would this reader consider the process valuable or interesting?
- Can I explain this process in a paragraph or an essay? (Is my topic too broad or too narrow?)

The last question—about the scope of your topic—is particularly important. Some processes (such as studying for a test or getting a high score on a computer game) can be explained in a paragraph or two. Other processes (such as how to succeed in college or how to use a computer program) might require a long essay or a book-length explanation. Choose a process or skill that is appropriate and interesting to your potential readers *and* that is narrow enough to explain in a paragraph or two. (In Chapter 13, you will learn how to write an essay about a more complex process.)

WRITING ACTIVITY 1

Read the topic sentences below and decide which ones are suitable for the following college assignment: ''Write a paragraph or two explaining how to do something. Your readers are your classmates in our composition course.'' On a separate piece of paper, explain why you think that each topic would or would not be suitable for this assignment.

1. Raising a happy, healthy child takes much time and effort.
2. There are several important steps to follow in order to prepare for a job interview.
3. Raking leaves can help you keep your sidewalk clean.
4. Changing a tire seems like a simple procedure, but it is actually quite a complicated process.
5. Building a dog kennel by yourself can save you money and time.
6. Choosing a college is an important decision, and there are several ways of making this decision.

7. You would be amazed at how much fun it is to shoot your own videotaped shows.
8. It is easy to get from my home to the bus station.
9. To stop smoking is difficult, but it is definitely worth the effort.
10. Members of the U.S. Department of Energy believe that Americans have many options for conserving energy.

Here is an example of a student's draft of a paragraph analyzing how to do a Heimlich maneuver to save someone from choking. Are the instructions clear enough for you to follow?

Recently, I saved my sister's life by performing the Heimlich maneuver on her as she lay on a restaurant floor, choking from the food that was caught in her throat. Everyone should know how to do this lifesaving procedure. The first step is to have someone hold up the choking victim so that you can stand behind the person. Next put your *comma form* arms around him or her. Then make a fist with one of your hands and put it against the person's abdomen, right above the navel and below the rib cage. Use your other hand to smash your fist into his or her abdomen in a quick upward thrust. Your goal is to force the air in the person's chest out hard enough to push the food out of his or her throat. Keep ramming your fist hard, upward into the person's abdomen until the food pops out of his or her mouth. Then get the person to a doctor or a medical technician as soon as he or she is breathing normally. Remember, if someone is choking and you don't perform the Heimlich maneuver on him or her, the person may die in four minutes.

What is the writer's topic sentence?

_____

_____

Is this topic appropriate for a paragraph-length process analysis? Why or why not?

_____

_____

_____

Could you perform the Heimlich maneuver by following the steps in this process analysis? Why or why not?

_____

_____

_____

_____

The preceding analysis of the Heimlich maneuver is effective because a person could use this set of instructions to perform the procedure. In addition, the paragraph has an interesting introduction and conclusion, both of which state the importance of learning the procedure. The steps in the process are arranged in a logical order, and the relations between the steps are indicated by appropriate transitions (*first, next, then*).

The writer of the paragraph on the Heimlich maneuver chose to write a ''how-to'' process analysis. As the following chart shows, there are other purposes for analyzing a process.

PURPOSES FOR WRITING
PROCESS ANALYSES _____

Some of the reasons for writing a process analysis include the following:

- To give directions or instructions about how to do, make, or prepare something
- To explain how something works
- To explain a mechanical, natural, or technical process
- To explain how to accomplish or achieve something

One of the most common process analyses that we read and write is the recipe—an explanation of the directions for preparing food. Here is a recipe for making a pie, written in 1920 by the novelist Ernest Hemingway. Can you follow his recipe?

Men have always believed that there was something mysterious and difficult about making a pie. Here is a great secret. There is nothing to it. We've been kidded for years. Any man of average office intelligence can make a pie at least as good as a pie of his wife.

All there is to a pie is a cup and a half of flour, one-half teaspoonful of salt, one-half cup of lard, and cold water. That will make pie crust that will bring tears of joy to your camping partner's eyes.

Mix the salt with the flour, work the lard into the flour, make it up into a good workmanlike dough with cold water. Spread some flour on the back of a box or something flat, and pat the dough around a while. Then roll it out with whatever kind of round bottle you prefer. Put a little more lard on the surface of the sheet of dough and then slosh a little flour on and roll it up and then roll it out again with the flour.

Command. → Cut out a piece of the rolled out dough big enough to line a pie tin. I like the kind with holes in the bottom. Then put in your dried apples that have soaked all night and been sweetened, or your apricots, or your blueberries, and then take another sheet of dough and drape it gracefully over the top. Cut a couple of slits in the top dough sheet and prick it a few times with a fork in an artistic manner.

Put it in the baker with a good slow fire for forty-five minutes and then take it out and if your pals are Frenchmen, they will kiss you. The penalty for knowing how to cook is that the others will make you do all the cooking.

This excerpt by Hemingway comes from a newspaper article that he wrote about his experiences camping out in the woods. Do you think that people who are inexperienced campers could follow Hemingway's recipe for preparing a good pie? Why or why not?

_____

_____

_____

_____

_____

_____

After you decide on a topic for your process analysis and your purpose for writing, use the prewriting techniques that you learned in Chapters 1 and 2 to generate ideas and details. Here is a sample of a student's prewriting notes for a process analysis paragraph:

Topic: How to Revise an Essay Using the SEARCH (or FIND) Command in a Word-Processing Program

Purpose: To provide step-by-step instructions so that students can use the SEARCH (or FIND) keys to revise an essay

Intro - explain uses (importance) of this command - maybe include a story about how I use it ??

STEPS

*① Determine how to begin the SEARCH keys to start the search command.
(Is it "SEARCH" or "FIND"?)*

② Command the program to search for the word or symbol (a string ??)

③ Tell the program what to do about capital letters (ignore?)

④ Decide what you want to do every time your program finds the word, symbol, or string that you told it to search for.

⑤ Shut off the SEARCH/FIND command after you have found all occurrences of the word, symbol, or string and after you've made all your revisions.

As this student reread his notes, he saw that he had assumed that his readers would know as much about computerized word processing as he does. He realized that he needed to clarify his audience for this assignment.

WRITING ACTIVITY 2

Reread your Idea Bank or your journal and put a check next to an entry that you might use to develop an analysis of how to do something or of how something works. (If you do not want to use the ideas in your Idea Bank, possible topics for this activity include how to cook something, how to fix something, how to break something, how to find and check out a book from your school's library, or how to impress someone on the first date.) Do some freewriting, brainstorming, or clustering about this topic. If you were going to develop a paragraph about this process, what would your purpose be? What would you want readers to know or be able to do? Also, write down who you think might be interested in reading about this process. How much do these readers already know about the process? What exactly might they need to know about it?

CONSIDERING YOUR READERS' NEEDS

Everything in a process analysis—from the level and amount of information to the vocabulary—depends on the writer's purpose and audience. Obviously, if you were writing a paragraph about the registration procedures at your school, you would need to include much more specific information if your readers were new students than if you were writing for students who had already registered for courses at least once. If a writer doesn't consider his or her readers' knowledge and expectations, he or she may write a process analysis that totally confuses readers. For example, the following process analysis paragraph was written by a student for a friend who was learning how to use a computerized database program. Do you think this reader could follow these directions? If not, why not?

"Searching" (or "Finding") is one of the more simple processes that a new user of dBASE III can follow. You begin by using the LOCATE command to check specific records in a database. If no record meeting the parameters of the syntax for the LOCATE command can be found, the SEARCH program will stop. You can continue searching by using the

CONTINUE command, which continues the search to determine if any other database record meets your parameters. If neither of these commands locates the record that meets your conditions, you can use the FIND and SEEK commands to search a database—if the database is indexed (since these commands can search only for the first occurrence of the specified syntax in *indexed* fields).

The paragraph has a clear topic sentence, precise and complete directions arranged in chronological order, effective transitions, and clear, correct sentences and grammar. Why, then, is it so difficult to understand? The writer did not consider his reader's level of knowledge of—and experience with—database processing. He assumed that the reader knows what a ''record'' or a ''syntax parameter'' is and knows which keys to press in ''using the LOCATE command.'' If the intended reader of this essay were a computer science teacher or a student in an advanced computing course, then these technical terms might have been appropriate. However, if the reader does not have specialized knowledge in this area, then he or she will be confused rather than enlightened by this set of instructions.

Remember to keep your purpose and your readers in mind as you brainstorm and answer the ''Reporter's Questions'' (What? Where? When? How? Why?) about the process you are analyzing. As you write down details, think about the information your readers will need in order to understand the directions that you are writing.

Here is one writer's attempt to shape his prewriting to suit his purpose and audience (based on the prewriting notes on page 202).

Notes for a Process Analysis

• Who are my readers, and would these readers consider this topic valuable or interesting?

My classmates – They might want to know how to use the SEARCH command because they have to write or revise an essay every week.

- What do these readers already know about this process, and what else do they need to know?

Some of them use WordPerfect, but the others don't, so I better explain what the SEARCH keys are in WordPerfect and how to use them.

I guess I also should spell out how to do every step. Also, students need to know that the steps are different in every program and that some programs refer to the SEARCH command as the FIND command.

Readers also probably need to know what to do whenever the program finds the string that it is searching for.

- What terms am I going to have to define or explain?

search, string, symbol, character

- Can I explain this process in a paragraph or an essay?

I think I can do it in a paragraph.

WRITING ACTIVITY 3

Develop a list of five topics that would be suitable for a paragraph about how to do something or how something works. Next to each topic, describe the audience who might be most interested in reading this paragraph. Then write one or two reasons why the topic would be important to these readers.

GROUP WORK 1

Form a group with two or three other students. Exchange the list of topics that you developed for the preceding Writing Activity. Discuss your answers to the following questions about *each* of your classmates' topics:

1. Is this topic or process valuable, important, or interesting? Why or why not?
2. Is this topic too broad or too narrow for a paragraph?
3. What do you already know about this topic or process and what else might you need to know about it?

WRITING ACTIVITY 4

Consider your classmates' responses to your list of topics in the preceding Group Work activity and select the topic that you think is most suitable for a paragraph-length process analysis. Write a topic sentence for this paragraph and then list all the steps that a reader might want or need to know.

Here is the topic sentence and prewriting list developed by the student who wrote the notes on pages 204 and 205. As you read this list, think about the additional information that you would need to know in order to follow these instructions.

Notes for a Process Analysis

Students can make revising easier by using the SEARCH (or FIND) command in any computerized word-processing program.

1. Use the SEARCH (or FIND) keys to command your program to search through a document to locate every instance of a word, symbol, or string of characters.

2. Decide what word, symbol, or string of characters you want to find.

3. Tell the program whether to ignore capital letters when it is

searching *or* to search for the string with the letters capitalized exactly as you typed them in.

4. Wherever the program finds the string that you told it to search for, you can correct it, type in a substitute for it, or rewrite it.

5. When you correct or rewrite a string, be careful not to replace one error with another.

6. Shut off the SEARCH (or FIND) command after you have found all the occurrences of the string you were searching for.

The notes above may be clear to the student, but they are confusing to the novice word processor. The writer did not explain what the ''SEARCH keys'' are or how to ''use'' them, nor did he explain how to ''tell'' the program what to do about capital letters. The writer left out many details that readers would need to understand how to do each step in this set of instructions.

WRITING ACTIVITY 5

Reread the student's notes above. Imagine that he is your classmate, and write him a brief letter explaining why you would or would not be able to follow his list of directions. Tell him which steps are confusing to you and why.

Here are some of the responses the writer's classmates gave him when he shared his list of notes with them:

I don't really understand the point of using this procedure. How does this make revising easier?

Leon — Step #2 should come before Step #1.

Help! How does a person "use" the SEARCH or FIND keys? And what are they?

How do you tell the program whether to ignore capital letters or not?

Leon — I think you should give some examples of what you mean by correcting or rewriting a string. I don't know what this means or how to do it.

The students who wrote these comments helped the writer realize that he needed to add more-specific details about exactly how to carry out this process.

DEVELOPING DETAILS FOR A "HOW-TO" ANALYSIS

As you move from prewriting to drafting, you should reconsider exactly what your reader will need to know in order to understand and to carry out the process you are explaining. Here are some guidelines for drafting these details.

GUIDELINES FOR DEVELOPING DETAILS FOR A PROCESS ANALYSIS

1. Describe any equipment, materials, or tools that readers will need to do the process successfully.
2. Define any key terms or technical words that readers might not fully understand.
3. Divide the process into manageable steps, each of which you can explain in a sentence or paragraph.
4. Tell the reader exactly what to do at each step and how and when to do it.
5. Explain the importance of each step.
6. Describe what the reader should *not* do (and why not).
7. Make the analysis coherent, so that readers will understand how each step leads to the next one.
8. Conclude by briefly stating the advantages, value, or importance of learning how to do this process.

Here is the discovery draft developed from the notes on pages 203–204, in which the writer tried to incorporate his classmates' suggestions.

Draft

Students can make revising easier by using the SEARCH (or FIND) command in any computerized word-processing program. For example, if you are writing a draft, and you cannot think of the exact words or the correct term for an idea, you can just type ?????? and continue writing. Then when you are revising, you can use the SEARCH command to find every place that you typed this series of question marks, and you can replace them with the appropriate or correct term or words. Doing this is easier than looking up words in a dictionary or a thesaurus while you are trying to get your ideas down. In addition, if you know you always misspell a word, you can use the SEARCH command to locate each instance of the misspelling, and then you can type in the correct spelling. This helps writers speed up their editing process.

In order to begin the SEARCH command (which is called the FIND command in some programs), you have to know which keys to press so that the program will search a document to locate every instance of a word, phrase, symbol, or "string" (any group of characters followed by a space). If you do not know which keys to use, look up this information in your documentation (book of instructions). Press the SEARCH command keys, and the program will indicate a place for you to type in the string of characters that you want to find. Type in this string of characters and hit the ENTER key. Then look at the monitor screen. The next thing that should appear on the screen in most programs is the question, "Ignore upper/lowercase?" or "Ignore capital letters?" If you want the program to search for your word or phrase exactly as you typed it in your writing, then type N for "No." If you want the program to find every instance of the word or phrase, regardless of whether it has capital letters in it, then type Y for "Yes."

Each time the program finds the word or phrase or string of characters that you told it to search for, it stops at the beginning of the string. This gives you the opportunity to examine the string and decide if you want to keep it, revise it, replace it, or add words to it. You can type in a word or a sentence if you want to add information, or you can correct the spelling of a misspelled word. The SEARCH command is also useful for revising your diction and vocabulary. You can use it to search for vague or "empty" modifiers (such as "a lot," "very," "extremely," "really," "awful," and so forth), and replace each of these words with a more precise word. In addition, you can search for any slang expressions or clichés that you use regularly. The SEARCH command can also be used to find errors in punctuation. For instance, if you ask the program to search for an apostrophe, you can check to see if you have used this punctuation correctly each time. All these revisions can be done in a minute instead of an hour. Thus, the SEARCH command is a handy tool for revising.

With his classmates' help, this writer has clarified the process that he wanted to analyze. He has provided detailed explanations of each step in the process and has organized these steps logically. In addition, he has provided "checkpoints" for readers to determine whether they are following the process correctly (for example, "Then look at the monitor screen. The next thing that should appear on the screen in most programs is the question . . ."). Now his discovery draft is clearer and easier to follow.

> **REMINDER** _____
> An effective analysis of a process states the goal of the process and explains exactly what readers need to know in order to accomplish the process or to understand how it works.

WRITING ACTIVITY 6

Trace the figure below with a pen or a pencil, so that you can draw it. Then copy the figure onto another piece of paper. Next write a paragraph explaining how to draw this figure. Give your set of written instructions to a friend or relative (or classmate), but do *not* show this person the figure. Ask him or her to draw the figure by following the directions in your paragraph. If the person has difficulty, ask him or her which directions in your paragraph were unclear and revise your paragraph in light of the responses.

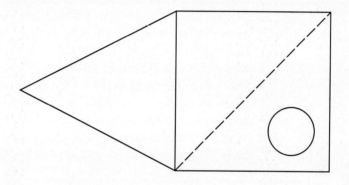

GROUP WORK 2

Here is a student paragraph that explains how to find a roommate. Form a group with two or three other students, and choose one person to record the group's answers to the questions that follow the paragraph (on a separate piece of paper).

Process Analysis Draft

When people move out, they often feel the need to live alone, but sharing a house or apartment with a roommate can be a great experience. You can get a roommate by advertising for one. Post your advertisement in all the places that you can think of. First, make up a flier that spells out the gender, age range, and social qualities of the kind of person you want to live with. Be very specific. Then describe yourself, and state the amount of rent that the roommate will have to pay. Then put the flier in your local newspaper and everywhere else you go. When people answer, interview them for clues about their personality and habits. Make sure you will be able to live with them. Choosing a person to live with is not easy, so try to choose well.

1. Underline the topic sentence of this paragraph.
2. Do you think this process was suitable for a one-paragraph explanation? If so, why? If not, why not?
3. Did the writer divide the process into manageable steps? If not, where did you get confused? Why?
4. Did you understand exactly what to do at each step and how and when to do it? If not, why not? Where should the author have added more specific details?
5. Was the time sequence clear and are the details organized logically? If not, where did you get confused? Why?

REMINDER _____

When you explain how to do or make something, remember to let readers know what they should do and what they should *not* do. Anticipate the likely problems that your reader will have and explain any potential mistakes and why it is important not to make those mistakes.

WRITING ACTIVITY 7

Imagine that a new school friend is coming to visit your home for the first time. Plan and write a paragraph or two that gives directions to get from school to your home. Begin by deciding which mode of transportation this friend should use: How do you usually get from school to your home—by foot, car, bus, or train? Next, break down the trip into a series of manageable steps. Remember to include details about specific distances, stoplights, stop signs, turns, landmarks, bus or train stations, and anything else that will help your new friend get to your home.

GROUP WORK 3

Exchange the paragraphs that you wrote for the preceding Writing Activity with a classmate. After you both have finished reading each other's directions, take turns telling each other how easy or difficult the directions were to follow. Did any instruction confuse you? Why? Where would you have gotten lost if you had actually tried to follow this set of instructions? After you finish discussing each other's papers, return them. Revise your paragraph in light of your classmate's comments.

DIFFERENTIATING BETWEEN A NARRATIVE AND A PROCESS ANALYSIS

Since all processes involve a series of steps or events in time, a process analysis is almost always organized chronologically. However, sometimes when writers relate a series of events in time, they are telling a narrative story rather than explaining a process. They may think that they are describing a process (about how to accomplish something), but what they are actually doing is narrating a series of events (about how they accomplished something). What's the difference? If a writer is telling about a series of events that happened and he or she does not explain how everyone can repeat or follow this sequence of events, then he or she is probably writing a narrative. If the writer wants to write a process analysis, he or she has to describe the series of events or steps that must be followed by anyone who wants to accomplish the goal or result that the writer is describing.

For example, if a student writes a paragraph describing the experiences he had the first time he tried to get a summer job, he is probably writing a narrative. Unless the events that he experienced are ones that all people experience or that they should follow in order to get a job, his story is not an analysis of a process. In order to turn his narrative into a process analysis, the writer would have to identify all the appropriate steps to take to get a summer job. He would also have to describe the materials students need (such as a résumé and letters of reference) and the exact procedures that they should follow in order to get the jobs they want.

Here is a draft of a student writer's explanation of the process of stopping a runaway horse. Is this paragraph a process analysis or a narrative?

The most frightening event of my life happened when I was nineteen years old and living on my uncle's cattle ranch in Waco, Texas. Right after I dismounted my favorite pony, a bee stung him, and he went crazy.

I was almost killed as my horse started kicking the air and running amuck. However, I knew that the trick to stopping a horse (or any animal) that is running away is to stay calm. So I moved slowly toward the horse, murmuring soft, calming words. When I was close enough to get his reins, I grabbed them very quickly. Then I pulled firmly on the reins to force the horse to turn its head to me. Once he realized that I was controlling him again, the horse quieted down and came to a halt. Stopping that panicky horse was a terrifying accomplishment.

Here is the writer's revision. How does it differ from the preceding draft?

If you ride horses or live on a ranch, you know that there are few things more frightening than the sight of a runaway horse on a wild rampage. The trick to stopping a horse (or any animal) that is running amuck is to stay calm. The first thing to do is slowly move toward the horse, murmuring soft, calming words. Never shout or scream; instead, smile and hum a song as you inch your way to the animal. When you are close enough to grab the horse's bridle or reins, do it very quickly. Then pull firmly on the reins to force the horse to turn its head to you. Once the animal realizes that you are controlling its reins or bridle, it will eventually quiet down and come to a halt. Finally, remember that the secret of stopping a panicky animal is staying calm and in control.

Do you see the difference between the narrative draft and the process analysis revision? The narrative describes a particular event in the writer's life. The writer turned this narrative into a process analysis by switching from the first person ''I'' to the second person ''you.'' (See page 186 in Chapter 6 on ''person''.) The writer also divided the experience into a series of steps that anyone can follow to accomplish the task (''of stopping a panicky animal'') and by explaining what the reader should not do (''Never shout or scream'').

WRITING ACTIVITY 8

Plan and write a paragraph or two describing the way your family or friends traditionally celebrate a holiday, a custom, or a special event. Does your family or your group of friends have a formal or an informal ceremony to observe this holiday, custom, or event? Describe the steps or stages of this celebration (beginning with the way you prepare for it). Do not write a narrative about a specific event; instead write an analysis of how your family usually celebrates this event.

ORGANIZING A PROCESS ANALYSIS

Reread the paragraphs on pages 213 and 214 about ''stopping a panicky animal.'' Note that the writer developed both the narrative and the process analysis versions of this piece using chronological order—the order in which the events occurred in time. Most analyses of how to do or make something or of how something works develop chronologically. As you develop details for your process analyses, think about what happens first, second, and so forth. Help your readers understand your analysis by explaining why they need to do one step before they do the next step.

Another strategy for helping your readers follow your steps is to connect them with chronological transitions, like the ones used by the writer of the two paragraphs on ''stopping a panicky animal'' (*after, first, when, then, once,* and *finally*). Here is a list of some of the transitions that you can use to make your process analyses more unified and coherent.

TRANSITIONS THAT INDICATE PROCESS ANALYSIS ORDER

Below are transitional words and phrases that signal the relations among the steps or stages of an explanation of a process:

first	*next*	*meanwhile*	*last*
second	*before*	*during*	*thus*
third	*after*	*when*	
then	*while*	*finally*	

WRITING ACTIVITY 9

Here is a list of brainstorming notes for a student's paragraph about how thunder and lightning occur. Rearrange this list so that the information makes sense and is easier to follow.

1. Scientists are not completely sure how lightning and thunder occur.
2. Wind and wet air swirl into thunderclouds high up in the sky.
3. The wind and the water smash against each other.
4. Scientists do know that an electric light is created by the rapid movement of water vapor and by friction.
5. Smashing wind and water generate electric charges.
6. Positive and negative electric charges are attracted to each other (like a magnet to steel filings).
7. The positive electric charges float to the top of the thundercloud.
8. The negative electric charges sink to the bottom of the thunder-cloud.
9. As the electricity flashes through the air, it sounds like a gigantic clap. That loud noise is thunder.
10. A stream of negative charges, called a ''leader,'' can rush out of a thundercloud.
11. The leader moves toward the positively charged top of another cloud.
12. Lightning is like static electricity: it jumps from cloud to cloud just like sparks jump from one piece of clothing to another.

GROUP WORK 4

Below is the revision of the student paragraph that appears on pages 211 and 212 of this chapter. Note that the writer added so many details that she had to expand her paragraph into an essay. Form a group with two or three other students, and choose one person to record the group's answers to the questions that follow the essay (on a separate piece of paper).

Second Revision

When people move out from their home, they often feel the need to live alone and make all of their decisions on their own. However, sharing a new home with a roommate can be a positive, rewarding experience. A roommate will share the burdens and the bills of a new apartment, he or she can help you meet new people and make new friends, and he or she can be a good person to talk with and go out with. The best way to find a roommate whom you will be compatible with is to advertise for one.

Begin by writing or printing a flier that spells out the gender, age range, and social qualities of the kind of person you could live with. It is best to be very specific about your potential roommate's characteristics. For example, indicate whether you want a person who is quiet or a person who is very outgoing, a "night" person or a "morning" person, a nonsmoker, a nondrinker, an athlete, and so forth. Also, briefly describe yourself ("Hispanic female college student, nonsmoker, 20 years old, seeks same to share 2 BR apartment"), and specify the amount of rent that the roommate will have to pay. Then pay to put the flier in your local newspaper, or copy it and post it all over school, at work, at your church or synagogue, and at any clubs you belong to.

Carefully interview everyone who responds to your ad. During the interview, examine the person for clues about his or her personality and habits. (Is he or she friendly or reserved? Neat or sloppy? Clean or dirty?) Ask the people you interview what kind of work they do and what other sources of money they have, so you will be assured that they will be financially responsible. In addition, find out how much cooking or cleaning they are willing to do and whether they have a girlfriend or a boyfriend whom they will be inviting over frequently. Finally, ask them what they are looking for in a roommate: Why do they want to share an apartment?

Choosing a roommate is not easy, but if you choose well, you will gain a friend who can help you out and who will share your problems and your joys.

1. What is the main idea of this revised paper?
2. Did the writer divide the process into manageable steps? Why or why not?
3. Did you understand exactly what to do at each step and how and when to do it? Why or why not?
4. How did the writer organize her details?

VARYING YOUR SENTENCE STRUCTURE

In Chapter 6, you practiced writing in the "first-person" point of view (*I, we*) and the "third-person" point of view (*he, she, it, they*). Most process analyses are written in a form of the "second-person" (*you*) point of view called the *imperative* ("command"). The subject of an imperative sentence is always *you,* but the pronoun *you* does not appear; it is "understood." For example, when Group Work activities direct you to "Form a group with two or three other students," you understand that the subject of this command is *you* ("*You* form a group with two or three other students").

If all the sentences in your process analyses are imperatives, then your paragraphs or essays will sound like monotonous orders. To avoid this, try varying your sentence beginnings so that they don't all start with the verb. Here is an example:

All Imperatives:

　　To cure insomnia, go to bed at the same time every night, including weekends. Wake up around the same time every morning. Develop a bedtime ritual and use it every night. Drink a glass of milk before retiring, but don't ever drink alcohol, because it disturbs sleep patterns. Finally, stop worrying about your insomnia; that will only make the problem worse. You'll fall asleep way before you die from lack of it.

Varied Sentence Beginnings:

　　Here are some tricks for curing insomnia. First, try going to bed at the same time every night and waking up around the same time every morning, including weekends. Since bedtime rituals prepare the mind to relax, develop a bedtime ritual and remember to use it every night. You might drink a glass of milk before retiring, but don't drink any alcohol because it disturbs sleep patterns. Finally, you should try to stop worrying about your insomnia; that will only make the problem worse. You'll fall asleep way before you die from lack of it.

The second version of this paragraph sounds less abrupt and more friendly and interesting than the first one. (For more information on sentence variety, see Chapter 16.)

WRITING ACTIVITY 10

Write a "how-to" paragraph about *one* of the topics below:

- Choose a college (or a university)
- Prepare for a job interview
- Select a major in school
- Stop smoking or drinking
- Build a campfire
- Lose (or gain) weight
- Buy a car
- Change a flat tire
- Learn another language
- Do your favorite hobby
- Do or make something that you do or make very well

Develop your ideas by prewriting—freewriting, brainstorming, or clustering. Then decide on a purpose for writing, and write a topic sentence about the advantages or importance of knowing how to do this process. List any materials or equipment that readers will need, and define any terms that they may not know. Then explain each step—in clear, specific language—in the order in which the steps are to be performed. When you finish writing, reread your paragraph from the point of view of an unknown reader: Will reading your details enable this person to carry out the process? Will he or she be able to follow the development of your ideas? Will the reader understand why the process is important or useful? If not, revise your details or add new ones.

USING PROCESS ANALYSIS ACROSS THE COLLEGE CURRICULUM

Many assignments in the natural and social sciences require analyses of processes. The "scientific method"—the general set of rules that guide scientists as they try to solve problems—is itself a process analysis. Here are its steps:

- State the problem and describe everything that you know about this problem (from your experiences, observations, and reading).
- Develop a hypothesis about the solution to the problem.
- Collect and record facts and data about the problem, and organize this information so that you can see patterns relating to your hypothesis.
- Evaluate your information and decide whether to revise your hypothesis.
- Develop and conduct an experiment to test the hypothesis.
- Draw conclusions about your hypothesis and test these conclusions further.

Much science writing consists of explaining how things develop, work, or occur. The following student paragraphs illustrate a typical scientific process analysis. This is the final version of the paragraph that was developed from the notes on page 216 of this chapter.

I have always been fascinated by the bolts of lightning that streak across the sky during a thunderstorm. Although scientists are not completely sure how lightning occurs, they know that it is a stream of electricity created by the rapid movement of water vapor and atmospheric friction. A thundercloud forms when moisture high in the sky starts swirling around because of high winds. As the water and wind inside the cloud smash against each other, their friction produces electric charges. The positive electric charges float to the top of the thundercloud and the negative charges sink to the bottom.

Positive electric charges in one cloud are attracted to the negative charges in other clouds (like a magnet to steel filings), but the moving wind between thunderclouds keeps them apart. When the accumulation of electric charges gets so great that they overcome the force of the wind, a stream of negative charges, called a "leader," rushes out of the cloud. This leader moves toward the positively charged top of another cloud or moves down to the earth, which is a conductor of electricity. As the electricity flashes through the air, it looks like a bolt of light and sounds like a gigantic clap—this sound is thunder. Thus, lightning is like static electricity: Leaders jump from cloud to cloud like sparks jump from one article of clothing to another.

GETTING READERS' RESPONSES

Here is a checklist to help you revise the drafts of your process analyses. Ask family, friends, and classmates to answer these questions.

PROCESS ANALYSIS CHECKLIST

1. Does the analysis have a clear, focused controlling idea that is neither too narrow nor too broad? If so, what is this idea? If not, can you suggest one?
2. Has the writer described the equipment, tools, or materials readers will need to complete the process successfully?
3. Do you understand all the key terms or technical words? If not, which ones should the writer define or explain more fully?
4. Can you tell what to expect at each step of the process? If not, why not?
5. Can you understand exactly what to do at each step and how and when to do it? If not, why not?
6. Has the writer explained the importance of each step? If not, where should he or she do so?
7. Did the writer let you know what you should *not* do (and why not)?
8. Is the analysis unified and coherent? Can you understand how each step leads to the next one? If not, why not?
9. Is the time sequence clear and are the details logically organized?
10. Does the analysis have an interesting conclusion that reminds you of the advantages, value, or importance of learning how to do the process?
11. Which sentences are confusing or have errors in them?
12. What suggestions do you have for improving this analysis?

■ EXPLORING FURTHER

The reading that follows is from a textbook titled *Consumer and Career Mathematics*. First the authors' method for solving problems in mathematics, "the five-step method," is analyzed. Next specific illustrations of this method—"using a physical model" and "listing all the possibilities"—are explained.

Problem-Solving Skills: A Five-Step Method

CONSUMER TOPIC

Sometimes you can read a computation problem and know exactly what to do to solve it. Other times, it is helpful to follow these five steps in your thinking.

A FIVE-STEP METHOD

Understand
- What am I to find?
- What facts are given?

Plan
- Is an estimate all that is needed to solve the problem?
- Can I solve the problem in one step? If so, what operation is required?
- Is more than one step required? If so, in what order should the steps be taken?
- Do I need additional data?

Solve
- Can I estimate the answer?
- Can the computation be done mentally, or should I use paper and pencil? Would a calculator make the work easier?
- In multiple-step problems, can I verify results as I go along by estimating?
- Is the plan working? Are the steps in the plan correct? Is the data correct?

Look Back
- Is the computed results reasonable for the problem?
  — Can I use an estimation method to check that the result makes sense?
  — Can I check the computation?
  — Can I check the result by using an alternate approach to the problem?
- Did I use the correct data?

Answer
- Do I need to round the computed answer (to the nearest cent, for example)?
- Did I use the correct label (dollars, inches, pounds)?
- Did I write a complete sentence stating the answer?

Problem-Solving Strategy: Use a Physical Model

RECREATION

There are sixteen students on the Yorktown High School student council. When the student council has a meeting, sixteen small square tables are arranged to form a large square, so that each member will have a place to sit.

Problem

The students at Yorktown High School elected four additional students to the student council. How can the members rearrange the sixteen tables into a new rectangular shape (with no holes in the middle), so that all twenty people will have a place to sit, and no seats will be empty?

Understand

You can often solve problems like this by *using a physical model.*

Plan

A. Cut out 16 squares of the same size to represent 16 square tables.
B. Arrange the small squares into as many different large rectangles as possible.
C. Count the number of seating positions for each arrangement.

Solve

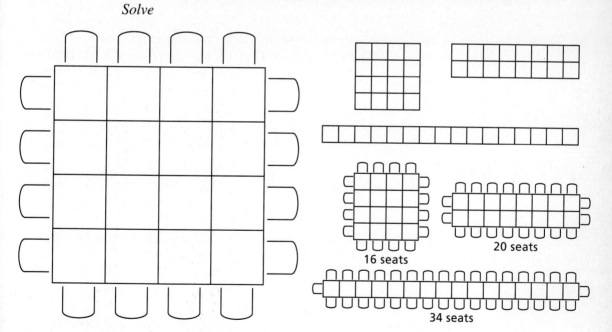

16 seats

20 seats

34 seats

Look Back
Check each arrangement to be sure you used exactly 16 tables.

Answer
The tables can be arranged into an 8-by-2 rectangle to seat 20 people.

Problem-Solving Strategy: List All the Possibilities

RECREATION

Each year, the pennant winners of the American League and the National League meet in baseball's World Series. The first team to win 4 games out of a maximum of 7 games wins the series.

In the 1986 World Series, the New York Mets played the Boston Red Sox. The Mets lost the first 2 games, won the next two, lost the fifth game, and then went on to win the series by winning the last 2 games.

In 1984, the Detroit Tigers won the series against the San Diego Padres. The Tigers won the first game, lost the second game, and then won the next 3 games. The series lasted only 5 games, because the winner was determined by the outcome of the fifth game.

In 1976, the Cincinnati Reds beat the New York Yankees in a 4-game series by winning the first 4 games in a row.

Problem
In 1981, the winner of the World Series was determined by the outcome of the sixth game. The Los Angeles Dodgers played the New York Yankees. The Dodgers lost the first 2 games and then won the next 4 games in this 6-game series. This series of loss-loss-win-win-win-win represents the way the Dodgers won the series. List all the arrangements of losses (L) and wins (W) that would result in a series winner at the end of the sixth game. How many ways could a team become a series winner in a 6-game series?

Understand
One way to solve this problem is to systematically *list all the possibilities.*

Plan
A. To win a 6-game series, a team has to win 4 games and lose 2 games. If a team has lost only 1 game by the end of the fifth game, it has won the series because it has won 4 games. A sixth game is not needed. Therefore, in a 6-game series, the series winner will never have a loss in the sixth game.
B. List all the ways a team can win a 6-game series if it loses the first game and one other game. The second loss can occur in the second, third, fourth, or fifth game. The series LWWWWL is not a possible way for a team to win a 6-game series.

C. List all the ways a team can win a 6-game series, if it wins the first game, loses the second game, and loses one other game.

D. List all the ways a team can win a 6-game series, if it wins the first 2 games, loses the third game, and loses one other game.

E. List all the ways a team can win a 6-game series, if it wins the first three games and loses the fourth game. Then find the total.

Solve

$$\left.\begin{array}{l} \text{L L W W W W} \\ \text{L W L W W W} \\ \text{L W W L W W} \\ \text{L W W W L W} \end{array}\right\} \text{4 ways}$$

$$\left.\begin{array}{l} \text{W L L W W W} \\ \text{W L W L W W} \\ \text{W L W W L W} \end{array}\right\} \text{3 ways}$$

$$\left.\begin{array}{l} \text{W W L L W W} \\ \text{W W L W L W} \end{array}\right\} \text{2 ways}$$

$$\left.\text{W W W L L W}\right\} \text{1 way}$$

Total: 10 ways

Look Back

Be sure you have not included an arrangement with a loss in the sixth game.

Answer

For a 6-game series, there are 10 different ways that a team can become a series winner.

WRITING ASSIGNMENT 1

Imagine that you are the editor of the Advice column of your school newspaper. Write a process analysis that explains how to solve a personal problem. You might want to analyze how people can solve financial problems, make friends, deal with a difficult relative, or make up with someone after a fight. What steps should people follow if they want to make up with someone with whom they have had a fight? Or what steps do you recommend for dealing with a friend who has lied to you? What should people do to recover from a romantic relationship that has recently ended badly or painfully? Explain to your readers (fellow students) what steps they should take to solve the personal problem that you have chosen to analyze.

WRITING ASSIGNMENT 2

Write a composition analyzing how to make or to do something. Imagine that your readers are classmates who do not know how to do or make this thing. Select a process that you know well. Begin with an introduction that explains the advantages of learning the process. Make sure that you tell readers what materials they will need to accomplish the process; also define any terms that they might not understand. Finally, explain each step of the process in detail and arrange these steps in the order readers must perform them.

✔ POINTS TO REMEMBER ABOUT PROCESS ANALYSIS

1. Make sure that your process is narrow enough to explain in a paragraph or an essay.
2. Keep your purpose and your readers in mind as you brainstorm the details for your process analysis. What exactly do you want them to know? What else might they want or need to know?
3. Make your introduction interesting and briefly explain the importance or advantages of the process.
4. Describe any materials, equipment, or tools that readers will need to perform the process.
5. Define any terms that readers may not understand.
6. Explain each step in the process clearly and in detail. Also, anticipate readers' confusion or mistakes, and explain what they should *not* do.
7. Use concrete, descriptive words and vivid images.
8. Make sure that your details are logically organized—in the order in which they are to be performed—and that you have included transitional words and phrases.
9. Experiment with different conclusions for your process analysis. Choose the ending that suits your purpose better.
10. Vary your sentence structure so that your process analysis is not a curt set of imperative commands.

8

COMPARISON AND CONTRAST

Comparison and contrast are involved in many decisions you make—from deciding what to eat to choosing your spouse. When you think about the similarities between two people, things, places, or points of view, you are comparing them. When you think about their differences, you are contrasting them. Consider how often you compare and contrast things—consciously or unconsciously—every day. For instance, when you buy an item, often you have compared and contrasted it to all the other things you could have bought.

In addition, every academic subject area requires comparison and contrast. For example, English teachers often ask students to analyze the similarities and differences between stories, poems, characters, settings, and authors. Political science instructors assign comparison and contrast essays about governments, leaders, parties, and theories. Physical science and mathematics courses require students to compare and contrast competing hypotheses and data. Social science teachers often assign papers asking students to explain how various theories and interpretations of behavior and events are similar or different. And art teachers ask students to compare or contrast paintings, sculptures, or artists.

If a teacher assigns a ''comparison'' paper, find out whether he or she expects you to compare *and* contrast the subjects. Some teachers do not state the direction ''contrast'' in their assignments, assuming that comparison papers analyze *both* similarities and differences.

DETERMINING THE TOPIC AND THE PURPOSE OF A COMPARISON-CONTRAST

If your instructor has not assigned a specific topic for your comparison-contrast paper, then you should choose two people, things, places, or viewpoints that you know well or that you feel strongly about. Consider selecting two subjects that seem different to you, but that also have several similarities. In fact, some of the most interesting comparison-contrast papers show the similarities between two objects that seem very different or the differences between two things that seem very similar.

For example, if you wanted to write a comparison-contrast paper about your child, you could explain how the child is similar to and different from other children. Or you could think of a possibly more interesting and original comparison; for example, you could compare or contrast your child and your pet. Here is a topic sentence for this comparison-contrast:

> Although a dog is not human, my puppy's love for me seems very similar to the love displayed by my son.

Some teachers and textbooks tell students to select ''comparable'' subjects to compare and contrast—subjects that are related or that share basic similarities. They warn writers, ''Comparing dissimilar things is like comparing apples and oranges.'' However, comparing apples and oranges might generate more interesting details than comparing two types of apples. For example, what are some similarities between apples and oranges? Write them below.

_____

_____

_____

Apples and oranges have more in common than people usually assume.

When you choose subjects for comparison-contrast paragraphs, look for points of resemblance between seemingly dissimilar things or points of difference between things that seem alike. Finding fresh comparisons takes effort, but it often results in a more thoughtful and interesting paper.

WRITING ACTIVITY 1

Examine the following pairs of subjects. In the space below each pair, list all the ways the two subjects are similar. The first one has been done as an example.

1. writing and swimming *activities requiring mental and physical effort, both improve with practice, both have different forms or types, both can help you feel better about yourself*

2. a person and an animal _____

_____

_____

3. a school and a zoo _____

_____

_____

4. talking and listening _____

_____

_____

5. being twenty-one years old and being sixty-five _____

_____

_____

6. basketball and football *Developed here (US),*
   uniform.
   body —— , plays z ball, ~~big & tall~~. , Very popular
   in US.
   professional players make ~lots' of money.
   4 st. game, referees,

7. the human brain and a computer _____

_____

_____

8. the United States and a quilt _____

_____

_____

Which of these eight pairs might you select for a comparison-contrast paragraph? Why?

_____

_____

_____

An effective comparison-contrast paragraph requires a clear purpose. Remember that the purposes for writing are to *express* something important to ourselves or to others, to *explain* something or share information with readers, or to *persuade* readers to think or feel or do something. The most common academic purpose in exploring topics by comparing and contrasting is to explain or to inform. Here are specific purposes for writing academic comparisons and contrasts.

PURPOSES FOR WRITING COMPARISONS AND CONTRASTS

Some reasons for writing comparison-contrast paragraphs are as follows:

- To explain and describe the similarities between two subjects (two people, things, places, or viewpoints)
- To explain and describe the differences between two subjects or the differences in your attitudes toward two subjects
- To analyze the similarities *and* the differences between two subjects

As with all of your writing, your purpose and your audience (your readers) govern the details you select for comparison and contrast paragraphs.

THINKING ABOUT YOUR AUDIENCE _____

Here are some questions to consider when you are planning a comparison-contrast paragraph.

1. Who exactly am I writing for? Who would be interested in reading this paragraph?
2. How much do my readers already know about the two subjects that I am comparing or contrasting?
3. What else do they need to know about these subjects?
4. What unfamiliar terms should I define or explain?
5. What are the most important or interesting features or characteristics of the subjects that I am comparing or contrasting?

WRITING ACTIVITY 2

Reread your Idea Bank or your journal and put a check next to an entry that you might use to develop a comparison or contrast paper. (If you do not want to use the ideas in your Idea Bank, some possible subjects for this activity include two friends, jobs, classes, teachers, musical groups, songs, works of art, popular magazines, or problems.) Do some brainstorming and clustering about this topic. (See pages 10–14 for reminders about how to brainstorm and cluster.) If you were going to develop a paragraph comparing or contrasting these two subjects, what would your purpose be? What would you want readers to know or to think? Also, write down who you think might be interested in reading this comparison-contrast. How much do these readers already know about the subjects? What else might they need to know about them?

Here is an entry from a student's Idea Bank.

The worst part of going back to school was leaving my son in day care. What was best for Carlos? Should I have hired a baby-sitter? What could I afford? I was — I STILL AM — so worried about his happiness.

Here are two paragraphs that the writer of the preceding Idea Bank entry developed for his writing course. As you read them, notice the way the writer used narration to develop his comparisons and contrasts. (See Chapter 6 on narration.)

The most difficult part of going back to school was selecting day care for my three-year-old son, Carlos. It took me a while to realize that a group day-care center was better in many ways than a baby-sitter. I knew that the best situation was custodial care—leaving Carlos with a baby-sitter who would watch only him. A good baby-sitter would take care of Carlos's food, clothes, and diapers and would play with him. However, all the baby-sitters I interviewed were extremely expensive (charging more than $6.00 per hour), and I simply couldn't afford that much money. So I looked for a less expensive alternative.

The only other type of day care was group day care. Unlike custodial care, group day-care centers take care of between ten and thirty children each day. Because there were twenty-five children at the day-care center I visited, I was concerned that Carlos's immediate needs would be ignored. However, the caregivers seemed very loving and attentive to the children. Also, the advantage of group day care was that Carlos would get to play with other children and learn how to share and cooperate. And the day-care center was only $3.50 per hour. Thus, I put Carlos into group day care. He loves the center, but I still worry about my son's happiness.

What was the writer's topic sentence?

_____

_____

Did his paragraphs convince you of his points? Why or why not?

_____

_____

_____

_____

_____

Which transitions helped you follow the development of his ideas?

_____

_____

_____

DEVELOPING A TOPIC SENTENCE FOR A COMPARISON-CONTRAST

The topic sentence of a comparison or a contrast paragraph should identify the subjects being compared or contrasted and should state your opinion about these subjects or about the similarities or differences between them. Here is the topic sentence from the preceding paper:

It took me a while to realize that a group day-care center was better in many ways than a baby-sitter.

The writer identifies his two subjects (group day care and a baby-sitter) and indicates that he will focus on their differences (group day care is *better* in many ways).

Here is a topic sentence that focuses on the similarities of its subjects.

The democratic principles of government in the United States today are quite similar to those that ruled in ancient Greece.

This sentence spells out the two subjects (the democratic principles of the United States and ancient Greece) and indicates the writer's intention to show their similarities.

Here is another topic sentence of a paragraph; this one focuses on the differences between the writer's subjects.

The people in Tallahassee, Florida, seem friendlier than the people in the city where I live now—Madison, Wisconsin.

This sentence also identifies its subjects (the people in Tallahassee and the people in Madison), and it indicates the writer's intention to shows the differences in the friendliness of these two groups.

Below is one more topic sentence. How is it different from the three preceding ones?

Animal shows and beauty pageants are similar in several ways, but animal shows treat dogs and cats with more respect than beauty pageants treat women.

Unlike the two preceding topic sentences, this one promises to explain *both* the similarities *and* the differences between its two subjects (animal shows and beauty pageants). However, the second half of the sentence indicates that the writer is going to focus on contrasting the types of shows—in particular, the differences in the way participants are treated.

The following writing activity will help you practice writing different kinds of topic sentences for comparisons and contrasts.

WRITING ACTIVITY 3

Follow the directions after each number below. The first sentence has been done as an example.

1. Write a topic sentence comparing and contrasting typewriters and word processors.

    Typewriters and word processors are both machines for typing, but word processors enable people to write, revise, and edit more easily.

2. Write a topic sentence comparing (noting only the similarities between) two teachers.

_____

_____

_____

3. Write a topic sentence contrasting (noting only the differences between) two films or videos.

_____

_____

_____

4. Write a topic sentence comparing television and narcotic drugs.

_____

_____

_____

5. Write a topic sentence contrasting someone's words and his or her actions.

_____

_____

_____

6. Write a topic sentence contrasting what you thought college would be like and what it actually is like.

_____

_____

_____

_____

7. Write a topic sentence comparing *and* contrasting two sports.

_____

_____

_____

_____

8. Write a topic sentence comparing *and* contrasting high school and college.

_____

_____

_____

_____

_____

DEVELOPING DETAILS FOR A COMPARISON OR A CONTRAST PARAGRAPH

The first step in developing supporting details is considering exactly what background information or unfamiliar terms your reader may need to know in order to understand the subjects you are comparing or contrasting. Next use prewriting techniques (freewriting, brainstorming, clustering) to develop details about the similarities and the differences between the two subjects.

You may find it helpful to make a chart or list of the similarities and/or differences between your two subjects. Here is an example of a student's brainstorming notes.

USA & Athens, Greece – when?
USA today and Athens about 600 BC similarities–

Both democracies USA - direct - How? Senate and House of Reps. People vote. Athens? only citizens - But they served in the Assembly and the Council of 500 - they made the laws.

Also USA today - all people have equal rights/ Ancient Athens - all citizens had equal rights. Other similarities ??? Majority rule Used in USA today by Congress and by juries. Used in Ancient Athens by Council to pass laws (and by juries)

Voting was <u>different</u> - USA has free elections/ Ancient Greece had lotteries

Also, USA has one a federal government but Greece had many city-states.

Similarities - Army - USA has a volunteer army. In Ancient Athens, all males served in the army.

Next the student turned his notes into a chart of similarities and differences between his subjects. Here is the chart.

Comparison-Contrast Chart: Democratic Principles of Government in the United States Today and in Ancient Greece (Athens, around 600 B.C.)

U.S. Today	Ancient Greece

(Democracy) –
Direct – Senate and
House of Reps let people
vote
more equal because
everyone can vote

citizens could serve
in – the assembly and
Council of 500

↓

(Equality) – all people
have equal rights
and the

all citizens had
equal rights

(Majority rules)
(by Congress – to
pass legislation –
and by juries)
Armed forces
Army / Navy / Air Force
volunteer army
& draft

majority rule used
to pass laws and
in trials.
(Army)
all male citizens
had to serve

Note that the writer circled the features on both lists that he felt were the most important. He then rewrote his list, elaborating on these points of similarity (the circled features). Here is his revised list.

Comparisons:	U.S. Today	Ancient Greece
Direct democracy	Senate and House of Representatives	Assembly and Council of 500 citizen-members
Equality	All people have equal rights	All citizens were equal and had equal rights
Majority rule	Is used by Congress and by juries	Used to pass laws and for all trials
Army	Volunteer army	All male citizens served

The writer now has a blueprint for a paragraph comparing his two subjects. Notice that the writer ignored his original ideas that did not relate to the four points of comparison he wanted to describe. Since this writer was still not sure whether he wanted to write about similarities or differences (or both), he also prepared a chart of the differences between his subjects. Here is this chart.

Contrasts:	U.S. Today	Ancient Greece
Direct democracy	Women and minorities can vote	Women and slaves could not be citizens
Voting	Elections and electoral college	Lotteries
Federalism	Federal government	Each city-state had its own government

GROUP WORK 1

Form a group with two or three classmates, and choose one person to write down the group's responses. For each pair of subjects below, decide whether you think they are more similar or more different. If the group decides that the subjects are more similar than different, prepare a comparison chart for the two subjects. If the group decides the subjects have more differences than similarities, prepare a chart of their contrasts.

1. Men's and women's average salaries (for the same jobs)
2. Mystery books and mystery films
3. Love for a parent and love for a spouse
4. A sports car and a family car
5. Board games and video games

ORGANIZING A COMPARISON OR CONTRAST PARAGRAPH

You can organize comparison and contrast paragraphs in two ways. One strategy is to develop details subject by subject; this is often called *block order,* because you are blocking out the important features of one subject and then of the other subject. With block order, you discuss all the features of one of the subjects you are comparing (or contrasting) before going on to discuss the next subject. Here is an example of a comparison paragraph organized by block order. The writer has selected three points of comparison, which he describes in the same order for each of his subjects.

DIRECT DEMOCRACY IN ATHENS

EQUALITY IN ATHENS

MAJORITY RULE IN ATHENS

The democratic principles of our government today are a legacy from ancient Greece. The concept of democracy—rule by the people—began in the city-state of Athens, Greece, around 600 B.C. Athens was ruled by an assembly of about a dozen nobles and by a council of 500 citizens. Anyone who was a citizen could volunteer for a government job, and all citizens were considered equal with equal rights. Athens also created the idea of "majority rule," which was used to pass laws. Thus, Athens was a model for the United States, which also enables its people

DIRECT
DEMOCRACY
IN THE USA

EQUALITY
IN THE USA

MAJORITY
RULE IN
THE USA

to participate in government. In the United States, we vote to elect our political representatives in the Senate and House of Representatives. In addition, the Fourteenth Amendment of our Constitution guarantees all American citizens equal rights. Finally, like the Athenian government, Congress uses a version of majority rule to pass bills and laws. Although the Athenian and American governments are separated by about 2,500 years, they are remarkably similar.

Another strategy for organizing comparison and contrast paragraphs is to develop ideas point by point, in *alternating order.* Here you alternate from one subject to the other. In an alternating pattern, first you decide on the points of comparison or contrast, and then you compose the paragraph or essay point by point, indicating how each point relates to both of the subjects that you are comparing or contrasting. In the paragraph below, the writer of the preceding paragraph reorganized the information into alternating order.

DIRECT
DEMOCRACY

⮕ Athens

⮕ USA

EQUALITY

⮕ Athens

⮕ USA

MAJORITY
RULE

⮕ Athens

⮕ USA

The democratic principles of our government today are a legacy from ancient Greece. The concept of democracy—rule by the people— began in the city-state of Athens, Greece, around 600 B.C. Athens was ruled by an assembly of about a dozen nobles and by a council of 500 citizens. Thus, Athens was a model for the United States, which also enables its people to participate in government. In the United States, we vote to elect our political representatives in the Senate and House of Representatives. Another similarity in the governing principles of ancient Athens and the modern United States is that by law, all citizens are considered equal, with equal rights. Finally, like the ancient Athenian government did, our Congress uses a version of majority rule to pass bills and laws. Although the Athenian and American governments are separated by about 2,500 years, they are remarkably similar.

WRITING ACTIVITY 4

Reread the two paragraphs on pages 240 and 241 on democratic principles of government in ancient Athens and modern America. Which order do you think communicates the information more effectively? Why? Write your answer on a separate piece of paper.

> **REMINDER** _____
>
> In planning a comparison-contrast paper, limit your focus to two subjects that seem similar but have some differences or that seem different but have some similarities. Then think of as many similarities or differences between your subjects as you can. Select the key features that you want to compare or contrast, and decide whether to organize them according to block or alternating order.

WRITING ACTIVITY 5

Think about two English or language arts courses that you took recently. Do some brainstorming about the ways these courses were similar or different. Then decide on the important points that you want to compare and contrast (for example, types of knowledge that you were expected to learn or amount and difficulty of required reading and writing). Write a chart comparing *or* contrasting these courses, using the points of comparison or contrast that you think are the most important.

GROUP WORK 2

Choose a partner and work together on this activity. Exchange the charts that you wrote for the preceding writing activity, and answer the following questions about your partner's chart:

1. If the writer used this chart to develop a paragraph, what would be the purpose of the paragraph? Can you tell what the author wanted to show or to prove?
2. Were the points of comparison or contrast that the author selected interesting or important? Did he or she ignore other significant similarities or differences between the two courses?

3. If the author emphasized the ways the courses were alike, did he or she include enough similarities? If not, where does he or she need to add more details?
4. If the author emphasized the ways the courses were different, did he or she specify enough differences? If not, where does he or she need to add more details?
5. Should the author use block order or alternating order to develop this paragraph? Why?

Comparison-Contrast Transitions. Reread the student paragraph on page 241 of this chapter. Notice the transitional words and expressions that the author used to introduce each of the similarities he wanted to describe: "was a model for," "also," "another similarity is," "finally," and "like." Transitions are the glue that holds together a paragraph. Here are some transitions you may find useful for comparing and contrasting.

> **TRANSITIONS THAT INDICATE**
> **COMPARISON AND CONTRAST** _____
>
> Comparison: *also, in addition, as well, furthermore, like, too, in the same way, similarly, too, as well as*
>
> Contrast: *although, though, however, nevertheless, in contrast, on the other hand, whereas, while, conversely*

WRITING ACTIVITY 6

After you read the contrast paragraph below, follow the directions that come after it.

There are two kinds of writers in this world: handwriters and people who use machines to write. Handwriters (people who write with a pen or pencil) are usually different from machine-writers (people who write with a typewriter or a computer). Most people who write by hand are conservative. They like the solid feel of a pen in their hand. Writing is a lot of work, no matter how you do it. Moving a pen across a page is simple and easy, and it involves little risk.

With a pen, words are "carved in stone." A paper isn't really a piece of stone, but you get the point. Machine-writers are more flexible and fluid. With a computer, words are formed with light. Word-processed sentences glide across the screen. They can be highlighted, deleted, made to reappear, or moved around with a flick of a few keys. Machine-writers are more willing to revise than are handwriters because revision is so easy with a word processor. Handwriters and machine-writers are different, but both types can produce wonderful writing.

Write your answers to these questions on a separate piece of paper.

1. Does the paragraph stick to one main point? If not, cross out every sentence that goes off on a tangent.
2. Does every sentence develop or support the topic sentence? If not, cross out the irrelevant sentences.
3. Which sentences need transitions to show their relation to the preceding sentences? Add the appropriate transitions with a caret (^).

WRITING ACTIVITY 7

Plan, write, and revise a paragraph or two about the subjects you worked on for Writing Activity 5 and Group Work 2 on pages 242–243 (comparing or contrasting two academic courses). Make sure that you use appropriate transitions. Then check to see that all the sentences in your paragraph support your main idea.

Often your subjects will have similarities *and* differences. If you want to write about both, you may have to write more than one paragraph. For example, the writer of the comparison paragraph on democracy in ancient Athens and the United States (on page 241) decided that he also wanted to contrast these subjects. Here is his comparison paragraph, followed by a paragraph that contrasts these two democracies. (The second paragraph is based on the chart on the bottom of page 239).

The democratic principles of our government today are a legacy from ancient Greece. The concept of democracy—rule by the people—began in the city-state of Athens, Greece, around 600 B.C. Athens was ruled by an assembly of about a dozen nobles and by a council of 500 citizens. Thus, Athens was a model for the United States, which also enables its people to participate in government. In the United States, we vote to elect our political representatives in the Senate and the House of Representatives. Another similarity in the governing principles of ancient Athens and the modern United States is that by law, all citizens are considered equal, with equal rights. Finally, like the ancient Athenian government did, our Congress uses a version of majority rule to pass bills and laws. Although the Athenian and American governments are separated by about 2,500 years, they are remarkably similar.

However, ancient Athenian democracy was far more limited than ours is in America today. Full democracy was limited to the city-state of Athens, whereas our federal government is elected by people from all fifty states. Moreover, in ancient Greece, women, slaves, and foreigners could never be citizens and thus were unable to participate in the government. In America, on the other hand, anyone who is eligible to vote can participate in elections. Elections themselves are another difference: In ancient Greece, government officials were chosen by lotteries rather than by votes. Still, even with these limitations, Athenian government embodied the principle that people can govern themselves, a guiding principle of our modern Constitution.

What clues did the writer provide to let you know that he wanted to emphasize that the two forms of government are more similar than they are different? Did you notice that the first paragraph was longer than the second? The writer devoted about 50 percent more words to the similarities than to the differences (not counting the last sentence of the second paragraph, which points out a similarity). The final sentence of the second paragraph returns to the idea in the first topic sentence—that the democratic principles of both governments are similar. Also, did you catch the transitional expression that this writer used to minimize the differences: ''Still, even with these limitations''?

WRITING ACTIVITY 8

Choose a pair of subjects from any of the preceding writing activities in this chapter. Develop a chart that compares them and a chart that contrasts them. Then decide whether you want to emphasize their similarities or their differences. Write a topic sentence indicating the emphasis you have chosen. Then write two paragraphs based on your chart—one comparing your subjects and the other contrasting them.

USING FIGURATIVE LANGUAGE TO COMPARE AND CONTRAST

In Chapter 5, you learned how to use figurative language to help readers understand your thoughts and feelings. You practiced writing *similes*—comparisons that use the words *like* or *as*. Do you remember this simile: ''His face was as white as the underside of a fish that had died several days ago''? You also practiced creating another type of figurative language—*metaphors*, comparisons that leave out the word *like* or *as* (''His face was an ashen sheet'').

Similes and metaphors can add energy and liveliness to your comparison-contrast paragraphs. For example, here is an excerpt from a television critic's review of the pilot program for the series ''Class of '96,'' a show about six freshmen on a fictional college campus.

> In these two hours not only the students are fresh—so are the shock of recognition, the rush of friendship, and the feelings of giddiness and terror. The series suggests that in this heady business of inventing a brand-new self, life is sometimes true or false, and sometimes an essay question.

The writer makes two comparisons to help us understand his point: He compares the ''freshness'' of first-year students with the freshness of the emotions they (and the audience) feel, and he compares life away at college to a test.

Similes and metaphors are effective supporting details in comparison and contrast paragraphs. They illuminate the meaningful similarities between seemingly dissimilar things. For example, the opening section of this chapter asked you to think about the similarities between a child and a pet. These similarities can be expressed in figurative language:

Puppies are as sweetly innocent and cute as human babies.   [simile]
Indeed, most people feel that their dogs are children who simply don't
ever talk back.   [metaphor]

GROUP WORK 3

Form a group with two or three classmates, and choose one person to
record the group's responses. For each word below, think of an interesting
comparison and express it as a simile or a metaphor. The first one has
been done as an example.

1. prejudice

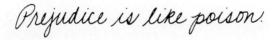

Prejudice is like poison.

2. love
3. fear
4. divorce
5. a blind date

WRITING ACTIVITY 9

Choose one of the comparisons that your group composed for the preceding activity *or* select a pair of subjects from the first writing activity
in this chapter (on pages 228–229). Make a comparison or a contrast
chart for your subjects, and write a topic sentence about them. (For
example, a topic sentence for the simile ''Prejudice is like poison'' might
be ''Like poison, prejudice seeps through one's blood and corrodes one's
heart and mind.'') Then compose and revise a comparison or a contrast
paragraph about your topic sentence.

USING COMPARISON-CONTRAST ACROSS THE COLLEGE CURRICULUM

Many academic assignments ask students to compare or contrast ideas, people,
objects, or events in order to illustrate the students' knowledge about these
subjects:

• Describe three peptides and explain how their molecules and their
   functions differ.   [contrast]

- How does the inflation that Germany experienced after World War I compare to German inflation today?   [comparison]
- How are descriptive linguistics and prescriptive linguistics similar? How do they differ?   [comparison and contrast]
- Why have scientists been able to build nuclear fission reactors but not nuclear fusion reactors?   [comparison and contrast]

Here is an English literature assignment that calls for comparing and contrasting:

Read aloud the following poem by the Native American writer N. Scott Momaday. Read it again silently, and follow the directions below it.

The Eagle-Feather Fan

The eagle is my power.
And the fan is an eagle.
It is strong and beautiful
In my hand. And it is real.
My fingers hold upon it.
As if the beaded handle
Were the twist of bristlecone.
The bones of my hand are fine
And hollow; the fan bears them.
My hand veers in the thin air
Of the summits. All morning
It scuds on the cold currents;
All afternoon it circles
To the singing, to the drums.

Write a paragraph or two about the central metaphor of this poem. To what is the poet-narrator comparing himself? What details does the poet provide to illustrate this comparison? What do the metaphors and similes in this poem show us about the poet's attitude toward his subject? How does your attitude toward this subject compare to the poet's?

This assignment asks students to explain the comparisons that the poet describes in the poem. In addition, it asks students to compare their attitudes toward the poem's subject to the poet's feelings about it.

The following student paragraphs illustrate a typical response to this assignment.

By comparing his hand to the feathers of an eagle fan, the poet-narrator of "The Eagle-Feather Fan" helps us understand the energy and power that he admires in this bird. The poet's language makes his comparison vivid. As he holds the fan in his hand, its feathers give him the power to fly, to "veer in the thin air of the summits" and "scud on the cold currents." The similes and metaphors in this poem support this image of the poet flying like an eagle. For example, the poet compares the handle of the fan to a cone high up on a pine tree. He also says that the bones of his hand are so "find and hollow" that the eagle fan can lift them up to "circle" in the air.

Obviously, the poet admires eagles and wishes he had their strength, their power, and their ability to fly. I enjoyed this poem, especially because the metaphor communicates the poet's feelings quickly and sharply. His descriptive language helped me visualize the fan (and the poet) gliding along in the air. Although I don't honor eagles the way this poet does, his image made me wish that I too could fly like an eagle and "circle to the singing, to the drums."

The student has fulfilled the requirements of the assignments by explaining his understanding of the poet's comparisons and by comparing his attitudes to those of the poet.

GETTING READERS' RESPONSES

Use the checklist below to help you revise your drafts. Ask family, friends, and classmates to answer the questions below honestly and fully.

COMPARISON-CONTRAST CHECKLIST

1. Does the topic sentence identify the two (or more) subjects that the writer is comparing or contrasting and indicate whether the writer will emphasize the subjects' similarities or differences?
2. Should the writer provide more information about his or her subjects or define any unfamiliar terms?

(Continued)

3. Are the points of comparison or contrast that the writer selected interesting or important?
4. Did the writer ignore other significant similarities or differences between his or her subjects?
5. If the writer emphasized the ways these subjects are alike, did he or she include enough similarities? If not, where does he or she need to add more details?
6. If the writer emphasized the ways the subjects are different, did he or she specify enough differences? If not, where does he or she need to add more details?
7. Did the author use block order or alternating order? Was this the most appropriate order? Why or why not?
8. Does every sentence develop or support the topic sentence? If not, which ones are irrelevant?
9. Which sentences need transitions to show their relation to the preceding sentences?
10. What suggestions do you have for improving this comparison or contrast?

■ EXPLORING FURTHER

The following essay has no title, and its author did not want to reveal his name. It is from a collection of students' essays on applications for admission to college—*Essays That Worked: 50 Essays from Successful Applications to the Nation's Top Colleges.* In this essay, the writer uses comparison and contrast to illustrate the way his perception of his father changed as the writer matured.

Name Withheld

Ever watch "My Three Sons" on T.V.? I'm not an avid television viewer, but whenever I'd watch it when I was little it always struck me as rather odd. "Pop" always smiled benevolently and gave wise counsel over dinner, while meals with my own "Pop" always consisted of an awkward silence occasionally punctuated by a sarcastic remark from my father in some impersonal restaurant. Just recently, however, my father and I met for dinner after a long and regrettable estrangement; what happened that night played more like a scene from "My Three Sons" than anything of my previous experience, and my reactions to it made me understand both my father and myself with greater insight and maturity than ever before.

Perhaps all children see their parents as demi-gods capable of incredible feats but incapable of fault or weakness. I'd always seen my father that way, but was awakened from this somewhat euphoric state early in my childhood when my parents' divorce and my father's apparent neglect shattered my ideal of fatherly perfection. Not only did my father not measure up to Fred MacMurray, but he seemed to have nothing but faults. My attitude spilled over into other areas of my young life; just as Plato had conceived of a perfect example of everything in his Theory of Forms, a little Jesse had already established in his mind certain idealistic standards for all people and things in his life. I must admit, these standards of perfection made me a somewhat compulsive little boy who was often left disillusioned.

The differences between my father and myself were further aggravated by a conflict of interests: Dad would visit on weekends, dragging me away from a good book for a game of baseball where my ineptitude left me feeling deeply embarrassed. In a way, though, I believe what I saw as my father's un-intellectuality made me strive all the more in the opposite direction. ''Chip'' may have had a sweet and doting father, but I'm willing to bet my socks that ''Chip'' can't read ancient Greek!

Thus, I found myself a bit surprised and confused when my father and I finally began to communicate. He told me that, although we didn't have common interests, he held a greater regard for mine, that he admired and was almost jealous of my strength of will in resisting his influence and in pursuing what I loved. He apologized for his inability to communicate and for the neglect that had prevented a close relationship between us, and he told me that he'd always been proud of me, of my achievements and performances and of the person I had become.

As he spoke, I realized that the very fact that we were speaking meant that, I, too, had long since purged the choler of my disillusioned resentment that had maintained the wall between us. This reconciliation left me feeling good, not only about my father but about myself. I understood how I had changed from a cynical little tot into an optimistic young man. I realize now that hoping for perfection, that creating idols, is a frustrating and fruitless pursuit; I am even grateful for imperfections in the people and things that I love because those imperfections allow me to more fully understand what love is, and because I sense that my own imperfections, too, are forgivable. This fall, I was outraged by a change my school had implemented in the direction of a more standardized curriculum, a change decidedly for the worse. I channeled my energy into a constructive campaign to rally student support and to offer alternate solutions. I was able to do this because I had come to realize that an institution may be flawed but still amenable to change, and that it is everyone's responsibility to work to perfect it rather than wallow in disillusioned resignation.

Perhaps my early experience of having my ideals shattered helped me to develop a realistic outlook. After a period of disillusionment, I believe I matured into a heightened awareness of myself and others. Compassion and self-awareness are qualities I prize most and ones that in some measure I now possess.

Whereas I was once an exacting perfectionist, I have grown into a person with an almost pathological need to understand and help other people. It is almost as if I am making up for lost time which I spent expecting too much from others; my adolescent life has been spent in efforts, both on a personal level and in schoolwide activities, to make others feel comfortable with themselves and proud of their own achievements. I believe very strongly in modesty and social courtesy; at the very least boasting makes others uncomfortable. My tendency to strive for excellence, however, has not disappeared, but evolved: now I see being "perfect" as being tolerant and compassionate, towards others and towards myself.

I believe that all children defy their parents and that part of growing up involves the gradual acceptance of faults. It may be that my parents' divorce interrupted this natural flow in my own life, but it also hastened it. I am better off having grown up with obstacles, and my reconciliation with my father has provided a vantage point from which I can look back and understand that I have finally achieved a balance between acceptance and perfectionism. Looking back now, I can't believe that I ever compared such a decent and complex man as my father to some two-dimensional character on a T.V. program that never got particularly good ratings anyway. And, when you get right down to it, how great could a man be if he names his son "Chip"?

Discussion Questions

1. What is the main point of this essay? What was the writer's purpose in writing this essay?
2. What might be another title for the essay?
3. Which details, similes, or metaphors were most effective in helping you understand the writer's perception of his father when the writer was young? Why were these details so powerful?
4. Which details were most effective in helping you understand the writer's current perception of his father?
5. What order did the writer use to develop his ideas? Was this order logical and effective?
6. How did the writer achieve unity and coherence?

WRITING ASSIGNMENT 1

Write a comparison and contrast composition about the way you viewed someone when you were a child and the way you view this person now. Choose a significant person in your life (a relative, a close friend, a hero or a heroine), and explain your perceptions of this person at a specific time in your life when you were young. Then compare and contrast these perceptions to your current views of and attitudes toward this person.

WRITING ASSIGNMENT 2

Examine a photograph of yourself today. Then get out a picture of yourself five years ago. What similarities and differences do you see? Write a composition comparing and contrasting yourself five years ago and yourself now. Five years ago, what were you like? What was your life like? How are you and your life similar today? How are you different? How do your attitudes and the way you view things today differ from your feelings, behavior, and personality five years ago?

You don't have to answer all the questions above—use them to help you narrow down your composition. Note that this assignment asks you to use narration and description to explain your comparisons and contrasts.

WRITING ASSIGNMENT 3

Choose one of the following pairs of subjects, and write a composition about them. Remember to compose planning charts (like the ones on page 239 of this chapter) to help you generate details.

1. Compare and/or contrast your conception of college before you began attending it and your perception of it now. What did you think college would be like? How do you think and feel about your experiences in college now?
2. Think about a product that you bought because of its description in an advertisement on television or in a magazine. Compare and/or contrast what the product was supposed to be or do (according to the advertisement) and what it actually was or did when you used it.
3. Compare and/or contrast the ways men and women are treated or respected in a particular profession (for example, doctors, police officers, or accountants) *or* in a specific professional sport (for example, tennis, basketball, or swimming).

✔ POINTS TO REMEMBER ABOUT COMPARISON
AND CONTRAST

1. If you have a free choice of topics, choose subjects whose similarities or differences are not immediately obvious.
2. Think about your purpose in comparing and/or contrasting your subjects. What do you want your readers to understand, to think, to feel, or to do?
3. Consider whether your readers need background information about your subjects or need any terms defined or explained.
4. Write comparison and contrast charts to help you explain all the similarities and differences between your subjects.
5. Select the points of comparison or contrast that you think will be interesting or important to your intended readers.
6. Include enough supporting details to clarify the similarities and/or the differences between your subjects.
7. Decide whether to use block order or alternating order to develop your details.
8. Use concrete, descriptive words, vivid images, similes, and metaphors to enliven your comparisons and contrasts.
9. Make sure that every sentence illustrates or supports the topic sentence (and cross out any irrelevant sentences).
10. Use transitional words and expressions to show the relations between your ideas and your sentences.

9

DIVISION AND CLASSIFICATION

Division and classification are basic thought processes. We divide and classify in order to make sense of the people and the things in our lives. By placing objects in categories, we see interrelations among different things that share common features. For instance, consider the ways you classify food. People divide the foods they eat in many ways (breakfast/lunch/dinner, home-cooked food/fast food/frozen food, meat/dairy/vegetables/grains, and so forth).

Dividing and classifying helps us make decisions. For example, how do the classifications in a menu help you understand what foods a restaurant is serving? Most chefs divide their menus into several categories and classify these categories (appetizers, main dishes, side dishes, and desserts) to help customers decide what they want to eat.

Division and classification are similar processes. When you divide, you break something down into its parts, types, or categories. With classification, you arrange several things or people into groups or categories based on features they share. This textbook itself illustrates the strategies of division and classification. It is divided into four parts, which are classified according to the skills that you can practice in each part: ''The Writing Process,'' ''The Writer's Portfolio'' (strategies of paragraph development), ''Essay Development,'' and ''The Writer's Handbook'' (sentence structure and grammar).

Effective division and classification paragraphs have the following characteristics:

- A clear focus and purpose that are appropriate for the intended audience
- A logical basis for dividing or classifying your subject

- Relevant examples and illustrations
- Appropriate transitional words and expressions

Division and classification are helpful ways of organizing and explaining information in our daily lives and in college courses.

WRITING ACTIVITY 1

Here is an activity that will illustrate how much you already know about dividing and classifying. Below is a student's cluster about buying his first car. The writer has already divided the topic *cars* into many subtopics or details (features of automobiles). Imagine that this writer has asked you to help him classify these details into logical groups or categories. Think of the different ways he could sort these details into groups (such as "body size" or "safety features"). Then take out a piece of paper and write down a heading for each group. List the details that fit under each heading.

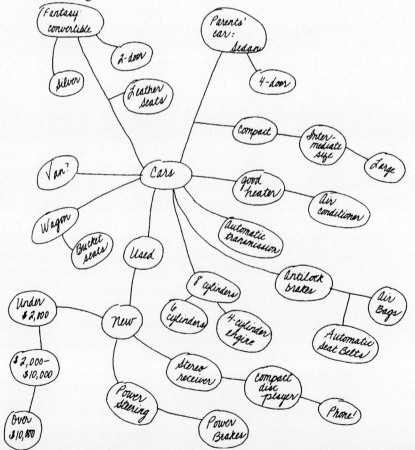

DECIDING ON A PURPOSE AND A TOPIC SENTENCE

Make division and classification easier by narrowing down your purpose before you begin. What exactly is your subject, and why are you dividing it into parts or classifying it? What do you want to learn? What do you want to express or explain?

PURPOSES FOR WRITING A DIVISION OR A CLASSIFICATION

Some reasons for writing division and classification paragraphs include the following:

- To gain a better understanding of an object, place, or concept by breaking it down into its parts and explaining how each part relates to the whole
- To explain how the types or parts of an object, place, or concept are similar or different
- To clarify your understanding of people, objects, places, or concepts by sorting them into groups according to characteristics or features that they share
- To increase your understanding of people, objects, places, or concepts by sorting them in different ways, according to different characteristics or features

---

One way to begin developing a purpose and a main idea for a division or a classification paragraph is to do some brainstorming about your topic and about the different ways you can divide it. Here is an example of a student's brainstorming about recreational reading, a topic that he was assigned in his English class.

Stuff I read - different books, many magazines, any comic

I like to read things that are different lengths - short, medium (50-100 pages), and long.

What do I enjoy reading most? <u>Books</u> What types?

(1) novels   (2) biographies   (3) collections of short stories

Fiction – Types of novels I like:
*   mysteries, adventure stories, spy thrillers, and science fiction*

Notice that as this writer brainstormed, he divided his topic in several different ways. Each time he did this, he used a different *organizing principle* to classify his groupings. For example, the writer's first organizing principle was the type of material that he reads for recreation (i.e., for pleasure). Next he divided his reading material by its length. Then he focused on the books that he enjoys most and divided them into types. Finally, he classified fictional books by their content. Here is an outline of the writer's classifications based on his four different organizing principles:

My Recreational Reading Materials

(Organized by Classification)

1. Types

   books

   magazines

   comics

2. Length

   short (fewer than 50 pages)

   medium (50 to 100 pages)

   long (more than 100 pages)

3. Favorite types of books

   novels

   biographies

   collections of short stories

4. Content of novels

   mysteries

   adventure stories

   spy thrillers

   science fiction stories

GROUP WORK 1

Form a group with two or three classmates and choose one person to write down the group's responses. Examine the list of characteristics below. Each describes a feature of a friend at a university. Together decide how you might divide and group the characteristics on this list (which aren't arranged in any particular order). For example, one category might be "responsibilities as a teacher" and another might be "favorite activities." (You can put a characteristic in more than one category.)

English professor	local PTA member
mechanic	Little League coach
card player	placement test scorer
marathon runner	father of two children
loyal friend	freshmen faculty adviser
vegetarian	writer of textbooks
Republican	baseball card collector
camp counselor	gardener
poet	school newspaper adviser
basketball player	loving husband
dog walker	supervisor of student teachers
cook	department chairperson
caring son	Dodgers fan

The best way to develop a topic sentence for a division or a classification paragraph is to think about what you want readers to understand about your topic. For example, when the writer of the brainstorming list on pages 257–258 thought about categories, he decided that the most important one was "favorite types of books." He wanted to explain each type. As he thought about these books, he experimented with several different topic sentences. In each one, he stated his topic and mentioned the organizing principle he had chosen to divide and classify this topic. Here are some of the topic sentences he developed.

(1) My favorite kinds of recreational reading are novels, biographies, and short stories.

(2) My recreational reading can be categorized by my three favorite types of books: novels, biographies, and collections of short stories.

(3) My favorite kinds of reading can be classified in three categories: novels, biographies, and collections of short stories.

Here is the topic sentence that the writer decided to use for his paragraph. He liked it because it clearly stated the organizing principle that he used to classify his categories:

The recreational reading I enjoy most falls into three categories: novels, biographies, and collections of short stories.

REMINDER _____
The topic sentence of a division paragraph or a classification paragraph should identify your topic and indicate the organizing principle you are using to classify your groups or types.

WRITING ACTIVITY 2

At a grocery store or a supermarket, examine the ways the store's manager has divided and classified its products. Are certain products grouped together in areas or on shelves? What are the organizing principles of this classification? (For example, are products divided by type into canned foods, dairy, produce, and so forth?) Write down all the categories of products in the store. Then, under each category, write down the names of at least five products in this category. Finally, develop a topic sentence for a paragraph about how this store's classification system helps (or does not help) shoppers.

WRITING ACTIVITY 3

Think of at least four different organizing principles for dividing and classifying the members of your family. For example, one way to divide them is by gender (male or female). On a separate piece of paper, divide the members of your family into four different groupings, each classified according to a different organizing principle.

GROUP WORK 2

Form a group with one or two classmates and choose one person to write down the group's responses. Together decide on an appropriate organizing principle for dividing and classifying each topic below. Then divide the topic into at least three categories according to the organizing principle that you have selected. The first one has been done as an example.

1. Baseball teams
   Organizing principle: *Players' positions*
   Categories: *pitchers, catchers, infielders and outfielders*

2. College teachers
   Organizing principle:
   Categories:

3. Pets
   Organizing principle:
   Categories:

4. Research papers (or term papers)
   Organizing principle:
   Categories:

5. Automobile drivers
   Organizing principle:
   Categories:

6. Video *or* board games
   Organizing principle:
   Categories:

WRITING ACTIVITY 4

Select three of the topics from the preceding Group Work activity and develop a topic sentence for each one (on a separate piece of paper). Here is an example of a topic sentence for a paragraph about the first topic:

> Baseball players can be classified in several ways, but the most common way is according to the positions they usually play.

Read the following classification paragraph and decide whether the writer achieved his purpose of explaining how we use classification to make sense of our surroundings.

Everyone, whether he realizes it or not, classifies the items he finds in his environment. Most speakers of English recognize a category that they call *livestock,* which is made up of other categories known as *cattle, horses, sheep,* and *swine* of different ages and sexes. An English speaker who is knowledgeable about farm life categorizes a barnyardful of these animals in a way that establishes relationships based on distinguishing features. For example, he feels that a *cow* and a *mare,* even though they belong to different species, are somehow in a relationship to each other. And of course they are, because they both belong to the category of Female Animal under the general category of Livestock. the speaker of English unconsciously groups certain animals into various sub-categories that exclude other animals:

LIVESTOCK				
	Cattle	**Horses**	**Sheep**	**Swine**
Female	cow	mare	ewe	sow
Intact Male	bull	stallion	ram	boar
Castrated Male	steer	gelding	wether	barrow
Immature	heifer	colt/filly	lamb	shoat/gilt
Newborn	calf	foal	yearling	piglet

A table such as this shows that speakers of English are intuitively aware of certain contrasts. They regard a *bull* and a *steer* as different—which they are, because one belongs to a category of Intact Males and the other to a category of Castrated Males. In addition to discriminations made on the basis of livestock's sex, speakers of English also contrast mature and immature animals. A *foal* is a newborn horse and a *stallion* is a mature male horse.

The conceptual labels by which English-speaking peoples talk about barnyard animals can now be understood. The animal is defined by the point at which two distinctive features intersect: sex (male, female, or castrated) and maturity (mature, immature, or newborn). A *stallion* belongs to a category of horse that is both intact male and mature; a *filly* belongs to a category of horse that is both female and immature. Nothing in external reality dictates that barnyard animals should be talked about in this way; it is strictly a convention of English and some other languages.

In contrast, imagine that an Amazonian Indian is brought to the United States so that linguists can intensively study his language. When the Indian returns to his native forests, his friends and relatives listen in disbelief as he tells about all the fantastic things he saw. He summarizes his impressions of America in terms of the familiar categories his language has accustomed him to. He relates that at first he was bewildered by the strange animals he saw on an American farm because each animal not only looked different but also seemed to represent a unique concept to the natives of the North American tribe. But after considerable observation of the curious folkways of these peculiar people, at last he understood American barnyard animals. He figured out that some animals are good for work and that some are good for food. Using these two components—rather than the Americans' features of sex and maturity—his classification of livestock is considerably different. He categorized *stallion, mare,* and *gelding* as belonging to both the Inedible and Work (Riding) categories. The *bull* also belonged to the Inedible category but it was used for a different kind of Work as a draught animal. He further placed a large number of animals—*cow, ewe, lamb, sow,* and so on—in the category of Edible but Useless for Work. Since his method of categorizing the barnyard failed to take into account the breeding process, which depends upon the categories of sex and maturity, he no doubt found it inexplicable that some animals—*ram, colt, boar,* and so on— were raised even though they could not be eaten or used for work.

To an American, the Amazonian Indian's classification of barnyard animals appears quite foolish, yet it is no more foolish than the American's system of classification by the features of sex and maturity. Speakers of each language have the right to recognize whatever features they care to. And they have a similar right to then organize these features according to the rules of their own speech communities. No one system is better than another in making sense out of the world in terms that can be talked about; the systems are simply different. A speaker of English who defines a *stallion* as a mature, male horse is no wiser than the Amazonian who claims it is inedible and used for riding. Both the speaker of English and the speaker of the Amazonian language have brought order out of the multitudes of things in the environment—and, in the process, both have shown something about how their languages and their minds work.

WRITING ACTIVITY 5

Explore your reactions to the preceding passage by answering the questions below.

1. The author of this excerpt is Peter Farb, a researcher who wrote books about the role language plays in human behavior. What is Farb's main point in this excerpt? Why do we classify everything around us?

_____

_____

_____

2. Why do you think an English speaker's classifications of barnyard animals might differ from an Amazonian Indian's categories? Why might they have different organizing principles for dividing and classifying these animals?

_____

_____

_____

_____

3. On a separate piece of paper, write a paragraph or two classifying a group of things that you know well (such as college courses, cars, books, television programs, video games, professional sports, and so forth). Begin by brainstorming or clustering and think of a purpose for writing about this topic. Develop a table, like Farb's, of the various sub-categories of your group. This can help you discover organizing principles for classifying your topic.

Here is a topic sentence from a student's paragraph about the topic "types of foods":

The most common way of classifying foods is by the nutrients that they contain.

Note that the writer identified the topic ("foods") and mentioned the organizing principle ("the nutrients that they contain"). Topic sentences for division or classification paragraphs often use language such as the following:

[*This topic*] can be divided into three main types: . . .
[*This topic*] can be classified according to how they . . .
[*This topic*] fall into three categories: . . .
Three kinds of [*categories*] make up [*this topic*]: . . .

> **REMINDER**
> Try out different words to describe the groups that you choose for your classification paragraphs. Instead of *groups,* use *types, categories, kinds,* or *classes.* (Look up these words in your dictionary or thesaurus to understand how they differ slightly in meaning.)

GROUP WORK 3

Work with one or two classmates on this activity. Your topic is "restaurants." Together think of at least three different organizing principles to divide and classify types of restaurants. Then write a separate topic sentence for each different way you have classified restaurants.

DEVELOPING SUPPORTING DETAILS FOR DIVISION AND CLASSIFICATION PARAGRAPHS

In order to accomplish your purposes (for your intended readers), think of examples and reasons that describe, explain, or illustrate each part or group you are classifying. Try freewriting, brainstorming, and clustering. After you have jotted down everything you can think of about your groups, try outlining your information.

An outline is useful for developing and grouping items for a classification paragraph. For example, here is a student's outline for the topic "types of foods." Note that she underlined the organizing principle in her topic sentence. Also look at the way the writer used indentation, numbers, and letters to arrange her headings and subheadings.

The most common way of classifying foods is <u>by the nutrients that they contain.</u>

    I. Carbohydrates

        A. sugars

           1. fruits

           2. honey

           3. milk

        B. starches

           1. bread

           2. potatoes

           3. pasta

        C. fibers

           1. vegetables

      2. fruits

      3. seeds

II. Proteins

   A. animal proteins

      1. meat

      2. fish

      3. poultry

   B. plant proteins

      1. beans

      2. nuts

      3. grains

III. Fats

   A. saturated

      1. meat

      2. milk

      3. butter

   B. unsaturated

      1. fish oil

      2. olive oil

      3. vegetable oil

Here is another student's outline for a classification paper about the same topic.

In order to stay healthy, you need nutrients from foods in <u>each of the four food groups.</u>

   I. Grains (4 or more servings per day)

   A. bread

      1. bread

      2. rolls

    B.   cereal

        1.   dry cereal

        2.   cooked hot cereal

    C.   pasta

        1.   noodles

        2.   shells

II.   Fruits/vegetables (4 or more servings per day)

    A.   fruits

        1.   tree fruits

        2.   vine fruits

    B.   green vegetables (vitamin C)

        1.   broccoli

        2.   spinach

    C.   yellow vegetables (vitamin A)

        1.   carrots

        2.   corn

III.   Dairy (2–3 servings per day)

    A.   milk

        1.   whole

        2.   skim

    B.   cheese

        1.   soft cheeses

        2.   hard cheeses

    C.   other milk products

        1.   yogurt

        2.   butter

IV.   Meat/beans or nuts (1–2 servings per day)

    A.   meat

      1.   red meat

      2.   white meat

         a) poultry

            (1) chicken

            (2) turkey

            (3) goose

         b) fish

            (1) finned fish

            (2) shellfish

   B.   beans or nuts

      1.   beans or bean paste

      2.   nuts or nut paste

These writers can use their outlines to describe and illustrate each of their subcategories.

An outline can also help writers evaluate their discovery drafts. For example, here is a draft based on the outline on pages 266–267. After you read it, reread the outline on which it is based. What information did the writer forget to include? Which categories did she discuss too briefly (compared to the amount of details she provided for the other two categories)?

The most logical way to classify foods is by the nutrients they contain. There are three main categories of nutrients: carbohydrates, proteins, and fats. Carbohydrates are the main source of energy for our bodies. Three types of carbohydrates are sugars (found in fruits, honey, and milk), starches (in bread, potatoes, and pasta), and fiber (in vegetables, fruits, and seeds). Fiber does not provide energy, but it helps move food through the digestive tract. The second type of nutrient is protein (animal proteins and plant proteins). Finally, our bodies need fats—for energy, for growth, and for absorbing vitamins. Unsaturated fats (such as fish, olive, and vegetable oils) are much healthier than saturated fats (meat, milk, and butter). Carbohydrates, proteins, and fats provide the materials and the energy for all of our bodies' activities.

Is the writer's discussion of the major types of nutrients balanced? If not, why not?

_____

_____

_____

What details from her outline might the writer include in her revision of this draft?

_____

_____

_____

In addition to using your outline to check the adequacy of your details, you can ask yourself questions about your discovery draft based on it. Here are some suggestions.

**CHECKING FOR EFFECTIVE SUPPORTING
DETAILS IN A DIVISION OR
A CLASSIFICATION PARAGRAPH** _____
Write down answers to the following questions:

1. Did I oversimplify when I divided my topic into categories or groups? Did I overlook an important category?
2. Does each group or category that I discussed include all parts or types of that group (or did I leave out any important parts or types)?
3. Did I describe or explain each part or type in approximately the same amount of detail (or did I write too little or too much about one of the groups or categories)?

ORGANIZING A DIVISION OR A CLASSIFICATION PARAGRAPH

Reread the paragraph on pages 269–271 about types of foods. Note that the writer arranged her categories from the most important nutrients to the least important. As you develop details for your division and classification paragraphs, organize them logically: either from least important to most important (or vice versa). Another strategy to consider is classifying people or things in order of their general familiarity (from best known to least familiar).

GROUP WORK 4

Form a group with two or three classmates, and choose one person to write down the group's responses. Together do some brainstorming about the topic "types of classes at our college." Then decide on an organizing principle to divide these types of classes (for example, "teacher's methodology"—lecture, workshop, or a mixture of the two). Use this organizing principle to develop at least three categories, and decide on a logical order for these categories. Develop a discovery draft of a paragraph or two about the types of courses at your college. (You can compose this paragraph individually or together in a group.)

Another strategy for helping your readers follow your ideas is to connect them with transitions. Here are some transitions that you can use to make your writing more unified and coherent.

TRANSITIONS THAT INDICATE DIVISION AND CLASSIFICATION _____

Here are some transitional words and phrases that signal division and classification.

> *first, second, third, next, last, finally*
> *the most common type of, kind of, class of . . .*
> *another type of, kind of, class of . . .*
> *the most important category of . . .*

REMINDER _____

Do not add *-ly* endings to transitions that do not need them. (Do *not* use the words *firstly, secondly,* and so forth.)

WRITING ACTIVITY 6

Plan, write, and revise a paragraph or two about *one* of the topics below. Make sure that you use appropriate transitions in your revision.

- Classify your talents or abilities.
- Classify your clothing.
- Classify the clubs you belong to.
- Classify employers for whom you have worked.

CONCLUDING A DIVISION OR A CLASSIFICATION PARAGRAPH

Sometimes writers forget to end classification paragraphs with a concluding sentence. Instead, they end with a sentence about the last part or final category of their topic. When you revise your paragraphs, check to make sure that you have ended with a point about your topic or about the entire paragraph.

For example, imagine that you have decided to write a paragraph about the types of problems that college athletes face. You decide to write about three problems: their lack of time to relax or socialize because of their studies and practices, their difficulty staying in shape all the time, and their temptations to take steroids to improve their performance. The conclusion to this paragraph should refer to all of these problems, not just the third one. Here is a possible conclusion:

> People who envy college athletes should consider the many problems caused by their attempts to succeed in school and on the field.

WRITING ACTIVITY 7

After you read this paragraph, write answers to the questions that follow it.

Many kinds of minerals are essential to our health. We need adequate amounts of calcium to build and maintain strong bones and teeth. We need to eat foods rich in iron so that our red blood cells can carry oxygen to our organs. Blood carries oxygen in molecules called hemoglobin. Some excellent sources of calcium are dairy products (such as milk, cheese, and yogurt) and dark green vegetables. In addition to minerals, our bodies need vitamins.

Iron is mostly found in meat, but it also can be found in dark green vegetables. Sodium is found in salt and in most foods. Phosphorus helps keep our bones and teeth strong. We get phosphorus from meat and from dairy products. The human body needs magnesium to regulate its fluids (the liquid in the cells). Fruits and vegetables provide the daily requirement of magnesium. These foods also provide potassium, which helps in fluid regulation.

Write your answers to these questions on a separate piece of paper.

1. Does the topic sentence clearly identify the writer's organizing principle? If so, what is it? If not, what would you suggest? How could the writer have divided and classified minerals in order to explain their importance in the body?
2. Does every sentence develop or illustrate the writer's main idea about minerals? If not, cross out any irrelevant sentences.
3. Which sentences need to be moved to a different place in the paragraph so they make more sense?
4. Which sentences need transitions to show their relation to the preceding sentences? Add the appropriate transitions with a caret (∧).
5. Does the paragraph have a conclusion? If it doesn't, suggest one.

USING DIVISION AND CLASSIFICATION ACROSS THE COLLEGE CURRICULUM

Almost every college course requires students to divide and classify ideas, things, or people in order to make sense of them. Here are some examples of these assignments.

- Describe the four categories that anthropologist Oscar Lewis used to characterize the culture of poverty.
- Describe the sections of the Bill of Rights and explain why each was necessary to amend the Constitution.
- Identify the two major groups of anesthetics and describe the parts of the body affected by each type in both groups.
- Develop a classification system for describing human communicable diseases.

Division and classification paragraphs in the social and physical sciences may require the use of numbers for clarity. Here is an example:

> People who do not want to get fat should know the four major categories of activity levels. Activity levels are usually classified by the amount of energy (or calories) used in performing at that level. (1) "Sedentary" activities, such as sleeping, lying down, and sitting, use up only about 50 to 100 calories per hour. Television watching, for example, does not require much energy. (2) In "moderate" activities approximately 100 to 250 calories per hour are used up. Such activities include walking slowly, making a bed, and gardening. (3) Activities such as walking fast, riding a bike, or washing a car are considered "vigorous" activities. In these activities about 250 to 350 calories each hour are burned. (4) Finally, "strenuous" activities, in which 350 calories or more per hour are used up, require much energy (running, exercising, and playing sports). The more calories you use per hour, the more fat your body will burn—and the more weight you can lose.

Note that each number in the preceding paragraph is enclosed in a set of parentheses that do *not* affect the sentence's punctuation.

GETTING READERS' RESPONSES

Use the checklist below to help you revise the drafts of your division and classification paragraphs.

DIVISION AND CLASSIFICATION CHECKLIST

1. Does the topic sentence identify the topic and indicate the organizing principle that will be used to divide or classify this topic?
2. Has the writer used only one organizing principle per paragraph?
3. Did the writer include all the parts or members of each object or group that he or she discussed?
4. Did the writer provide approximately the same amount of detail about each group, part, or type that he or she classified?
5. If the writer was classifying parts of an object or a concept, did he or she explain how each part relates to the whole?
6. How did the writer organize his or her details? Is there a more appropriate or logical way of organizing the details?

7. How can the writer improve the unity and coherence of this draft? Where are additional transitions needed?
8. Does the paragraph end with a concluding sentence that sums up the writer's analysis of the topic?
9. Which sentences have errors in them?
10. What suggestions do you have for improving this draft?

■ EXPLORING FURTHER

The topic for the writing assignment that follows is "American families." Instead of including a paragraph or essay for you to read, this assignment begins with a list. Here are some types of families in the United States today.

- married couples without children
- unmarried couples without children
- single fathers with children
- single mothers with children
- couples with each other's stepchildren
- couples with foster children
- gay couples with children
- married or unmarried couples with biological or adopted children
- married or unmarried couples with grandchildren
- married or unmarried couples with biological or adopted children and with stepchildren
- sisters and brothers living together with or without children
- single grandparents with grandchildren
- single parents and foster children

The writing assignment that follows is based on the preceding list. Before you do the assignment, use the list to answer the following questions on a separate piece of paper.

1. Were any types of families omitted from this list? If so, what are they composed of?
2. What point or points might you want to make about this list? What purpose can you think of for writing about the different types of families in this country today?
3. What audience might be interested in this topic?
4. The writing assignment that follows asks you to write a paragraph on the types of families in America today. Which prewriting strategies could you use to develop your ideas for this paragraph—free-

writing, brainstorming, clustering, asking the five Reporter's Questions—or all of these strategies? Use them to develop ideas and details about the types of families in our country today and to classify these types.

WRITING ASSIGNMENT

When you finish writing down everything you can think of about types of families, decide on the point you want to make and how you can use classification to support this point. Choose an organizing principle and use it to organize your material into groups or categories. Then experiment with different topic sentences. Next write a discovery draft of a paragraph (or two) classifying the types of families in the United States today. Finally, use the techniques that you practiced in Chapter 4 of this book to revise, edit, and proofread your draft.

✔ POINTS TO REMEMBER ABOUT DIVISION AND CLASSIFICATION

1. Do you want to divide your topic into its parts or categories? Do you want to classify these categories based on the features they share?
2. Think about your purpose in classifying your topic. What do you want your readers to understand, to think, or to feel (based on your classification)?
3. Consider whether your readers need background information about your topic or need any terms defined or explained.
4. Select an organizing principle that makes sense to you and that seems interesting. Use this organizing principle to classify the parts or subgroups of your topic.
5. Include supporting details and examples to illustrate each part or subgroup.
6. Decide how to organize your classification logically so that readers will understand your points.
7. Cross out any irrelevant sentences or details that do not fit into the categories that you have created with the organizing principle you selected.
8. Use transitional words and expressions to show the relations between your ideas and your sentences.
9. End with a conclusion that refers to your topic (not to one of its categories).

DEFINITION

Novelist Kurt Vonnegut offers a useful bit of advice about writing: "You say what you have to say. But you have to learn to say it in such a way that the reader can see what you mean." Defining is an effective strategy for helping readers "see what you mean." When you define a word or a subject, you communicate what the word or subject means to you. This is certainly a valuable skill.

Why is it important to know how to write clear definitions? Why not simply look up unfamiliar terms in a dictionary and quote the dictionary's meanings? We can answer this question by examining a dictionary's definitions for the term *slide*. Most people associate this word with the dictionary's first definition for it: "to move along in constant contact with a surface or a substance (as in "The boxes slide down the chute like ducks on ice"). However, to children a slide is "an inclined track or chute used for fun." Musicians might define a slide as a "U-shaped section of tubing that is moved to change the pitch of brass instruments." To scientists, a slide is "a small glass plate used as a mounting for objects to be examined under a microscope." Park rangers think of a slide as "the fall of a mass of rock, snow, or earth down a slope," whereas baseball players define it as "the movement of dropping down and skidding along the ground toward a base to avoid being tagged out by the baseman." Clearly, a person's definition of a word depends on his or her topic, purpose, and audience's expectations!

USING A DICTIONARY TO DEVELOP A DEFINITION

Chapter 19, on vocabulary and diction, will show you how to use dictionaries to discover the meanings of words. However, a dictionary can provide only the *denotations* of a word—its objective, literal definitions at the particular time that the dictionary was written. For example, the dictionary definitions of the word *discriminate* include "to differentiate, recognize as being different" and "to make distinction as in treatment." These denotations are neutral; neither implies that "discriminating" is a good or a bad action.

In addition to having denotative meaning, a word can have *connotations*—emotions or feelings that people associate with the word. For example, for some people *discriminate* has a positive connotation ("to judge carefully and accurately"). For others, the same word has a negative connotation ("to treat people unfairly because they are members of a particular group"). (See pages 520–522 in Chapter 19 for practice in using denotations and connotations.) Connotations can have strong effects on readers, so you need to consider them carefully as you write.

In addition, remember that almost all words have shades or layers of meaning. The meaning of a word varies depending on its context—on who is using it and on where and why it is being used. For example, can you think of a context in which the word *bad* might mean something totally different from its traditional definition as "not good, defective"?

WRITING ACTIVITY 1

Look up the dictionary definition of each of the following words:

slim, slender, thin, skinny, gaunt

What meanings do these words have in common?

_____

_____

_____

_____

How do their connotations differ?

_____

_____

_____

_____

Often, a dictionary definition of a word doesn't really help a reader understand its meaning. Here is a quotation about this point by French writer Marcel Ayme:

From time to time I find myself terribly limited by the dictionary.

Don't let yourself be limited by dictionary denotations. As you plan definition paragraphs, consider your personal interpretations of a word and the meanings that it holds for you.

GROUP WORK 1

What do you think Marcel Ayme meant when he wrote the sentence quoted above? Did you ever find yourself "terribly limited by the dictionary"? How? Why? Form a group with two classmates and discuss his statement. Choose one person to write the group's responses and to share these with the class.

WRITING ACTIVITY 2

Below is a list of six terms. Look up the dictionary definition of each one. Write the dictionary's first definition in the appropriate space. Then write what the word means to *you*. The first one has been done as an example.

1. law and order

   Dictionary definition: *"the condition existing when people obey the rules of conduct, established and enforced by the authority or custom of a community"*

My definition: *rules set down and enforced by the police and the courts (or by sheriffs and posses in the 1800s)*

2. courage

Dictionary definition: _____

_____

My definition: _____

_____

3. liberal

Dictionary definition: _____

_____

My definition: _____

_____

4. maturity

Dictionary definition: _____

_____

My definition: _____

_____

5. handicap

Dictionary definition: _____

_____

My definition: _____

_____

6. ignorance

Dictionary definition: _____

_____

My definition: _____

_____

_____

One way to define a word is to supply a *synonym*—a word that shares the same general meaning but that has a slightly different meaning:

Prejudice is *the unfair biases* that people hold about others.

The problem with using synonyms to define words is that some synonyms have very strong positive or negative connotations, which affect the way people understand them. (See pages 520–522 in Chapter 19 for a discussion of how synonyms can suggest different meanings.) For example, here are three terms that some people might say are synonyms: ''Black,'' ''African-American,'' ''Negro.'' Do these terms have the same denotation? Do they have the same connotations? Which word do you use? Why?

_____

_____

_____

WRITING ACTIVITY 3

Plan, write, and revise a response to the following question: Why might some people want to be called ''Native Americans'' and others prefer to be called ''Indians''? Some people feel that the two terms mean the same thing. Others believe that the terms have almost nothing in common. Put yourself in the place of a person descended from people who lived in

America long before Christopher Columbus arrived here, mistakenly believing that he had landed in India. Which term might you prefer? Why?

_____

Definitions should tell readers what the term or the subject means to the writer. Here is an example of the way a writer defines what *handicap* and *ignorance* mean to her. These paragraphs are excerpted from an essay by a fourteen-year-old champion disabled runner, Sarah Reinertsen:

> It's interesting to compete in other countries because I think other cultures are less ignorant about people with disabilities. There is a type of prejudice in the United States against people who have handicaps. It was hardest when I was younger. In junior high and high school, kids are pretty mature; but on a younger level, if someone wants to hurt you, they pick on your obvious weakness, which in my case was my artificial leg. When I was younger, if the other children made fun of me in school—and they did—I didn't say anything to them. I felt sorry for *them* because I figured if that's the way their minds worked, *they* were handicapped—not me.
>
> The other way that people show their ignorance is by staring. When I was young, it used to bother me, because I didn't realize that they didn't understand my disability. Kids would say to their parents, "Hey, Mom, look at that!" and the parent would say, "Shh, don't ask questions." It always made me angry, because I think it's important for everyone to know the full story. Unless people learn about disabilities early on, they won't really accept the physically challenged as normal people.

What does the writer mean by the statement "other people were handicapped—not me"?

_____

_____

_____

_____

_____

PLANNING A DEFINITION PARAGRAPH

How long should your definition be? You know the answer: as long as you need to accomplish your purpose for your intended readers. Sometimes a phrase or a sentence is sufficient to define a term: "Sexism is discrimination based on a person's gender." A sentence definition may be appropriate when you are writing for readers who are familiar with your topic and with the vocabulary you are using. Often, however, you will need to write a paragraph to define a word or a term, especially if your readers do not have background knowledge about your subject.

Here is a student's first attempt at defining the term *sexism:*

Sexism means when people feel prejudice toward women.

Does this definition help you understand what the writer means by the term *sexism*? If not, why not?

_____

_____

_____

The writer of this definition discussed it in her writing workshop group, and her classmates pointed out several problems with her definition. First they noted that "sexism" cannot be a "when." The word *when* refers to a time or an event, and sexism is not a time. It is a kind of belief or behavior.

Next the writer's classmates pointed out that she had defined an abstract term (*sexism*) with another abstract word (*prejudice*), and they did not know what she meant by either term. They also pointed out that sexism could mean prejudice toward men. Finally, they asked her for one or two specific examples of what she thinks *sexism* means. Here is the writer's revision:

Sexism is the unfair treatment of women or men based on the belief that their gender is inferior. At one point in American history, sexism was legal. Our laws denied women the right to go to school, to vote, to own property, and to enter many professions. Nowadays, sexism consists of more subtle forms of discrimination. For example, more men get higher-status jobs than women do, and men typically make more money than women in the same occupation (with the same qualifications and same number of years of service). Sexism is illogical, and it is wrong.

The revised definition enables readers to understand exactly what the writer means when she used the term *sexism*. By giving examples of sexism, the writer increases our understanding of *sexism* and makes a statement about some of the consequences of it.

The writer of the definition paragraph on page 283 began with a topic sentence that identified the term and explained the term's main characteristic. According to this writer, the main characteristic of *sexism* is its unfair treatment based only on gender. This characteristic distinguishes sexism from other types of discrimination (such as racism, chauvinism, and ageism). The topic sentence illustrates a formal definition.

WRITING A FORMAL DEFINITION

A *formal definition* has three parts: (1) the word, term, or subject that the writer is defining, (2) the general class or category to which the term belongs, and (3) the features or characteristics that distinguish the object, person, or idea from all others in this class or category. Here are examples:

Word or Term	Class or Category	Distinguishing Features

SEXISM / is the unfair treatment of women or men / based on the belief that their gender is inferior.

AN OBOE / is a double-reed woodwind instrument / that has a range of three octaves and a high, penetrating tone.

A PEDIATRICIAN / is a doctor / who takes care of sick children and adolescents.

A PRÉCIS / is a brief written summary / that states—in the writer's own words—the main ideas in a long document.

PLAGIARISM / is writing down words or ideas / that someone else said or wrote and presenting these words or ideas as if they were your own.

> **REMINDER** ————————————————————————
> Do *not* use a word to define itself. For example, do not write "Tabescense is the physical process of becoming tabescent." This kind of definition is known as a "circular" definition because it sends readers around in circles trying to figure out what the term means. A better definition of this word might use synonyms: "Tabescense is the physical process of wasting away, withering away, or becoming too thin to survive."

When you write formal definitions, use precise, specific language to state the general class or category to which the word you are defining belongs *and* to describe its distinguishing characteristics. If your category or your characteristics are vague, readers may not understand your meaning. Here is an example of a formal definition that is too vague:

A stethoscope is a thing doctors use to listen to people's organs.

After reading this definition, you may still be confused about exactly what a stethoscope is. What kind of "thing" is it? How do doctors "use" it? (And are doctors the only people who use stethoscopes?) Here is a more precise version of this definition:

A stethoscope is an instrument that is used by medical practitioners to listen to the sounds of internal organs, such as the heart and lungs.

The following activity will give you the opportunity to practice writing a formal definition: Think about the word *power*. How would you define this term? What is power? What general category or class does it belong to? (Is it an object or a feeling? If not, what is it?) What characterizes power?

In the space below, write a formal definition of this term. (Remember, "power" is not a *when* or a *where*. *When* refers to a time, and *where* refers to a location; "power" is neither.)

Power is _____

_____

_____

_____

Below is a definition of *power*. Note that the writer of this definition stated the term and the general category in the first sentence and the distinguishing characteristics in the second sentence.

Power, properly understood, is the ability to achieve purpose. It is the strength required to bring about social, political, or economic changes.

This definition was written by Martin Luther King, Jr. How does your definition of power compare to King's?

GROUP WORK 2

Work with one or two classmates on this activity. For each of the following terms, write a topic sentence for a formal definition of the word. (You may want to consult a dictionary. See pages 524–525 in Chapter 19 about how to read dictionary entries.) The topic sentence for the first term has been written as an example.

1. hydroponics

Hydroponics is the science of growing plants without soil.

2. biology
3. acrophobia
4. AIDS
5. electricity
6. family
7. euphemism

WRITING ACTIVITY 4

Do some brainstorming and clustering about the qualities or behavior of a "good teacher." Then develop a topic sentence for a paragraph about the definition of a "good teacher." (Don't write the paragraph; just write the topic sentence.)

GROUP WORK 3

Form a group with three or four other students and take turns reading your topic sentences defining a "good teacher." Which characteristics did all group members mention? Which ones would you add to your definition? Did you disagree with any classmate's definition of a good teacher? Why?

GROUP WORK 4

Reread the excerpt by Gloria Naylor on pages 192–195 of Chapter 6. In this essay, Naylor explores how words get their meanings. The two words she defines are *nigger* and *girl*. Form a group with two or three other students and answer the following questions. Choose a recorder to write the group's answers.

1. What different definitions does Naylor offer for the term *nigger* in this essay? What does each mean?
2. Did Naylor convince you that the meaning of the word *nigger* varies depending on who says it to whom and why? If so, which details in the essay did you find most convincing? If not, why not?
3. How does your dictionary define the word *girl*? What are the similarities and the differences between your dictionary's definition of this word and Naylor's definition?
4. How does Naylor develop her definitions? Where in her essay does she use narration to define a word? Where does she use description? Where does she use comparison and contrast? What do these examples tell you about how *you* can develop written definitions?

As with all writing, the topic sentence and the details you develop for your definition paragraphs depend on your topic, your purpose, and your readers' knowledge and expectations. Here are some questions to consider as you plan your definitions.

DEFINING FOR SPECIFIC PURPOSES AND READERS

Determine the details and the strategies you will use to develop your definitions by considering your purpose and your audience. Ask yourself these questions:

1. Do I want readers to understand an unfamiliar term or subject?
2. Do I want readers to get a new or fresh understanding of a familiar word or topic?
3. Do I want to explain how the meaning of a word has changed over time (or from one generation to the next)?
4. Do I want to explain why a term is often misunderstood or used incorrectly?
5. Do I want to argue for a particular definition of a word or a subject?
6. How much do my readers already know about the term or subject I am defining?
7. What else do readers need to know about the subject or about me in order to understand my definition?
8. What examples and explanations would best accomplish my purpose in writing this definition for these readers?

WRITING ACTIVITY 5

Reread the ideas that you wrote for Writing Activity 4 and Group Work 3 on page 286 of this chapter. If some of your friends asked you to write a paragraph defining a "good teacher," what qualities or behaviors would you include in your definition?

_____

_____

_____

What might some of your purposes be in writing a definition of a good teacher for your friends?

_____

_____

_____

Plan, write, and revise a paragraph that accomplishes one of these purposes.

SELECTING A STRATEGY FOR YOUR PURPOSE AND AUDIENCE

Strategies for defining words or terms vary. Depending on your purpose and readers, you might simply write a synonym for the term. Or you could look up a word in a dictionary and quote its definitions—its dictionary meanings. You might write a subjective definition that communicates your personal interpretation of the term. You could define something by comparing it to or contrasting it with other things. Or you could write a formal definition that identifies the class or category to which the term belongs and explain how it differs from others in that class. All of these strategies have the same goal: to explain your understanding of what something is and what it is not.

DEFINITION STRATEGIES ━━━━━━━━━━━━━━━━━━━

Here are examples of different ways to define terms.

- *Use a synonym: Prejudice—the unfair biases* people have about others—can lead to discrimination.
- *Quote a dictionary definition:* According to my dictionary, prejudice is "a judgment or opinion formed before the facts are known."
- *Give a personal example:* When I hear people of different ethnic backgrounds tell me how amazing it is that I have succeeded, I know I am experiencing their prejudice.
- *Make a comparison or a contrast:* Prejudice and discrimination are both based on irrational negative attitudes, but Dr. Martin Luther King, Jr., illustrated the difference between them when he said, "The law may not make a man love me, but it can restrain him from lynching me."
- *Develop a formal definition:* Prejudice is a negative attitude or opinion that a person holds without knowing the facts about someone or something or in spite of facts that contradict this attitude or opinion.

Remember that you can use all the strategies that you have been practicing in this book to define words. Here are five topic sentences, each illustrating one of the strategies described in the preceding five chapters. The term defined is *nurse*.

DESCRIPTION: A nurse is a man or a woman who is trained to take care of people too sick, injured, or elderly to take care of themselves. [The remainder of the paragraph will provide examples that describe these nursing responsibilities.]

NARRATION: My experiences as a man in the nursing profession have provided me with many insights into what a nurse is and what he or she does.

PROCESS ANALYSIS: Becoming a good nurse requires a graduate degree in nursing, experience taking care of sick people, and compassion and patience.

COMPARISON AND CONTRAST: Although nurses do not have the same training and skills that doctors have, they can perform many medical procedures.

DIVISION AND CLASSIFICATION: Nurses can be classified according to their major responsibilities, such as: surgical, pediatric (children), or geriatric (the elderly).

Here is an example of how a student used several strategies to develop a paragraph defining the word *nurse.*

My experiences as a man in the nursing profession have provided me with many insights into what a nurse is and what he or she does. Officially, my job responsibilities are the same as those of any other nurse: taking care of people who are too sick, injured, or elderly to take care of themselves. I give patients medicine and shots, I change bandages and clean wounds, and I monitor temperatures and pulse rates. In addition, I do other things that I consider part of being a nurse. I listen to patients, and I try to comfort them. When a patient dies, I talk to the family and help console them. Doing all of these things has helped me realize how important it is for a nurse to have comprehensive professional training and excellent "people" skills. It has also helped me see that nursing focuses on helping patients and their family and friends cope with illness. I don't look like the stereotype of a nurse—a woman in a white uniform and white nursing cap—but I think I am an example of a good nurse. Not a "male nurse"; just a "successful nurse."

WRITING ACTIVITY 6

Plan, write, and revise a paragraph defining *success.* First decide on a purpose for writing this paragraph and think of an audience who might like to know your definition of *success.* Then do some prewriting about this term. What does success mean to you? To your family? To your friends? In your opinion, what public figures embody success? Why do you consider these men and/or women successful?

Use one or more of the five strategies described above (description, narration, process analysis, comparison and contrast, or classification) to develop details for a paragraph defining success.

WRITING ACTIVITY 7

Plan, write, and revise *another* paragraph defining *success*. This time, use a different strategy or strategies (description, narration, process analysis, comparison and contrast, or classification) to develop your paragraph.

In Chapter 4, you learned how to use facts, statistics, and testimony to support your topic sentence. These kinds of details provide an excellent way of developing a definition paragraph, as illustrated by the student paragraph below.

In the recent competition to admit more minority students to their schools, college administrators are playing around with the definition of "minority." My school's financial forms define a minority as "a person of African, Hispanic, Asian, Native American, or other non-European ancestry." I didn't know what to check on the form, since my great-grandmother was Irish and my great-grandfather was Chicano-American. Does that make me a minority? Or is the term *minority* defined by numbers and percentages? According to a recent report of the Quality Education Minorities Project (*Education That Works*), people "of non-European ancestry" account for about one-third of all Americans and about 30% of American college students. This report notes that by the year 2075, "minorities" will account for the majority of people in America. How will we define "minority" then?

GROUP WORK 5

Form a group with two other students and choose one person to record the group's answers to the following questions about the preceding paragraph.

1. What is the writer's topic sentence and purpose?
2. Which detail—or details—are most convincing in supporting this topic sentence?
3. What source does the writer cite for these facts and statistics?
4. Is this source reliable? Why or why not?
5. The preceding paragraph is a draft. What suggestions do you have for revision?

If you don't remember how to use facts, statistics, and testimony in your definition paragraphs, read "Guidelines for Using Statistics as Supporting Details" on pages 115–116 and "Guidelines for Using Testimony as a Supporting Detail" on pages 117–118 (in Chapter 4).

WRITING ACTIVITY 8

Plan, write, and revise a paragraph or two defining the term *minority*. Use one or more of the strategies that you learned about in this chapter. In addition, try to find relevant facts, statistics, and/or testimony to support your topic sentence.

REMINDER _____

Strategies for developing strong definition paragraphs include using a synonym, quoting a dictionary definition, describing examples, narrating a story, analyzing a process, making comparisons or contrasts, and classifying the term or subject into groups or types.

DEFINING BY NEGATION

Yet another strategy for supporting the main point of your definition paragraphs is to explain what the term does *not* mean (or what it might be mistaken for) before you explain what it does mean. Here is an example.

Many people think that a nurse is a smiling woman, in a white uniform and cap, whose main jobs are to take your temperature and change your bedpan while you're in the hospital. However, this stereotype of a nurse is not correct. Today's nurses are both male and female. They are trained professionals who offer comfort and assistance to people who are ill or who are experiencing great physical or mental stress. Nurses work in hospital bedrooms and in operating rooms; they also help people in institutions and provide professional home care. Using their medical and psychological training, nurses plan and implement patients' care and help patients recover from illnesses. Finally, a good nurse also teaches his or her patients how to stay healthy.

Note that the writer began by describing what she thought were readers' preconceived notions of what a nurse is. Then she explained what a nurse is and what nurses do.

WRITING ACTIVITY 9

Choose *one* of the terms below, and define it by negation. Plan a paragraph that begins by explaining what this term does not mean. Then use one or more of the strategies discussed in this chapter to explain what the term does mean. After you plan and write this paragraph, revise it using the techniques that you practiced in Chapter 4.

- intelligence
- courage
- sex appeal
- failure
- disability
- honor

REMINDER ━━━━━━━━━━━━━━━━━━━━━━━━━━━━━━━━━
Defining a concrete object (which people can experience through one or more of their senses) is different from defining an abstract term. Abstract terms (such as *love, freedom,* and *integrity*) represent ideas or concepts, so their meaning is subject to differing interpretations. When you define an abstract term, use precise language and give examples of exactly what you mean by this term.

As you read the student paragraph below, think about the strategies that the writer used to define the abstract word *beauty*.

The old cliché "beauty is in the eyes of the beholder" is not always true; sometimes beauty can be judged through a person's ears. To me, beauty is the voice of Marian Anderson, the first famous black soloist. Her voice embodies all the things we usually associate with beauty: elegance, grace, sweetness. Its velvety richness, stretching across three octaves, is exquisitely pleasing and satisfying to hear. I remember the first time I heard her voice streaming from a recording of spiritual music. I was overcome by its loveliness. None of Anderson's successsors (Leontyne Price, Jessye Norman, and Kathleen Battle) can match the perfection of her vocal gifts. When Marian Anderson died, the world lost a truly great beauty.

ORGANIZING A DEFINITION PARAGRAPH

Definition paragraphs can be organized from the least important example to the most important one—or vice versa. You can also try organizing your details or examples in order of their general familiarity (from best known to least familiar). If you are using narration to develop a definition paragraph, then chronological order is probably the most appropriate way of organizing your stories and examples.

Here are some transitions that can make your definitions more unified and coherent.

> **TRANSITIONS THAT INDICATE DEFINITION** ━━━━━
> The following transitional words and phrases often signal definition.
>
> *For example, . . . for instance, . . . by definition, another type of . . .*

WRITING ACTIVITY 10

Look up the dictionary definition of the word *abortion*. Write it here:

_____

_____

What are some synonyms that people use for *abortion* (such as "fetus murder" or "a woman's choice")? Look through newspapers, magazines, and journals to find the synonyms people use for *abortion* and the different ways they define this term. Write these synonyms and definitions below:

_____

_____

_____

_____

_____

Plan, write, and revise a paragraph or two defining what *abortion* means. Include your personal interpretation of this word, facts, and testimony (definitions that you have read).

USING DEFINITION ACROSS THE COLLEGE CURRICULUM

Many academic assignments ask students to define terms, concepts, places, or objects in order to illustrate the students' knowledge about these subjects:

1. Explain the differences between a geologist's definition of the term *pitch* and a machinist's definition of this word.
2. Write a definition of Piaget's concrete operational stage that would enable a student in an introductory psychology course to understand this concept.
3. Define *neurosis* and *psychosis* and then compare and contrast them.

4. Define *deviance*. Is there such a thing as positive deviance? If not, why not? If so, define this and describe at least two examples.

Definitions for writing in college courses depend on one's purpose and readers.

WRITING ACTIVITY 11

Do you know your college major yet? If not, what career or discipline are you most interested in now? Choose a word that is important in this major or field but that most people who are not in the field would not know or do not really understand. (For example, if you are majoring in economics, you would know what the terms *bimetallism* or *coincident indicators* or *monetarist* mean, but most of the general public would not.) Write this term at the top of a piece of paper and then explain what it means to you. Next write down a dictionary definition of this word and a definition provided by one or more of your textbooks in the discipline from which you have selected the word. Then do the following:

1. Imagine that you are answering a take-home examination in a course in your major area. Plan, write, and revise a one- or two-paragraph definition of this term for the professor of the course, who wants to evaluate your understanding of this term.
2. Imagine that you are writing a definition of this term for your English teacher, who knows almost nothing about the term. Plan, write, and revise a one- or two-paragraph definition of the term for this teacher, who wants to evaluate your ability to write definitions.

GETTING READERS' RESPONSES

Use the checklist below to help you revise the drafts of your definition paragraphs.

DEFINITION CHECKLIST

1. Does the definition have a clear, focused topic sentence that is neither too narrow nor too broad? If so, what is it? If not, what might it bc?
2. Do the examples and explanations in the paragraph support the topic sentence? Should the writer cross out or revise any of them? (If so, which ones?)

---

3. Did the writer use precise words that helped you understand exactly what he or she means by the term? If not, which words or sentences were too vague?

4. Did the writer help you see what the term does *not* mean (in addition to what it does mean)? If not, should he or she add this ''negative'' definition? If so, where?

5. Did the writer create a circular definition by using a word—or a form of that word—to define itself?

6. How did the writer organize his or her details? Is there a more appropriate or logical way of organizing the details?

7. How can the writer improve the unity and coherence of this draft? Where are transitions needed?

8. Does the paragraph end with a concluding sentence that sums up the writer's interpretation of the term?

9. Which sentences have errors in them?

10. What suggestions do you have for improving this description?

■ EXPLORING FURTHER

The poet Robert Frost once said, ''Home is the place where, when you have to go there, they have to take you in.'' (Note that Frost's use of *where* in this explanation is appropriate because he *is* defining home as a place.) What is a ''home''? Take out paper and do some freewriting, brainstorming, and/or clustering about what the word *home* means to you.

When you finish writing your notes, read the following definition of the word *home.* It is a newspaper editorial by the writer Jonathan Van Meter.

Homes Don't Have to Pretend

Home is not the loft I live in. There are too many useless pipes and rattling windows for it to be called a home. It is too big and boxy to ever be thought of as sweet. The loft I live in pretends to be my home, but it is not. It has an ulterior motive. All filled up with 50's furniture, good light and open space, it is an esthetic environment, carefully arranged and decorated in an attempt to impress myself—to prove that I have good taste.

There are too many locks on the doors, too many mice, too little understanding of what it used to be, too many people above and below me, whom I don't know and don't care to know, too many cold spots, too few closets, too many lamps and chairs that never actually get used and too few people living in it to call it home. And, most crucially, the kitchen has never been anything but an oversized coffee maker and a place to keep the milk (for the coffee) cold.

The place where I live and the home of my mind will never match. Mostly because the place where I live is a very physical, very obvious attempt to distance myself from my home—a place that served the exact opposite purpose of the loft I live in now. Function was the point. It was very honest about what it was. It was a place that had exactly enough beds for the seven people who lived there. A phone, a bathroom, a couch. No answering machines, no remote controls, no original art. The kitchen was so overused it seemed to wear out every couple of months. Things were replaced or removed when they didn't work any longer, not when they began to bore someone or fell out of style. Nothing reflected anyone's taste, good or bad, and the colors of everything always seemed wrong.

But there were drama and people and voices and no locks on the doors. And now it is November, and home is where my heart wants to go. Unfortunately I can never go there again. My family has moved away, and a psychologist from the Bronx has moved in. He has no children and all his plants are dead.

Discussion Questions

1. What was your response to Van Meter's definition of his home?
2. What might be another title for this essay?
3. What was the writer's purpose in this essay? What did he want to show or convince his readers of?
4. Which details were most effective in enabling you to understand what the writer means by the term *home*?
5. What did the writer mean when he stated, "The place where I live and the home of my mind will never match"? Reread your notes about the word *home*. Does a home have to be a place? If so, what kind of place is it? If not, can a home be a state of mind or a feeling?

 WRITING ASSIGNMENT

Plan, write, and revise a paragraph or two defining what a home means to you. Develop your details and examples using one or more of the strategies that you practiced in this chapter. Decide on a logical order for your details, and end with a conclusion that sums up your personal interpretation of this word.

✔ POINTS TO REMEMBER ABOUT DEFINITION

1. Think about your purpose in defining your topic. What do you want your readers to understand, to think, or to feel after they read your definition?

2. Which strategies might accomplish this purpose best (for your intended readers)?

3. Consider whether readers need background information about your topic in order to understand your definition.

4. Consult a dictionary, but do not copy the dictionary's definition. Instead, explain your interpretation of what the term means.

5. If you are writing a formal definition, make sure that you have included details that really distinguish the term from other terms in its class or category.

6. Decide how to organize your definition logically so that readers will understand your points.

7. Cross out any irrelevant sentences or details that do not expand your definition.

8. Use transitional words and expressions to show the relations between your ideas and your sentences.

9. End with a conclusion that sums up your interpretation of the word or topic you are defining.

10. Revise and edit your definition for clarity and correctness.

C H A P T E R

CAUSE-AND-EFFECT ANALYSIS

Cause-and-effect analysis helps people make sense of the events, conditions, and problems in their lives. This kind of analysis answers the questions "Why?" "What made this happen?" "What will happen as a result of this?" When you explain causes and effects, you show how events, conditions, or problems are connected.

Every academic course requires you to analyze causes and effects. All disciplines ask students to break down problems—to explain why and how a problem occurred, to explain or predict what its consequences were (or may be), and to consider ways of solving the problem. An important part of thinking and understanding is the ability to explain why events, conditions, or problems happened and to indicate their consequences.

In the paragraph below, a student writer explains some causes for people's seasonal eating habits. The writer supports her analysis with personal interpretations, facts, and expert testimony.

Thanksgiving is over, my family is thinking up new ways to cook leftover bird, and I'm wondering why Americans almost always serve turkey at this holiday. Why do we eat certain foods at certain holidays or times of the year? Why do we drink eggnog at Christmas and not at Easter? And why do many of us eat heavy foods like meat and pudding in the winter and lighter foods like salads and iced desserts in the summer? The commonsense answer to these questions is that our seasonal eating habits are cultural. We grow up associating specific foods with specific holidays or times of the year. We learn from parents, friends, and neighbors to serve up special foods for special holidays. But seasonal eating has other causes. Some foods, like certain fruits or vegetables, are available only in some months. In addition, food has psychological meaning for people. Most of us associate barbecues and ices with being outdoors in the summer, and we think of hot chocolate as a great food for cuddling up with indoors during the cold months. Furthermore, researchers have found that we crave different foods in different seasons in order to regulate our bodies' needs. For instance, in the summer when we sweat, we need fruits and salads to replace the water in our system. In the winter, our metabolism slows and we eat more fat and protein to heat up our bodies. So although we may not be aware of why we crave hot dogs at summer picnics or turkey at Thanksgiving, seasonal eating is a fact of our lives.

Note that the writer clearly identified the phenomenon that she wanted to explain—seasonal eating. Instead of beginning with a topic sentence, she began with the question that the paragraph would answer: "Why do we eat certain foods at certain holidays or times of the year?"

The writer accomplished her purpose—to explain seasonal eating habits—by providing several specific examples and facts. She examined obvious causes *and* less apparent underlying causes. In addition, she developed her details logically, moving from subjective interpretations to objective, research-based facts.

This cause-and-effect analysis illustrates critical-thinking skills. The writer did not stop after she explained her first "commonsense" cause for seasonal eating habits. Instead, she realized that most effects result from many interrelated causes, and she mentioned three causes in her paragraph (cultural habits, food availability, and physical needs). Be a critical thinker: Remember that most events, conditions, and problems have multiple causes *and* multiple effects.

DECIDING ON A PURPOSE AND DEVELOPING A TOPIC SENTENCE

One of the best sources of topics for cause-and-effect compositions is your own life. Novelist Eudora Welty noted that "writing a story or a novel is one way of discovering sequence in experience, of stumbling upon cause and effect in the happenings of a writer's own life." Have you been keeping an Idea Bank, like the one described on pages 4 and 5 in Chapter 1? Have you been using it to try to analyze the causes of "happenings" in your life? If not, it's never too late to start. Remember that an Idea Bank is a notebook in which writers record their observations, thoughts, and feelings.

Read through your Idea Bank to find appropriate topics for cause-and-effect analyses. Look for an important decision that you wrote about. You might want to examine the reasons why this decision was a difficult one to make. Could you explain how and why you reached your decision? Could you describe the results or the consequences of this decision? If this does not seem interesting to you, then look for a problem that you described in your Idea Bank or that you are having now. Could you write about the people or things that caused this problem? Or about some ways you might solve it? Could you predict some effects of solving this problem?

After you select a topic for a cause-and-effect analysis, you need to decide on your purpose for writing.

**COMMON PURPOSES FOR WRITING
CAUSAL ANALYSES** ━━━━━━━━━━━━━━━━━━━━━━━━━━━

Here are some purposes for explaining causes or effects:

- To express and support an opinion (a subjective interpretation) about the reasons for or the results of a particular condition, event, or problem
- To explain the causes or effects of a particular condition, event, or problem that readers may not be informed about
- To persuade readers that your analysis of causes or effects is logical and convincing

---

The topic sentence of a cause-and-effect analysis should state the event, condition, or problem you are analyzing and indicate whether you are empha-sizing causes or effects. In a single paragraph, it is probably wise to focus on either causes or effects rather than discuss both. For example, imagine that your teacher has asked you to write a paragraph or two about "childhood problems." You have narrowed your focus down to "children's problems with popularity." Here is a possible topic sentence for a paragraph that focuses on causes:

There are several reasons why some children are unpopular.

And here is one for a paragraph focusing on effects:

Children who are rejected by their peers can develop long-lasting emotional scars.

WRITING ACTIVITY 1

Write a topic sentence for each of the following subjects. The first one has been done as an example.

1. Effects of having a pet

   Although a pet is a big responsibility, it provides its owner with much affection and happiness.

2. Reasons why students have part-time jobs

   _____

   _____

3. Effects of going to school and working at a job

   _____

   _____

4. Reasons why we need to stop polluting the air

   _____

   _____

5. Effects of air pollution

   _____

   _____

6. Reasons why teenagers drink alcoholic beverages

_____

_____

7. Effects of moving to a new place

_____

_____

8. The grade that you think you will receive in one of your courses and the reasons why you think you will receive this grade

_____

_____

_____

 GROUP WORK 1

Work with one or two classmates on this activity. Below are the first seven subjects of the preceding Writing Activity. Take turns reading aloud your topic sentences for each subject. Decide which person's topic sentence is the most interesting and write it in the space next to each subject. Then together develop at least three causes or effects for each topic sentence. The first one has been done as an example. When you do this activity, use a separate piece of paper to write your causes and effects.

1. Effects of having a pet

Best topic sentence: _Although a pet is a big responsibility, it provides its owner with much affection and happiness._

Three effects:

1. Pets can provide their owners with unconditional love or affection.
2. Playing with one's pet can be relaxing and very enjoyable.
3. Taking good care of a pet makes a person feel better about himself or herself.

2. Reasons why students have part-time jobs

Best topic sentence: _____

_____

Three or more causes: _____

_____

3. Effects of going to school and working at a job

Best topic sentence: _____

_____

Three or more effects: _____

_____

4. Reasons why we need to stop polluting the air

Best topic sentence: _____

_____

Three or more causes: _____

_____

5. Effects of air pollution

Best topic sentence: _____

_____

Three or more effects: _____

_____

6. Reasons why teenagers drink alcoholic beverages

Best topic sentence: _____

_____

Three or more causes: _____

_____

7. Effects of moving to a new place

Best topic sentence: _____

_____

Three or more effects: _____

_____

DEVELOPING DETAILS FOR A CAUSE-AND-EFFECT ANALYSIS

Developing and selecting details for cause-and-effect paragraphs requires you to think carefully about the amount of background information you will need to provide for your reader. Here are questions to help you think about this.

ANTICIPATING READERS' NEEDS AND EXPECTATIONS

Write answers to the following questions:

1. Who are your readers, and what background information might

they need about the event, condition, or problem you are analyzing?
2. How familiar are readers with some of the causes or effects
that you are analyzing?
3. Which causes or effects might readers feel strongly about? Will
their feelings make them challenge your interpretation of certain causes or effects?
4. What evidence should you provide to convince readers of the
soundness of your analysis?

Depending on your focus, your purpose, and your readers' expectations, you can use any of the strategies that you already have practiced in this book to develop a cause-and-effect paragraph. For example, here is a student paragraph in which the writer used narration to support his topic sentence about the effects of childhood unpopularity.

Children who are rejected by their peers can develop long-lasting emotional scars. I know this only too well because I am twenty-two years old and I still feel the effects of being unpopular as a child. I still have problems making and keeping friends. When I was younger, I was a quiet, studious child. The other kids called me names like "geek" and "nerd" because I would always rather read than play. I only had one or two friends as a teenager and I always felt lonely and sad. I longed to be part of a crowd, but I couldn't figure out how to join any group. Today I am a straight-A student, but I'm miserable. I still feel jerky and "uncool." In fact, being the schoolboy nerd made me paranoid. Now when classmates talk to me or are nice to me, I always suspect them of wanting my help with their work or of wanting to borrow my notes. I don't know how to respond naturally to their conversations, and I often feel nervous and awkward. I'm seeing a social worker for therapy now, and I'm doing better in social situations. However, I don't think I'll ever get over being rejected as a child.

This writer narrates a story to support his main point. In Chapter 6, you learned that narration is a technique for relating events that happened over time. Since *effects* are events, conditions, or problems that follow *causes* in time, narration is an effective strategy for developing a cause-and-effect analysis. But you can use the other strategies that you practiced in this book to explain causes and effects. For example, here is a paragraph that offers facts and personal examples to make its point.

One of the most painful parts of growing up is being rejected by other children. There are several reasons why some children are unpopular. Often it seems that unpopular kids are different. They don't like to do the things that others kids do. They're often loners or they don't follow the crowd. Also, many unpopular children alienate other kids by their behavior. Some are overly aggressive or bossy; others are very passive and aloof. This behavior is often a symptom of more serious problems. Children who seem different and lonely often lack the social skills that other children develop naturally. Unpopular children don't know how to start conversations or join groups. I see this in my son's behavior. He just doesn't seem to be able to "read" social cues. He doesn't pick up on the other kids' reactions to what he says and does. So other children perceive him as "different" or immature and they don't want to play with him. He is working with the school psychologist now, and he's learning how to listen, to cooperate, and to get along better with other children. However, there is nothing he can do about another cause of childhood unpopularity: kids' desires to exclude other children (to pick on them and keep them out). In order for some children to be the "in" group or club, they have to reject or exclude other children. Regardless of the reasons for their problems, unpopular children suffer greatly.

The writer of this paragraph has obviously given much consideration to the different reasons why some children are unpopular. Her details support her main point clearly and effectively.

The details you select and develop for cause-and-effect analyses depend on your purpose. For instance, if you wanted to share your feelings about the causes of a problem, you could describe the personal experiences and observations that influenced your beliefs. On the other hand, if you wanted to persuade readers to believe your analysis, you would need to provide them with factual evidence for your assertions.

WRITING ACTIVITY 2

Choose an event in your life that had significant or long-lasting effects on your emotions and/or your behavior. Describe this event and explain its effects. If you have difficulty thinking of an event, here are some possibilities:

- Getting into the college of my choice
- Being rejected by the college of my choice
- Having a terrific teacher
- Going into military service
- Becoming a parent
- Becoming a grandparent
- Becoming an aunt or an uncle

> **REMINDER** ————————————————————————
> If you want to support a cause-and-effect analysis with facts, statistics, or testimony, see pages 115 through 118 in Chapter 4 for guidelines about how to do this correctly.

Sometimes when you are describing a complex condition, event, or problem, you may find it difficult to distinguish between causes and effects. For instance, read the draft paragraph below. Which details are causes? Which are effects?

Many of us drift away from our childhood friends as we grow older. Friendships often fade and die when friends go their own ways. For example, when our friends move away, it becomes increasingly difficult to stay in touch with them. Phone calls to distant friends can't replace face-to-face conversations with pals who live close by. So we often find ourselves talking to faraway friends less and less, and finally we discover that we don't have much to say to them anymore. It's difficult to keep a long-distance friendship alive.

Did you notice that several details in this paragraph are both causes *and* effects? The causes and effects in this paragraph work like a chain reaction: Each effect becomes the cause of another effect. Here is a summary of the chain reaction—or *causal chain*—in the preceding paragraph.

When friends move away, we find it increasingly difficult to stay in touch with them, which causes us to talk to them less frequently, which causes us to have less and less to say to them, which causes the friendship to end.

As you evaluate the cause-effect relations between events or conditions, consider the possible causal chain reactions and explain them in detail.

UNDERSTANDING CAUSE-EFFECT RELATIONS

In Chapter 4, you learned about reading and thinking critically. Remember that critical thinking involves questioning the logic and the effectiveness of a piece of writing. As you develop a cause-and-effect analysis, remember that most events, conditions, or problems have more than one cause. For instance, you might be having a problem with a parent or with a child and you might assume that the other person's behavior is causing this problem. However, if you think critically about the problem, you may realize that it has other causes, such as the person's reactions to your own attitudes or behavior. You might even determine that the current problem is part of an ongoing problem related to the ways all the members of your family treat one another.

When you develop ideas for a cause-and-effect analysis, think carefully about the relations between the events or conditions that you are describing. Avoid the two common errors in cause-and-effect analyses. These errors, sometimes called "logical traps" or "logical fallacies," are explained below.

TWO COMMON LOGICAL FALLACIES
IN CAUSE-AND-EFFECT ANALYSIS

Critical thinkers and writers do *not* do the following:

1. *Oversimplify* the causes of an event, a condition, or a problem by stating that it has only one cause. Here is an example of an

oversimplified cause-effect statement: ''The children in my son's class exclude him because they are all mean and nasty.'' Maybe the children in this boy's class reject him because he behaves unacceptably. Keep in mind that most effects have several causes.

2. *Make a false assumption* that something caused an event, a condition, or a problem just because it happened right before the event or the condition. Here is an example of this problem: ''My son must be unpopular because several children in the class refused to play with him after school this week.'' Maybe these children could not play with the writer's son because they had to do chores after school or go places with a parent. Remember that a cause and an effect that seem related may actually have occurred coincidentally (and may not be causally related at all).

Critical thinkers consider all the possible causes of an effect and decide which ones are logically related. For example, imagine a situation in which a student thinks she is doing really well in a course, but she keeps receiving grades of *C* on her papers and tests. Here are some reactions she might have:

1. My teacher doesn't like or respect female students.
2. My teacher doesn't like or respect me.
3. My teacher isn't grading my work fairly.
4. My teacher's standards and grading criteria are too high.
5. My teacher thinks I'm not improving enough.
6. My teacher thinks I could work harder and do better.
7. I'm misinterpreting my teacher's assignments or instructions.

As the student thinks about each possibility, she dismisses the first two as immature reactions because she doesn't have any evidence to support them. She decides to explore the third and fourth possible causes by talking with classmates and examining their essays and grades. Finally, she decides to make an appointment with her teacher to discuss the other three possible causes of her low grades. After talking with her classmates and teacher, this student concludes that the last two causes are the reasons for her grades. This conclusion is based on logical and relevant evidence, and it enables her to plan a course of action for improving her writing and her grades.

 GROUP WORK 2

Form a group with two or three classmates and choose one person to write down the group's responses. Examine each topic sentence.

What is the problem (or problems) with the logic of the cause-and-effect analysis in each statement?

1. If teenagers watched less television, they would do better in school.
2. My typed essays receive higher grades from my English teacher than do my handwritten essays, so typing must improve the quality of my writing.
3. Asian-American students do better in college and graduate in larger numbers than do other minority groups in America because they are so much smarter.
4. Sexual harassment in high school isn't taken seriously by administrators because most of the principals and deans are men and they dismiss it as "boys being boys."
5. Union members who strike are selfish and greedy.
6. Most unwed mothers give up their infants for adoption because they can't take care of them.
7. Automobile insurance rates are higher for teenage drivers than they are for adults because teenagers are worse drivers than adults.
8. Many professional athletes take drugs to help them deal with the intense psychological pressure of being superstars.
9. Information about sex and sexually transmitted diseases leads to increased sexual activity among teenagers.
10. Many college students drop out of college because they cannot afford the high tuition.

When you use cause-and-effect analysis to solve problems, you are explaining why the problem has happened and what you (or the people involved) should do about it. The first step in solving a problem is figuring out exactly what the problem is and its probable causes. The next step is thinking about all the possible solutions to the problems and considering the consequences of each solution.

Here are some questions to consider as you use cause-and-effect analysis to describe and explain problems and solutions.

USING CAUSE-AND-EFFECT ANALYSIS TO SOLVE PROBLEMS ━━━━━━━━━━━━

Think critically about the many possible causes and effects of the problem that you are analyzing.

- What and who caused this problem? How? Why?
- Are there any other possible causes of this problem?
- What are the effects of this problem (for everyone involved in it)?
- What are the possible solutions to the problem?
- Who can I talk to about the pros and cons of each solution?
- What consequences would each solution lead to?
- What is the best solution? Why?

WRITING ACTIVITY 3

Write a ''Letter to the Editor'' for your school newspaper, analyzing the school's most serious problem. What is this problem? What are the obvious causes of this problem? What other conditions might be causing this problem? Can you recommend any solutions?

WRITING ACTIVITY 4

Think about the best teacher you ever had *or* the best course that you have ever taken. How do you define ''best''? (See Chapter 10 about defining terms.) Do some prewriting about the possible reasons why you think the teacher or the course was so effective. You might want to make a list of reasons why you liked or admired this teacher or why you enjoyed or benefited from this course. Develop your ideas into an analysis that explains why you think this teacher or course was so important for you.

ORGANIZING A CAUSE-AND-EFFECT PARAGRAPH

The organization of a cause-and-effect paragraph depends on whether you are emphasizing causes or effects and on the supporting details that you have developed. If you are narrating events or describing a causal chain, you might want to develop your details chronologically. If you are explaining the reasons why a condition or a problem exists, you might use emphatic order (least important reason to most important). Another strategy for organizing your details is the one illustrated in the paragraph on seasonal eating on pages 300–301 of this chapter. This writer moved from personal reasons to objective or research-based facts. Logical organization helps readers follow your ideas and understand which causes or effects are minor and which are major.

Here are some transitions you can use to organize your details and to make your cause-and-effect analyses more unified and coherent.

TRANSITIONS THAT INDICATE
CAUSE-AND-EFFECT ANALYSIS ━━━━━━━━━━━━━━━━━

These transitional words and phrases signal causes and effects.

Causes: *one reason why, because, another reason is that, first, next, the most important cause, finally*

Effects: *for this reason, thus, therefore, as a result, another consequence, the most significant effect, since, accordingly, consequently, hence*

GROUP WORK 3

Form a group with two or three classmates and choose one person to record the group's responses. Together develop ideas for *one* of the following cause-and-effect topics: ''Reasons College Students Cheat'' or ''The Effects of Cheating in College.'' Together choose which topic to consider and experiment with different topic sentences. Then list all the causes or effects that the group can think of.

WRITING ACTIVITY 5

Write a paragraph or two based on the topic sentence and ideas that your group developed for the preceding Group Work activity. When you revise your paragraph, make sure that you have included appropriate transitions to signal the relations between your ideas.

USING CAUSE-AND-EFFECT ANALYSIS ACROSS THE COLLEGE CURRICULUM

Many academic assignments ask students to define terms, concepts, places, or objects in order to illustrate the students' knowledge about these subjects:

1. Do you agree or disagree that watching violent television increases children's violent or aggressive behavior?
2. What causes hurricanes? What causes tornadoes? How are these causes similar? How do they differ?

3. Discuss the causes of schizophrenia and explain how these causes interact with one another.
4. What are the current and future effects of the increasing unemployment in our city?
5. Predict the consequences of the recent changes in Medicare laws. What consequences will these changes have for people who depend on Medicare? What consequences will they have for taxpayers? Provide evidence to support your predictions.

All of these assignments require writers to use the strategies that you have been practicing in this chapter:

- Thinking about readers' knowledge of the topic and their expectations
- Considering all possible causes and effects
- Figuring out which causes or effects are the most logical
- Providing adequate evidence to support the cause-effect relations
- Organizing details logically and coherently

GETTING READERS' RESPONSES

Use the checklist below to help you revise the drafts of your cause-and-effect analysis paragraphs.

CAUSE-AND-EFFECT CHECKLIST

1. Does the analysis have a clear, focused topic sentence that is neither too narrow nor too broad? If so, what is it? If not, what might it be?
2. Is the writer's purpose clear?
3. Do readers need background information about the topic in order to understand the analysis?
4. Do the examples and explanations in the paragraph support the topic sentence? Should the writer cross out or review any of them? (If so, which ones?)
5. Did the writer oversimplify causes or effects?
6. Did the writer make any errors in logic (for example, stating that one event caused another simply because it preceded the other—when in reality the two events were related only by coincidence)?
7. Did the writer explain each cause or effect clearly and specifically and provide enough evidence to convince you of the accuracy of his or her analysis?

(Continued)

8. How did the writer organize his or her details? Is there a more appropriate or logical way of organizing the details?
9. Does the paragraph end with a concluding sentence that sums up the writer's analysis?
10. What suggestions do you have for improving this draft?

■ EXPLORING FURTHER

In 1993, the Ms. Foundation for Women declared April 28 Take Our Daughters to Work Day, a day on which many parents, particularly mothers, take their daughters to work in order to increase girls' awareness of the wide range of opportunities open to them today. The Ms. Foundation created this event in response to recent research indicating that girls' self-esteem and self-confidence decreases greatly between the ages of nine and twelve. In addition to helping girls understand their own importance and opportunities, other goals of this day are for daughters to learn about the valuable things that their mothers have done and for mothers to reflect about the kinds of roles they set for their daughters.

Here are two viewpoints about Take Our Daughters to Work Day. The first is a student essay about some reasons why the writer plans to take her daughter to work next April 28. The second, by a journalist, describes some consequences of going to work with his mother when he was younger.

My Daughter/Myself

Next April 28, the next Take Our Daughters to Work Day, I am inviting my ten-year-old daughter Annette to spend the day with me to learn about my present and her future. In fact, I think we should all take our daughters to work on a regular basis so that they see that they can achieve their potential and become whatever they want to be. And so that we can achieve our potential too.

Before I take Annette to my job, I will probably ask her to come to my college with me. I know that she sits in her classes with girls who hesitate to speak their mind, whose most common response to their teachers' questions is ''I don't know'' or ''I'm not sure.'' So I want her to hear all the brilliant women in my classes and see that ''nice'' women can be the first ones to answer the question. I also want her to watch how well the female teachers and administrators perform their jobs—to see articulate women who are confident and powerful. Then I will take Annette to a session with my college adviser so that she and I can hear about the many careers options in my major. I want Annette to hear the possibilities roll off my adviser's tongue: doctor, medical technician, laboratory director, science teacher, and on and on. Then

I will take my daughter out to lunch in an elegant restaurant for a meal that neither of us shopped for or cooked!

Finally, I will fulfill the day's title and take Annette to work with me. She will watch me perform my job as an assistant operations control manager in the business office of the Lake Grove Power Station. I know my daughter will be proud of me. I also know that she will wonder why I haven't been promoted. She'll probably ask me why men who are less qualified and less experienced than I am keep getting promoted while I am still an assistant manager. She'll probably ask me why the male assistant managers make more money than I do. As I struggle to answer her questions, I will agonize over my answers. Why can't I demand and get what I deserve? If I don't, what kind of role am I modeling for my daughter?

So I am taking my daughter to work—to improve her future and mine.

—Rachel Finzi

Discussion Questions

1. What was Ms. Finzi's purpose in her essay? What did she want to show or to convince readers of?
2. Did she accomplish this purpose? Why or why not?
3. Which details did you find the most interesting or effective in Ms. Finzi's essay? Why?
4. Was her cause-and-effect analysis logical? What evidence did she provide to support this analysis?
5. What other situations or information can you think of that support—or that contradict—Ms. Finzi's analysis?

Mother's Gifts Aren't Just for Girls

My mother once worked for a tiny company known as Irving B. Bleistern, Paper Bags and Paper Products, in a storefront office on the Lower East Side, in the city, a few blocks from where we lived. I used to go there a lot.

This was in the 1950s. My mother was way ahead of her time. She was a single parent, a working mother, and a woman with a child-care problem.

This problem she solved, during the time I was between about 8 and 12, by ordering me to report to her office after school. Sometimes I did homework there. Sometimes I'd go from there to the Boys Club, or a friend's house. But I always had to check in at Bleistern's, the way other kids had to check in at home. It was where mom was.

This comes up because tomorrow has been designated as Take Our Daughters to Work Day, a special occasion that is being promoted by the Ms. Foundation as a way for grownups to show young girls that they can be—to steal that very ambiguous phrase from the U.S. Army recruiting advertisements—all that they can be.

It's a nice enough idea, especially if words like "empowerment" and "validation" speak to you, but I think it misses half the point, which is boys.

This boy would not know half of what little he knows about humanity if he had not seen his mother at work. A widow, she was our one and only breadwinner.

She was, officially, the bookkeeper. But at Bleistern's, which they referred to in those pre-correct days as a "one-girl office," she was also the office manager, accountant, sales director, payroll department and, occasionally, the one who would stand outside with a clipboard, directing the loading of the trucks by the warehousemen.

Mr. B., as she called the boss, was a decent guy who wore a suit and tie to the office and whose mother, known as Mrs. B., came most days to sit and watch and answer phones and do what she referred to as help out.

It was my impression—though, granted, my view was somewhat partisan—that my mother ran the place. Anyway, the people in the office treated her like she did, and in turn, treated me like a prince.

Bleistern gave me my first job, sharpening pencils and emptying pencil sharpeners: 50 cents a week, which he put in a pay envelope, just like he would every Friday for the warehouse guys and the salesmen, who were mainly Spanish-speaking men who sold Mr. B.'s products in all the bodegas and hole-in-the-wall stores from the Bowery up to the Grand Concourse.

The office was tucked in between the stoops of tenement buildings along 11th Street, between Avenues B and C, in a neighborhood that was predominantly Puerto Rican. The fact that it was Puerto Rican I remember mostly because of the way people there addressed my mother: in the third person. *La Secretaria.*

She was probably a figure of some mystery and awe in the neighborhood. Not many women worked, and very few who did were ever seen loading trucks on a warehouse dock. There was an incident one summer that summed it up.

In this neighborhood, and throughout the city, whenever the temperature reached a certain unbearable level, people opened the fire hydrants. Kids would take turns aiming the powerful gush of water, using a soda can opened at both ends to spray passing cars and people, to make gigantic rainbow arches in the air, and generally to shut down all activity on the street except for water.

One August afternoon when this happened on 11th Street, my mother was stranded at the office door, waiting for a waterfall to cease so she could walk up the street. Somebody spotted her and yelled out in Spanish to stop the water and let her pass. *"La Secretaria!"* he said, and the water stopped, and all the people watched her go by.

I tell you this because I believe that boys need as much as girls to see their mothers part the waters of the world. Maybe more so.

So since this is America, I throw in my two cents: Take your sons to work, too, moms.

My mother would later have much better jobs than the one at Bleistern's. She would get a degree in accounting, have an office with a window and nice furniture in it. She would like those jobs better than the one at Bleistern's.

And I would be proud of her. But I could never be prouder of her than when she was *La Secretaria* of 11th Street.

—*Paul Vitello (Newsday)*

Discussion Questions

1. What was Mr. Vitello's purpose in his essay? What did he want to show or to convince readers of?
2. Did Mr. Vitello accomplish this purpose? Why or why not?
3. Why does Mr. Vitello think it is important for mothers to take their sons to work with them?
4. What are some of the effects that going to work with his mother had on Mr. Vitello?
5. Why was Mr. Vitello more proud of his mother's role as *La Secretaria* than he was of her other, "better" jobs?
6. What do you think Mr. Vitello learned from going to work with his mother?

WRITING ASSIGNMENT

What is your response to Take Our Daughters to Work Day? Do you think it is a good idea or a bad idea? What are some reasons why mothers (and fathers) should take their daughters (and sons) to work? What are some positive effects that may result from this event? Might any problems or negative effects result from having children attend work with their mothers?

Plan, write, and revise a paragraph or two answering *one* of the following questions:

• Should mothers bring their daughters to work on Take Our Daughters to Work Day? Why or why not?

or

• Should parents bring their children to work with them on a regular basis? Why or why not?

or

• Imagine having an eleven-year-old daughter. How would you want her to feel about her future? (Or if you have a daughter, how does she feel about her future and what would you like her to feel?) How might you help your daughter (or future daughter) feel confident that she can achieve her goals in life?

Develop your details and examples using one or more of the strategies that you practiced in this chapter. Decide on a logical order for your details, and end with a conclusion that leaves your reader thinking about the main point that you wanted to communicate in this piece of writing.

✔ POINTS TO REMEMBER ABOUT CAUSE-AND-EFFECT ANALYSIS

1. Think about your purpose in analyzing causes or effects: What do you want readers to understand, think, or feel after they read your analysis?
2. In a single paragraph, focus on causes or effects.
3. Consider the background information about your topic that readers may need to know in order to understand your cause-and-effect analysis.
4. Choose strategies and supporting details that are appropriate for your purpose and your readers.
5. Check to make sure that you have not created any logical fallacies. Did you oversimplify the causes that you are analyzing? Or did you make a false assumption that two events, conditions, or problems were causally related simply because they occurred next to each other in time?
6. Organize your analysis logically so that readers will understand your points.
7. Cross out any irrelevant sentences or details that do not expand your analysis.
8. Use transitional words and expressions to show the relations between your ideas and your sentences.
9. End with a conclusion that sums up your points.
10. Revise and edit your analysis for clarity and correctness.

ARGUMENTATION

Everyone knows how to argue—how to try to get someone to understand or to agree with your point of view. When people argue face-to-face or over the phone, they may get very emotional. In taking a stand and trying to convince others to join them, some people try to overwhelm their listeners with their feelings. Strong emotional appeals may—or may not—work in persuading people to agree with you. In academic writing, however, they rarely are appropriate. The aim of written argument is to influence others through logic and evidence rather than through emotional appeals. The goal is to persuade rather than to overpower.

Argument differs from other strategies that you have been practicing for your Writer's Portfolio chapters. In fact, argument isn't really a strategy; it's a purpose—to convince people that something you think or feel is valid, reasonable, or right. When you argue in writing, you use one or more of the strategies that you have learned (describing, narrating, analyzing a process, comparing, contrasting, dividing, classifying, defining, and analyzing causes or effects) to illustrate and explain your point or position. One of the keys to writing strong arguments is to select effective strategies that will encourage readers to share your viewpoint. You can express your feelings or entertain readers in an argument, but the main objective is to convince readers that your viewpoint is valid.

DEVELOPING A TOPIC SENTENCE

You can't convince readers to adopt your position or believe in it unless you know exactly what your point of view is. As you begin planning your argument, remember that your topic or opinion must be *arguable*. It must be open to debate, and other people may have different views about it. If you take a position that no one doubts or disagrees with, then why bother defending it in writing? Examples of assertions that are not arguable are facts and statements of opinions:

Drinking alcohol impairs people's ability to drive.   [statement of fact]
I have always disliked alcohol.   [personal opinion]

One way to test whether your position is arguable is to state your viewpoint using the word *should* or *ought* (or *should not* or *must not*). If you cannot do this, then the position is probably a fact or a personal opinion. If you can state your position using *should* or *should not,* then examine it to see if it is so general that no one would oppose it. Here is a student's first draft of an argumentative topic sentence:

People *should not* drink and drive.

Is this a debatable position or point of view? Would anyone disagree with it? Probably not, so it is a weak main point for an argument. The writer must revise it so that it presents an opinion, a reason, or a solution:

People who drink and drive should be punished.

This topic sentence can be debated, but it's still too vague for an academic paragraph. What does the writer mean by "should be punished"? Here is the writer's final revision.

People convicted of drunk driving should have their licenses taken away

for two or three years.

This statement is clear and specific, and people could argue against it. Thus, it is an appropriate topic sentence for an argument paragraph.

GUIDELINES FOR CHECKING A TOPIC SENTENCE FOR AN ARGUMENT ━━━━━━━━━━━━

Here are some characteristics of effective topic sentences for argumentative writing:

1. The position or viewpoint is worth arguing about. (It's not merely a statement of your personal preference.)
2. People may disagree with your position. (If everyone agrees with it, then it's probably a statement of fact, not a point of view.)
3. Your position is neither too narrow nor too broad. (It requires evidence to support it, and you can develop this evidence in a paragraph.)

WRITING ACTIVITY 1

Examine each of the following topic sentences and decide if it would be appropriate for an argument paragraph. If it isn't, why not? The first one has been done as an example.

1. Economics is a better major than history.

   no - This is a statement of a personal opinion that cannot be proved.

2. Many people discriminate against physically-disabled adults.

   _____

   _____

3. College admissions tests are unfair.

   _____

   _____

4. The people of the world need a cure for AIDS.

   _____

   _____

5. Women are not allowed to serve in many combat roles in the armed forces.

_____

_____

6. Smoking a pipe or cigarettes can cause health problems.

_____

_____

GROUP WORK 1

Work with two or three classmates on this activity. On a separate piece of paper, revise each of the statements in the preceding Writing Activity so that it is an appropriate topic sentence for an argument paragraph. The first one has been done as an example.

1. Economics is a better major than history.

    Students should consider majoring in economics because this major can prepare them for a variety of rewarding careers.

CONSIDERING READERS' KNOWLEDGE AND OPINIONS

If you don't have a specific audience in mind as you develop an argument, try to imagine or create one. Think about readers who either have no opinion about your topic or who disagree with your position. In order to convince these readers of your position, you will have to consider their knowledge of and attitudes toward your topic.

QUESTIONS TO ANSWER ABOUT
YOUR AUDIENCE ———————————————

Here are some questions that you should answer as you plan a topic sentence for an argument paragraph:

- What do my readers already know about my topic?
- What values, beliefs, or concerns do readers share with me about this topic?
- What objections might readers have to my position or my point of view?
- Why is their viewpoint different from mine? What reasons do they have for disagreeing with me?
- What kinds of evidence might convince them to believe (or to consider) my point of view on this topic?

 GROUP WORK 2

Form a group with two or three classmates and work on this activity together. Below are five positions that could serve as topic sentences for arguments. For each topic sentence, identify readers who might support the position and write one or two possible reasons for their support. Then identify readers who would oppose the position and list one or two reasons for their objections. The first one has been done as an example.

1. Wearing a seat belt is so important to automobile safety that cars should not be able to start until all the passengers have buckled their seat belts.

   Supporters: *Parents - They would want their children to be forced to wear seat belts and they would want anyone who drives their children to wear one.*

   Opponents: *People who like to take risks - They would resent being forced to wear*

*a seat belt and they might feel that
it infringes on their rights.*

2. There is so much to be learned in junior high and high school
   that the secondary school year should be extended to twelve
   months.

   Supporters: _____

   _____

   _____

   Opponents: _____

   _____

   _____

3. Physical-education courses should not be required in college.

   Supporters: _____

   _____

   _____

   Opponents: _____

   _____

   _____

4. If the directors of the college food service want more students to
   eat in their cafeterias, they should serve fresher, better-tasting
   food.

   Supporters: _____

   _____

   _____

Opponents: _____

_____

_____

5. People must develop new ways to recycle their garbage so that we can save the earth's dwindling natural resources.

Supporters: _____

_____

_____

Opponents: _____

_____

_____

BUILDING AN ARGUMENT WITH RELEVANT EVIDENCE

In order to be convincing, the supporting details in an argument must be relevant to the topic and to readers. Good reasons support a writer's points by providing specific examples that readers can understand. And, of course, good reasons vary from purpose to purpose and from audience to audience. For some arguments, you may be able to use reasons and evidence that come from your experiences or observations or that are common knowledge. For instance, here is an assertion that you could support with evidence from your personal experiences or from your observations of other students:

Most college students who do not have jobs find it almost impossible to

buy all the books and materials they need for school.

Imagine that the author of this topic sentence is writing a letter to his family asking them to send money. Here is his argument:

Dear Mom, Dad, and Grandma Rae,

I miss you, and I hope you are all fine. I am not. I am having so much trouble paying for books, folders, and other school materials that I may have to skip some meals to save money. I have tried my best to economize, but I cannot skimp on school necessities. Is it possible for you please to send me an additional $50 a week? If you could, you would make my life so much better. I am *really* having a hard time making ends meet. If you want me to get A's, I have to study all evening, so I can't get a part-time job. And I can't study if I'm starving. So please help me out!

Love,

Brad

The writer resorts to emotional appeals that he hopes will work with his family (such as "I am *really* having a hard time making ends meet" and "I can't study if I'm starving"). Now imagine that the writer of this letter is writing to his school's scholarship-fund committee. He has the same goal as he had in the letter to his family: to convince them to send him more money. Can he use the same appeals?

Here is the writer's letter to the committee. Do you think it would accomplish his goal? Why or why not?

To Whom It May Concern:

Currently, I am the grateful recipient of your scholarship stipend of $75 per week. I am writing to ask whether there is any possibility of increasing this amount to $125 a week. If there isn't, I do not think I can continue attending college full-time.

I use your money to pay for food, utilities, clothes, school supplies, and school fees. The total amount of these bills comes to approximately $130 per week. Since I do not work and my family cannot afford to send me the additional $55 I need to spend each week, I have tried to economize. I have started skipping meals, and I am borrowing my roommate's clothes. However, I am still behind on my payments.

I know that I am not allowed to work (under the conditions of your scholarship), but if you cannot find any additional money for me, I will have to get a part-time job. I don't see any alternatives. Can we please meet to discuss this?

Thank you.

Sincerely,

Bradley O'Connor

The argument to the scholarship fund includes many kinds of reasons that you have practiced using in earlier chapters: examples, explanations, facts, and statistics. It differs from the argument in the first letter, which is based mostly on appeals to the audience's emotions.

    The introduction of this chapter noted that readers of academic writing often expect to see appeals to logic rather than appeals to emotion in written arguments. That doesn't mean you cannot—or should not—appeal to your readers' feelings to try to get them to understand your point of view. As you plan an argument, think about your own emotional responses to your position. Can you narrate an experience or describe a situation using language that will evoke similar emotions in readers? Advertisers do this all the time. In fact, many advertisers rely almost exclusively on emotional appeals instead of logical reasons to convince readers to buy their products or use their services. Here is an example of an advertisement that uses dramatic images and connotative language to personalize the ''product'' and convince readers of its value.

"LETTING MY SON JOIN THE ARMY
WAS THE HARDEST THING I'VE EVER DONE.
IT WAS ALSO ONE OF THE SMARTEST."

"Russ has always been the baby of our family, so I was terribly upset the day he
left us for the Army. Even though I knew he had good reasons for joining—especially the
money he'd be earning for college—I also knew how tough the Army could be. And
I worried about how he would cope.

Then, three months later, I was invited to Russell's graduation from basic training. As
I watched him standing there—looking so strong, so mature, so self-confident—I realized
the Army had done something really important for my son. It had helped him grow up.
And believe me, if you think Russell felt proud that day, you should have seen his mother!"

To find out more about what the Army can do to help your son or daughter get
an edge on life, call 1-800-USA-ARMY, Ext. 100.

ARMY. BE ALL YOU CAN BE.

Army materials provided courtesy of the U.S. Government, as represented by the Secretary
of the Army

GROUP WORK 3

Form a group with two or three classmates and answer the questions below. Choose one person to record the group's responses.

1. Who is the advertiser and what "product" does it sell?
2. What is the main point of this advertisement? What does the advertiser want you to think or feel or do?
3. Where does the advertisement use narration to make its point?
4. What emotions or feelings is this narration supposed to evoke in readers? Did it elicit these feelings from you?
5. Does the advertisement make any appeals to logic? If so, what reasons or evidence does it provide to support its point?
6. Would this advertisement convince you to do what the advertiser wants you to do? Why or why not?

Thinking about your readers' knowledge and attitudes will help you balance appeals to emotion and appeals to logic in your arguments. If you decide that emotional appeals are inappropriate for your topic and readers, then provide logical reasons, including examples, facts, statistics, and expert testimony. (See pages 115–116 for guidelines on including facts and statistics in your paragraphs and pages 117–118 for guidelines on including testimony.)

> **REMINDER**
> An effective argument has a clear topic sentence stating a position or viewpoint that is open to debate and that can be supported by specific examples, reasons, and facts.

If you are having difficulty coming up with logical reasons to support a position or point of view, try brainstorming about different categories of reasons (such as "emotional," "physical," "social," "financial," "environmental," and "political"). Here are different types of reasons, followed by an example of each. The topic sentence is "Our town government should enact legislation to curb air pollution."

1. *Physical:* The air in Linden Township is so polluted that people's eyes burn and tear on smoggy days.
2. *Mental/emotional:* Many Linden Township parents are very worried about the chemical pollution of our air and its effects on their children's nervous systems.

3. *Financial:* The increasingly polluted air in Linden Township is damaging the quality of life in this town, and people are having difficulty selling their homes at fair prices.
4. *Social:* Strong disagreements about what to do about the air pollution in this town are contributing to the breakup of old friendships.

WRITING ACTIVITY 2

What is your position about sex education in secondary schools (junior and senior high schools)? Should secondary schools teach students about sex, sexually-transmitted diseases, and/or contraception? If so, why? If not, why not?

If you have difficulty thinking of reasons, consider the emotional, physical, social, and financial consequences of teaching sex education in secondary school. Then consider the consequences of *not* teaching this subject. Plan, write, and revise a paragraph or two defending your position on this issue.

WRITING ACTIVITY 3

What problem at your school really concerns or upsets you? Write a letter to the editor of the school paper about this problem. As you draft the letter, think about the kinds of details that readers might want to know. What evidence can you present to convince readers that the problem is a significant one? What kinds of logical and emotional appeals would be appropriate for convincing readers of your points? If you propose a solution to the problem, include evidence that supports your recommendation.

ANTICIPATING OPPOSING ARGUMENTS

In order to convince readers that your position is valid or reasonable, consider their viewpoints and their objections to your position. If you can anticipate your readers' objections, then you can respond to them effectively. A technique for thinking about opposing viewpoints is to brainstorm a ''for/against'' (or a ''pro/con'') list. Here is an example of a student's list about the issue of whether women in the armed forces should serve in combat roles.

WOMEN IN COMBAT ROLES
IN THE ARMED SERVICES

FOR	AGAINST
women are qualified and deserve the same opportunities as men have	women shouldn't kill or be killed
women are physically capable of serving in combat roles	women should not have to be pulled away from their families to fight far away
women already proved they could serve as well as men (in Operation Desert Storm)	If servicewomen have children, they will miss their mothers terribly
It is just as wrenching for a family to lose a father as it is to lose a mother	Women should stay with their families and let men do the fighting

Here is the paragraph that the writer developed from this list. Underline the sentences that present possible objections to the writer's position on this issue.

If this country is ever involved in another war, I want to be at the front, as a woman proudly commanding an air squadron of men and women risking their lives in combat missions. The time has come to allow all qualified women to compete on an equal basis with men for assignments that involve possible combat roles. I know that many people are horrified at the idea of a servicewoman being pulled away from her family (especially her children) if she is needed in a war zone on the other side of the world. I also know that the thought of women killing or being killed in combat horrifies people. However, both of these have already happened (in Operation Desert Storm in 1992), and society didn't fall apart. Moreover, it is just as intolerable (and just as wrenching for a family) to have "Daddy" come home in a body bag as it is to have "Mommy" die in combat. Servicewomen who are physically qualified for combat deserve the same rights to learn the technical skills of combat specialties, to earn the extra money that these specialties pay, and to serve their country as servicemen have.

Notice the writer's analysis of possible objections to her argument: "I know that many people are horrified at the idea of a servicewoman being pulled away from her family (especially her children) if she is needed in a war zone on the other side of the world. I also know that the thought of women killing or being killed in combat horrifies people." By responding to these objections in the remainder of her paragraph, the writer shows readers that she has thought carefully about differing views on this issue before deciding on her position. She did not let her personal convictions blind her to other people's points of view.

As you develop details for your argument, try to anticipate your readers' reactions. Reach into your own experiences and observations and imagine a situation in which you might feel very differently about your topic than you feel about it now. Also, imagine that you are the intended reader, and ask yourself why this reader might not agree with the assertions in your paragraph. Build a bridge to readers who disagree by showing respect for them and for their points of view.

GROUP WORK 4

Work with another student. Together choose *five* of the following assertions to work on for this activity. Select one person to write down all the reasons he or she can think of to support the assertion. The other group member should write down all the reasons why this assertion is wrong or will cause problems.

As you do this activity, *ignore* your personal beliefs about each issue and try to imagine how a person who supports or opposes the assertion thinks and feels about it.

1. Working and making money are more important than going to college and graduating with a degree.
2. English should be the only official language of the United States.
3. Convicted murderers should be executed.
4. College courses should be graded "pass/fail" rather than with letter grades.
5. People who are convicted of drunk driving should lose their licenses forever.
6. Colleges should not require admissions tests.
7. People who live in this country should buy products produced here rather than imported products.
8. People should live together before getting married.
9. Cable television should be free.
10. Everyone's taxes should be increased to pay for building homes for homeless people.

WRITING ACTIVITY 4

Choose the assertion in the preceding Group Work that most interests you. Develop a "for/against" list of reasons supporting and opposing the assertion you have selected. Then plan, write, and revise a paragraph explaining why this assertion is correct or why readers should believe the assertion. Next plan, write, and revise a paragraph explaining why this assertion is not true or is wrong.

When you finish writing both paragraphs, answer the following question: How were your thoughts or feelings about this topic affected by developing arguments for and against it?

AVOIDING LOGICAL FALLACIES

A *fallacy* is a mistake in reasoning that leads to an illogical statement. People often make logical fallacies when they argue because their strong feelings overwhelm them, and they begin thinking with their hearts instead of their heads. Here is an example:

> Please, you have to buy me a compact disc player because everybody has one. It's the only way to listen to music.

If "everybody" buys something, does that make the object good or worth buying? Moreover, is there only one way to listen to music?

Faulty logic can sabotage persuasive writing by making readers think that the writer does not know what he or she is writing about. In Chapter 11, you learned about two logical fallacies that advancing writers often make in cause-and-effect analysis:

1. *Oversimplifying* the causes of an event or a condition by stating that it had only one cause: "More people should be hired to help at registration so that students could register more quickly." Reasons other than the lack of staff may be causing registration to take a long time. Solving the problem of speeding up registration requires an analysis of all the reasons for its slow pace. Most conditions or events have multiple causes and multiple effects. If you ignore important causes, readers will question your judgment.

2. *Making a false assumption* that something caused an event or a condition just because it happened right before the event or the condition: "Our school's computerized registration system cannot manage senior registration because the computer breaks down every time seniors try to register." The computer system's problems may have nothing to do with the status of the students who are registering. The computer may "break down" every time it processes a student who has not yet declared a major. Don't assert a cause-effect connection between two conditions or events unless you can support your assertion with convincing evidence.

Here are other logical fallacies to avoid in your persuasive paragraphs. Analyze your drafts and look for these errors in reasoning.

3. *Overgeneralizing* by making broad statements that you cannot support in a paragraph (or an essay): "The registration process at my school gets worse every semester because no one in the administration really cares about students." The writer cannot prove that every administrator does not "care about" students or that problems in the registration process are related to administrators' feelings. Remember

that a single example or instance is not sufficient to support a main point about "all" people or "all" things.

4. *Citing a false authority* by supporting a point with a quotation from a person who is not an expert on your topic: "Several seniors have pointed out that the registration process at our college is becoming increasingly difficult because of mismanagement by the registrar's staff." Unless the writer can show that these seniors have evidence of mismanagement, he cannot use their assertions to support his point. Find convincing evidence to support your assertions by consulting appropriate sources (experts, books, journals, and magazines).

5. *Circular reasoning,* or trying to prove one's point by repeating it in different words: "Students should be able to register at home on their computers because computers are the best way to register." This assertion states the writer's opinion twice (in different words), but it doesn't provide any reasons or evidence to support or illustrate the point. Readers get bored or annoyed reading the same assertions over and over again. Instead, provide specific facts, examples, and observations to support your points.

6. *Majority rule or "bandwagon" reasoning* occurs when a writer assumes that if most people are doing something, then it must be reasonable or right: "All the students I know are so annoyed at our college's registration procedures that they are ready to transfer to a different school." If a group of people believe something, does that make their belief correct or valid? Readers will not be convinced that your position is right simply because the majority of people you know agree with you. Instead of discussing what "everyone else" is thinking or doing, find more convincing reasons to support or to prove your assertions.

7. *Using either-or reasoning* by stating—or implying—that there are only two "sides" or viewpoints or alternatives, when there actually are many (that the writer has not considered): "If students are so unhappy with the registration procedures at this college, then they should go to a different college." The writer of this assertion is ignoring the many other actions that "unhappy students" can take (including trying to improve the registration procedures or trying to cope more effectively with these procedures). When you write an argument, consider other ways of perceiving your topic by interviewing people who are knowledgeable about the topic and by consulting sources of public information about it.

8. *Stereotyping* appeals to people's prejudices: "The registration process is getting worse because the registrar keeps hiring foreigners who don't speak English well." This assertion reveals the writer's unreasonable emotions and prejudices, which are almost certainly

untrue and which will antagonize readers who do not share this prejudice. Examine the evidence in your arguments to determine whether they are factual or simply reflect prejudices and stereotypical thinking. Find facts and examples that can serve as convincing evidence.

WRITING ACTIVITY 5

Read the following topic sentences and, in the space below each, explain the logical fallacy that it illustrates.

1. Women should get custody of children in divorce cases because children need their mothers more than they need their fathers.

2. The country will never be able to provide national health care for everyone because people infected with AIDS will drown any national health-care system with their bills.

3. Plagiarism used to be considered cheating, but it's no longer a bad action because most students plagiarize in their research papers.

4. Women should have the opportunity to serve in combat roles in the armed forces because women have the same rights as men.

5. According to my parents, the main reason why English should be the only official language in this country is because it would make immigrants adapt to our culture more quickly.

WRITING ACTIVITY 6

This activity will help you identify potentially foggy thinking and writing habits. Below is a photograph of three women. Examine it carefully for a few minutes. Then plan and write a paragraph about these women. Before you begin writing, you may want to answer the questions that follow the picture.

1. What exactly do you see in the picture?
2. Who and what are these women? What do you think their jobs are?
3. What evidence *in the photograph* helped you decide what these three women are and what they do? Be specific.

CONSULTING PUBLIC SOURCES OF INFORMATION

Many topic sentences for argument paragraphs can be supported by personal experiences and observations that illustrate the writer's reasons for his or her point of view about the topic. However, often you may decide that your argument requires more objective types of supporting details, especially if you are defending a controversial position or if your readers disagree strongly with your position. This is the time to consult public sources: to do extensive reading and interviewing. Journalist and writer Anna Quindlen once explained how she plans her arguments by consulting sources:

> I begin by reading, reading, reading. I have to understand my subject before I interview people; otherwise I won't understand the terms they use or the issues they raise. Also, I have to understand where they're coming from.

If you're going to get testimony from experts on your topic, follow Quindlen's suggestion and read about it first so that you are prepared for the interviews. Here are some tips for getting testimony in interviews.

INTERVIEW TECHNIQUES FOR GETTING EXPERT TESTIMONY

These are guidelines for preparing for an interview:

1. As you read about your topic, write down questions that occur to you or that seem important.
2. Revise your questions into the actual questions that you will use in the interview. Make sure that each question will elicit a full answer, as opposed to a "yes" or a "no." If you must ask a "yes/no" question, follow it up with "Why?" (or "Why not?").
3. Use a tape recorder to tape the person's responses to your questions so that you can listen carefully. If you don't have a tape recorder, take accurate notes.
4. Make sure that you have spelled the person's name and professional affiliation correctly.

In Chapter 4, you learned how to use facts, statistics, and testimony to support or prove your topic sentence. (See pages 115–118 to review the guidelines for including these types of details in your paragraphs.) Academic disciplines have different styles for citing the sources of paraphrases and quotations in paragraphs and essays. If your teacher does not tell you which style manual to use for citing sources, use the *MLA Handbook for Writers of Research Papers* (published by the Modern Language Association in 1984).

The two most common methods of "documenting" or giving credit to the authors whose works or ideas you are summarizing, paraphrasing, or quoting are illustrated below, following an excerpt about stress from a book titled *Your College Experience: Strategies for Success,* by A. Jerome Jewler and John Gardner.

Stress is natural. So, to the extent that stress is a sign of vitality, stress is good. Yet most of us, as we grow and develop, don't really learn how to cope effectively with stress-producing situations, and the result is that stress can overwhelm us, interfering seriously with our ability to perform. The primary way to manage stress is to modify it with something that enhances our feeling of control in the situation. Relaxation is very important in counteracting stress.

If you do not mention the writers' names in your paraphrase or quotation, then you must write their last names and the page number(s) of the source within parentheses at the end of the sentence. Note that the names and the page number are *not* separated by any punctuation mark.

Paraphrase: Stress can sabotage our adjustment to college life if we don't learn how to cope with it. In fact, experts on the college experience have noted that allowing stress to build up without counteracting it by relaxing can impair our ability to perform in college (Jewler and Gardner 227).

Quotation: Experts on the college experience have indicated that stress can impair our ability to perform in college: ''Most of us, as we grow and develop, don't really learn how to cope effectively with stress-producing situations, and the result is that stress can overwhelm us, interfering seriously with our ability to perform'' (Jewler and Gardner 227).

If you do mention the writers' names in your sentence, then put only the page number(s) of the source in parentheses at the end.

Paraphrase: Stress can sabotage our adjustment to college life if we don't learn how to cope with it. In their recent book on succeeding in college, Jerome Jewler and John Gardner noted that allowing stress to build up without counteracting it by relaxing can impair our ability to perform in college (227).

Quotation: In their recent book on succeeding in college, Jerome Jewler and John Gardner noted that ''most of us, as we grow and develop, don't really learn how to cope effectively with stress-producing situations, and the result is that stress can overwhelm us, interfering seriously with our ability to perform'' (227).

PREPARING A LIST OF YOUR SOURCES

If you paraphrase or quote sources in your argument, you must provide a list of the works that you cited, arranged alphabetically according to the authors' last names. Here is a sample of a partial list that follows the guidelines of the *MLA Handbook for Writers of Research Papers:*

Works Cited

Boyer, Ernest. The Undergraduate Experience in America. New York: Harper & Row, 1987. [a book with one author]

Jewler, A. Jerome, and John J. Gardner. Your College Experience: Strategies for Success. Belmont, CA: Wadsworth, 1993. [a book with two authors]

Luciano, Lani. "Finding a School That Fits." Money (September 1992): 18–19. [an article in a magazine]

Wiener, Harvey. Personal interview. 25 May 1993. [an interview with an expert]

WRITING ACTIVITY 7

The excerpt on page 340 discusses the effects of stress on college students. Plan and develop an argument about the topic "stress." Begin by doing some freewriting, brainstorming, or clustering about the kinds of stress that you and your friends are experiencing in college. One possible approach to this topic is stating and supporting an assertion about the causes of the greatest stress for college students. Another possibility is making and supporting a recommendation for the best way (or ways) of coping with stress in college. Use the techniques you have learned in this chapter to plan and write your paragraph (or two).

WRITING ACTIVITY 8

Revise the paragraph that you wrote for the preceding Writing Activity by including facts, statistics, or testimony to support your points, if you have not already added them. Do research or interviews, and include paraphrases or quotations as supporting evidence for your assertions. Follow the guidelines for including this evidence on pages 115–118 in Chapter 4.

ORGANIZING AN ARGUMENT

One strategy for arranging the examples and reasons in an argumentative paragraph is to begin with your *second-strongest* reason, end with the *strongest* reason, and arrange the reasons in the middle from least to most compelling. This organization lets you create powerful initial and final impressions on readers.

If you are discussing possible objections to your position or viewpoint, you will have to decide where to raise and counter these objections. There are no rules to guide you in deciding how to arrange your details because the organization of an argument depends on the kinds of details and strategies the writer is using. For example, if you choose to illustrate the reasons for your belief or position by narrating one or more experiences, you will probably arrange your details chronologically. On the other hand, if you choose to discuss causes and effects to support your viewpoint, you may have to follow the causal ''chain'' of your ideas. (See pages 310–311 in Chapter 11 about causal chains.) Here is an example of how a writer can use a causal chain to develop and organize an argument.

Our college is ignoring the learning potential of the Nintendo generation. New computer technology could open a whole new world of learning for many students. Most of us were raised with computers and video games, so we're comfortable interacting with a video screen and keyboard. If teachers could package courses on computer networks, we could master a subject at our own pace in a place and time of our own choosing. As we work through our individualized lessons in the comfort of our homes, we would be saving hundreds of dollars by not having to commute to school. And if we see that we are having difficulty, we could call up an on-line tutorial that would provide specific instruction. Moreover, interactive computerized instruction doesn't have to be individualized seminars. If students' computers could be linked on a network, the students could work together to create solutions to problems and to help each other learn. Nintendo teenagers, who are used to playing in small groups and teaching each other strategies to succeed, would really benefit from computerized peer-group work, and learning would be much more enjoyable. Interactive multimedia computer programs have the power to transform the way we learn. Our school could enhance learning and save money if it would only take advantage of the technological revolution in education.

Could you follow this writer's cause-effect reasoning? Did she convince you of her point? Why or why not?

Did you also notice how the writer of the preceding paragraph used transitions to make the paragraph unified and coherent? Here are some transitional words and expressions that you might use in your arguments.

TRANSITIONS THAT INDICATE ARGUMENTATION ────────────

Providing reasons and examples:
first, another reason why, moreover, since, finally

Anticipating opposing points of view:
on the other hand, although, nevertheless, even though

Drawing conclusions:
thus, therefore, consequently, in conclusion

USING ARGUMENT ACROSS THE COLLEGE CURRICULUM

Not only is the ability to write convincing argument a required skill in college, it is also necessary to get into many colleges. Most college and scholarship applications ask students to write a paragraph or an essay explaining why they want to go to the school or why the school should accept them or give them a scholarship. In almost every college subject, teachers ask students to state a position and support or defend it with relevant evidence. Assignments that call for arguments include essays, critiques, position papers, proposals, research papers, memos, and evaluations. Here are some examples:

1. Does watching violent television programs affect children's violent or aggressive behavior? Write an essay explaining your position about this issue. Support your position with relevant evidence from our readings and from other sources.

2. What causes hurricanes? What causes tornadoes? How are these causes similar? How do they differ? Develop a theory about the differences in these two weather phenomena and defend your theory with appropriate evidence.

3. Discuss the causes of schizophrenia and explain how these causes interact with one another. Support your analysis with relevant theory and research.

4. Write two essays. In the first essay, describe the current and future effects of the increasing unemployment in your city. Explain your reasons for predicting these effects. In the second essay, describe one

or two actions that your city government should take to reduce unemployment. Explain why you think this action (or these actions) would work.

All these assignments require one or more of the strategies you have already practiced (describing, narrating, analyzing a process, comparing, contrasting, dividing, classifying, defining, and analyzing causes or effects) to explain and support a theory, a position, or a solution.

WRITING ACTIVITY 9

One of the most common academic and professional writing assignments is the proposal, a statement that tries to get readers to agree with the writer's project or solution. A proposal tells readers what needs to be done, why it is worth doing, how it will be done, and what it will require.

Write a proposal about a course that you would like to take but that does not exist at your school. What subject or ideas would you most want to study? How should the course be taught (lecture, seminar, small groups, individualized tutorial)? What should the teacher do? What would students be required to do? Plan and write a proposal describing this ideal course and convincing college administrators that it should be developed soon. Explain why the course is necessary or valuable, how it should be conducted, and what it will require. Consider why readers might object to your recommendations and address their concerns.

GETTING READERS' RESPONSES

Ask family, friends, and classmates to answer the questions in the following checklist honestly and fully.

ARGUMENT CHECKLIST

1. Does the argument have a clear, focused topic sentence that is neither too narrow nor too broad? If so, what is this idea? If not, what might it be?
2. Do you understand the writer's purpose in writing this paragraph? Did the writer accomplish this purpose? (If so, how? If not, why not?)
3. Are the writer's reasons logical? Are there any examples or reasons that confuse you or that are illogical?

(Continued)

4. If the writer made emotional appeals, did they work to per-suade you to see things from his or her perspective? If so, how can these appeals be made even better? If they didn't work, why not?
5. Did the writer anticipate your (or any) objections to his or her position? Did the writer counter these objections effectively? If not, why not?
6. If the writer included paraphrases or quotations, did he or she use and cite them correctly? If the writer did not use facts, statistics, or testimony, should he or she do so?
7. How are the details organized? Is there a more appropriate or logical way of organizing the details?
8. How can the writer improve the unity and coherence of this draft? Where are additional transitions needed?
9. Which sentences have errors in them?
10. What suggestions do you have for improving this argument?

■ EXPLORING FURTHER

Before you read the essay that follows, write your answer to this question: Should colleges hire qualified women to coach male athletic teams? Why or why not? (Write a brief response below.)

_____

_____

_____

_____

Now read an editorial essay on this topic by Phil Taylor, which appeared in *Sports Illustrated*.

No Skirting This Issue

It's time athletic directors considered top women for men's college basketball jobs

Some of the most interesting action during a Final Four weekend takes place at the National Association of Basketball coaches' headquarters hotel, where it seems nearly every college coach in the country is hanging out in the lobby. Athletic directors like to come in and chat up the coaches, in many cases buttonholing prospective candidates to fill a vacancy. Last weekend in New Orleans, I saw several athletic directors working the lobby of the Sheraton, each searching for someone to lead his men's team, but none of them asked me for advice.

That's too bad, because if they had consulted me, I would have told them about a terrific candidate they haven't even considered, someone who took a stagnant program and built it into a two-time national champion. This coach runs a program that has an excellent graduation rate, has never had a hint of scandal and has a national recruiting base. What's more, this coach teaches the technical aspects of the game as well as anyone. The athletic directors might assume I'm talking about Mike Krzyzewski of Duke, but in fact I'm describing Stanford women's coach Tara VanDerveer.

That's right, I would have suggested a woman as the next head coach at a Division I school with that opening in its men's program. Sure, there would be some professional risk for any athletic director who took that step, and there might be some embarrassment if it didn't work out. But look at what's happening now. This season the men's coaches at California, Utah State and Army were all fired because they made playing basketball seem like going to boot camp. And think about Bobby Cremins of Georgia Tech . . . I mean South Carolina . . . no, I mean Georgia Tech, waffling over which job he wanted. What could be more embarrassing than that?

Every school wants a coach who will cast its athletic program in a positive light, look out for its athletes and win games. There are women coaches capable of doing all that, just as there are women who have distinguished themselves as athletic directors and university presidents. If women can teach men chemistry and political science on college campuses, surely they can teach them the matchup zone.

If they thought it through, most athletic directors would agree with me. If they had bothered to ask me in New Orleans, I would have told them of another coach who consistently produces an outstanding defensive team, recruits well in urban areas and serves as an exceptional role model, especially for black players. That description may fit John Chaney of Temple or John Thompson of Georgetown, but I would have been talking about Vivian Stringer of Iowa.

Or maybe I would have told them about a coach whose team regularly contends for the Pac-10 crown and has become a hot ticket in town. Arizona's Lute Olson? Well, yes, but also Washington women's coach Chris Gobrecht.

This isn't to say that any of these top women coaches are longing to move to the men's game. The point is, they should get the same consideration for a men's coaching job as promising male coaches receive. But some women's coaches think this is a bad idea, that having women cross over to the men's game would imply that coaching females is somehow less important than coaching males. Washington athletic director Barbara Hedges has even said that hiring Gobrecht for the vacant Huskie men's job would unfairly damage the women's program.

There's nothing wrong with opening the search for a men's team coach to all qualified coaches, regardless of gender—which is what usually happens when an athletic director is searching for someone to coach the women's team. It used to be that men coached women's teams because women were considered neophytes. But in case you haven't noticed, the women have caught up to the men, if not in their ability to play the game, at least in their ability to teach its principles.

Anyone who argues that young men couldn't accept being coached by a woman is underestimating most college basketball players. Don't we constantly hear players talk reverentially about their mothers and about growing up in households headed by a woman? The idea of a woman in authority wouldn't be a shock to many of them. Also, it's easy to imagine a woman being better than a man at persuading a high school star's parents that she is interested in more than just their son's basketball ability, that she would make sure he goes to class and eats properly and gets in at night. Listening to a woman's recruiting pitch would be like hearing Chaney talk about his 6 a.m. practices at Temple: She would scare off some players, but the ones who came would really want to be there.

And let's not get bogged down in the woman-in-the-locker-room issue. Men who coach women's teams have handled it without difficulty, and women would do the same.

It's not as if the idea of hiring a woman to coach men's basketball is totally foreign. In 1990, Kentucky coach Rick Pitino hired Bernadette Locke-Mattox, a former All-America at Georgia, to be one of his assistants. (She's still the only woman assistant on a major-college men's team.) The same year, Virginia interviewed its women's coach, Debbie Ryan, who went to the Final Four three times in the last four years, before hiring Jeff Jones to coach the men's team. This winter, after coach Lou Campanelli was fired for verbally abusing his players, Cal athletic director Bob Bockrath said one alumnus had urged him to contact VanDerveer.

Bockrath should have gone ahead and done it.

—*Phil Taylor*

Discussion Questions

1. What is Taylor's main point? What does he want to convince readers to believe?
2. What reasons does he give to support his position?

3. What emotional appeals does he make to support his position?
4. Which reasons or appeals did you find particularly interesting or compelling? Why?
5. What strategies did Taylor use to develop his points (for example, where does he use description, narration, and so forth)?
6. Did Taylor's essay change (or affect) the way you think or feel about this issue? If so, how and why? If not, why not?

Evaluating Your Evidence

Take out the composition that you wrote for Writing Activity 6 on page 339 of this chapter. How did you describe the women in the photograph on page 339? What evidence in the picture contributed to your assumptions about these women?

From left to right, the photograph shows Doctors Karen Ambroise, Paula A. McKenzie, and Deborah Arrindell. All three are surgeons at Kaiser Permanente Medical Center in Maryland. Reevaluate your description of these women in light of this fact.

WRITING ASSIGNMENT 1

Several paragraphs in this chapter focused on the issue of equality of opportunities for women. Plan, write, and revise a paragraph or two about this topic. Do some freewriting, brainstorming, or clustering to decide on a focus. What aspect of this topic would you like to discuss? Do you feel strongly about a particular issue involving women's rights? Can you compose a position that you could defend? (This position might focus on women's rights to equal pay for equal work or women's rights to political positions—including the presidency.) Or do you feel strongly that women who take advantage of equal—or superior—opportunities are creating problems for men (or for their families)? Develop a position on this issue that you can illustrate and support in a one- or two-paragraph argument.

WRITING ASSIGNMENT 2

Imagine that you are a powerful national legislator and you are proposing a law (or other piece of legislation) that would improve this country by improving the economy, a particular social problem, or the quality of people's lives. What law would you propose? What piece of legislation does our country need most now? Why? (You might want to consider what would happen if this law were passed and enforced.) Who would object to this law? What would their reasons be for opposing it and how can you counter their objections? What experiences, observations, examples, and reasons can you present to support your position? Plan, write, and revise a composition proposing this law and defending the need for it.

✔ POINTS TO REMEMBER ABOUT ARGUMENTATION

1. Make sure that your topic or opinion is *arguable* (is open to debate) and that other people may have different views about it.
2. Consider what you want readers to understand, think, feel, or do after they read your argument.
3. Make sure that your position (your topic sentence) is neither too narrow nor too broad and that it requires evidence to support it.
4. Consider the background information about your topic that readers may need to know in order to understand your point of view. Why might their viewpoint differ from yours? What kinds of evidence might convince them to believe (or to consider) your point of view?
5. Choose strategies and supporting details that are appropriate for your purpose and your readers.
6. Decide whether you want to make emotional appeals, logical appeals, or both types.
7. Do not make any logical fallacies.
8. Anticipate readers' objections and respond to them effectively.
9. If you are defending a controversial position or if your readers disagree strongly with your position, consult public sources of information about your topic. Cite these sources correctly.
10. Decide how to organize your argument logically so that readers will understand your points.
11. Cross out any irrelevant sentences or details.
12. Use transitional words and expressions to show the relations between your ideas and your sentences.
13. End with a clincher sentence that emphasizes your point.
14. Revise and edit your analysis for clarity and correctness.

PART

3

Essay
Development

13

MOVING FROM PARAGRAPHS TO ESSAYS

A strong essay has the same five qualities of good writing that characterize a strong paragraph:

A Clear Focus:	The main point of a paragraph is the *topic sentence*. The main point of an essay is the *thesis statement*.
Adequate Development:	Each sentence in the paragraph and each paragraph in the essay supports the main idea with specific details.
Unity:	Each paragraph (and the entire essay) sticks to one main point.
Coherence:	Each paragraph (and the entire essay) is organized logically and flows smoothly.
Correctness:	Each paragraph has complete sentences that are relatively error-free.

If you can write paragraphs, you can write essays. The major difference is that an essay is more fully developed than a paragraph. Thus, writing an essay requires you to choose a broader topic and to develop more details than writing a paragraph does. (The typical college essay is approximately 250 to 1,000 words long: 2 to 10 double-spaced typewritten pages.)

You have already practiced crafting and revising strong paragraphs for a variety of purposes. Now you are ready to apply the principles and strategies that you've learned to writing effective essays. These include the following:

- Focusing on a central idea for a clearly defined purpose and audience
- Deciding what strategies are appropriate for achieving your purpose (description, narration, process analysis, comparison and contrast, division and classification, definition, cause and effect, and argumentation)
- Developing your main point with specific experiences, descriptions, observations, facts, statistics, and testimony
- Arranging details and paragraphs in a logical order
- Including transitional words and expressions to help readers understand the development of your ideas
- Writing an effective introduction and conclusion
- Revising for clarity, unity, and coherence
- Editing for correctness

PLANNING AN ESSAY

Both a paragraph and an essay are composed of three sections: an introduction, a "body," and a conclusion. The introductory paragraph in an academic essay often includes a sentence or two stating the main or controlling idea of the essay—the *thesis statement*. A thesis statement serves the same function as a topic sentence: It gives the main idea that the writer wants to communicate to readers and it limits what the writer can discuss. A good thesis statement is a focusing guide for the writer and for the reader. The student essay below illustrates how the thesis statement provides both writer and reader with a clear idea of what the rest of the essay will discuss.

Many of us drift away from our childhood friends as we grow older. We change, they change, and the reasons for staying friends change. For a variety of reasons, it is difficult to stay close with childhood friends.

Friendships often fade and die when friends go their own ways. For example, when friends move away, it becomes increasingly difficult to stay in touch with them. Phone calls to distant friends can't replace face-to-face conversations with pals who live close by. So we often find ourselves talking to far-away friends less and less, and finally we discover that we don't have much to say to them anymore.

In addition to separating geographically, friends can also drift apart

vague   *explan*

socially. Intense careers and expanding families leave people with little time to meet and talk with old friends. Instead of finding time to spend with old friends, many people make new friends in their new social circles: colleagues at work, parents of their children's friends, and spouse's friends.

Metaphor

Another friendship killer is jealousy. As people grow, they change, and some friends can't accept these changes. They envy their old *or also* friends' dates, spouses, children, careers, or lifestyles. And this envy eats away at the friendship, corroding old bonds of love and concern. Some people cannot even understand the changes in their old friends. They get angered or threatened by their friends' growth, decisions, and changing values.

The nursery rhyme is true: "Make new friends, but keep the old. One is silver, and the other is gold." Old friendships can be wonderful, like antique silver. But they can also tarnish and be painful. Thus, we make new friends to take the emotional place of old ones.

WRITING ACTIVITY 1

Answer on separate paper the questions below about the preceding essay.

1. Reread the writer's thesis statement (underscored). What examples or reasons supported this thesis most effectively? (Summarize these reasons in the space below.)

_____

_____

_____

_____

_____

_____

_____

2. Which transitional words made the essay coherent?

_____

_____

_____

3. What did you like about the essay?

_____

_____

_____

_____

 GROUP WORK 1

This writing task will help you explore some of the differences between a paragraph and an essay. Form a group with two or three classmates and decide who will write down the group's responses.

The essay on pages 354–355 of this chapter is an expanded version of the paragraph on pages 309–310 of Chapter 11. Here is that paragraph.

Many of us drift away from our childhood friends as we grow older. Friendships often fade and die when friends go their own ways. For example, when our friends move away, it becomes increasingly difficult to stay in touch with them. Phone calls to distant friends can't replace face-to-face conversations with pals who live close by. So we often find ourselves talking to far-away friends less and less, and finally we discover that we don't have much to say to them anymore. It's difficult to keep a long-distance friendship alive.

Together, compare this paragraph and the essay on pages 354–355 and answer the following questions (on a separate piece of paper):

1. What is the topic sentence of the paragraph? What is the thesis statement of the essay? How do they differ?
2. What are some differences between the opening sentence of the paragraph and the introductory paragraph of the essay?
3. How many examples or reasons did the writer include in the paragraph? What other examples or reasons did the writer include in the essay?
4. How does the conclusion of the essay differ from the concluding sentence in the paragraph?

NARROWING THE SUBJECT AND DEVELOPING A THESIS STATEMENT

Narrowing a subject for an essay is the same process as selecting a topic for a paragraph. Many times, your instructor will give you a broad subject for an essay, and you will have to decide which aspect of the topic you want to focus on. For example, if your essay assignment is "space exploration," you would need to consider what interests you about this subject, what you already know about it, and what else you might want to know about it. Thinking about these issues can help you narrow or limit the assignment to a subject that is manageable in a brief essay. You might decide to write about the benefits of the space shuttle voyages, or the need for a space station in outer space, or why funding on space exploration should be reduced. You might even decide to write a personal essay about why you would (or would not) want to be an astronaut.

Here is an example of how a student used brainstorming and clustering to narrow the broad topic "role models."

Role Models

Person who is everything you want to be
Hero or heroine to imitate   Someone who

inspires you   Famous? (not necessarily)
I have many role models - my dad, my
uncle Bill, Patrick Ewing, Arthur Ashe.
Who's the most important. Well of course I
love my dad. But the person I admire most
is Arthur Ashe Why?   He $\cancel{\text{X}}$ was so
smart and good and dignified.

> **REMINDER** _____
> Narrow your subject by using the prewriting techniques you have learned: freewriting, brainstorming, and clustering. Keep in mind the fact that the "bigger," or more complex, your subject is, the longer your essay will be.

WRITING ACTIVITY 2

Here are ten broad subjects from courses across the college curriculum. Select *three,* and narrow each into a subject that you could write about in an essay of five or six paragraphs. (Do this on a separate piece of paper.)

sex education	role models
pollution	compact disc technology
physical fitness	divorce
political parties	birth control
the armed services	friends
television	ecology

Like a topic sentence, a thesis statement should focus on only one subject. In addition, it must be narrow enough to allow you to discuss your topic in a manageable length. Here are features of thesis statements:

> **SIMILARITIES BETWEEN TOPIC SENTENCES**
> **AND THESIS STATEMENTS** _____
> The topic sentence of a paragraph and the thesis statement of an essay both:
>
> - Communicate a main idea or point in a complete sentence that is clear and precise
> - Include key words that convey the writer's attitude toward the topic
> - Are not too narrow (mere statement of facts requiring little support) or too broad (an assertion that would require a book to support it)

Many professional authors write a *draft* thesis statement that they use to guide the development of their ideas and details. Writing a draft thesis statement—and putting it at the end of the essay's introductory paragraph—will help you keep your essay focused on its main idea. Your examples and reasons will evolve from this draft thesis, and every time you lose track of your point, you can return to the end of your introduction to remind yourself of your goal in writing the essay.

Remember that a thesis statement is always a preliminary assertion. As you revise the various drafts of your essay, you will probably develop new points that support a different thesis. When you are finished revising your essay, revise your thesis statement so that it is more focused and reflects the examples and details in the essay.

Here is the draft thesis statement of the essay on pages 354–355 of this chapter.

It's hard to stay close to the friends you had as a kid.

And here is the revision that the student wrote after he finished writing his essay:

For a variety of reasons, it is difficult to stay close with childhood friends.

The revised thesis statement is clearer and more specific. It will help the writer remember that all the details in the essay must explain the ''reasons'' for the assertion that ''it is difficult to stay close with childhood friends.''

GROUP WORK 2

Form a group with two other students, and choose one person to write the group's responses on a separate piece of paper. Below are several sentences. Decide if each one would make a good thesis statement for an essay. If not, explain why not and revise it to make it into an effective thesis statement. The first one has been done as an example.

1. *Kwanzaa* is an African American holiday that begins on December 26 and lasts for several days. *Too narrow - just a statement of fact*

   REVISION:
   The holiday of Kwanzaa is an important celebration of african american history and culture.

2. This essay will discuss the difficulties of being a parent.
3. Traveling through Europe by train is great, but you need to do many things to prepare for this kind of trip.
4. Racism is a problem in American society.
5. The military provides excellent opportunities for college graduates who are still undecided about their careers.
6. Tuition hikes are really bad for everyone.
7. There are many reasons why couples should live together before making the commitment that marriage represents.
8. My favorite teacher was great.

WRITING ACTIVITY 3

Examine the following brainstorming list that the student writer developed in response to the assignment "Write an essay predicting what education will be like in the next century." After you read the list, write *at least two* different thesis statements that you could develop or support with details in this list.

- Twenty-first century schools will be different.

- All sorts of technological advances.

- No more boring lectures or blackboard drills.

- No classrooms/just huge telecommunication networks.

- All lessons will be "hands-on."

- Everyone will be computer literate.

- Computers will be cheaper than TV sets.

- Students will access information from computers, compact discs, and interactive laser videos.

- Teachers and students will be able to download information and data from satellite dishes.

- Teachers will be "coaches."

- Teachers will select themes for students to explore (in projects).

- All subjects will be taught together in big projects.

- Students of different ages will work together on teams.

Thesis statement 1 _____

_____

_____

_____

Thesis statement 2 _____

_____

_____

_____

KNOWING YOUR PURPOSE AND AUDIENCE

How might you begin developing details for an essay? The first step is to consider your purpose and audience: Why are you writing this essay, and who are your intended readers? Too often, advancing writers feel that their only purpose in writing is to please their teacher. They forget that they must also have their own purpose for writing. Do you remember the purposes that were discussed in the chapters on writing strong paragraphs? They are the same for writing essays:

- To *express* something important to ourselves or to others
- To *explain* something or share information with readers
- To *persuade* readers to think or feel or do something

WRITING ACTIVITY 4

Here are six subjects for essays. Write a possible purpose and audience for an essay about each subject. Then craft a sentence (or two) that states your viewpoint about the subject and that you could support in an essay of five to eight paragraphs.

1. A problem in my school
   Purpose: _____
   Audience: _____
   Thesis statement: _____

   _____

   _____

2. The difficulties of being an only child *or* of having sisters and/or brothers
   Purpose: _____
   Audience: _____
   Thesis statement: _____

   _____

   _____

3. Why I need (or don't need) a car
   Purpose: _____
   Audience: _____
   Thesis statement: _____

   _____

   _____

4. The uses of a computer for doing academic work
   Purpose: _____
   Audience: _____
   Thesis statement: _____

   _____

   _____

5. The worst mistake I ever made
   Purpose: _____
   Audience: _____
   Thesis statement: _____

   _____

   _____

6. The advantages of being an older college student
   Purpose: _____
   Audience: _____
   Thesis statement: _____

   _____

   _____

SUPPORTING A THESIS WITH DIFFERENT TYPES OF PARAGRAPHS

In the Writer's Portfolio section of this book (Chapters 5 through 12), you learned eight different strategies for developing paragraphs. How do you decide which ones to use for the "body" paragraphs of your essay? You probably know the answer to the following questions by thinking about your topic, the purpose and audience for your essay, and the details that you have explored in your prewriting activities. Ask yourself, "How can I best achieve my purpose in this essay? By narrating experiences? By describing, defining, comparing, or contrasting people, things, conditions, or events? Or should I analyze causes and effects or argue for a particular action or point of view?" Often the topic itself (and your ideas about it) suggest the types of strategies you can use to develop your essay.

Your purpose and audience should govern the development of your essays, from the way you narrow your subject to the way you edit your grammar. For example, imagine that your teacher has assigned an essay on careers. Here are several possibilities for developing this essay, based on different purposes and audiences:

1. **Purpose:** To describe the career I want
   Audience: Classmates
   Possible strategies: Describe what clinical psychologists do, contrast their jobs to those of other types of psychologists, and/or explain why I want this career
2. **Purpose:** To explain how one becomes a pharmacologist
   Audience: Students interested in this career
   Possible strategies: Describe what pharmacologists do and classify different types of careers in pharmacology or analyze the process of preparing for a career in pharmacology
3. **Purpose:** To explain why students should seriously consider a career as an elementary school teacher
   Audience: Students who haven't decided on a major
   Possible strategies: Narrate a story that illustrates the rewards of

teaching, explain why our community needs more good elementary school teachers, explain why teaching is an excellent career.

Here is another example of how one's purpose and audience influence the development of the body paragraphs of an essay. A teacher asked students to write an essay about sexual harassment. After doing some freewriting, brainstorming, and clustering on this subject, one student decides that she wants to write about the different kinds of sexual harassment that are taking place at her college. She uses her notes to compose a discovery draft of an essay that is purely descriptive. Here is an outline of this draft:

Paragraph 1:   Introduction with the thesis statement: "Sexual harassment at Winston College is widespread and takes many forms."

Paragraph 2:   Description of the kinds of sexual harassment the writer has experienced

Paragraph 3:   Description of the kinds of sexual harassment her friends and classmates have experienced

Paragraph 4:   Description of how the number of sexual harassment incidents at the college is growing each year

Paragraph 5:   Description of how the writer and her friends try to combat sexual harassment

Paragraph 6:   Conclusion

Suppose this writer read her draft and decided that she wanted to change her purpose. Now she wants to write an essay that will convince college administrators that they are not doing enough to stop sexual harassment at her college. For this purpose and audience, she would have to develop a new thesis, which she could support with different strategies:

Paragraph 1:   Introduction with the thesis statement: "Sexual harassment at Winston College is widespread. It is sick and harmful, and it must be stopped."

Paragraph 2:   *Definition* of what the writer means by sexual
                 harassment

Paragraph 3:   *Narration* of the writer's experiences being sexually
                 harassed by male students

Paragraph 4:   *Description* of the kinds of sexual harassment the writer
                 has heard about from friends and classmates

Paragraph 6:   *Cause-and-effect analysis* of why sexual harassment is
                 so widespread at her school

Paragraph 7:   *Process analysis* of the steps that college
                 administrators must take to reduce sexual harassment
                 at the school

Paragraph 8:   Conclusion

Notice that the essay outlined above is an *argumentative* essay, in which the
writer uses five different paragraph development strategies to support her point.

REMINDER ━━━
The strategies that you use for the ''body'' paragraphs of an essay will
develop naturally from your purpose, audience, and thesis. Don't worry
about what strategy to use; just concentrate on developing as many details
as you can to explain, illustrate, or support your thesis (for your intended
readers).

Here is the revised essay that resulted from the student's notes on ''role
models''—on pages 357–358 of this chapter. The different strategies the writer
used to develop each paragraph are identified in the margins.

A role model is a person who exemplifies all the
things you want to be. He or she is someone you admire,   **definition**
look up to, and learn from. As long as I can remember, my
role model has been Arthur Robert Ashe, Jr. He was
everything I want to be: smart, successful, committed to
helping his people, and devoted to his family.

If I close my eyes, I can still see him. Tall and thin, with the bulging leg muscles of a runner, he looked like a stallion. Whether he was hitting a Grand Slam winner on the tennis court or making a speech in the boardroom, Arthur Ashe was always calm and focused. Quiet and graceful, he was a man of steel. He could stare down anyone and make that person listen to him.

description

In his oversized spectacles, he looked like a professor, which in a way, he was. After a heart attack ended his tennis career in 1979, he decided to try to teach others. In fact, he took on the mission of educating people about the sports history of African Americans. He wrote a three-volume book on this topic (*A Hard Road to Glory*), which he adapted into an award-winning television program. He also wrote instructional articles on tennis for various sports magazines and essays on African Americans for newspapers. In addition to teaching people through his scholarship, Ashe taught in many other ways. He started the African American Athletic Association, which counsels inner-city high school athletes, and he joined TransAfrica, a think tank that produced policy papers about the USA's relations with Africa.

description

narration

description

In addition to being a champion tennis player and a scholar, Arthur Ashe was a great sportsman. Never selfish or self-centered, he always played fair, and he tried to help other athletes. He was the founding father of the tennis players' union, the Association of Tennis Professionals. Unlike sports stars who concentrated on their careers only,

description

Ashe traveled the world looking for young minority players, **cause-and-**
like Yannick Noah, whom Ashe helped become a **effect**
champion. It is no wonder that *Sports Illustrated* magazine **analysis**
named Ashe their "Sportsman of the Year" for 1992.

But Arthur Ashe was much more than an athlete and
an educator. He was a loving husband and father, **description**
spending hours with his family. His greatest agony was
having to tell his young daughter that he had gotten AIDS
from a blood transfusion.

When Arthur Ashe died in 1993, the world lost a hero.
More important, we lost a role model for young people of
color. We must continue to learn about him and to try to **argument**
model our lives after his. We must keep the memory of
this great man alive.

What is the writer's thesis and purpose in this essay?

_____

_____

_____

Did the writer accomplish this purpose? Why or why not?

_____

_____

_____

_____

WRITING ACTIVITY 5

The following student essay is based on the draft that appears on pages 209 through 210 in Chapter 7. Each paragraph below is numbered. Write answers to the questions that follow the essay.

(1) By now, most college students know that using a computer to word-process their drafts makes writing easier and less time-consuming. Although a computer cannot do our thinking or writing, it certainly can help us write more effectively. In particular, students can become more efficient revisers and editors by using the SEARCH (or FIND) command in any computerized word-processing program.

(2) The SEARCH command is helpful at almost every stage of the writing process. For example, if you are writing a draft and you cannot think of the exact words or the correct term for an idea, you can just type ??? and continue writing. Then when you are revising, you can use the SEARCH command to find every place that you typed this series of question marks, and you can replace them with the appropriate or correct term or words. Doing this is far easier than looking up words in a dictionary or a thesaurus while you are trying to get your ideas down.

(3) In addition, if you know you always misspell a word or make the same error over and over, you can use the SEARCH command to locate each instance of the misspelling or error and then you can type in the correction. This helps writers speed up their editing process.

(4) In order to begin the SEARCH command (which is called the FIND or the HUNT command in some programs), you have to know which keys to press so that the program will search a

document to locate every instance of a word, phrase, or symbol (or any group or "string" of characters followed by a space). If you do not know know what keys to use, look up this information in your documentation (book of instructions). Press the SEARCH command keys, and the program will indicate a place for you to type in the string of characters that you want to find. Type in this string of characters and hit the ENTER key. Then look at the monitor screen. The next thing that should appear on the screen in most programs is the question, "Ignore upper/lowercase?" or "Ignore capital letters?" If you want the program to search for your word or phrases exactly as you typed it in your writing, then type N for "No." If you want the program to find every instance of the word or phrase, regardless of whether it has capital letters in it, then type Y for "Yes."

(5) Each time the program finds the word or phrase or string of characters that you told it to search for, it stops at the beginning of the string. This gives you the opportunity to examine the string and decide if you want to keep it, revise it, replace it, or add words to it. You can type in a word or a sentence if you want to add information, or you can correct the spelling of a misspelled word. The SEARCH command is also useful for revising your diction and vocabulary. You can use it to search for vague or "empty" modifiers (such as "a lot," "very," "extremely," "really," "awful," and so forth) and replace each of these words with a more precise word. In addition, you can search for any slang expressions or clichés that you use regularly. The SEARCH command can also be used to find errors in punctuation. For instance, if you ask the program to search for an apostrophe, you can check to see if you have used this punctuation correctly each time.

(6) The SEARCH command allows writers to concentrate on composing and organizing ideas. They know that when they are done with a draft, they can search it, revise it, and edit it in minutes instead of hours. Thus, the SEARCH command is a handy tool for revising.

1. What is the writer's thesis and purpose?

_____

_____

_____

2. Was the introduction effective in making you want to read the rest of the essay? Why or why not?

_____

_____

_____

3. What point is the writer making in paragraph 2, and what strategy did she use to develop this point?

_____

_____

_____

4. What point is the writer making in paragraph 3, and what strategy did she use to develop this point?

_____

_____

_____

5. What point is the writer making in paragraph 4, and what strategy did she use to develop this point?

    _____

    _____

    _____

6. What point is the writer making in paragraph 5, and what strategy did she use to develop this point?

    _____

    _____

    _____

7. Is the conclusion effective? Does it sum up or reinforce the writer's points? Explain your answer.

    _____

    _____

    _____

Sometimes, as you think about your purpose and audience for an essay, you may realize that you need to do more brainstorming and clustering to generate additional ideas. These new details may suggest a different strategy for developing a particular paragraph or for the entire essay.

If you decide that your draft needs additional supporting details, try *branching* it to evaluate your details and to generate new ideas for your revision. Branching lets you see exactly where you do not have enough supporting details. (For additional information on branching as a revision strategy, see pages 110–111 in Chapter 4.) Here are guidelines for branching a draft:

- Write the thesis statement in a circle in the middle of a sheet of paper.
- Write each supporting point in its *own* circle and connect it to the main circle.
- Draw branches out from each supporting point and write in the specific details you used to develop each supporting point.
- Evaluate each supporting point by asking yourself if it clearly sup-

ports or illustrates your thesis and if it can serve as the topic sentence for each ''body'' paragraph.
- Decide if you need additional examples, reasons, facts, statistics, or testimony to support each main point.
- Cross out irrelevant details.
- Develop new details for the circles that do not have enough branches (enough supporting details).

Here is an example of this strategy. Below is a draft of the student paragraph discussed on page 186 in Chapter 6. Following this paragraph is the writer's attempt to branch this draft.

I remember seeing my son in the hospital after his accident and worrying that he was going to die before I could tell him I was sorry and tell him I loved him. Before the accident, we had a fight and we didn't make up. Then he was in intensive care, and all I could think was that he was going to die hating me. He was a mess. I didn't know what to do. He eventually woke up. That hour was the longest one of my life. But we made up and everything was okay. I learned not to stay in a fight with my kids.

Branching her draft paragraph helped this writer develop and organize new details to explain and illustrate her experience. Here is the final version of this writer's essay.

Fights between children and their parents seem a natural part of being in a family. In our struggle to cope with each other's needs and demands, families feud and make up and then fight again over the same issues. However, five years ago, I learned something that forever changed me and my relationships with my children. I learned that sometimes God may not give us the chance to "kiss and make up," and we may have to live with the bitterness of our fights forever.

On that fateful day five years ago, I had a typical screaming fight with my thirteen-year-old son, Bobby. I have long forgotten what it was that we fought about, but I will never forget how angry he was when he left the house. He slammed the door, screaming, "You hate me! You're mean and unfair and I can't take it anymore!" I was upset, but I remember thinking that he would calm down and be home in time for dinner, as he always was after a fight. But dinnertime came and went and there was no Bobby. When the phone rang, I knew something was really wrong.

The police who drove me to the hospital told me that Bobby had been running down Main Street when he was hit by a car whose driver didn't see him. I was frozen with fear. When I finally reached Bobby, all I saw was a still mass under white sheets, tubes covering his face and arms. I sat by his side for an hour. I didn't hear any of the nurses and doctors who tried to talk to me. All I heard was Bobby's voice echoing inside my brain: "You hate me!" "I can't take it anymore!" My son was going to die before I could tell him how sorry I was and how much I loved him.

Bobby was in a coma for a week, and I was consumed by guilt. If only I had been able to go with him. If only I had taught him to be more careful. If only I had not fought with him before he left the house. I knew I would be condemned to hear his angry words over and over again every day of my life. How I wished I could go back in time and make up with him. If we had both calmed down and made up, Bobby would not have stormed out in blind anger.

Bobby finally woke up from his coma, and eventually he recovered fully. He forgave me, and I finally forgave myself. But because of this incident, I vowed never to let him or my other children walk out in anger. To this day, we always resolve our arguments before any of us leaves the house. It helps us remember how much we love and value each other.

WRITING ACTIVITY 6

Examine the single-paragraph assignments that you wrote for Chapters 5 through 12. Select one that you really like or one that you want to work on again. Expand your main point of the paragraph into a thesis statement for an essay. Then develop your ideas in more detail and write an essay based on your paragraph.

ORGANIZING AN ESSAY

The order of the paragraphs in an essay depends on the nature of the supporting details. If you are narrating a story or explaining a process, then the most natural order is a chronological one (in which details are organized as they occurred—or would occur—in time). If you are describing objects, you might use spatial order. Or if your details lead you to describe, define, or analyze several factors, examples, reasons, causes, or effects, then the most logical order is an emphatic one—with details organized from least important to most important.

The body paragraphs of an essay can also be arranged from general to specific. The essay about using the SEARCH command, on pages 369–371 of this chapter, is organized this way.

WRITING ACTIVITY 7

Plan, write, and revise an essay for your English instructor on your feelings about writing. Here are some questions for you to consider: Have your feelings about writing changed since the beginning of this course? If so, how and why? If not, why not? Have your writing strengths and problems changed? If so, how and why? If not, why not? (You don't have to answer these questions in your essay; just think about them to get started.)

Do some freewriting, brainstorming, or clustering about this topic. Develop a thesis statement and compose a discovery draft of an essay. Examine your details and decide whether the way that you organized them is logical. Could you reorder your details in a more effective organization?

WRITING ACTIVITY 8

Here are five subjects. Choose *one* of them to develop in an essay of five or six paragraphs. Follow the guidelines given after the subjects.

1. Who is your role model? Why do you want to be like him or her?
2. Where and how should children learn about sex? Why?
3. If you had more free time, what would you most like to spend this time doing? Why?
4. What is your school's worst problem? What can be done about this problem?
5. Should all students know how to use a computer? If so, why? If not, why not?

Guidelines

Do ten minutes of freewriting on the topic you chose. Write down any experiences that you have had relating to this subject, observations that you have about it, and any facts that you know about it. Narrow your focus for this essay: What point do you want to make about your subject? Decide whom you are writing for: What is this audience like? How familiar are they with the topic? How do they feel about it? Make a list of all the things that they will need or want to know about this topic. Then decide on your purpose: What exactly do you want to explain or describe or prove? What do you want your audience to feel or think or do after reading your essay?

On a separate piece of paper, do five minutes of brainstorming about what you want to explain or illustrate or prove to readers. When you finish brainstorming, circle the words or phrases that seem most important or useful, and draw lines between the circles that seem related. Select one circle from your brainstorming and do five minutes of clustering about it. Next write a sentence that explains what your clustering is about. Turn this sentence into a preliminary thesis statement, and write a discovery draft of an essay (four to six paragraphs) that explains, illustrates, or supports this thesis statement. Branch the draft to determine where you need to add additional details or explanations. Revise your essay using the techniques you learned in Chapter 4.

WRITING INTRODUCTIONS

You'll find it helpful not to think about the introduction to your essay until you have a draft that is worth introducing. Rarely does a writer fully understand his or her thoughts and feelings about a subject until he or she has finished writing a discovery draft about it. So you shouldn't write an introduction until you have a clear idea of what you want your essay to communicate. This doesn't mean that an introductory paragraph is not important. The introduction is actually the most crucial paragraph because it makes the reader decide whether or not to continue reading. In addition, it creates an image of you for readers and helps readers understand why your subject is important or interesting.

Below are several strategies for capturing your reader's attention in your introduction. Each is illustrated by an introduction from an essay by the writer Anna Quindlen.

1. Begin with your thesis statement or with the reason why you are writing the essay's subject.

   There is nothing like a tag sale to force you to confront the hard choices in life. To junk the class notes from Introduction to Psychology and give away the trunk that houses them; to stare with hard, unromantic eyes at the cake plate your husband's great-aunt gave you as a wedding present and tote it out to the car; to look upon a size-8 suit and accept for all time that the body it fits is no longer yours—these things mark milestones, besides providing much-needed closet space.

2. Start with a general statement about your subject. Then narrow your point until you reach the end of the paragraph and present your thesis.

It was always the look on their faces that told me first. I was the freshmen dormitory counselor, and they were the freshmen at a women's college where everyone was smart. One of them would come into my room, a golden girl, a valedictorian, an 800 verbal score on the SATs, and her eyes would be empty, seeing only a busted future, the devastation of her life as she knew it. She had failed biology, messed up the math; she was pregnant. That was when I became pro-choice.

3. Begin with a direct quotation.

The most hateful words I've heard in the last three years were "He'll need surgery." It was not major surgery, thank God; we brought him in early in the morning and carried him out at sunset. But giving anyone permission to open up the blue-white body of your two-year-old is dreadful.

4. Tell a brief story that will lead to your thesis.

When I was a little girl, I loved Halloween because it was the only day of the year when I was beautiful. I had friends who went out dressed as hobos and clowns and witches, but I never would. I was always a princess or a ballet dancer, Sleeping Beauty or Cinderella.

5. Introduce the importance of the subject by presenting facts, statistics, or testimony.

In 1971, *The New England Journal of Medicine* reported the discovery of a connection between a rare form of cancer in young women and a synthetic estrogen called diethylstilbestrol. The drug, which became known familiarly as DES, had been given to pregnant women thought to be in danger of miscarrying, and the cancer was occurring in some of their daughters. It was not until two years after the reports that I found out that I was one of the young women at risk.

6. Startle readers with an eye-opening statement.

Well, another year has gone by and still the Nobel Prize has not been awarded to the inventors of the Snugli baby carrier. I can't figure it.

WRITING ACTIVITY 9

Reread some of the paragraphs that you wrote for the activities in Chapters 5 through 12. Select one to develop into an essay. When you finish writing a discovery draft of this essay, write *two introductions* for it. Use a different technique for composing each introduction.

Here are some common problems that characterize weak essay introductions. Avoid them or revise them in your writing:

> **PROBLEMS IN ESSAY INTRODUCTIONS** —————————
>
> Don't bore readers with the following introductions:
>
> 1. A question that does not have a satisfactory answer:
>
> Will people of the world ever learn to live in peace?
> When will adults stop abusing children?
>
> 2. An apology for lack of knowledge or information:
>
> Although I don't know too much about this topic, . . .
> I am not an expert in this area, but . . .
>
> 3. Announcements about the content of the essay:
>
> In this essay, I will discuss . . .
> Now I am going to tell you about . . .
>
> 4. Overused beginnings such as dictionary definitions, familiar quotations, and clichés:
>
> According to *Webster's Dictionary, love* is . . .
> ''Where there's smoke, there's fire.''

GROUP WORK 3

Choose a partner or two to work with on this activity. Exchange an essay that you wrote for an assignment in this book or another assignment in your English course. Answer the following questions (on a separate piece of paper) about your partner's essay introduction:

1. What strategy did the writer use to develop the introduction?
2. Was this introduction effective in making you want to read the rest of the essay? Why or why not?
3. How else might the writer have introduced his or her topic?
4. What suggestions for revision do you have?

WRITING CONCLUSIONS

An effective conclusion is as important as a good introduction. A strong conclusion leaves readers feeling that the writer has supported his or her thesis. It also gives the essay a satisfactory ending so the reader isn't left hanging. Just as there are several approaches to writing effective introductions, there are a variety of ways of writing interesting conclusions. (The examples below are also from Anna Quindlen's essays.)

1. Briefly summarize the essay's main points.

> I would like to maintain the obscenity standards set so well by my mother and me that afternoon in our living room. She exercised her personal right to throw a dirty book at the wall, and I exercised my personal right to read it and discover that it was not really dirty at all. It worked just fine then, and it will work just fine now.

2. Make an interesting comparison or image.

> They are not homeless. They are people who have no homes. No drawer that holds the spoons. No window to look out upon the world. My God. That is everything.

3. Suggest an action or an idea that readers should consider in light of your essay.

> Of course, between one [housekeeper] leaving and the other arriving, I have thought the same thing: Do it yourself. No one can do it as well as you. That's not true, actually; each one of them did certain things better than I did, gave something that I simply don't have in me. It is hard to find someone who will give your children a feeling of security while it lasts and not wound them too much when it is finished, who will treat those children as if they were her own, but knows—and never forgets—that they are yours.

4. Speculate about what your thesis implies for the future.

> I will try to teach my sons about sex, after I've explained fertile periods and birth control and all the other mechanics that are important to understand but that never really go to the heart of the matter: I believe I will say that when you sleep with someone, you take off a lot more than your clothes.

5. Make a brief remark that sums up your feelings.

> I was born a Catholic and I think I will die one. I will ask for a priest to give me Extreme Unction, as it was given to my

mother, and to her mother before her. At the end, as in the beginning, I will ask for the assistance of the church, which is some fundamental part of my identity. I am a Catholic.

As you write conclusions, try to avoid the following common problems:

PROBLEMS IN ESSAY CONCLUSIONS _____

Here are some "do not's" for writing conclusions:

1. Don't reword your introduction.
2. Don't discuss a completely new idea or another supporting detail.
3. Don't announce what you have done. (For example, do not write statements, that begin with "This paper proved that . . ." or "In this essay, I tried to show that . . .")
4. Don't use familiar quotations or clichés.

REVISING YOUR ESSAYS FOR COHERENCE AND UNITY

Here is a checklist to help you evaluate the coherence and unity in your writing.

**CHECKLIST FOR EVALUATING AN
ESSAY'S COHERENCE AND UNITY** _____

- Make sure that every paragraph supports or develops the essay's thesis statement *and* the paragraph's topic sentence.
- Check to see whether each sentence is logically related to the ones that precede and follow it.
- Organize the essay (and each paragraph within it) in a logical order.
- Use appropriate transitional words and phrases to signal the relations between the paragraphs and the relations among the ideas in each paragraph.
- Repeat the key words that limit the focus of the thesis statement (or of the topic sentence of each paragraph).
- Use pronouns and synonyms to keep your main point echoing throughout the essay.

 GROUP WORK 4

Form a group with two or three students and choose someone to record the group's answers to the questions that follow the essay below.

Sometimes it seems that people who study teenage crime don't bother talking or listening to teenagers. Ivory-tower professors often assert that teenage crime is a "socioeconomic" problem. "Minority males," they say, often commit juvenile crime to get respect from their peers, to get money to survive, and to fight racism and the "system." Psychologists have related theories about why teenagers commit crimes. They say that male teenagers commit crimes to feel powerful, especially teenage boys who come from fatherless homes. A look at the real world does not support these theories at all.

Many male teenagers raised by single mothers do not commit crimes. The crime rate among wealthy teenagers is rising higher than the rate of lower-income teens. The number of crimes committed by teenage girls is becoming almost as high as the number committed by boys.

The most probable cause of teenage crime is the desire for peer group acceptance. Teenagers steal to be "cool," to show off, and to take socially approved risks. If you talk to teenage criminals from different social classes, you will hear them echo the same sentiment: "Crime is fun." They don't seem to know—or to care—about "right" and "wrong." They are cut off from society's norms, doing what their friends think is cool.

Teenage crime reflects the fact that our society is becoming increasingly violent—in the media and in reality. Kids hear audiences clap as the hero or heroine on the screen pumps bullets into somebody's head. Even the cartoon that teenagers watch are violent: The Simpsons are forever abusing each other and getting immense enjoyment from this.

If we look more carefully at the teenagers who are really

committing crimes today, we can see that they don't resemble the criminals in academic articles or psychological reports. The causes of teenager crime are complex and often confusing.

1. What is the writer's thesis? Does the essay stick to this main point? If not, where does it go off on a tangent?
2. Examine each paragraph: Does it have any sentences that are not clearly related to the main idea? If so, which ones?
3. Is every sentence logically related to the one that precedes it and to the one that follows it? If not, which sentences should be crossed out, rearranged, or rewritten?
4. Which sentences need transitions to show their relation to the preceding sentences?
5. Which paragraphs need transitions to show how they relate to the ideas in the paragraph that precedes them?
6. What other revisions can you suggest to improve this essay?

GROUP WORK 5

Form a group of three students. Examine an essay that you wrote for one of the Writing Activities in this chapter. Exchange essays and read your classmate's essay. Write answers to the six questions in the preceding Group Work activity. When you get your classmate's comments back, revise your essay based on his or her responses to it.

REMINDER ━━━━━━━━━━━━━━━━━━━━━━━━━━
Signal the connections between your ideas by repeating the key words in your thesis statement (and in each topic sentence), by using transitions, and by using pronouns and synonyms that refer back to the main point of the essay.

WRITING ACTIVITY 10

Plan, write, and revise an essay on *one* of the following subjects:

- The most interesting person or place you know
- A person who influenced your decision to go to college
- An ideal place to live

- An experience that taught you an important lesson
- How to build something or how to fix something
- The similarities and the differences between two jobs
- Types (or categories) of problems that you have experienced being in college
- What makes a person a "good parent" or a "good sibling"
- Why you like or dislike your job
- What happens when parents overprotect their children
- Why companies should or should not test their employees for drug use

GETTING READERS' RESPONSES

Use the checklist below to help you revise the drafts of your essays. Ask family, friends, and classmates to answer the questions below honestly and fully.

ESSAY CHECKLIST ─────────────────────────────

1. Does the essay have an interesting introduction that includes a clear statement of the writer's main point?
2. Is this main point appropriate for an essay or is it too general or too narrow?
3. Does each supporting paragraph include details that are appropriate for the writer's purpose and audience?
4. Are there enough details to accomplish the writer's purpose?
5. Are there any details or sentences that do not illustrate or explain the essay's main idea?
6. Which details include specific and concrete language? Which details are too vague or abstract?
7. Can you follow the order in which the details are developed? If not, why not?
8. Has the writer used transitions appropriate to link ideas within paragraphs and between paragraphs?
9. Is each paragraph coherent? Is the entire essay coherent? If not, why not?
10. Does the essay have an effective conclusion?
11. What suggestions do you have for improving this draft?

■ EXPLORING FURTHER

On pages 366 through 368 of this chapter, you read a student essay about Arthur Ashe. Here is an essay by Ashe that he wrote for the *New York Times* and the *Washington Post* in 1977.

Since my sophomore year at UCLA, I have become convinced that we blacks spend too much time on the playing fields and too little time in the libraries. Consider these facts: for the major professional sports of hockey, football, basketball, baseball, golf, tennis and boxing, there are roughly only 3170 major league positions available (attributing 200 positions to golf, 200 to tennis and 100 to boxing). And the annual turnover is small.

There must be some way to assure that those who try but don't make it to pro sports don't wind up on street corners or in unemployment lines. Unfortunately, our most widely recognized role models are athletes and entertainers—"runnin' " and "jumpin' " and "singin' " and "dancin'."

Our greatest heroes of the century have been athletes—Jack Johnson, Joe Louis, and Muhammad Ali. Racial and economic discrimination forced us to channel our energies into athletics and entertainment. These were the ways out of the ghetto, the ways to get that Cadillac, those regular shoes, that cashmere sport coat.

Somehow, parents must instill a desire for learning alongside the desire to be Walt Frazier. Why not start by sending black professional athletes into high schools to explain the facts of life?

I have often addressed high school audiences and my message is always the same. "For every hour you spend on the athletic field, spend two in the library. Even if you make it as a pro athlete, your career will be over by the time you are 35. You will need that diploma."

Have these pro athletes explain what happens if you break a leg, get a sore arm, have one bad year or don't make the cut for five or six tournaments. Explain to them the star system, wherein for every star earning millions there are six or seven others making $15,000 or $20,000 or $30,000. Invite a bench-warmer or a guy who didn't make it. Ask him if he sleeps every night. Ask him whether he was graduated. Ask him what he would do if he became disabled tomorrow. Ask him where his old high school athletic buddies are.

We have been on the same roads—sports and entertainment—too long. We need to pull over, fill up at the library and speed away to Congress and the Supreme Court, the unions and the business world.

I'll never forget how proud my grandmother was when I graduated from UCLA. Never mind the Davis Cup. Never mind the Wimbledon title. To this day, she still doesn't know what those names mean. What mattered to her was that of her more than thirty children and grandchildren, I was the first to be graduated from college, and a famous college at that. Somehow, that made up for all those floors she scrubbed all those years.

Discussion Questions

1. What is Ashe's thesis in this essay?
2. Whom do you think he imagined as his readers, and what was his purpose in writing this essay for these readers?
3. What might be another title for this essay?
4. What strategies did Ashe use to support his thesis?
5. What is the point he is trying to make in his conclusion?
6. Did Ashe convince you of his thesis? Why or why not?
7. How did he achieve unity and coherence?

WRITING ASSIGNMENTS

Here are four writing assignments. Before you respond to any of them, read the prewriting questions that follow the fourth assignment. Answering these questions will help you get ideas for these assignments.

WRITING ASSIGNMENT 1

Write an essay responding to the points that Arthur Ashe made in his essay. Do you think that teachers and coaches should encourage African American children and teenagers to spend more time in the library and less time playing sports or music? Why or why not? As you think about your response, consider the fact that Ashe himself represents a possible counterargument to his thesis. As a brilliant, multitalented African American athlete, he was widely respected and admired by people of all racial and ethnic backgrounds. Because he was a ''superstar,'' his words and actions helped break down damaging stereotypes of African Americans.

WRITING ASSIGNMENT 2

Write an essay describing yourself. (You may want to look at the paragraph that you wrote for assignment 2 on page 166 of Chapter 5, which asked for a similar description.) Begin by thinking of the one word that best describes you at this point in your life. Decide on a purpose and an audience for this essay. For example, you might write a description that will convince a person whom you find attractive to go out on a date with you. Or write a description that will convince a potential employer to hire you. Or write a description that will convince a school to which you might want to transfer to accept your application.

WRITING ASSIGNMENT 3

Write an essay describing the most important decision that you ever made. Decide on a purpose and an audience for this essay. Help readers understand your decision and why it was easy or difficult to make. Also let readers know how this decision affected your life (then and now).

WRITING ASSIGNMENT 4

Why do you think the Golden Rule is such an important moral value in so many cultures? This rule—"Do unto others as you would have them do unto you"—is universal. For example, in the New Testament, Saint Matthew instructs us, "All things whatsoever ye would that men should do to you, do ye even so to them; for this is the law and the prophets." The Jewish Talmud states, "What is hurtful to yourself do not do to your fellow man. That is the whole of the Torah, and the rest is commentary." According to Islamic tradition, "No one of you is a believer until he loves for his brother what he loves for himself." And Buddhist doctrines warn us, "Hurt not others with that which pains yourself." Finally, the Hindu god Mahabharata tells us, "This is the sum of duty: Do not do to others which if done to thee would cause thee pain." Write an essay about the Golden Rule.

Prewriting Questions

1. What is your focus? Is it too narrow or too broad?
2. What else do you need to find out about your subject or your focus, and where will you look for this information?
3. What do you want readers to understand, or think, or do after they finish reading your essay?
4. Should you describe your observations about specific people, places, or things? If so, what do they look/sound/smell/feel/taste like?
5. Should you narrate a story or a sequence of events? If so, what background information will readers need to know?
6. Should you define your key terms and offer some examples of what you mean by them?
7. Should you explain the similarities or differences between the things that you are discussing?

8. Should you analyze the categories, or the types, or the causes and re-sults of specific events or behaviors?

9. Should you argue the worth or importance of specific ideas or actions? If so, should you offer any facts, data, or testimony to illustrate or sup-port your points?

✔ POINTS TO REMEMBER ABOUT PLANNING, WRITING, AND REVISING ESSAYS

1. Begin with a clear sense of your purpose and your readers.

2. Develop a thesis statement that states your main point in a specific, complete sentence.

3. Consider background information about your topic that readers may need to know in order to understand your explanations.

4. Choose strategies and supporting details that are appropriate for your purpose and audience.

5. Think about whether you should include facts, statistics, and testimony to clarify or support your thesis statement.

6. Organize your essay logically so that readers will understand your points, and use transitional words and expressions to show the relations between your ideas and your sentences.

7. Check to make sure that you have not made any logical fallacies.

8. Reread every supporting detail to make sure that it is relevant to the topic sentence. If it isn't, cross it out.

9. Make sure every detail includes specific, concrete language and descrip-tive words that appeal to readers' five senses.

10. Branch each paragraph to see where it needs additional supporting details.

11. Make sure that your revised details are organized logically in an order that readers can follow.

12. Make sure that each sentence is logically related to the ones that pre-cede and follow it.

13. End with a conclusion that sums up your points.

14. Edit every paragraph to make it relatively free of errors in sentence structure, grammar, spelling, punctuation, and capitalization. (If you are writing with a word-processing program, use the spell-check and the grammar-check functions.)

PLANNING AND WRITING ESSAY TESTS

Almost every college course requires students to take essay examinations or timed writing tests. In one sense, these tests seem unfair. The pressure of time in the testing situation prevents students from producing their best writing. Also, timed writing tests make it difficult to do what this book has taught advancing writers to do: plan and compose thoughtfully, revise several times, and edit slowly and carefully. Most teachers take this into consideration when they evaluate timed writing. They know that even the best writers may not produce strong paragraphs and essays in timed essay tests.

On the other hand, writing against the clock prepares students for the timed writing situations they will face in their future careers. Think of the kinds of writing that most professionals do—reports, interoffice memos, letters, and proposals. Much of this writing is done on the spot to meet a deadline. For instance, corporate executives don't need—or have—an hour to brainstorm ideas for a technical memo. Doctors and lawyers don't have time to think about the writing strategies that would be most appropriate for reports to their clients. And police officers don't have time to revise their accident reports for better organization and tone. All these professionals must produce clear, coherent writing under the pressure of time and stress. You can learn to do this too.

PREPARING FOR ESSAY EXAMINATIONS

Essay examinations help determine how well students understand the content and skills taught in a course. The best way to prepare for these exams is to keep up with the readings and the assignments throughout the semester. Last-minute cramming cannot substitute for reading and taking notes over a period of weeks or months. In order to demonstrate your understanding of the concepts and content of a course on an essay test, you must know the material well. Thus, you should study for each of your courses each night or on a weekly basis.

Another way to prepare for an essay exam is to keep a *double-entry notebook.* This is a book in which you can write your notes and also write comments about your notes. Here is a sample from a student's double-entry notebook:

Here are guidelines for keeping a double-entry notebook.

HOW TO KEEP A DOUBLE-ENTRY NOTEBOOK

Prepare your notes for studying by doing the following:

1. Instead of writing on every page of your notebook, write your notes on the right-hand pages only. Take careful notes on class

lectures and the material in your assigned (and optional) read-ings, and write these notes only on the right-hand pages.

2. On the left-hand pages, write your responses to the notes on the right-hand pages. As you read your notes (on the right-hand pages), think about your reactions to what you are reading and write your questions, comments, and reactions on the left-hand pages.

3. If you jot down any questions on the left-hand pages, remember to write answers to these questions.

Keeping a double-entry notebook and studying the course material daily are the surest means of learning and of doing well on exams.

UNDERSTANDING ESSAY QUESTIONS

Essay questions often provide clues about how the teacher expects students to respond. Read each essay question twice and look for these clues. One type of clue in every essay question is the *cue verb*—the instruction that tells writers what strategies to use in developing and writing their response. Here are some cue verbs and the strategies that they suggest:

Analyze:	Describe each part of a process, object, idea, or problem separately and show how they relate to one another and to the whole.
Argue:	State your point of view and provide support or evidence for it.
Classify:	Separate people, objects, ideas, or problems into groups according to characteristics that all members share.
Compare:	Describe or explain similarities and differences.
Contrast:	Describe or explain differences (only).
Define:	Explain the meanings of the word, idea, or theory and provide examples to illustrate these meanings.
Describe:	Provide specific sensory details so that readers can experience your topic from your perspective.
Evaluate:	Explain the worth or value of something or someone by examining its good and bad points.
Explain:	Give examples and reasons.
Identify:	Define and explain who, what, when, where, why, and how.
Illustrate:	Describe several examples.
Narrate:	Relate a sequence of events.

Outline: List the main ideas and the most important secondary points.

Summarize: Select the main points and briefly describe them in a paragraph or two.

Trace: Begin with the first occurrence of the event and describe its progress up to the present.

Here is an example of a question with two cue verbs. Read the student response that follows the question and decide whether the student has provided the information that the teacher asked for.

Q: Identify the NBER and explain its functions.

> The NBER is the National Bureau of Economic Research, an independent organization that decides officially when the peaks and troughs of each business cycle occur. The NBER members do this by examining and interpreting changes in the economic indicators. The NBER does not make an official decision about a turning point in the business cycle until all of the members agree that it has occurred. This makes the NBER trustworthy for all the government and business economists who try to predict economic changes.

Every time you read an essay question, circle the cue verb (or verbs) and do what it asks you to do. Many well-prepared students fail tests because they ignore or misinterpret these cue verbs. They write excellent responses to questions that they have *not* been asked! Here is an example of this problem:

Q: Analyze the internal and external factors affecting the American business cycle. (10 points)

The business cycle is the pattern of change in the general economic activity of the country. It consists of four phases that come one right after another: expansion, peak, contraction, and trough. In the trough (the lowest point), the economy remains in a decline until people start to buy more goods and services. The increase in the demands for these goods and services puts the economy into the expansion phase (the first phase) of another cycle. Clearly the business cycle affects the way that individuals and businesses in the United States spend money.

The writer of the preceding response ignored the cue verb *analyze*. Instead of describing the factors affecting the business cycle, the writer defined what the cycle is. The answer is excellent, but it won't get any credit because it does not answer the question—it does not analyze the factors driving the busines cycle. Here is how another writer responded to this question.

Q: (Analyze) the internal and external factors affecting the American business cycle. (10 points)

The American business cycle has many internal and external factors driving it. The external factors are the ones that take place outside the economy. The most important one is international relations. Imports, exports, and wars can expand or contract a nation's economy. Another external factor consists of political policies (about welfare, immigration, taxation, etc.). The third external factor that affects our economy is new discoveries.

Four internal factors cause changes in the business cycle: (1) capital investment (of money and equipment), (2) changes in the sizes of inventories, (3) aggregate (overall) demand for goods and services, and (4) the *government's control of the money supply.*

All of these internal and external factors are related. A change in one usually leads to changes in the others.

Note that this writer circled the cue verb and underlined the key words—the terms and ideas that the teacher expects to see in students' responses to the question.

> **REMINDER** ────────────────
> Read the entire question carefully and circle every cue verb. Then under-line key words and ideas. Use these key words or ideas to develop your topic sentence or thesis statement.

GROUP WORK 1

Form a group with two or three classmates and examine the essay questions below. Together circle every cue verb and underline key terms and ideas. Then, in the space below each question, write down what you think the assignment is asking you to do. Do *not* write an answer to the question; write what you might do to answer the question effectively. The first one has been done as an example.

1. (*English*) Trace the changes in the <u>character</u> of Shakespeare's <u>Hamlet</u>.

Describe how Hamlet's behavior, words, and personality change from the beginning of the play to the end of the play.

2. (*History*) Analyze the causes of the fall of the Berlin Wall.

3. (*Economics*) Which of the health-care policies that we analyzed is the fairest to all Americans? Justify your selection.

4. (*Music History*) Outline the contemporary musical trends we discussed this semester. Then choose two of these trends and compare them.

5. (*Political Science*) Select one of the congressional bills that we have discussed and describe its development from a draft bill into the current law.

Sometimes teachers will use a vague cue verb such as *discuss* or *examine* in an essay question. These catchall cues usually mean ''explain'' or ''analyze and illustrate.'' If an essay exam question asks you to ''discuss'' a topic (and does not provide any other cue verbs), respond to the question by describing each important part of the topic, explain the importance of each part, and support your explanations with examples or other relevant evidence. Here is an example of a student's notes prepared for a question with vague cues:

This section of the test is worth 25 points. Write a brief essay in which you examine the economic indicators of the business cycle and discuss the relations between these indicators and general economic activity.

NOTES Economic Indicators - tools for predicting changes in the economy
1. Leading Indicators - 12 variables affecting production & employment (work week, layoff rate, new orders, vendor performance,

business formations, contracts, building
permits, inventory changes, price changes,
stock prices, changes in liquid assets,
changes in the money supply)

2. Coincident Indicators (occur at same time) —
employment, personal income, production
and sales, and the composite index

3. Lagging Indicators — changes that happen
after economy changes (business, labor,
debt, and interest)

WRITING ACTIVITY 1

Read each of the following essay questions. Circle the cue verbs and underline the key terms and ideas in each question. Then write down what students would have to include in their responses to answer the question effectively. The first one has been done as an example.

1. In a brief paragraph, discuss economic aggregate demand.

The answer should define what "economic
aggregate demand" means and should describe
one or two examples.

2. Describe Pavlov's experiment with dogs. Explain Pavlov's original purpose and explain his important discovery.

3. Discuss Erik Erikson's eight psychosocial stages of human development.

4. Define *cult* and discuss why teenagers may be attracted to cults and join them.

5. Discuss the main causes of environmental pollution.

A final word of wisdom about interpreting essay questions: Before you begin your responses, circle and number each part of the question. Often an essay question will contain two or three parts (with a separate cue verb for each part). Some students get so caught up responding to the first part of the question that they ignore or forget to answer the other parts. For example, how many parts are there in the following essay question?

As we mature, we often see things from different perspectives. Write an essay describing a person whom you know now and whom you knew well when you were a child. Be specific so that readers can experience this person the way that you did as a child. Then describe your perception of the person today. How and why did your perception of this person change? (25 points)

This question is deceptive. It may look easy, but it is quite complex. It has five parts:

1. *Identify* a person whom you know now and whom you knew well when you were a child.
2. *Describe* this person from your perspective as a child.
3. *Describe* your perception of the person today.
4. *Explain* how your perception changed.
5. *Explain* why your perception of this person changed.

Here is a student's response to this question:

As we mature, we often see things from different perspectives. Write an essay describing a person whom you know now and whom you knew well when you were a child. Be specific so that readers can experience this person the way that you did as a child. Then describe your perception of the person today. How and why did your perception of this person change? (25 points)

My uncle, Kyle Peterson, has been a second father to me since I was born. When I was young, Uncle Kyle always seemed so old (even though he is only ten years older than me). Uncle Kyle often baby-sat for me, and he was a strict disciplinarian. He'd punish me if I lied or did something I wasn't supposed to do, but he never yelled at me — he was always calm and serious. I knew how much he loved me and that he wanted me to learn right from wrong. Uncle Kyle was my all-powerful protector and guide.

Today our roles have reversed. Uncle Kyle is very ill, and I take care of him. He is frail and fragile now. He rests his pale bony arm on my shoulder as I guide him places. As he gets weaker he seems almost to be getting younger: more self-centered and less aware of the consequences of his words and actions.

Obviously Uncle Kyle has changed. But I have changed too. I am wiser now. I love Uncle Kyle, but I see that he always had weaknesses and problems that I simply ignored in my childish desire to see him as my great protector.

If this writer had not responded to all five parts of the question, the essay would not receive full credit. Remember to circle and number each part—or cue verb—in every essay question.

BUDGETING YOUR TIME

Before you pick up your pen or pencil, read the entire test to get an overview of what it includes. Read every question and note its point value (the number of points or credit the teacher will give to its response). Determine the total amount of time you have for the entire test and decide how many minutes you should spend responding to each question. (You might want to note this number in the margin next to each question.) This will enable you to budget your total test time wisely.

The worst mistake students can make in writing a response to an essay question is to waste time recopying a draft. Many students fail tests because they run out of time as they are recopying their drafts or they don't leave enough time to edit what they have recopied. Plan the time that is allotted to each question on a test. Compose the first draft in your head or write scratch notes and outlines on scrap paper before you write the essay. Leave time and space for revising and editing. (If you can, write on every other line so that you will have a place for your revisions and corrections.)

The more you practice responding to timed essay questions, the better you will get at writing effective answers in one draft. A key part of preparing for essay exams is learning to budget your time effectively on practice tests. Here are some suggestions:

- Read the test information booklet or ask your teacher or adviser about the test's time limit. Know in advance exactly how long you will have to answer each essay question.
- If there is more than one essay question on the test, choose the one that you know the most about—not the one that you feel the most strongly about. Sometimes when students select a controversial topic on an essay test, they get so caught up in their emotional responses to the topic that they forget to include logical reasons and supporting evidence.
- If you have to answer several essay questions, examine the point value of each question and allot your total time accordingly. Spend the most amount of time planning, writing, and editing the response to the essay question that is worth the most points.
- Make up practice questions similar to the ones on the test and time yourself as you respond to these practice questions. Budget your time. For example, if the time limit for each question is a half hour, you might budget five minutes for brainstorming and writing notes, five minutes for focusing and arranging your ideas, fifteen minutes for writing the essay, and five minutes for revising and editing. Check the time every five minutes so that you can determine how far behind or ahead of your planned time you are.

WRITING ACTIVITY 2

Practice the techniques above by planning a response to the following questions. Do *not* write the essays; just plan how you would go about responding to these essay questions. Then answer the questions that follow the essay questions.

Essay Examination: You have one hour to write and edit essay responses to *both* questions below. Please write your essays on a separate piece of paper.

A.   What were the purposes and goals of your writing course? Write a brief essay describing your interpretation of the purposes and goals of the course for which you are using this textbook. (25 points)

B.   How has this course (and/or this textbook) changed your writing? Write a brief essay describing the effects of this course (and/or this book) on your writing processes or compositions. (75 points)

1. Which question would you answer first? Why?

_____

_____

_____

2. How much time would you allot to each question? Why?

_____

_____

_____

_____

WRITING THE ESSAY

After you finish writing your notes and planning your response to an essay question, decide which strategy it calls for:

• **Describing** a person, place, object, process, or point of view as he, she, or it relates to the topic

• **Narrating** an experience that reflects your ideas or feelings about the topic

• **Analyzing** the parts or categories of an object, idea, or event *or* explaining how to do or to make something

- **Comparing** or **contrasting** two or more people, objects, processes, events, or concepts by describing points of similarity and difference between them
- **Classifying** people, things, processes, events, or viewpoints into groups according to characteristics that are shared by all members of the group
- **Defining** the topic by explaining its distinguishing characteristics and by illustrating it with examples of what you mean by it
- **Analyzing** the causes or the effects of an event, a condition, or a behavior
- **Arguing** your point of view by using several of these strategies.

Make sure that your thesis statement, topic sentence, or main point repeats the key words in the essay question. Here is an example:

QUESTION: What are the *four phases of the business cycle?* Describe each in detail.

THESIS: The *four phases of the business cycle* are expansion, peak, contraction, and trough.

WRITING ACTIVITY 3

Reread the two essay questions in Writing Activity 2, on pages 401–402 of this chapter. On a separate piece of paper, plan, write, revise, and edit two essay responses to these questions. Limit yourself to the one-hour time limit indicated in the essay exam instructions.

RESPONDING TO AN ESSAY TEST OF WRITING SKILLS

Teachers use essay examinations to evaluate students' learning and to assess their ability to apply their knowledge to new problems and situations in a discipline. Essay tests of students' writing skills have a different purpose. Colleges administer these tests to determine whether students have the academic writing skills necessary to perform well in school and in the careers for which college is preparing them. Placement tests are used to place students into appropriate courses, competency tests determine students' readiness to do upper-level work, and exit or proficiency tests determine students' readiness to exit a course or graduate.

   The writing skills that you have learned in this book are the same skills that you need to use for any writing test. All essay exams and writing tests require you to do some thinking and prewriting about the topic, to develop a clear thesis, to provide specific details arranged in logical paragraphs, and to revise and edit your essay so that it is clear, coherent, and relatively correct. A timed test, however, necessitates speeding up the time that you devote to each stage of the writing process (prewriting, planning, writing, revising, and editing).

Before you take any writing test, you should find out as much as you can about it. What kinds of questions does it include? What is the time limit for each question? How are responses scored? Are there any sample test questions to practice with?

The most important thing to remember when your writing skills are being evaluated is to try to relax. Don't freeze up or let anxiety overwhelm you. Keep reminding yourself that you know how to write a strong response. You have a variety of prewriting strategies for developing your response to the test topic and a variety of techniques for revising and editing your answer. Here are some additional tips:

TIPS FOR WRITING WELL
ON TIMED ESSAY TESTS ───────────────────────────

1. If you have a choice of topics or questions to answer, choose the topic that you know the most about.
2. Do some prewriting. Freewrite, brainstorm, cluster, or branch in order to get a sense of what you know about the topic.
3. Write a very brief introduction, and make sure that it includes your thesis statement or point of view about the topic.
4. Be specific and concrete. Don't write vague generalizations or clichés. Use experiences, observations, and the knowledge you have gained from reading to support and illustrate your assertions.
5. Write one draft. Skip lines and leave room to put in your revisions and corrections.
6. Wear a watch and check the time. Plan how much time you will need to write, revise, edit, and proofread your response.

WRITING ACTIVITY 4

The CUNY Writing Skills Assessment Test is used to evaluate the writing skills of more than 35,000 students at The City University of New York every year. Here is a sample form of this writing test. Follow the directions and write your response on a separate piece of paper.

THE CITY UNIVERSITY OF NEW YORK
WRITING SKILLS ASSESSMENT TEST

Form WF

Directions

You will have 50 minutes to plan and write the essay assigned below. You may wish to use your 50 minutes in the following way: 10 minutes planning what you are going to write; 30 minutes writing; 10 minutes rereading and correcting what you have written. You should express your thoughts clearly and organize your ideas so that they will make sense to a reader. Correct grammar and sentence structure are important.

You must write your essay on *one* of the following assignments. Read each one carefully and then choose either A *or* B.

A. Job security is more important than the opportunity to change the kind of work one does. People should be guaranteed a steady job for the rest of their working lives (even if the daily routine never changes) rather than have the freedom to change jobs along with the risk of having no job at all.

Do you agree or disagree with what this passage says? Explain and illustrate your answer from your own experience, your observations of others, or your reading.

B. Recent laws make it possible to punish teenagers as if they were adults. This is unfair, because teenagers are often unaware of the seriousness of the crimes they commit. They should not be condemned to spend years of their young lives in jail.

Do you agree or disagree with what this passage says? Explain and illustrate your answer from your own experience, your observations of others, or your reading.

✔ POINTS TO REMEMBER ABOUT WRITING EFFECTIVE ESSAY TESTS

1. Prepare for tests by keeping a double-entry notebook and by studying nightly (or weekly).
2. Compose practice essay questions based on your lecture notes and as-signed readings. Write timed essays in response to your questions.

3. When you take an essay test or a writing test, read the test's directions, time limits, and point value for each question. Budget your total time appropriately.

4. Circle and number the parts and cue verbs in each question and make sure that you respond to all of them.

5. Think about the strategy that each cue verb calls for.

6. Write a thesis statement that uses key words from the question.

7. Write scratch notes on scrap paper. Do *not* write a draft and recopy it.

8. Skip lines in your essay so that you will have room to make neat additions, substitutions, and corrections.

9. Keep an eye on the clock and make sure you will have enough time to finish answering all the questions.

10. Leave time to revise, edit, and proofread your essay carefully.

PART

4

The Writer's
Handbook

C H A P T E R

15

SENTENCE STRUCTURE

A common concern voiced by many student writers is, "I don't know how to write good sentences." Do you share this concern? If you do, this chapter will help you see that you already know how to create effective sentences. Indeed, if you worry about your ability to compose and use sentences, think about this fact: Although you may not be able to explain exactly what sentences are, you have been speaking them since childhood and writing them since first grade. This chapter will give you many opportunities to craft clear sentences, and it will also help you identify and correct errors in your sentences.

UNDERSTANDING THE SENTENCE

English sentences have a number of identifying features, many of which you already know. Here are some of these characteristics:

1. A sentence is a group of words that expresses a complete thought: "Prof. Allan Brick likes his students."
2. A sentence has a word or a word group that serves as its subject: "*Prof. Allan Brick* likes his students."
3. A sentence has a word or a word group that serves as its verb: "Prof. Allan Brick *likes* his students."
4. A sentence begins with a capital letter and ends with a mark of final punctuation (a period, an exclamation point, or a question mark): "Allan Brick likes his students."

A sentence must have a subject and a verb. The *subject* is the person, place, thing, or idea that the sentence is about or that is doing the action of the sentence. The *verb* expresses the action that the subject is doing or the condition being experienced by the subject. The verb also indicates the sentence's tense (the time of the action or condition expressed in the sentence).

If you can speak English, you can identify the subject and the verb of any sentence by using your natural language ability to read sentence clues. For example, what is the subject of the "sentence" below? What is its verb?

The grandiths flubbered on the plash.

Your knowledge of English word order, sentence parts, and word endings lets you identify subjects and verbs even in nonsense sentences. To find the subject of this sentence, you probably asked yourself, "Who or what is this sentence about?" The answer is *grandiths*. The subject of a sentence is often a *noun* (a person, place, thing, quality, or idea) or a *pronoun* (*he, she, it, they,* and so forth).

To find the verb in the nonsense sentence, you probably asked yourself, "What word tells what the subject did or experienced?" The answer is *flubbered*. Note that the *-ed* ending on *flubbered* lets you know that this action took place at some time in the past.

A verb can consist of more than one word. For example, here are some verbs that consist of a verb preceded by a *helping verb:*

has studied	*will* study	*has been* studying
had studied	*will have* studied	*was* studying

Remember that you cannot use the *-ing* form of a verb (*studying*) as the verb of a sentence unless you include a helping verb. Here are examples of word groups that are not complete sentences because the helping verb has been left out of each verb:

A. The graduate student studying for a final exam.
B. She hoping to get an *A* on her essay test.

Compare the word groups above to the sentences below:

A. The graduate student *was* studying for a final exam.
B. She *is* hoping to get an *A* on her essay test.

The verb of a sentence can be an *action verb*—a verb that expresses the action that the subject is performing—or it can be a *linking verb*—a verb that expresses the relation between the subject and another word (or words) that identifies or describes the subject. Common linking verbs are *be, appear, become,* and *seem.* Here are examples of each type of verb.

Action Verbs:
Lourdes *wrote* five drafts of her first essay, and then she *revised* her final version two more times.

Linking Verbs:

Lourdes *is* the best writer in our class, and she *feels* confident about her ability to succeed in college.

WRITING ACTIVITY 1

Read each sentence below. Draw a circle around the subject of the sentence and then underline the verb that tells what this subject is doing or experiencing. The first one has been done as an example.

The (portfolio project) in my English class is helping me to improve my writing. The project requires each student to keep a portfolio. A portfolio is actually a folder of one's writing. In this folder, students put their drafts and revisions. Each day, the student takes out a draft to revise or edit. Sometimes he or she reads aloud a draft or a revision to a group of classmates. They help the writer see problems in his or her writing. In addition, classmates can help one another to feel more confident about their writing. This process also reveals how much our essays have improved. At the end of the semester, we will select the three best pieces from our portfolio. Our teacher will evaluate these for our final grades. Meanwhile, I am really pleased with my progress.

IDENTIFYING AND CORRECTING FRAGMENTS

In Chapter 4, you learned about the importance of editing your writing for academic English conventions. One of the most important of these conventions is sentence completeness. Most readers, especially teachers and employers, expect to see complete, correct sentences in a piece of writing. They do not expect to see *fragments*—parts of sentences punctuated as if they were complete sentences. For example, how do you think readers would react to the following three fragments?

Playing basketball, my favorite sport ever since I was about five years old. When I shoot hoops with my friends on the courts in our neighborhood. A glorious and satisfying experience.

None of these statements about basketball is a complete sentence; each is a fragment. These fragments are annoying to read because the reader has to slow down and figure out what the writer meant by each incomplete thought. Compare the fragments above with the complete sentences below. Which brief paragraph is easier to read?

Playing basketball has been my favorite sport ever since I was about five years old. When I shoot hoops with my friends on the courts in our neighborhood, I feel healthy and happy. It is a glorious and satisfying experience.

As the example above illustrates, a sentence communicates a complete idea; it is easier to understand than a fragment.

A fragment is *not* simply a short sentence. The following sentences are all complete sentences; none is a fragment:

I came. I saw. I conquered.

Here is an even shorter complete sentence: ''Stop!'' The subject of this sentence is not present, but most speakers of English understand that it is *you.*

Often fragments sound like complete ideas, especially when you read them aloud. In the example below, only the first and last sentences are complete. Can you tell why the other word groups are fragments?

Every mother knows the vocabulary of her baby's cries. From listening to the different cries and observing the baby's behavior. Crying from hunger, the most common type of crying. Continues even after a baby is picked up. Although the baby enjoys being comforted. Boredom creating a different kind of crying with a lower pitch. Yet another type of baby cry. Differing from the others in intensity. Occurring when the baby is sick. By listening carefully to her baby's cries and observing the child's responses. A mother often knows what her baby is communicating.

Understanding the different causes of fragments may make it easier for you to identify them in your writing. The preceding paragraph includes the four most common types of fragments. These types are listed below:

1. *Missing-subject fragments:* ''Continues even after a baby is picked up.'' [What ''continues''? This fragment is missing a subject that would tell readers what continues.]

2. *Missing-verb fragments:* ''Yet another type of baby cry.'' [What about this ''cry''? This fragment is missing a verb that tells what this cry is or does.]

3. *-ing/-ed/-en fragments:* "Boredom creating a different kind of crying with a lower pitch." [What does "boredom" do, and when does it do it? This fragment is missing a verb that tells when the action occurs, such as *creates, has created,* or *will create.*]

4. *Dependent-word fragments:* "Although the baby enjoys being comforted." [Where is the rest of this idea? This fragment is missing an idea that would complete the thought.]

Below are some suggestions for finding and correcting each type of fragment.

Missing-Subject Fragments. Missing-subject fragments often occur because writers assume that the subject of one sentence applies to the word group that follows the sentence. Circle the missing-subject fragment in each example below:

A. The criminal was a notorious con man. A charming smooth talker with very believable stories.
B. Several people were fooled by this con man. Changed his name every time he changed his swindle.

In the examples above, reread the second word group in each set. In set *A,* does "A charming smooth talker with very believable stories" sound like a complete idea? It does not because it is a fragment that should be connected to the sentence preceding it. In set *B,* the word group, "Changed his name every time he changed his swindle" is also a fragment because it does not tell *who* "changed his name." The person who "changed his name" is the "con man" of the preceding sentence. Thus, this fragment must be connected to the sentence that precedes it. Here are corrected versions of both fragments:

The criminal was a notorious con man, a charming smooth talker with very believable stories. Several people were fooled by this con man. He changed his name every time he changed his swindle.

There are two ways to correct missing-subject fragments:

1. Attach the fragment to the sentence that precedes or follows it
2. Add a subject to the fragment

Below is a sentence followed by a fragment:

A virus is a tiny organism that is smaller than bacteria. *Responsible for a wide range of infectious illnesses.*

Here are two ways of correcting the fragment above:

1. *Attach the fragment to another sentence:*

A virus is a tiny organism that is smaller than bacteria and is responsible for a wide range of infectious illnesses.

2. *Add a subject to the fragment:*

A virus is a tiny organism that is smaller than bacteria. It is responsible for a wide range of infectious illnesses.

WRITING ACTIVITY 2

Underline the fragment in each set of word groups below. Then use one of the two methods noted above to correct each fragment. The first one has been done <u>both</u> ways as an example.

1. Comets are often thought of as stray members of the solar system. <u>Flying in and out of our skies every decade or so.</u>

    Comets are often thought of as stray members of the solar system, flying in and out of our skies every decade or so.

    Comets are often thought of as stray members of the solar system. They fly in and out of our skies every decade or so.

2. However, a comet's orbit is as regular as a planet's. And can be calculated to the exact place each minute.

3. Comets are very different from planets. Formed of particles of matter contained in an envelope of gas.

4. Comets are much smaller than planets. Being relatively invisible until they come close to the earth.

5. Halley's Comet is the most famous of all comets. Discovered by the British astronomer Edmund Halley.

6. Last seen in 1986. Halley's Comet takes seventy-six years to orbit the sun.

Missing-Verb Fragments and Relative Pronoun Fragments. As their name indicates, missing-verb fragments are word groups that are incorrectly punctuated as sentences because they lack a verb. Circle the missing-verb fragment in each example below:

C. The criminal was able to convince many people with his lies. Especially elderly men and women.

D. Several people were fooled by this con man. Among them my grandparents and their neighbors.

In set *C*, does "Especially with elderly men and women" sound like a complete idea? It does not because it does not say what these people did or what happened to them. This fragment should be connected to the sentence that precedes it. Similarly, the fragment in set *D*, "Among them my grandparents and their neighbors," needs to be attached to the preceding sentence, which tells what happened—they "were fooled." Here are the corrected versions of both of these fragments:

The criminal was able to convince many people with his lies, especially elderly men and women. Several people were fooled by this con man, among them my grandparents and their neighbors.

Missing-verb fragments can also result from incorrect use of the following words: *who, whom, which, that,* and *whose.* These words are called *relative pronouns.* They are used to refer back to a noun in the sentence or to begin a word group that gives additional descriptive information about the subject. Here is an example of each of these uses:

1. The con man gave victims phone numbers *that* were actually the numbers of his criminal friends.   [The pronoun *that* refers back to the word *numbers.*]

2. The con man, *who* was a convicted felon, was trying to get people to reveal their credit card numbers.   [The pronoun *who* refers back to the noun *con man* and gives additional information about him.]

As you can tell from the sentences above, a relative pronoun needs its own verb included in the sentence. In sentence 1, the subject is *con man* and its verb is *gave.* The relative pronoun is *that* and its verb is *were.* (The verb is *were* because the noun it is referring back to—*numbers*—is plural.) The subject of sentence 2 is *con man,* and its verb is *was trying;* the relative pronoun is *who* and its verb is *was.*

If you write a word group with a subject and a relative pronoun and only one verb, you will create a missing-verb fragment. Here is an example:

The con man who was telling believable stories. He fooled everyone.

In the first word group above, the relative pronoun *who* is the subject of the verb *was telling,* and there is no verb for the subject of the sentence, *con man.* This sentence specifies a particular con man (the one "who was telling believable stories"), but it does not say anything about this con man. It is an incomplete idea. In order to correct the fragment, the writer must add a verb or connect the fragment to a complete sentence.

The con man *who* was telling believable stories finally was caught. He fooled everyone.

or

The con man *who* was telling believable stories fooled everyone.

There are two way to correct missing-verb fragments:

1. Attach the fragment to the sentence that precedes or follows it. (You may have to cross out the subject of the fragment *or* the subject of the sentence to which it is being connected.)
2. Add a verb to the fragment.

Here are two fragments, followed by each type of correction:

Viruses as deadly as bacteria. Are responsible for many human diseases.

1. *Attach the fragments to form a sentence:*

   Viruses as deadly as bacteria are responsible for many human diseases.

2. *Add a verb to each fragment:*

   Viruses are as deadly as bacteria. They are responsible for many human diseases.

Cowpox, a virus that can have painful effects on milk cows. Does not have serious effects on humans.

1. Cowpox, a virus that can cause painful effects on milk cows, does not have serious effects on humans.
2. Cowpox is a virus that can have painful effects on milk cows. It does not have serious effects on humans.

WRITING ACTIVITY 3

Underline the fragment in each set of word groups below. Then use one of the two methods noted above to correct each fragment. The first one has been done <u>both</u> ways as an example.

1. The videotape is a fairly recent invention. <u>Only about seventy years old.</u>

The videotape is a fairly recent invention, only about seventy years old.

The videotape is a fairly recent invention. It is only about seventy years old.

2. The idea of storing information on a magnetic tape first occurred to Valdemar Poulson. A famous Danish scientist.

3. The videotape that Poulson created. It was a band of stretched plastic.

4. The plastic covered by a film of magnetic iron oxide.

5. The iron oxide has tiny particles in it. Particles with the ability to carry an electric current.

6. A magnetic recording head emits electric signals. These signals, which change the currents in the iron oxide particles.

7. The sound or sight that a person wants to record. It is converted into electric signals by the recording head.

8. The signals of the recording head that correspond to the patterns of the sight or sound. They permanently change the currents on the magnetic tape.

9. The changes in the currents on the videotape. These currents are what produces sight and sound when the tape is played back.

-ing/-ed/-en **Fragments.** The section on sentences (pages 409–411 of this chapter) explained that every sentence needs a verb that expresses the time, or tense, of the action in the sentence. Some verbs are composed of more than one word. For example, the verb in the sentence, ''The man *is telling* me stories,'' is composed of a *helping verb* (*is*) and a *main verb* (*telling*). The verb in the sentence, ''The man *might have been telling* lies,'' is composed of three helping verbs (*might, have,* and *been*) and a main verb (*telling*). Sometimes writers create fragments by forgetting to use helping verbs. If a word group has a verb that ends in *-ing, -ed,* or *-en* and is missing its helping verb, it is a fragment. Here is an example:

That man telling me lies.

Below is a chart of common helping verbs.

HELPING VERBS (ALSO KNOWN AS AUXILIARY VERBS) ———————

is	*are*	*was*	*were*	*will be*
has	*have*	*had*		*will have*
has been	*have been*	*had been*		*will have been*
does	*do*	*did*		
can		*could*		*will*
may		*might*		*must*
shall		*should*		*would*

Here are four more examples of *-ing/-ed/-en* fragments:

E.　The con man *telling* very believable stories.
F.　Several people *fooled* by this con man.
G.　*Taken* in hook, line, and sinker by his tales of woe.
H.　Their reason *being* that he seemed so convincing.

Each of these word groups is a fragment because it is missing a helping verb. To correct these fragments, add a helping verb to each or change the form of the *-ing/-ed/-en* verb:

Past tense: The con man *was* telling very believable stories. Several people *were* fooled by this con man, and they *were* taken in hook, line, and sinker by his tales of woe. Their reason *was* that he seemed so convincing.

Present tense: The con man *is* telling very believable stories. Several people *are* fooled by this con man and *are* taken in hook, line, and sinker by his tales of woe. Their reason *is* that he seems so convincing.

There are two different ways to correct *-ing/-ed/-en* fragments:

1.　Add a helping verb before the *-ing/-ed/-en* verb or change the form of the *-ing/-ed/-en* verb.
2.　Attach the fragment to the sentence to which it is logically related. (You may have to cross out the subject of the sentence *or* the subject of the fragment when you connect them.)

Below is an *-ed* fragment followed by a sentence:

The many different diseases caused by viruses. These vary in intensity from head colds to AIDS.

Here are two ways of correcting the fragment above:

1. *Add a helping verb to the fragment:*

   Many different diseases are caused by viruses. These vary in intensity from head colds to AIDS.

2. *Attach the fragment to another sentence:*

   The many different diseases caused by viruses vary in intensity from head colds to AIDS.

WRITING ACTIVITY 4

Underline the *-ing/-ed/-en* fragment in each set of word groups below. Then use one of the methods noted above to correct each fragment. The first one has been done <u>both</u> ways as an example.

1. Coffee <u>introduced from Arabia during the sixteenth century</u>. It became one of the most popular beverages of all time.

   Coffee was introduced from Arabia during the sixteenth century. It became one of the most popular beverages of all time.

   Introduced from Arabia during the sixteenth century, coffee became one of the most popular beverages of all time.

2. An African legend saying that coffee first grew in Kaffa, a small town in Ethiopia. It was discovered by a farmer named Kaldi.

3. Noticing his goats were behaving strangely after they ate some berries. Kaldi examined the berries.

4. Heating the berries in some boiling water. Kaldi noticed the berries dissolved.

5. The berries made a delicious liquid. The reason being that the heat released the berries' flavor.

6. Kaldi shared the brew with his friends. His friends naming the drink coffee in honor of their town.

Dependent-Word Fragments. Dependent-word fragments occur when writers use a dependent word to begin a word group and forget to connect this word group to a complete sentence. Below is a list of common dependent words.

DEPENDENT WORDS ――――――――――――――――――――――――――

Here is a partial list of dependent words (also known as *subordinators* or *subordinating conjunctions*):

To show time: *after, as, before, once, until, when, whenever, while*

To show cause: *because, if, in order that, since, so that*

To show concession: *although, even though, though, when*

To show place: *wherever*

To show manner: *how*

If a word group begins with one of these dependent words, it cannot be punctuated to stand alone, because it is an incomplete thought. A dependent-word fragment "depends on" the preceding sentence or the following sentence to complete its meaning, so it must be attached to that sentence. For example, if I had not connected the two word groups in the first sentence of this paragraph, I would have created a dependent-word fragment:

If a word group begins with one of these dependent words. It cannot be punctuated to stand alone, because it is an incomplete thought.

Circle the four dependent-word fragments in the brief paragraph below.

The criminal was a notorious con man. Because he was a charming smooth talker. Wherever he went. He concocted believable stories. After several people were fooled by this con man. The police put together a profile of his behavior. Although the con man changed his name every time he changed his swindle. He was finally caught and jailed.

These fragments can be corrected by connecting them to the complete sentences in the paragraph. Here is an example, with dependent words underlined:

The criminal was a notorious con man <u>because</u> he was a charming smooth talker. <u>Wherever</u> he went, he concocted believable stories. <u>After</u> several people were fooled by this con man, the police put together a profile of his behavior. <u>Although</u> the con man changed his name every time he changed his swindle, he was finally caught and jailed.

Thus, you have two ways to correct dependent-word fragments:

1. Omit the dependent word.
2. Attach the fragment to the sentence to which it is logically related.

Here is a fragment, followed by a sentence:

Although viruses are living organisms. They cannot reproduce or grow unless they are inside the cells of an animal or a plant.

Below are two ways of correcting this fragment:

1. *Omit the dependent word:*

   Viruses are living organisms. They cannot reproduce or grow unless they are inside the cells of an animal or a plant.

2. *Attach the fragment to another sentence:*

   Although viruses are living organisms, they cannot reproduce or grow unless they are inside the cells of an animal or a plant.

Note that you should use a comma to connect a dependent-word fragment to the *beginning* of another sentence:

When I yawn, I feel sleepy.

However, you do not need to insert a comma if you connect the dependent-word fragment to the *end* of another sentence:

I feel sleepy *when I yawn.*

WRITING ACTIVITY 5

Underline the fragment in each set of word groups below. Then use one of the two methods noted above to correct each fragment. The first one has been done <u>both</u> ways as an example.

1. <u>When people yawn.</u> They think it is a sign that they are tired.

   People yawn. They think it is a sign that they are tired.

   When people yawn, they think it is a sign that they are tired.

2. Because many of us do yawn when we are tired. We assume that yawning is our body's way of telling us to go to sleep.

3. However, when we yawn. Our body is signaling us that our lungs need more oxygen.

4. When we are tired or sleepy. Our body's cells are not working efficiently to get enough oxygen from our blood.

5. Resting or sleeping restores our body's cells. Because we breathe more deeply and take more oxygen into our lungs.

6. So if you find yourself yawning. Either take a nap or go into the fresh air and take some deep breaths.

REMINDER

There are four different causes of fragments:

- Omitting a subject
- Omitting a verb
- Omitting the helping verb before a verb that ends in -*ing*, -*ed*, or -*en*
- Beginning a word group with a dependent word

Correct each fragment using the strategy that seems most logical.

WRITING ACTIVITY 6

Each word group in the paragraph below is numbered. Above each word group, write an *F* if the word group is a fragment or an *S* if it is a sentence.

(1) My mother, Maria Aguilar, has always been my primary role model (2) ever since I was a young child (3) I studied her gestures, her behavior, and her style (4) the many qualities that I admired about my mother (5) her grace, her honesty, and her compassion (6) her most special quality was her ability to listen carefully to whoever was speaking to her (7) if someone had a problem and asked for her advice (8) she would lean in toward the person and focus all her attention on him or her (9) I always tried to imitate my mother (10) I

also vowed that when I grew up and became an adult woman (11) I would behave just like her (12) now I am grown up and I am a mother myself (13) sometimes, when I listen to my children (14) I am delighted to realize that I look and sound like my mother did.

GROUP WORK 1

Form a group of three students and choose one student to record the group's responses on a separate piece of paper. Examine each of the word groups in the preceding Writing Activity. Then, as a group, decide how to correct each fragment. Rewrite the corrected paragraph on a separate piece of paper.

WRITING ACTIVITY 7

Below is a paragraph with all *four* kinds of fragments. After you find each fragment, decide which method to use to correct it. Then write the corrected paragraph over on a separate piece of paper.

My grandfather was really a *grand* kind of father to me. Kind and gentle and endlessly patient. Since the time I was an infant. He lavished attention on me. He would listen to all my stories and problems. And would pay careful attention to what I was saying. Unlike all the other adults I knew. He never interrupted me. Unless he felt that I had done something wrong. If he felt that I had done something wrong. He would gently ask me why I did it. Suggesting that I think about how it affected the other person or people. He would share his wisdom and experience with me. I loved listening to his advice. The reason being that he never criticized me. Or made me feel stupid or silly. Not only was my grandfather a caring friend. But he was also an inspiring teacher. He took me on trips to museums and shows. Teaching me how to examine art carefully. My favorite place to go with him. Was the Museum of African-American Art. A museum that exhibited great paintings and sculptures. Although I didn't know much about art. My grandfather respected my reactions to it. If I didn't understand something. He would explain it patiently over and over again. My grandfather taught me how to be a caring and loving man. When my grandfather died. I lost my best friend and my favorite relative.

GROUP WORK 2

Form a group with two classmates and exchange your corrected version of the paragraph in Writing Activity 7 above. Examine the differences in the way that your classmates and you corrected each fragment. Explain why you chose the correction method that you used.

HOW TO CORRECT FRAGMENTS: A REVIEW

- •Reread each sentence in your paragraph or essay, starting with the *last* one first. Does each one make sense as a complete idea and sentence?
- •Make sure each sentence has a subject and a verb that expresses what the subject is doing or experiencing.
- •Each time you used an *-ing/-ed/-en* verb, check to see that you used a helping verb.
- •If a sentence includes a dependent word, make sure that the word group that begins with this word is connected to a complete idea.

IDENTIFYING AND CORRECTING RUN-ONS

Another common sentence error that many writers make is the *run-on*. A run-on consists of two or more sentences (complete subject-verb units) incorrectly punctuated as one sentence. Like fragments, run-ons confuse readers, who have to read them over several times to figure out where one idea ends and another begins. For example, compare the run-on in word group *A* below to the sentence in word group *B*. Why is *B* easier to read than *A*?

A. Basketball is a terrific sport for weekend athletes it provides healthy exercise and fun.
B. Basketball is a terrific sport for weekend athletes since it provides healthy exercise and fun.

The two complete ideas are incorrectly joined in word group *A*. Sentence *B* is correct, and it is clearer because the word *since* in sentence *B* shows the relation between the two complete ideas that are being joined into one sentence.

Just as a fragment is not simply a short sentence, a run-on is not merely a long sentence. A sentence can be hundreds of words long and be perfectly correct, as long as it is punctuated correctly. For example, here is a correct sentence that is over three hundred words long. It comes from Martin Luther King, Jr.'s, "Letter from a Birmingham Jail."

Perhaps it is easy for those who have never felt the stinging darts of segregation to say, "Wait." But when you have seen vicious mobs lynch your mothers and fathers at will and drown your sisters and brothers at whim; when you have seen hate-filled policemen curse, kick and even kill your black brothers and sisters; when you see the vast majority of your twenty million Negro brothers smothering in an airtight cage of poverty in the midst of an affluent society; when you suddenly find your tongue twisted and your speech stammering as you seek to explain to your six-year-old daughter why she can't go to the public amusement park that has just been advertised on television, and see tears welling up in her eyes when she is told that Funtown is closed to colored children, and see ominous clouds of inferiority beginning to form in her little mental sky, and see her beginning to distort her personality by developing an unconscious bitterness toward white people; when you have to concoct an answer for a five-year-old son who is asking: "Daddy, why do white people treat colored people so mean?"; when you take a cross-country drive and find it necessary to sleep night after night in the uncomfortable corners of your automobile because no motel will accept you; when you are humiliated day in and day out by nagging signs reading "white" and "colored"; when your first name becomes "nigger," your middle name becomes "boy" (however old you are) and your last name becomes "John," and your wife and mother are never given the respected title "Mrs."; when you are harried by day and haunted by night by the fact that you are a Negro, living constantly at tiptoe stance, never quite knowing what to expect next, and are plagued with inner fears and outer resentments; when you are forever fighting a degenerating sense of "no-bodiness"—then you will understand why we find it difficult to wait.

Note that Dr. King used semicolons to separate his dependent clauses (all of which begin with the word *when*) and he connected them all to the final independent clause, which begins, ''then you will understand . . .''

Length does not determine whether a word group is a sentence or a run-on. Remember that a run-on is two or more sentences that are punctuated as one sentence. Here is an example:

s   v   s   v

The dictionary was brand-new its cover was smooth and shiny.

If you insert a comma between the independent clauses, does that make the run-on a correct sentence?

The dictionary was brand-new, its cover was smooth and shiny.

Inserting a comma does *not* correct this run-on. Instead the comma turns this word group into a run-on with a special name: a *comma splice*. A comma cannot be used to correct a run-on because a comma is not an acceptable mark of punctuation for separating two complete sentences.

Many writers have difficulty identifying their run-ons because they sound like complete ideas when they are read aloud. For example, read the following paragraph aloud. As you are reading, try to identify each run-on.

> All mothers know the vocabulary of their baby's cries, they know this from listening to the different cries and observing the baby's behavior. Crying from hunger is the most common type of crying it continues even after a baby is picked up. Boredom creates a different kind of cry this type has a lower pitch. By listening carefully to her baby's cries, a mother gets to know how they differ, she also gets to know what her baby is communicating.

Every sentence in the brief paragraph above is a run-on. Let's examine the last run-on in this paragraph: ''By listening carefully to her baby's cries, a mother gets to know how they differ, she also gets to know what her baby is communicating.'' Note that this run-on consists of a dependent-word group that is connected to two complete sentences. Here is how this run-on should be corrected:

s   v

By listening carefully to her baby's cries, a mother learns how they differ.

s   v

She also knows what her baby is communicating.

When you begin a word group with a pronoun (*he, she, they* or *it*) that refers back to a noun in a preceding word group, check to make sure that you haven't written a run-on.

There are four methods of correcting run-ons:

1. Separate the two clauses with a period and a capital letter.

   The dictionary was brand-new. Its cover was smooth and shiny.

2. Insert a comma and a *coordinator* after the first clause. The seven English coordinators are *and, but, yet, for, or, nor,* and *so.* (See pages 457–458 for a discussion of the uses of coordinators.)

   The dictionary was brand-new**,** *and* its cover was smooth and shiny.

3. Insert a *dependent word* (or *subordinator*) where it seems most logical. (See page 420 for a list of dependent words.)

   Because the dictionary was brand-new, its cover was smooth and shiny.

4. Separate the two clauses with a semicolon (;). (See page 426 for more information on using semicolons to join ideas that are short and closely related.)

   The dictionary was brand-new**;** its cover was smooth and shiny.

How do writers decide which method to use to correct their run-ons? Experienced writers often try them all and select the method that best conveys the relation between the ideas in the two independent clauses. For example, here is a run-on:

Sun exposure is bad for you, it can cause skin cancer and damage your immune system.

In your opinion, which of the four methods of correcting this run-on best expresses the relation between the two ideas?

A. Sun exposure is bad for you. It can cause skin cancer and damage your immune system.
B. Sun exposure is bad for you, for it can cause skin cancer and damage your immune system.
C. Sun exposure is bad for you because it can cause skin cancer and damage your immune system.
D. Sun exposure is bad for you; it can cause skin cancer and damage your immune system.

All four sentences are correct. None is ''better'' than the other three. All of these sentences express the same meaning, but they differ in emphasis. The coordinator in sentence *B* and the semicolon in sentence *D* signal a close relation between the two ideas and give each the same emphasis. The subordinator in sentence *C* also signals a closeness in ideas, but *because* moves the sentence's emphasis to the independent clause that precedes it. The period in sentence *A* signals that the relation between the two ideas is not close enough to justify combining them into one sentence.

Here is another run-on, followed by each type of correction. Which correction communicates the meaning most clearly?

Run-on: Viruses are microscopic organisms, they can cause very large epidemics.

A. Viruses are microscopic organisms; they can cause very large epidemics.
B. Viruses are microscopic organisms. They can cause very large epidemics.
C. Viruses are microscopic organisms, but they can cause very large epidemics.
D. Although viruses are microscopic organisms, they can cause very large epidemics.

Sentence 4 probably communicates the meaning most clearly because it uses the dependent word *although* to show the relation between the two ideas and to put emphasis on the second idea.

WRITING ACTIVITY 8

In the space under each run-on below, try out *all four* methods of correcting it. The first one has been done as an example.

1. Many people imagine they can see a man on the moon, they see shapes that look like a face.

   1- Many people imagine they can see a man on the moon. They see shapes that look like a face.

   2- Many people imagine they can see a man on the moon, for they see shapes that look like a face.

   3- Many people imagine they can see a man on the moon since they see shapes that look like a face.

4- Many people imagine they can see a man on the moon; they see shapes that look like a face.

2. The patterns on the moon look like facial expressions, they are actually huge mountain ranges.

3. The mountain ranges are shadowed from the sun's light. They look like big black holes.

4. These holes are shaped like eyes, a nose, and a mouth they do seem to compose a face.

5. Satellite pictures of the moon reveal only mountains, they don't show any men.

6. There is not a man in the moon, maybe there is a woman there.

WRITING ACTIVITY 9

Choose one of the four methods to correct each run-on below.

1. The legend of Midas is thousands of years old, it gave rise to the expression ''the Midas touch.''
2. According to the legend, King Midas did good deeds for his people, he earned a great reward.
3. The god Dionysus heard about Midas's goodness he granted him one wish.
4. Midas wished that everything he touched would turn to gold, it came true.
5. His golden touch caused Midas great problems he turned everything and everybody to solid gold.
6. Midas was starving, his touch turned even his food to gold.
7. Midas lost everything that was important to him, he began to regret his wish.
8. Midas begged Dionysus to take back the gift, Dionysus did so.

GROUP WORK 3

Form a group with two other students. Each person should take turns explaining the method that he or she used to correct each run-on in Writing Activity 9 above.

GROUP WORK 4

Below is a draft that a student wrote about his brother. Form a group with two other students and decide which person will record the group's decisions. Together identify and correct every run-on below.

My brother's triumph over his disability inspires everyone who knows him. Hector was born fourteen years ago with Down's syndrome, it is a condition that results from a genetic mutation. Down's syndrome babies have an extra chromosome, this disorder causes many problems. From the beginning, Hector never looked like our family, he had the typical squashed, flat nose and concave, slanting eyes of Down's syndrome children, people were always making thoughtless, mean comments that we all ignored. Hector also had problems growing and learning. At four he was diagnosed as having mental retardation, that didn't stop Hector from trying to do everything that his family and friends did, also it certainly didn't stop any of us from loving him totally. He has always been sweet, good natured, and happy he's also a lot of fun to be with. Hector is doing very well now, he went to a special school and learned how to read and write. Recently he learned how to use a computer, he is doing basic work for a friend's computer company. His happiness and brave spirit make us all so proud to know him.

HOW TO CORRECT RUN-ONS: A REVIEW ———————

- Reread each sentence in the paragraph or essay that you are revising, starting with the *last* one first. Is each one a complete idea and sentence?
- Check to see if you accidentally combined two sentences together (with or without a comma).
- Check each word group that begins with a pronoun that refers back to the subject of the previous word group. Make sure that you have not created a run-on.
- Decide which of the four correction methods is most appropriate for correcting each run-on that you find in your writing.

IDENTIFYING AND CORRECTING DANGLING AND MISPLACED MODIFIERS

In addition to errors in sentence completeness, other types of sentence errors can make your writing unclear. Two of these sentence errors are caused when writers do not use modifiers correctly. A *modifier* is a word or group of words that describes a sentence's subject or that tells when, where, or how the action of the sentence occurs or occurred. Here is an example of a modifier that is correctly placed next to the word it is modifying:

> A computerized word-processing program *with a mouse* is a wonderful tool for composing an essay.

The modifier "with a mouse" describes a specific type of computer. How clear would the sentence be if the writer put this modifier at the end?

> A computerized word-processing program is a wonderful tool for composing an essay *with a mouse.*

Can you "compose an essay" with a "mouse"? No, but you can compose an essay using a "computerized word-processing program *with a mouse.*"

As you can see from this example, a misplaced modifier can change the meaning of a sentence in ways that the writer did not intend. Here are examples of sentences with modifier errors. As you read these sentences, consider whether they sound awkward or confusing.

A. Julio found that studying helps him do better on tests *the night before.*   [*When* does Julio take his tests?]
B. Julio *almost* answered all the questions on his math test.   [Did he answer *any* questions?]
C. Julio saw several failing tests *standing near the teacher's desk.*   [Can tests *stand*?]

D. *Despite studying for days,* mistakes were made on several of the problems.   [Is there a *person* in this sentence who did the studying and made the mistakes?]

E. *While looking at the test,* his body missed the chair and fell down.   [*Who* looked at the test and *who* fell?]

Sentences *A, B,* and *C* have *misplaced modifiers:* The descriptive words are not next to the words that they are describing. These sentences should be rewritten as follows:

F. Julio found that studying *the night before* helps him do better on tests.   [Now the sentence clearly communicates that Julio studies the night before his tests.]

G. Julio answered *almost* all the questions on his math test.   [This sentence now says that he responded to ''almost all the questions'' rather than he ''almost'' responded to them.]

H. *Standing near the teacher's desk,* Julio saw several failing tests.   [Now this sentence makes clear that it was Julio who was ''standing near the teacher's desk,'' not the failing tests!]

Sentences *D* and *E* have *dangling modifiers:* The word that each modifier is describing is missing from the sentence. Both sentences have to be rewritten so that the subject is present, not merely implied.

I. *Despite studying for days,* Julio made mistakes on several of the problems.   [This correction says that Julio was the one who studied for days and made several mistakes.]

J. *While looking at the test,* he missed the chair and fell down.   [This correction makes it clear that Julio—not his body—was ''looking at the test.'']

As you edit your sentences, check to make sure that every modifier is next to the subject or verb it is describing. In addition, if you begin a sentence with a modifier, make sure that the word it is describing follows directly after the modifier.

WRITING ACTIVITY 10

Each of the sentences below has a misplaced or dangling modifier. Circle the error in each sentence and rewrite it correctly on separate paper. The first one has been done as an example.

1. While jogging this morning, a thought came into my mind.

While jogging this morning, I had a thought.

While I was jogging this morning, a thought came into my mind.

2. I wondered why people don't do more exercise huffing and puffing down the street.
3. So many people complain about being overweight and stiff who don't exercise.
4. Thinking about why people dislike exercise, the morning sped by.
5. Much more time than usual, I jogged for an entire hour.
6. I decided that people might exercise more if they started gradually dripping with sweat.
7. Starting with ten minutes a day and adding ten minutes each week, the rewards can be inspiring.
8. By the time thirty minutes is reached, new muscles can be seen and felt.
9. I decided to write an essay in the shower about my belief.
10. I discovered I had many interesting ideas about exercising while getting dressed.
11. I composed an essay about the benefits of exercising in about an hour.
12. While revising the essay, new ideas about exercising kept coming to me.
13. I put the ideas in the essay that seemed most unique.
14. After editing and proofreading the final draft, the essay made me very proud of myself.

HOW TO CORRECT MISPLACED AND DANGLING MODIFIERS

- Make sure that every modifier has a noun or pronoun (a person, place, thing, or idea) or a verb that it is describing.
- Read each sentence one at a time, looking for each word that describes a noun, pronoun, or verb. Make sure that the descriptive word (or words) is next to the noun, pronoun, or verb that it is modifying.
- Check for the modifiers *almost, only, even,* and *hardly.* These should be placed immediately *before* the word that they are describing.

IDENTIFYING AND CORRECTING FAULTY PARALLELISM

Another type of sentence error is caused by using words that are not in the same grammatical form. When you write a sentence that includes a series of words or ideas, these words or ideas must be in *parallel* grammatical form:

> Chung Mei's favorite hobbies are *reading mysteries, writing poems,* and *riding a motorcycle.*

If one of the words in the series is written in a different grammatical form than the others, it makes the sentence confusing:

> Chung Mei's favorite hobbies are *reading mysteries, writing poems,* and *to ride a motorcycle.*

The sentence above sounds unbalanced. Each of the verbs should be in the same—parallel—grammatical form (*reading, writing,* and *riding*).

Here is an example of the dramatic effect of using parallelism correctly. It is excerpted from Martin Luther King, Jr.'s, "I Have a Dream" speech.

> *Go back to* Mississippi, *go back to* Alabama, *go back to* South Carolina, *go back to* Georgia, *go back to* Louisiana, *go back to* the slums and ghettos of our northern cities, knowing that somehow this situation can and will be changed.

In the pairs of sentences below, the *A* sentence has a parallelism error; the *B* sentence illustrates one way of correcting the error.

1A. My favorite forms of exercise are jogging, swimming, and to play basketball.   [The first two verbs have *-ing* endings; the third verb should also.]

1B. My favorite forms of exercise are *jogging, swimming,* and *playing* basketball.

2A. After I exercise, I not only feel healthy and trim but I also feel hunger.   [The first two feelings are written as descriptive words; the third one should also be written that way.]

2B. After I exercise, not only do I feel *healthy* and *trim* but I also feel *hungry.*

3A. Basically I exercise because it helps me stay thin, it maintains my stamina, and exercising keeps me sane.   [The first two dependent clauses begin with *it* plus a verb: *it helps, it maintains;* the third one should begin the same way.]

3B. Basically I exercise because *it helps* me stay thin, *it maintains* my stamina, and *it keeps* me sane.

WRITING ACTIVITY 11

Circle the faulty parallelism in each sentence below and rewrite the sentence correctly on separate paper. The first one has been done as an example.

1. I am going to college to gain more knowledge, to prepare for a profession, and it will make my parents proud.

    I am going to college to gain more knowledge, to prepare for a profession, and to make my parents proud.

2. College is providing me with fascinating courses, great teachers, and I have friends who are new and interesting.
3. The keys to doing well in college seem to be planning time effectively, I study carefully for tests, and learning from one's mistakes.
4. The most difficult part of college is finding time, energy, and it's difficult to find privacy.
5. My typical college day consists of getting up early to study, going to classes, going places with my roommates, and to study more at night.
6. I prefer studying in places that don't have much noise, are spacious, and that are well ventilated.
7. While studying, I not only reread the text and my notes, but I also am highlighting the key ideas with a yellow marker.
8. College will enable me to fulfill my career dreams if I work very hard and if I am achieving my academic goals.
9. After I graduate, I have a choice to make: go to graduate school to get an advanced degree or taking a job to earn some money.
10. Whatever I decide, I will be proud that I have gotten a higher education, broadened my horizons, and taking advantages of the opportunities college has to offer.

WRITING ACTIVITY 12

Below are four quotations that illustrate how the rhythm of parallelism emphasizes the writer's meaning. On separate paper, write a sentence imitating each quotation's parallelism. The first one has been done as an example.

1. "Education makes people easy to lead, but difficult to drive; easy to govern, but impossible to enslave" (Lord Brougham).

Freedom makes people happy to work, but difficult to exploit; happy to share, but impossible to dominate.

2. "I have nothing to offer but blood, toil, tears, and sweat" (Winston Churchill).
3. "In those days, only three things in the world scared me: jail, a job, and the army" (Malcolm X).
4. "Perhaps it is better to be irresponsible and right than to be responsible and wrong" (Winston Churchill).

GROUP WORK 5

Form a group. Together write a sentence for each of the sample quotations that imitates its parallel structure.

1. "I came; I saw; I conquered" (Julius Caesar).
2. "Ask not what your country can do for you; ask what you can do for your country" (John F. Kennedy).
3. "If this is a country where one stops being Vietnamese or Italian, this is a country where one begins to be an American" (Richard Rodriguez).

HOW TO CORRECT FAULTY PARALLELISM: A REVIEW _____

- Check every sentence for a pair or a series of nouns, verbs, or descriptive words. Make sure that the words in the pair or the series are in parallel grammatical form and that they all have the same ending.

REMINDER _____
Experiment with your sentences to determine which method of correcting the errors communicates your meaning most clearly.

The chart below indicates typical errors in Academic Written English sentence structure (based on the chart on page 95 in Chapter 3). Each error is preceded by the correction symbol that your teachers may use when they mark your writing and is followed by the number of the page in this chapter that discusses the error.

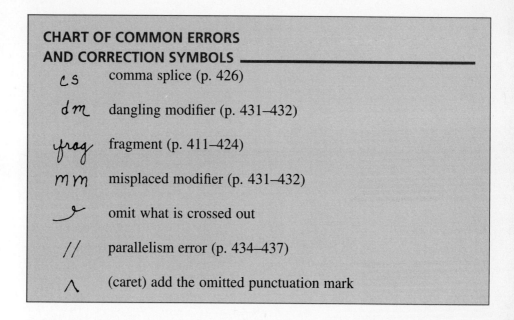

**CHART OF COMMON ERRORS
AND CORRECTION SYMBOLS** _____

cs   comma splice (p. 426)

dm   dangling modifier (p. 431–432)

frag   fragment (p. 411–424)

mm   misplaced modifier (p. 431–432)

⟋   omit what is crossed out

//   parallelism error (p. 434–437)

∧   (caret) add the omitted punctuation mark

✔ POINTS TO REMEMBER ABOUT SENTENCE STRUCTURE

1. Make sure that each sentence expresses a complete idea and that it begins with a capital letter and ends with a period, a question mark, or an exclamation point.
2. Read each sentence, one at a time, to see if it has a subject and a verb.
3. Check each sentence, one at a time, to determine that it is a complete sentence and not a fragment or a run-on.
4. Correct missing-subject fragments by adding a subject or by connecting the fragment to the sentence that precedes it.
5. Correct missing-verb fragments by adding a verb or by connecting the fragment to the sentence that precedes it.
6. Correct *-ing/-ed/-en* fragments by adding an appropriate helping verb or by changing the verb to a form that communicates the tense and time of the action in the sentence.
7. Correct dependent-word fragments by deleting the dependent word or by connecting the fragment to the sentence that precedes or follows it.

8. Correct each run-on by separating the two complete ideas with a period, a semicolon, or a comma and a coordinator, or by inserting a dependent word in front of the word group where it would make sense.
9. Make sure that every modifier is next to the word or words that it is describing.
10. Make sure that words in a pair or in a series are in the same grammatical form.

16

SENTENCE VARIETY AND STYLE

There is more to writing effective sentences than simply composing complete, correctly punctuated sentences. Crafting strong sentences involves developing a sophisticated *style* of writing—an interesting way of choosing and arranging words. To do this, you must become more aware of the many possibilities that you have every time you shape a sentence. Inexperienced writers often play it safe, writing sentences in the same few patterns over and over again, because they believe that varying their sentence structures will cause them to make errors. What results are repetitious sentences that all seem to have the same pattern and rhythm—sentences that are correct but boring. This chapter will show you some choices you have for crafting sentences that communicate the complexity of your ideas.

ACHIEVING SENTENCE CLARITY AND VARIETY

Effective sentences communicate a writer's meaning clearly and directly. However, being "clear" and "direct" is not easy, and it is not achieved merely by keeping every sentence short and simple. For example, read the paragraph below, which is composed of complete, correct sentences. What are your reactions to these sentences? Are they clear and interesting? Do they communicate the writer's ideas effectively and show the relations among these ideas?

I fell in love with music. I was five years old. I attended my first

concert. I had heard music all my life. I don't remember enjoying it. Most of it was babyish and boring. This was my first time experiencing classical music. I clearly remember the sensation it produced. It was a physical sensation. The violins played. Their bell-like sounds made me shiver. Then the horns played. Now I know that these horns were clarinets and oboes. They started gurgling their sounds. I felt like I was breathing music. I felt like my lungs were moving with the bassoon. I also felt my heart. It thumped out the rhythm of the drums. I heard the clash of the cymbals. It made me jump in my seat. The music stopped. The silence made me cry. I was so overwhelmed. I could not even clap.

Sometimes short, simple sentences, like the ones in the paragraph above, are perfect for expressing one's ideas. However, an entire paragraph composed of these sentences is often choppy, boring, and difficult to read. Note this paradox: A series of short, simple sentences is easier to *write* but more difficult to *read* than a series of varied sentences that express the relations among the ideas. For example, below is a revision of the preceding student paragraph. These sentences have been combined into longer, more detailed sentences.

I fell in love with music when I was five years old and I attended my first concert. I remember that I had heard varied types of music all my life, from the nursery rhymes that my parents quietly hummed to the popular songs that *Sesame Street* loudly serenaded me with. However, I don't remember enjoying any of this music since most of it was babyish and boring. The concert was my first time experiencing classical music, and I felt like I was breathing the music. My lungs moved with the sounds of the bassoon, and my heart beat rhythmically with the drums. When the concert ended, I was extraordinarily overwhelmed.

This revision is easier to understand and more interesting than the original sentences because it spells out the writer's ideas and the ways these ideas are related to one another.

There are several ways to make your sentences more lively, varied, and precise:

- Add adjectives and adverbs (words that modify and describe other words in a sentence) to clarify your exact meaning.
- Add descriptive phrases (groups of words), such as prepositional phrases, phrases that begin with *-ing/-ed/-en* verbs, and appositive phrases.
- Combine sentences by coordinating or subordinating them.

This chapter will explain each of these strategies.

ADDING ADJECTIVES AND ADVERBS

One of the easiest ways to improve your sentence variety and style is to expand your sentences by adding adjectives and adverbs to them. An *adjective* is a word that is used to modify (describe) a noun or a pronoun by telling "how many," "what type," "which one," "what color," "what size," and so forth. An *adverb* is a word used to modify a verb, an adjective, or another adverb; it tells "how," "when," "how often," "where," and "to what degree." Here are some examples of how writers use adjectives and adverbs to clarify meaning:

I have one small Italian violin.   [The adjectives *one, small,* and *Italian* modify the noun *violin.*]
It is magnificent.   [The adjective *magnificent* modifies the pronoun *it.*]
I play it carefully and loudly.   [The adverbs *carefully* and *loudly* modify the verb *play.*]
Plucking this violin is a consistently thrilling experience.   [The adverb *consistently* modifies the adjective *thrilling,* which is modifying the noun *experience.*]
I play this violin extremely well.   [The adverb *extremely* is modifying the adverb *well,* which is modifying the verb *play.*]

Adjectives and adverbs enable readers to experience your ideas from your unique perspective. The preceding student draft (on page 439) and revision (on page 440) illustrated this point. Below is a sentence from the draft, followed by the revision, which includes additional nouns, verbs, adjectives, and adverbs.

Original: I had heard music all my life.

Revision: I remember that I had heard varied types of music all my life, from the nursery rhymes that my parents quietly hummed to the popular songs that *Sesame Street* loudly serenaded me with.

In the revision, the writer decided to illustrate what he meant by "music" by including two examples of the kind of music that he heard in his early life and by using adjectives and adverbs to describe these examples. This helps us understand his meaning, and it makes his sentences more interesting.

WRITING ACTIVITY 1

Below are five pairs of words. The first word in each pair is an adjective, and the second is an adverb. Write a sentence using each word (in the space provided). The first one has been done as an example.

1. fast *My aunt enjoys driving fast cars.*

   fast *My aunt ran fast in this year's marathon.*

2. careless _____

   _____

   carelessly _____

   _____

3. thorough _____

   _____

   thoroughly _____

   _____

4. late _____

   _____

   late _____

   _____

5. fair _____

_____

fairly _____

_____

Let's look at another example of how adding adjectives and adverbs clarifies a writer's precise meaning. Below is a short, simple sentence. What image or mental picture does it communicate to you? Does it help you "see" what "the building" looks like?

The building was a wall.

This sentence is confusing. It seems to be saying that "a building looked like a wall," but it is very unclear. Now let's add some adjectives to clarify the image.

The apartment building was a serene black wall.

The picture is getting clearer, but it still needs additional adjectives and adverbs.

In the darkness, the apartment building on the other side of the avenue was a serene black wall.

Below is the sentence with a few more adjectives and adverbs. This final version is a sentence by the writer Tom Wolfe.

In the darkness, the apartment building on the other side of the avenue was a serene black wall holding back the city's sky, which was steaming purple.

As you revise your sentences, try to paint word pictures, the way Tom Wolfe did, to make your sentences fuller, clearer, and more descriptive. Tune in more closely to your senses and use the techniques described in Chapter 5 of this book.

REMINDER ━━━━━━━━━━━━━━━━━━━━━━━━━
Expand your sentences with adjectives and adverbs that make your ideas clearer and more precise. Use specific, concrete words that let readers see, hear, smell, taste, and feel the things and actions you are describing.

Adjectives and adverbs can be added just about everyplace in an English sentence. Let's expand a simple sentence to illustrate this point. Here is the sentence:

The music was loud.

We can add details before and after the subject so that we specify exactly what we mean by ''music'' and ''loud'':

The *rap* music *blasting from the overhead speakers* was *so* loud *that it rattled the silverware on our table.*

The added sensory details clarify the meaning and make the sentence more interesting.

WRITING ACTIVITY 2

Here is a simple sentence:

The audience enjoyed the performance.

Expand this sentence on a separate piece of paper by following the directions below.

1. Rewrite the sentence, adding adverbs that describe *where* the audience was. (Where was the performance taking place? Exactly what did this place look like?)
2. Rewrite the original sentence or your sentence from (1) above, adding adjectives and adverbs that describe the performance. (Who was performing? What were he/she/they performing? How did they look, behave, and sound?)
3. Rewrite the original sentence or your sentence from (1) or (2) above, adding adjectives and adverbs describing how the audience looked or behaved. (How were the people acting or what were they doing?)

GROUP WORK 1

Form a group of three students. Together expand each sentence below by adding adjectives and adverbs before and after the subject and the verb. Choose a recorder to write the group's revision on a separate piece of paper. See how many words you can add to each blank place in the sentence, but you do *not* have to add words to every blank space. The first one has been rewritten two different ways as an example.

1. _____ I heard _____ music _____.

> *Suddenly last night I heard classical music swelling up from the orchestra pit. Last night, I heard outrageously loud music blasting from the stage.*

2. The _____ music _____ was _____ loud _____.

3. The singer's _____ voice created a _____ mood and made

   me feel _____.

4. _____ I started dancing _____ to the _____ beat of the drums.

5. The _____ rhythm of this _____ music sounded like _____
   to me.

6. _____ I waved my arms to the _____ beat _____.

Here are some guidelines for helping you decide where to add adjectives and adverbs to the sentences in your drafts.

QUESTIONS TO ASK ABOUT EXPANDING A SENTENCE

Ask yourself the following questions about the sentences in your drafts and revisions.

- What adjectives can I add to describe the subject of this sentence more fully?
- What adjectives and adverbs can I add to clarify what the subject is doing or experiencing?
- What adverbs can I add to clarify where and when (or for how long) the action of this sentence is occurring?
- What adverbs can I add to clarify how and why the action of this sentence is taking place?

WRITING ACTIVITY 3

Choose *one* of the topics below to develop into a paragraph or a brief essay. When you finish composing and revising your writing, examine every sentence—one at a time—to see where you can expand it by adding more adjectives and adverbs.

- Describe your favorite music and explain why it is your favorite type.
- Describe your favorite musical group and explain why it is your favorite.
- Describe the music you most dislike and explain why you dislike it.
- Describe a musical performance that made a deep impression on you and explain how and why this performance affected you.

ADDING DESCRIPTIVE PHRASES

Another strategy for making your sentences more interesting and varied is to add groups of descriptive words such as prepositional, participial, and appositive phrases. Each type of phrase is explained below.

Prepositional Phrases. A *prepositional phrase* is a group of words beginning with a preposition and ending with a noun or a pronoun. It can be an adjective phrase (telling who or what the subject is) or an adverb phrase (telling where, when, how, or why the action in the sentence occurs or occurred). Here are some examples:

> A madrigal is a song *for several voices* unaccompanied *by any musical instruments.* Singing madrigals about romance was a popular form *of entertainment in Europe during the sixteenth and seventeenth centuries.*

There are many prepositions in English. Some of the most frequently used ones are listed below.

COMMON PREPOSITIONS			
about	below	in	over
above	beside	into	through
across	between	near	to
around	by	of	toward
at	during	off	under
before	for	on	with
behind	from	onto	

To vary your sentences, add prepositional phrases that describe the sentence's subject and that describe where, when, how, or why the action in a sentence occurred. Here is an example of using prepositional phrases to add these details to a sentence:

Draft: The shy young girl ran away.

Who? The shy young girl *from Vietnam* ran away.

Where? The shy young girl from Vietnam ran away *down the stairs*.

How? The shy young girl from Vietnam ran away down the stairs *on trembling legs*.

Why? The shy young girl from Vietnam ran away down the stairs on trembling legs *at the piercing sound of the alarm*.

WRITING ACTIVITY 4

Expand each of the sentences below by adding one or more prepositional phrases to each of the blanks. Rewrite them on a separate piece of paper. The first one has been done as an example.

1. I left school _____ to hear a new band _____ play _____.
                   when?   what?   where?

I left school before 2:30 p.m. to hear a new band of reggae musicians play at the Town Center.

2. _____ I arrived _____, I found a seat _____.
   when?   where?   where?

3. The musicians _____ were playing _____ _____.
                 where?   what?   how?

4. I sat _____ _____ and listened _____.
         how?   where?   what?

5. One _____ was playing a bass guitar _____.
       who?   how?

6. _____ the show was over, and the band went _____.
   when?   where?

7. I decided to go _____ _____ _____
   where?   how?   why?

Another way to vary your sentence patterns is to shift prepositional phrases to different places in your sentences. Here is an example:

Original: The shy young girl from Vietnam ran away **down** the stairs **on trembling legs** at the piercing sound of the alarm.

Shift 1: Down the stairs the shy young girl from Vietnam ran away on trembling legs at the piercing sound of the alarm.

Shift 2: On trembling legs the shy young girl from Vietnam ran away down the stairs at the piercing sound of the alarm.

Shift 3: At the piercing sound of the alarm, the shy young girl from Vietnam ran away down the stairs on trembling legs.

Which one sounds best to you? Which one communicates the idea most precisely? The answer really depends on what the writer wants to emphasize. Shifts 1, 2, and 3 all express the same idea, but they emphasize different parts of the sentence. Shift 1 emphasizes where the subject went, Shift 2 emphasizes how the action occurred, and Shift 3 emphasizes why the action happened.

WRITING ACTIVITY 5

On a separate piece of paper, rewrite the seven sentences from Writing Activity 4, shifting the prepositional phrases to different places in each sentence. For example, here are two possible revisions of the first sentence:

1. I left school *before* 2:30 p.m. to hear a new band *of* reggae musicians play *at* the Town Center.

   Before 2:30 p.m., I left school to hear a new band of reggae musicians play at the Town Center.

To hear a new band of reggae musicians play at the Town Center, I left school before 2:30 p.m.

> **REMINDER** _____
>
> Add adjectives, adverbs, and descriptive phrases before and after your subjects and verbs to make your sentences clearer and more precise. Then experiment with adding prepositional phrases and with shifting these phrases to different places in your sentences.

WRITING ACTIVITY 6

Plan, write, and revise a paragraph describing a typical school day. When and how do you wake up? What do you do next? How do you get to school? How long is your school day? What usually occurs? Where do you usually go after school? What do you do when you get there? When you finish revising, examine every sentence. Where can you add prepositional phrases to clarify your meaning or to vary your sentence patterns? Rewrite the paragraph and underline every prepositional phrase that you added.

Participial Phrases (Phrases Beginning with *-ing/-ed/-en* Verbs). A *participial phrase* is a group of words beginning with a participle—a verb that ends in *-ing, -ed,* or *-en* (also called a *verbal*). In Chapter 15, you learned how to use helping verbs and verbs that end in *-ing, -ed,* or *-en* to write clear, correct sentences. You learned that if you leave out the helping verb, you can create a fragment:

    A. The con man *telling* very believable stories.
    B. Several people *fooled* by this con man.
    C. These people *taken* in hook, line, and sinker by his tales of woe.

In Chapter 15, you learned that one way to correct these fragments was to add a verb (or a subject and a verb):

    D. The con man *telling* very believable stories **visited** elderly couples.
    E. Several people *fooled* by this con man **lost** thousands of dollars.
    F. These people **were** *taken* in hook, line, and sinker by his tales of woe.

In sentences *D, E,* and *F,* the participial phrases that begin with *-ing/-ed/ -en* verbs are functioning as adjectives, *not* as verbs. In sentence *D,* the phrase "telling very believable stories" is describing the "con man." Similarly, in sentence *E,* the phrase "fooled by this con man" describes the "people." In sentence *F,* the phrase "taken in hook, line, and sinker by his tales of woe" also describes these people ("they").

Note that the *-ing/-ed/-en* phrases can be moved to the beginning of these sentences to add variety:

G. *Telling very believable stories,* the con man visited elderly couples.
H. *Fooled by this con man,* several people lost thousands of dollars.
I. *Taken in hook, line, and sinker by his tales of woe,* they lost everything.

A simple way to practice using *-ing/-ed/-en* phrases to expand and vary your sentences is to write pairs of sentences with the same subject and then combine them. Here are some examples:

Draft:
Braille was created by Louis Braille in 1829.
Braille consists of an alphabet of raised dots.

Possible Revisions:
Created by Louis Braille in 1829, braille is an alphabet that consists of raised dots.
Braille, created by Louis Braille in 1829, is an alphabet consisting of raised dots.
Consisting of raised dots, braille is an alphabet created by Louis Braille in 1829.

WRITING ACTIVITY 7

Practice writing using *-ing/-ed/-en* phrases by combining each pair of sentences below. You may have to change some verb endings; others are already in the appropriate *-ing, -ed,* or *-en* form. The first one has been done in two different ways as an example.

1. Last night I was scared breathless. I was awakened by a booming thunderstorm.

   Last night I was scared breathless, awakened by a booming thunderstorm.

Awakened by a booming thunderstorm, last night I was scared breathless.

2. I heard an extraordinarily loud burst of thunder. I buried my head beneath my pillows.
3. I didn't want to leave my bed. I was terrified by the crashing, tearing noises.
4. I looked up. I realized the thunder was growing weaker.
5. I was struck by a sudden fear. I looked out the window.
6. Our oak tree covered the driveway. It was split into dozens of tiny pieces.

WRITING ACTIVITY 8

Take out a paragraph or an essay that you wrote for an earlier chapter in this book. Circle the sentences that seem to have the same pattern or that seem to all begin in the same way. On a separate piece of paper, rewrite these sentences. Add descriptive words and prepositional phrases to expand them and vary their structure. See if any sentences can be reduced to *-ing/-ed/-en* phrases and inserted into other sentences. When you finish experimenting with revising your sentences in different ways, rewrite the final version on another piece of paper.

Appositive Phrases. An *appositive* is a word or phrase that renames (gives another name or a brief definition of) the noun or pronoun that it follows. Here are two sentences that include appositive phrases:

> Kurt Masur, *the famous conductor,* is directing the Philharmonic this season. The orchestra is playing his favorite piece, *Mahler's Symphony No. 1.*

How are appositives formed? If you examine the two sentences above, you can see that each is created from two ideas:

1. Kurt Masur is *the famous conductor.* He is directing the Philharmonic this season.
2. The orchestra is playing Masur's favorite piece. It is *Mahler's Symphony No. 1.*

Appositive phrases function like *-ing/-ed/-en* phrases. For example, suppose you wrote the following sentence:

The Nobel Prize is awarded annually to researchers in physics, chemistry, and medicine and to a writer.

Now suppose that you want to add information to this sentence explaining what the prize consists of. You can do this in several ways:

1. Add a relative clause (a word group that begins with the pronouns *which, that, who, whom,* or *whose*)

   The Nobel Prize, *which consists of a large sum of money and a gold medal,* is awarded annually to researchers in physics, chemistry, and medicine and to a writer.

2. Add an *-ing* phrase

   The Nobel Prize, *consisting of a large sum of money and a gold medal,* is awarded annually to researchers in physics, chemistry, and medicine and to a writer.

3. Add an appositive phrase

   The Nobel Prize, *a large sum of money and a gold medal,* is awarded annually to researchers in physics, chemistry, and medicine and to a writer.

All three sentences communicate the same idea and emphasis, but the third one does it with the fewest words. This does *not* mean that the third sentence is the "best" one. Deciding which option is best for a particular sentence depends on one's meaning and on the patterns of the surrounding sentences. A series of sentences with appositives can be just as repetitive and tedious to read as a series of short, simple sentences. You will have to experiment with the different techniques you are learning in this chapter in order to select the one that sounds best for each sentence.

WRITING ACTIVITY 9

Combine each pair of sentences below into a single sentence by changing one of them into an appositive and inserting it into the other sentence. The first one has been done as an example.

1. Many people are afraid of tornadoes. Tornadoes are a particularly violent form of weather.

Many people are afraid of tornadoes, a particularly violent form of weather.

2. A tornado can be terrifying. A tornado is a violently revolving storm.

3. In the center of the tornado is an area of calm air. The center of the tornado is known as the ''eye.''

4. This eye is formed by the air spiraling around it. This eye is simply a hollow space.

5. A tornado formed at sea sucks water and sand up into its eye. A tornado formed at sea is a ''waterspout.''

VARYING SENTENCE BEGINNINGS

If many sentences in your paragraph or essay begin the same way, they may bore your readers. For example, reread the paragraph on pages 439–440 of this chapter. How do most of the sentences in this paragraph begin? What is the effect of these similar sentence beginnings?

You can vary your sentence beginnings by using all the techniques that you have learned in this chapter. As you revise your sentences, add adjectives, adverbs, and descriptive phrases, and shift these to the front of the sentences. Experiment with your sentences. Begin some with adjectives, begin others with *-ing/-ed/-en* verbs, and begin others with prepositional phrases. Here is an example of this process:

When I learned how to read music, I discovered that I had perfect pitch. I could sing any musical note. I did this by remembering the notes in my head. I didn't even have to hear the note on an instrument. I was frightened by this musical ability, I almost stopped singing. I spoke to my music teacher. She showed me how lucky I was.

To help me understand my special skill,

to have this gift.

Another problem that can cause sentences to sound weak and boring is repeated use of *''dummy subject''* beginnings such as *There* and *It*. Some English sentences do require a dummy subject. For instance, English-speaking people use *It* to describe the weather (''It's raining'' or ''It's sunny''). In this case, the *It* has no meaning; it simply provides a dummy (a meaningless) subject. However, we often use dummy subjects to begin sentences that already have a ''real'' subject: ''*There is* a tornado forming five miles away'' (instead of ''A tornado is forming five miles away'').

Beginning with an unnecessary dummy subject weakens a sentence because it moves the focus away from the actual subject. A series of sentences with dummy subject openers is also boring to read. Realizing this, a student revised the following paragraph:

~~There is~~ A *Mozart is* concert about to begin. ~~It is a Mozart concert.~~ There are *are* several hundred people waiting to get into the concert hall. ~~There is~~ A *es* person announcing that the concert has been oversold: *The hall does not have* ~~There simply are~~ ~~not~~ enough seats for everyone who is waiting. ~~There are~~ Many people on the line ~~who~~ get angry, *but* ~~There~~ is not much that they can do about it.
(I think this one is okay.)

WRITING ACTIVITY 10

Rewrite the following sentences on a separate piece of paper. Delete every unnecessary dummy subject and change whatever else is necessary to make each sentence complete and correct. The first one has been done as an example.

1. It was about 10:00 p.m. when we arrived at the rap show.

About 10:00 p.m., we arrived at the rap show.
or We arrived at the rap show about 10:00 p.m.

2. There were many of our friends already at the show.
3. There were about ten people sitting down near the stage.
4. There were dozens of seats available.
5. There were two groups who performed, and we sang along with each one.
6. It was obvious that we loved singing with the bands.

GROUP WORK 2

Form a group with two other students. Together revise the paragraph below by varying the sentence beginnings and by deleting unnecessary words. Choose one student to record the group's final version.

It is good for women to exercise. Exercise helps women look attractive. It makes them look thinner and trimmer. Exercise also helps women gain strength. It makes them stronger. It helps prevent bone loss. Bone loss is a serious problem for many women. Exercise keeps a woman healthier as she grows older. It strengthens her heart. It makes her heart less prone to disease. There are also many ways that exercise improves a woman's self-esteem. It helps her feel good about her body. It gives her a growing sense of independence. It is a way of making a woman feel more in control of her body. Many women have discovered the rewards and joys of regular exercise.

Sentence variety makes writing more interesting to read. However, sometimes deliberately repeating a sentence pattern or a sentence opener effectively energizes your writing. For instance, what is your response to the parallel sentence beginnings in the following paragraph by Senator Bill Bradley? This paragraph comes from a discussion of what he learned from his African-American teammates when he played for the New York Knicks:

Besides learning about the warmth of friendship, the inspiration of personal histories, the family in each of their lives, I better understand distrust and suspicion. I understand the meaning of certain looks and certain codes. I understand what it is to be in racial situations for which you have no frame of reference. I understand the tension of always being on guard, of never totally relaxing. I understand the pain of racial arrogance directed my way. I understand the loneliness of being white in a black world. And I understand how much I will never know about what it is to be black in America.

WRITING ACTIVITY 11

Using Bradley's paragraph as a model, write a paragraph about an important lesson that you learned or an event that gave you new understandings. Begin many of the sentences with ''I understand that'' or ''I learned that.'' When you finish writing and revising this paragraph, rewrite it. Change the sentence beginnings and patterns, using the techniques that you have learned in this chapter. Then examine both versions. Which one is more effective? Why?

SENTENCE VARIETY REVIEW ━━━━━━━━━

Below are the strategies that you have learned for varying your sentence patterns and beginnings and for improving your sentence style.

- Use short and long sentences in the same paragraph.
- Add adjectives and adverbs that expand your sentences and clarify your exact meaning.
- Add prepositional phrases, phrases that begin with *-ing/-ed/-en* verbs, and appositives to your sentences.
- Experiment with moving adjectives and descriptive phrases to the beginning of your sentences.

COMBINING SENTENCES

Teachers often tell students to write ''clear, direct'' sentences, and students often interpret this to mean that they should write short, simple sentences. Is sentence clarity related to sentence length? Here is an experiment that will help you answer this question. Ask five people whether the sentences in *A* or *B* below are easier to read and to understand:

A. Gerontology is the study of old age. It is a new field. This field is fascinating. Gerontology is in psychology.

B. Gerontology, the study of old age, is a fascinating new field in psychology.

Each of the sentences in passage *A* has seven or fewer words. Each sentence is shorter and simpler in structure than the single sentence in *B,* which has thirteen words. Yet probably everyone will say that the sentence with thirteen words is clearer than the four short sentences. One long sentence that omits repeated words and that spells out the relation among its ideas is often easier to understand than are several short sentences. Combining short, simple sentences into longer ones enables you to express the relations among your ideas more precisely, and it also makes your sentences clearer and more interesting to read.

You have already practiced combining sentences by changing them into prepositional phrases, *-ing/-ed/-en* phrases, and appositives. Here is an example of each strategy:

Uncombined Sentences:
My parents approve. They approve of my major. This major is in gerontology. They are very supportive.

Combined with Prepositional Phrases:
My parents approve *of my major in gerontology*. They are very supportive.

Combined with an Appositive Phrase:
My parents approve of my major, *gerontology*. They are very supportive.

Combined with an *-ing/-ed/-en* Phrase:
Approving of my major in gerontology, my parents are very supportive.

The remainder of the chapter will provide you with opportunities to practice two other sentence-combining techniques: coordination and subordination. These two techniques will help you improve your sentence style.

Coordination. *Coordination* involves combining two or more complete sentences with a comma and a *coordinator* (sometimes called a *coordinating conjunction*). Here is an example:

I need to narrow my professional goals, and then I must select the appropriate major.

Combining these two sentences with the coordinator *and* does not change their meaning or add any new information. It does, however, show readers the relation between the two ideas, and it makes the writer's style less choppy.

English has only seven coordinators, listed below.

COORDINATORS _____
and indicates that the second clause provides similar or additional information:

Kiesha knows the terrible effects of smoking, *and* she is worried about her inability to stop.

(Continued)

but and *yet* indicate that the second clause provides contrasting or different information:

> Kiesha knows the terrible effects of smoking, *but* she cannot bring herself to stop.

for indicates that the second clause provides reasons for the information in the first clause:

> Kiesha knows the terrible effects of smoking, *for* she has been reading literature from the American Cancer Society.

or indicates that the second clause provides an alternative to or consequence of the information in the first clause:

> Kiesha knows that she should stop smoking now, *or* she will have to pay the price later.

nor indicates that the second clause continues a negative statement begun in the first clause:

> Kiesha knows that smoking it is not good for her, *nor* is it healthy for the people around her.

so indicates that the information in the second clause is caused by the information in the first clause:

> Kiesha knows the terrible effects of smoking, *so* she is trying to break this habit now.

REMINDER _____

Note that you should insert a comma after the first clause, *before* the coordinator. (See pages 457–458 about commas.) Also note that you can combine two sentences with a semicolon and a transition (also called a *conjunctive adverb*). (See the chart of transitions on pages 87–88 of Chapter 3 and page 426 about semicolons.)

WRITING ACTIVITY 12

Below is a series of sentences, each followed by a coordinator and a space. In the space, write a sentence that makes sense connected to the first sentence with the coordinator. The first one has been done as an example.

1. I need a job, and *I am going to several employment agencies to get one.*

2. I have been searching for a job every afternoon, but _____

    _____.

3. It is critical for me to find employment, for _____

    _____.

4. I will do word processing, or _____

    _____.

5. Ideally, I would like to make $10.00 an hour, but _____

    _____.

6. I am willing to do typing and filing, and _____

    _____.

7. If I can't find a job that pays a decent salary, I will have to quit

    school, so _____

    _____.

Subordination. *Subordination* is another method of combining related ideas into a single sentence. You subordinate a sentence by adding a *subordinator* (a *subordinating conjunction*) to its beginning. Here is an example:

Because

∧ I am exercising frequently͵,I am able to eat more without gaining weight.

Combining the two sentences above produces a more readable, mature style because the reader does not have to "work" hard to figure out the writer's meaning. By combining the ideas with the subordinator *because,* the writer makes it clear that the second idea is caused by the first. When you revise your sentences, look for connections among them and experiment with combining them. Do the hard work of clarifying the relations among your ideas so that your readers don't have to!

Like coordination, subordination connects ideas so that readers can understand the relations among them. However, when you coordinate two ideas, you are presenting them as equally important:

A. I am trying to work out more frequently, but I still dislike exercising.

To "subordinate" means to treat something as less important than or as dependent on something else. When you subordinate the two ideas in example *A,* the idea that begins with the subordinator is perceived as less important:

B. *Although* I am trying to work out more frequently, **I still dislike exercising.**

The independent clause ("I still dislike exercising") is a complete sentence, so it is the idea that gets emphasized.

If you wanted to emphasize the first idea, you could shift the subordinator so that it begins the second idea:

C. **I am trying to work out more frequently** *although* I still dislike exercising.

Read sentences *A, B,* and *C* aloud. All three express the same ideas and the same relation, but they differ in pausing and in emphasis.

No one can tell you which clause to emphasize when you combine sentences. *You* have to decide precisely what you are trying to communicate, and you have to experiment with coordinating and subordinating your clauses until they emphasize the idea that you want to stress.

There are many subordinators in English. Below is a brief list of common ones, arranged according to the relation that they indicate between clauses. You will probably recognize these subordinators as the "dependent words" that were discussed in the section on fragments on page 420 in Chapter 15.

SUBORDINATORS _____

although, even though, and *unless* indicate that the clause that follows provides contrasting or different information from the independent clause:

> *Even though* Kiesha knows the terrible effects of smoking, she

cannot bring herself to stop.

because, since, in order that, and *so that* indicate that the clause that follows provides reasons for the information in the independent clause:

> Kiesha knows the terrible effect of smoking *because* she has been

reading literature from the American Cancer Society.

if, provided that, and *once* indicate that the clause that follows explains under what condition the idea in the independent clause occurs or occurred:

> Kiesha knows that she can stop smoking *if* she follows her doc-

tor's plan.

before, while, when, during, and *after* indicate that the clause that follows explains when the idea in the independent clause occurs or occurred.

> Kiesha is planning to stop smoking *after* she graduates this June.

Note that when a sentence begins with the subordinated clause, you should put a comma after this clause. However, when the sentence begins with the independent clause, you do *not* need to put a comma after it:

> Because I think revision leads to better writing, I am rewriting every essay about three times.   [comma]

> I am rewriting every essay about three times because I think revision leads to better writing.   [no comma]

WRITING ACTIVITY 13

The sentences below are composed of two sentences linked by a coordinator. On separate paper, rewrite the sentence using an appropriate subordinator.

1. I use my computer program's spell-checker every time I write, for I am not a particularly good speller.
2. I have been able to improve my ability to compose and revise my ideas, but I seem unable to learn how to spell correctly.
3. Often I can identify the words that I have misspelled, yet I do not know how to correct them.
4. I am unsure of the spellings of many common words, so I cannot even look them up in a dictionary.
5. I no longer worry about my spelling errors, for my spell-checker can find and correct almost all of them.

Subordination with Relative Pronouns. In Chapter 15, you learned about using relative pronouns (*who, whom, which, that,* and *whose*) to correct fragments. These pronouns can also be used to subordinate ideas. If you want to combine two sentences that have the same subject, replace the second subject with the appropriate relative pronoun. Here is an example of this technique for combining sentences:

Albert Einstein was a scientist, ~~Albert Einstein~~ *who* developed the theory of relativity, ~~This theory~~ *which* states that everything in the universe is moving and that all motion is connected.

Combining the three sentences above with relative pronouns links the ideas more closely and reveals the relations among them. It also makes the writing flow more effectively by eliminating words that are repeated unnecessarily.

PUNCTUATION POINTER:
COMMAS AND RELATIVE CLAUSES ————————————

Here are guidelines for deciding whether you need to use commas to insert a relative clause into another sentence.

• Do not use commas before and after a relative clause that is necessary for the reader to identify the subject that the clause is describing:

> Einstein's theory *that time is a fourth dimension* enables scientists to measure the speed of moving things more accurately.

There are no commas surrounding the subordinated clause, ''that time is a fourth dimension,'' because it is essential for letting the reader

---

know which one of Einstein's many theories is being discussed. An essential clause, which cannot be left out without changing the sentence's meaning, is called a *restrictive clause* and is *not* set off by commas.

- Put a comma before and after a relative clause that adds information that is not necessary for identifying the subject it is describing:

> Einstein's unified field theory, *which describes the dimensions of space and time,* enables scientists to measure the speed of moving things more accurately.

Commas surround the subordinated clause, ''which describes the dimensions of space and time,'' because this clause is not essential for letting the reader know which of Einstein's theories is being described. If this clause were omitted, the reader would still know that the sentence is describing Einstein's unified field theory. This kind of clause is called a *nonrestrictive clause.*

Let's look at how writers can make their sentences clearer and more interesting by subordinating them. Here is the paragraph that appeared on pages 439–440 of this chapter.

I fell in love with music. I was five years old. I attended my first concert. I had heard music all my life. I don't remember enjoying it. Most of it was babyish and boring. This was my first time experiencing classical music. I clearly remember the sensation it produced. It was a physical sensation. The violins played. Their bell-like sounds made me shiver. Then the horns played. Now I know that these horns were clarinets and oboes. They started gurgling their mellow sounds. I felt like I was breathing the music. I felt like my lungs were moving with the bassoon. I also felt my heart. It thumped out the rhythm of the drums. I heard the clash of the cymbals. It made me jump in my seat. The music stopped. The silence made me cry. I was so overwhelmed. I could not even clap.

Here is the writer's final version.

I fell in love with music *when* I was five years old *and* I attended my first concert. I had heard music all my life, but I don't remember enjoying it *because* most of it was babyish and boring. This was my first time experiencing classical music, *and* I clearly remember that the sensation it produced in me was physical. *When* the violins played, their bell-like sounds made me shiver. Then the horns, *which* I now know were clarinets and oboes, started gurgling their mellow sounds. *Feeling* like I was breathing the music, my lungs bellowed with the bassoon *and* my heart thumped out the rhythm of the drums. The clash of the cymbals made me jump in my seat. *When* the music stopped, the silence made me cry. I was so overwhelmed *that* I could not even clap.

The revised paragraph is clearer, less choppy, and more sophisticated in style.

SENTENCE-COMBINING QUESTIONS ⎯⎯⎯⎯⎯⎯⎯⎯⎯⎯⎯⎯
Use the questions below to evaluate the effectiveness of different ways of combining sentences.

1. Would the reader understand my ideas more clearly if I wrote them as separate sentences?
2. Which way of combining my sentences communicates my meaning and my intended emphasis most clearly?
3. Which combination sounds best?

WRITING ACTIVITY 14

Below is a paragraph that was rewritten as a series of short, simple sentences. Draw arrows between the sentences that you think would sound better combined. Experiment with different methods of combining them: Coordinate them, subordinate them, change one into an *-ing/-ed* *-en* phrase, or change one into an appositive phrase. On a separate piece of paper, write your final version. Be prepared to explain why you combined the sentences that you did and why you chose the method that you used to combine each set.

Sometimes people experience stress. They experience this stress physically. They experience it in the form of a psychosomatic illness. Psychosomatic illnesses are disorders. These disorders are caused by problems. The problems are psychological. These disorders are not imaginary. People develop these disorders. They do become sick. Some people have overwhelming stress in their lives. These people can develop rashes. These people can also develop migraine headaches. These diseases are genuine. They are not imagined. However, they may be triggered by problems. These problems are psychological. For example, a person is trying unsuccessfully to deal with a very stressful situation. He or she may get nervous and frustrated. He or she may break out in hives. When this occurs, it is evidence. His or her mind is displacing the mental stress. It is displacing this stress onto the body. In order to control his or her hives, this person must medicate the rash. This person must develop a better way of dealing with the frustration. The frustration is in his or her life.

GROUP WORK 3

Form a group of three students and choose one person to record the group's revisions. Below is a student paragraph that was rewritten as a series of simple, short sentences. In the spaces below each set, try out different ways of combining these sentences to make longer, clearer ones. Then delete all repeated or unnecessary words. Two possible combinations for the first set have been done as an example.

1. There are women.
2. They live in underdeveloped countries.
3. These countries are in the Third World.
4. The women are achieving progress.
5. This progress is remarkable.

1- Women who live in underdeveloped countries in the Third World are achieving progress that is remarkable.

2- Women living in underdeveloped Third World countries are achieving remarkable progress.

6. For example, Pakistani women are struggling.
7. They are trying to help their families.
8. They want their families to survive.
9. They are also struggling to protect something.
10. That something is their environment.

_____

_____

_____

_____

11. Most of these women face problems.
12. These problems are extremely difficult.
13. One of these problems is lack of food.
14. Another of these problems is lack of water.

_____

_____

_____

_____

15. They are combating these problems.
16. They are working together.
17. Together they grow food.
18. Together they build reservoirs.

_____

_____

_____

_____

19. These women are trying to ensure something.
20. They want a better future.
21. They want this future for their families.
22. They want this future for their environment.

_____

_____

_____

_____

_____

_____

✔ POINTS TO REMEMBER ABOUT SENTENCE
VARIETY AND STYLE

1. Be willing to ''play'' with your sentences. Experiment with rewriting
   them in different ways for a different focus or different emphasis.
2. Examine every sentence for places where you might add descriptive
   words and phrases in order to communicate your ideas more precisely.
3. Add adjectives and adverbs that enable readers to share your perceptions
   and experiences.
4. Vary the lengths of your sentences.
5. Add prepositional phrases that explain how, where, why, and in what
   way.
6. Add participial phrases (which begin with *-ing/-ed/-en* verbs) and appositive phrases.

7. Vary your sentence beginnings. Try shifting a phrase within a sentence to the beginning of the sentence.
8. Combine sentences with a coordinator or with a subordinator.
9. Combine sentences by changing one sentence into a prepositional phrase, a phrase that begins with an *-ing/-ed/-en* verb, or an appositive phrase.
10. Combine sentences by changing one sentence into a relative clause.

GRAMMAR AND USAGE 1: NOUNS, SUBJECTS, AND VERBS

Grammar is the study of the way a language works. Most people think that *grammar* means the rules for using words and sentences correctly. Most of us also assume that every language has one clear set of rules for "correct" or "good" grammar. However, the rules for "correct" grammar can differ from community to community. For example, the rules for correct American English usage differ from those for correct British English usage. Moreover, the rules for correct Ozark Mountain American English are different from those for correct Urban Black American English.

The way a community uses its language is called a *dialect,* and there are more than a dozen dialects of American English, each with slightly different grammatical rules. The grammar and usage rules in this chapter describe the dialect called Academic Written English (sometimes called Standard Written English), which is the dialect generally used for writing in schools, business, the government, and the news media.

EDITING ACADEMIC WRITTEN ENGLISH GRAMMAR AND USAGE

You already know many of the conventions of Academic Written English. You know that it is written from left to right and that each new paragraph is indented to the right. You also know that every Academic Written English sentence begins with a capital letter and has a subject and a verb. The remainder of the chapter will discuss other conventions of Academic Written English grammar (structure) and usage (rules for using the grammar correctly).

In writing, as well as in speaking, grammar and usage depend on one's subject, purpose, and audience. For instance, someone might say the following sentence to a friend:

My brother ain't happy 'cause he can't do nothing 'til he get out of the hospital.

The speaker has communicated her message without worrying about whether her grammar was "correct." If the listener didn't understand the speaker, she would probably respond with "What did you say?" or "What do you mean?" However, if the speaker had written this sentence in the final version of an academic paragraph, her teacher might find it unacceptable. The writer would need to edit the sentence so that it follows Academic Written English conventions:

My brother isn't happy because he can't do anything until he's out of the hospital.

The writer might have made the statement even more formal by omitting the contractions:

My brother is not happy because he cannot do anything until he is out of the hospital.

Effective writers examine their writing from the perspective of their intended readers. As you revise your paragraphs and compositions, think about the Academic Written English conventions that your readers will expect. If you don't follow these conventions, readers may not understand your ideas and may get distracted or annoyed. In school and at work, edit your writing to make it conform to the basic conventions of Academic Written English.

Nouns and Verbs. As you learned in Chapter 15, the building blocks of sentences are nouns and verbs. A *noun* is a word that names a person, place, thing, quality, or idea (such as *woman, Texas, peace*). A *verb* is a word that expresses an action, a condition, or a state of being (such as *write, become, is*). Some words can be used as a noun and as a verb:

I *walked* to the corner because I enjoy taking a *walk* every day.

The *smoke* from my father's cigar is so strong that it annoys our neighbors, who *smoke* only cigarettes.

Some nouns are in the process of becoming acceptable as verbs. For example, many professional writers use the words *critique* and *dialogue* as both a noun and a verb:

I was asked to *critique* your *critique* of Prof. Fernandez's most recent play.

The two screenwriters should *dialogue* with each other more frequently about the *dialogue* in their movie.

Other writers strongly object to this use of nouns as verbs. A recent edition of the *Broadview Book of Common Errors in English* (a reference guide that is popular with teachers) asserts that *critique* and *dialogue* are nouns, *not* verbs. Yet many people continue to use them as verbs and prefer this usage.

Verb Forms. Remember that a sentence is a group of words that includes a subject and a verb and expresses a complete thought:

Prof. Fernandez was reciting a poem.

The subject is the person, place, thing, or idea that the sentence is about. The verb states what the subject is doing or experiencing. In the sample sentence above, the subject is *Prof. Fernandez,* and the complete verb is *was reciting.*

"*You're a good man, Washbourne. I like the way you use nouns as verbs.*"
Drawing by Dana Fradon; © 1984 The New Yorker Magazine, Inc.

In English, the time of the action or condition expressed by the verb is called its *tense*. Verb tense tells when the action or the experience in the sentence happens—in the past, in the present, or in the future:

PAST: Prof. Fernandez *recited* a poem.

PRESENT: She *recites* a poem.

FUTURE: She *will recite* a poem.

The present tense describes what is happening *or* what is true right now *or* what happens regularly *or* what is generally true:

Prof. Fernandez *recites* (or *is reciting*) a poem now.
She *recites* poems every weekday morning at 10:00.
Her students often *recite* poetry with her.

For most English verbs, the present tense is the form of the verb that follows the word *to,* as in *to recite* or *to like*. This form, which is called the *infinitive,* is the form of the verb that you would look up in the dictionary. (For an explanation of the *-s* ending on the verb *recites* in the sample sentences above, see page 488 in this chapter.) The *-ing* form of the present tense is ordinarily used to indicate that the action or condition expressed by the verb is occurring at the moment that the writer is writing the sentence.

My sister *repairs* broken carburetors.   [*Repairs* indicates that she does this action on a regular basis.]

My sister *is repairing* a broken carburetor.   [*Is repairing* indicates that she is doing this action at the moment that the writer is writing about it—that the action is continuing.]

The future tense expresses an action or a condition that is yet to happen. You know how to form the future tense of a verb: Put the helping verb *will* or *shall* in front of the present-tense form:

Prof. Fernandez *will recite* some poems later today.

WRITING ACTIVITY 1

On separate paper, write five sentences, each of which uses the present-tense form of one of the following verbs: *discover, determine, imagine, succeed, regret.* (For fun, see if you can write these five sentences about the same topic, or if you can make them relate to one another.)

The past tense indicates that the action of a sentence has been completed or that the condition described in the sentence has ended. The past tense of most English verbs is formed by adding *-ed* to the end of the infinitive form (or just *-d* if the verb already ends in an *e*):

Prof. Fernandez *recited* new poems yesterday morning.

WRITING ACTIVITY 2

On separate paper, write a sentence using the past-tense form of each of the following verbs: *learn, provide, claim, finish, produce.* (Can you write these five sentences about the same topic? Can you make them relate to one another?)

English verbs also have two other past-tense forms. The *present-perfect* form indicates that the action or condition described in the sentence began in the past and is still occurring. (The name of the tense—"perfect"—has nothing to do with quality; it comes from the Latin word for "completed": *perfectus.*) To compose the present-perfect form of most English verbs, use *has* or *have* as a helping verb with the past-tense form of the verb:

Prof. Fernandez *has recited* three poems a day for almost five years. Her students *have listened* attentively to her readings.

The present-perfect verb tense is also used to describe an action or a condition that occurred sometime in the indefinite past and is related to the present. Here are some examples:

Prof. Fernandez *has recited* poetry many times, but she still feels nervous about doing it. Most of her students *have* never *recited* poetry, but some think they might like to try it.

If you want to refer to an action or a condition that has been occurring over a period of time and that is still occurring, you can combine the present-perfect form of the verb *to be* (*has been* or *have been*) and the *-ing* form of the verb:

Prof. Fernandez *has been reciting* poetry for about five years.

WRITING ACTIVITY 3

On separate paper, write a sentence that uses the present-perfect form of each of the following verbs: *influence, require, qualify, fulfill, flourish.*

Try to write these five sentences about the same topic or to make them relate to one another.

The *past-perfect* verb tense form is used to indicate that the action or condition described in the sentence occurred further back in time than another past action or condition that the sentence mentions. To compose the past-perfect form of most English verbs, use *had* as a helping verb with the past-tense form of the verb:

Prof. Fernandez *had recited* poetry in private for many years before she felt brave enough to recite it in front of her students. She *had feared* their reactions until she heard them clap and ask for another poem.

WRITING ACTIVITY 4

On separate paper, write a sentence that uses the past-perfect form for each of the following verbs: *decide, fail, realize, check, triumph.* (Can you write these five sentences about the same topic? Can you make them relate to one another?)

WRITING ACTIVITY 5

The following paragraph is written in the present tense. Change the time of the paragraph to the past by doing the following:

1. Cross out each underlined present-tense verb.
2. Write its past-tense form above it.

The first two have been done as examples.

decided

was About 1000 A.D., the kings of East and West Africa de~~ci~~de that it ~~is~~ important for them to have a written history of the events and laws of their communities. The kings notice a serious problem. As they add more and more laws to the existing ones, the people start to forget some of the laws. The kings want all the laws to be written down in one place. In addition, they also need a written history of their kingdoms because they want to tell their children who their ancestors <u>are</u> and what they <u>accomplish</u>. Thus, the kings <u>hire</u> "griots" to write their laws and their history. Griots <u>are</u> a special group of men who <u>learn</u> how to read and write. They <u>serve</u> as recordkeepers, historians, and political advisers to the chief. In effect, they <u>function</u> as living memories or libraries for entire African communities.

The *future-perfect* verb tense form is used to express an action or a condition that will be completed before another future action or condition takes place. There are two ways to compose the future-perfect form. The first way is to use *will have* or *shall have* as helping verbs with the *-ed* or the *-en* form of the verb:

> By the time Prof. Fernandez retires, she *will have recited* poetry for about twenty years. She *will have gotten* used to reciting poetry in public.

The second way of forming the future-perfect tense is to use *will have been* or *shall have been* as helping verbs with the *-ing* form of the verb:

> By the time Prof. Fernandez retires, she *will have been reciting* poetry for more than twenty years.

VERB FORM AND TENSE REVIEW

Infinitive	Present Participle	Past	Past Participle
recite	*reciting*	*recited*	*recited*

Present tense: I *recite* poetry. I am *reciting* poetry.
Past tense: Yesterday I *recited* poetry.
Yesterday I *was reciting* poetry.
Present-perfect tense: I *have recited* poetry daily for about ten years.
Past-perfect tense: I *had recited* long poems before I decided to choose shorter ones.
Future tense: I *will recite* poems again tomorrow.
Future-perfect tense: By the time I leave, *I will have recited* hundreds of poems. I *will have been reciting* poems for almost twenty years.

Regular and Irregular Verbs. The technical name for the verb form that you use with the helping verbs *has, have,* and *had* to create the perfect tenses is the *past participle.* The past-tense form and the past-participle form of most English verbs are the same:

> Today Prof. Fernandez *recited* the poem that she had *recited* for her husband on their first date. Her students *listened* attentively. Her husband has *listened* to her recite poems many times since then.

If the past-tense form and the past-participle form of a verb are both produced by adding *-d* or *-ed* to the infinitive form, the verb is called a *regular* verb. Most English verbs are regular verbs. They have only two forms: the present (the infinitive) and the past (with an *-ed* ending). As the chart on the preceding page shows, the future tense of most verbs is composed of *will* plus the infinitive form, and the perfect-tense form is the same as the past-tense form. The present tense poses a problem for some writers because they forget to add an *-s* ending on present-tense verbs that they use with "third-person-singular subjects":

> I *recite* poetry. You *recite* poetry. He *recites* poetry.

Confused? Don't worry. We'll clear this up soon (on page 488).

The only problem that the past and perfect tenses may present for writers is that you may forget to add the *-d* or *-ed* ending when you don't pronounce these endings. For example, look at the sentence below. It is clear that the writer is expressing a past-tense action:

> Yesterday Prof. Fernandez recite the poems that she loves most.

However, like many English speakers, the writer probably does not pronounce the *-d* ending of a word that is followed by a word beginning in a *th-, d-,* or *t-*. Thus, he left off the past-tense *-d* ending on the verb *recite.* Academic Written English requires this *-d* ending to indicate the past tense.

Some writers have a similar problem with the *-ed* ending on adjectives (words that describe nouns) that are created from the past participle. Here is an example:

> I am buying a *use* car, since I cannot afford a new one.

The *car* in this sentence was *used* by someone; thus, it is a *used* car. The adjective *used* is actually the past-participle form of the verb *to use.* Therefore, this adjective needs an *-ed* ending on it.

Here is an excerpt from a humorous essay by the writer and journalist William Safire. It describes the problems that some people have with *-ed* endings.

> The problem of the disappearing *d* or *-ed* manifests itself in that second usage, when the spelling does not match the pronunciation. *Old-fashion* looks funny in print before a noun—"served with old-fashion peach

cobbler,'' as it says on the menu—but it sounds right. Why should we insist on the *-ed* ending, when we readily accept *ice cream*? After all, we do not mean ''the cream of the ice'' but mean *iced cream.*

''Throughout the centuries,'' Prof. John Algeo of the University of Georgia tells me, ''English has tended to reduce a group of consonants at the end of a word by losing the last one.'' For example, a thousand years ago, we pronounced the *b* in *lamb,* and really hit that *g* in *long* (as a few Lawn Guylanders still do). ''So some English speakers today, in the vanguard of continuing the process of change, drop the final consonants in words like *world* and *blind,* which come out 'worl' and 'bline.' Judging from the past, those are advanced pronunciations—the wave of the future.''

The final *d* or *-ed* is getting kicked in the head by the rise of the attributive noun—that word for a thing that is used to modify another thing, like *killer* whale, *fashion* color, *lead* pencil and *call* girl. No wonder so many people follow that analogy to dispense with the *d* in making similar phrases, using stripped-down participles as if they were attributive nouns: *corn beef, whip cream, toss salad, skim milk, barbecue chicken, candy apples,* even *string instrument* and *stain glass.*

This brings us to the controversial rap singer Ice-T. Politicians complaining about violence in his lyrics miss the significant cultural controversy in his name—namely, should he be ''Iced-T''? Nobody, of course, pronounces the *-ed* in *iced tea;* as Professor Algeo notes, ''Since *-ed* in the first stands for the sound of *t,* it is lost before another *t* sound, just as *for goodness' sake* is usually pronounced like *for goodnesake,* with the final *s* sound of *goodness* lost before the initial one of *sake.* . . . *Iced tea* and *ice tea* would usually be pronounced alike in speech of normal tempo, thus inviting the simpler spelling.''

Does this change mean we must adopt pronunciation as our standard in spelling, and reject meaning? No. We do not write *for cry sake,* though that is our pronunciation of *for Christ's sake;* even when we write *for Chrissake,* we retain enough of the original meaning to remind readers that Jesus is being invoked.

Ears are sloppy and eyes are precise; accordingly, speech can be loose but writing should be tight. If it has taken a thousand years to lose the *b* in *lamb,* let it take a couple of generations at least to drop the *-ed* in the written *whipped cream.*

REMINDER ━━━━━━━━━━━━━━━━━━━━━━━━━━━━━━━━━━
If you write a past-tense verb, a past participle, or a past-participial adjective, check to make sure that you have written the correct ending (usually *-ed* or *-en*) even if you don't pronounce this ending.

If you look up a regular verb in the dictionary (under its *to,* or infinitive, form), you will see that many dictionaries do not list any other forms of the verb. Dictionary authors assume that you know how to create the future form (with *will*) and the past and participle forms (with *-ed*) of regular verbs.

However, a number of English verbs are *irregular:* Their past and/or past-participle forms are *not* created by adding *-d* or *-ed* to the infinitive form. Instead, the past-tense form and the past participle are produced by changing the spelling of the infinitive form. If you look up an irregular verb in the dictionary, it will list the past-tense form and the past participle directly after the pronunciation of the verb. Here is an example:

be•gin (bi-gin′) *v.* **-gan, -gun**

If you are ever unsure about the past-tense form or the past-participle form of a verb, just look up the infinitive form in the dictionary. For example, what is the past participle of the verb *hide*? If you know the answer, write it now. If you don't, look it up in your dictionary. You will discover that the past participle is *hidden,* as in ''The dog has hidden its bone.''

The most commonly used irregular verb is *to be,* which can be more confusing than other verbs because it is the only one that does *not* use its infinitive form for the present tense.

FORMS OF THE VERB *TO BE*

Present	Past	Past Participle
I *am*	I *was*	I *have been*
You *are*	You *were*	You *have been*
He or she *is*	She *was*	He *has been*
We *are*	We *were*	We *have been*
They *are*	They *were*	They *have been*

The only way to master the forms of irregular verbs is to use them frequently and memorize them as you use them. Below is a list of the principal parts of common irregular verbs, grouped according to their spelling patterns.

COMMONLY USED IRREGULAR VERBS

Infinitive	Past Tense	Past Participle
Begin, Began, Begun Pattern:		
begin	*began*	*begun*
drink	*drank*	*drunk*
ring	*rang*	*rung*

Infinitive	Past Tense	Past Participle
sing	sang	sung
sink	sank	sunk
spring	sprang	sprung
swim	swam	swum

Break, Broke, Broken Pattern:

break	broke	broken
choose	chose	chosen
freeze	froze	frozen
steal	stole	stolen
speak	spoke	spoken

Blow, Blew, Blown Pattern:

blow	blew	blown
draw	drew	drawn
fly	flew	flown
know	knew	known
throw	threw	thrown

Drive, Drove, Driven Pattern:

drive	drove	driven
ride	rode	ridden
rise	rose	risen
strive	strove	striven
write	wrote	written

Bleed, Bled, Bled Pattern

bleed	bled	bled
creep	crept	crept
feed	fed	fed
feel	felt	felt
lead	led	led
leave	left	left
mean	meant	meant
weep	wept	wept

Bring, Brought, Brought Pattern:

bring	brought	brought
buy	bought	bought
catch	caught	caught
fight	fought	fought

(Continued)

Infinitive	Past Tense	Past Participle
teach	taught	taught
think	thought	thought

Verbs Without a Pattern:

be	was, were	been
do	did	done
eat	ate	eaten
find	found	found
forget	forgot	forgotten
go	went	gone
run	ran	run
see	saw	seen
take	took	taken
tear	tore	torn

GROUP WORK 1

Do this activity with one or two classmates. Below are ten sets of three sentences. The first sentence in each set uses the present-tense form of a verb. Do the following in each set:

1. Fill in the past-tense form of the verb used in the first sentence in the space in the second sentence.
2. Fill in the past-participle form of the verb in the space in the third sentence.

The first one has been done as an example.

1. My brother Frank *is* a great pitcher. He ____*was*____ always a

   talented baseball player. He has ____*been*____ a pitcher for the

   past four years.

2. Frank *throws* a curve ball at about sixty miles an hour. Last

   month, he _____ a fast ball at seventy-one miles an

   hour. The fastest he has ever _____ a ball is seventy-

   five miles an hour.

3. Most pitchers *take* a long time to loosen up before pitching. Last

   year, Frank _____ about ten minutes to warm up. He

   has never _____ more than fifteen minutes to get ready.

4. Sometimes pitchers *fall* after they throw a very hard pitch. A

   few weeks ago, Frank _____ down so hard that he hurt

   his back. He had _____ only once before that fall.

5. Usually Frank *brings* a good-luck charm to help him pitch. This

   morning he _____ his ''lucky'' hat. In the past he has

   _____ a rabbit's foot.

6. Frank *speaks* to almost no one during a game. Yesterday he ____

   only a few words to the catcher. In past games he has _____

   only to the coach.

7. Frank *drives* other teams crazy with his pitches. In his last two

   games his slider _____ the batters to distraction. In

   other games his knuckleballs have _____ some batters

   into constantly striking out.

8. Frank also *catches* rather well. Last week he _____ a

   hard fly ball at the wall. He has always _____ line

   drives and grounders like a professional.

9. Now Frank *strives* to be good at everything. In the past he ____

   to be a great pitcher. Before that he had _____ to be

   the best ''all-around'' baseball player in the league.

10. The coach usually *chooses* Frank as his starting pitcher.

Yesterday he _____ someone else to start. When the

team lost, everyone said that the coach had _____ the

wrong starting pitcher.

Reread the list of irregular verbs on pages 478–480. Notice that we form most of them by changing the spelling of the infinitive rather than by adding a *-d* or an *-ed* (which is the way to form the past and past participles of regular verbs). Some writers find this confusing, and they add *-ed* endings to the past tense or the past participle of irregular verbs. For example, they may write, "I wish I had *throwned* out that letter before I *spoked* to you," instead of "I wish I had *thrown* out that letter before I *spoke* to you." Irregular verbs do *not* need *-d* or *-ed* endings in the past tense. Below are some other places where you do *not* have to add a *-d* or an *-ed* ending to a verb.

WHEN *NOT* TO USE A *-d* OR AN *-ed* ENDING ON VERBS

1. Don't add an ending to the infinitive form of a verb (the form that follows the word *to*):
   We wanted to move [*not* "to moved"] to Arkansas.
2. Don't add an ending to a verb that follows the helping verbs *do, does,* or *did*:
   We really did love [*not* "did loved"] the people and the scenery in Arkansas.
3. Don't add an ending to a verb that follows the helping verbs *can, could, should, would, may* or *might*:
   We could move [*not* "could moved"] to Kansas instead.

WRITING ACTIVITY 6

Write a sentence that uses the present perfect (*has/have* + past participle) *or* the past perfect (*had* + past participle) for each of the following verbs: *choose, begin, be, see, do, know*. See if you can write these six sentences about the same topic or if you can make them relate to one another.

WRITING ACTIVITY 7

Edit the following paragraph so that all its verbs are in Academic Written English forms. Cross out each incorrect past-tense form and each incorrect past participle. Then write in the correct version above it. The first one has been done as an example.

shown

Biofeedback has been sho~~w~~ed to work as well as medicine to cure certain illnesses. Recently, I learn that I can use biofeedback to control my blood pressure. My doctor had warn me that my blood pressure was getting too high, but I ignore his advice. When I seen him at my last visit, he tole me that I would have a stroke soon if I didn't do something to lower my blood pressure. This time, he really frighten me. I wented to a technician who shown me how to use a biofeedback machine. He hook me up to the machine and point out how its wavy lines indicate my blood pressure and heartbeat. Slowly I discover how to calm myself and make my blood pressure go down. As I relax and thinked about lowering my blood pressure, the lines on the machine show that my blood pressure actually was dropping. I have spoke to many friends about this experience, and several of them try it out. They have also acquire the skill of controlling their heartbeat or blood pressure through biofeedback. Biofeedback may have save our lives.

GROUP WORK 2

Below are some irregular verbs that were *not* included in the list on pages 478–480. Form a group with one or two classmates, and look up each verb in the dictionary to find out its past-tense and past-participle forms. Together compose one sentence using the verb in the past tense *and* a second sentence using the verb in the present-perfect tense (*has/have* + past participle) *or* the past-perfect tense (*had* + past participle).

Take turns writing these sentences on a separate piece of paper. Here are the verbs: *bite, grow, shake, show, shrink, thrive.* (You should write twelve sentences: two for each of the verbs.)

WRITING ACTIVITY 8

The sentences below follow the rules for forming the past and perfect tenses in other dialects. "Translate" each sentence into Academic Written English. Cross out the verb forms that are not Academic Written English. (If you are not sure, look them up in the dictionary.) Then write in the Academic Written English form of the past tense or the past participle. The first one has been done as an example.

1. Many of the problems in my high school classes be the students' fault. *are*
2. For example, I remember when the teacher say that the class wasn't participating enough.
3. She say, "You been sitting here like lifeless lumps."
4. That was when I realize that I been the only one who ask questions all semester.
5. Most of the class done no participating and very little work.
6. I had ask the students I knew why they didn't talk a lot in class.
7. They answer that they didn't understand the material.
8. I done tell them to listen more carefully and ask questions but they ain't care.
9. When these students fail, they didn't had anyone to blame but themselves.
10. I be trying my best to improve, so I am expecting an *A*.

WRITING ACTIVITY 9

Write a paragraph about what your life would be like now if you had not decided to go to college. What would you have done? How would you have felt? Try to use as many past participles as you can to describe what your life might have been like if you had not gone to college. (Some examples of past participles include "would *have gone* to work" or "would *have learned* a trade.")

Verb-Tense Consistency. If you are writing about events that took place or that will take place at different times, you may need to switch verb tenses in the middle of a sentence or a paragraph. Here is an example:

> Roger *is* angry at himself for not studying biology because he *thinks* that he *will fail* his final exam.

The time of the action in this sentence is the present (now), and two of the three verbs in this sentence are written in their present-tense forms: *is* and *thinks*. However, the ''exam'' that the sentence mentions has not yet occurred. It will take place in the future, so the correct verb-tense form to refer to it is the future form: *will fail.*

Problems occur when writers switch tenses for no obvious reason. Verb-tense shifts that don't communicate different time periods are very confusing. Here are some examples:

> When Roger told his parents that he had earned a *B+* in biology, they hug him and tell him that they are very proud of him. He was thrilled with their response and promises himself to do even better next semester.

There isn't any logical reason for this writer to shift back and forth from the past tense to the present. The writer should have used the past tense for all the verbs:

> When Roger *told* his parents that he had earned a *B+* in biology, they *hugged* him and *told* him that they *were* very proud of him. He *was thrilled* with their response and *promised* himself to do even better next semester.

Generally, when you are writing about a piece of literature, you should use the present tense:

> In Mark Twain's *The Adventures of Huckleberry Finn,* Huck *speaks* a strange dialect of English, which *reveals* that Huck *does* not really know how to write.

Many teachers also consider it acceptable to use the past tense to discuss literature:

> In Mark Twain's *The Adventures of Huckleberry Finn,* Huck *spoke* a strange dialect of English, which *revealed* that Huck *did* not really know how to write.

What is *not* acceptable is shifting tenses for no logical reason:

> In Mark Twain's *The Adventures of Huckleberry Finn,* Huck *speaks* a strange dialect of English, which *revealed* that Huck *did* not really know how to write.

> **REMINDER** ━━━
> Edit your verbs to make sure that they are consistent in tense. If the time that you are writing about does not change, then don't change verb tense.

WRITING ACTIVITY 10

The following student essay does not exhibit consistent verb-tense usage. Decide whether the essay would sound more logical in the present tense or the past tense. Then cross out the verbs that are not written in the tense you have selected, and rewrite them in the verb tense that you have chosen. Do *not* change any of the verbs in the quoted material. (The numbers in the parentheses are the page numbers for the quotations.)

Many writers capture the sounds of spoken dialect in writing. The most famous attempt was Mark Twain's The Adventures of Huckleberry Finn. In this book, Huck's words and grammar reveal him as a poor country boy without much formal education. For example, the book opened with Huck saying, "You don't know about me without you have read a book by the name of The Adventures of Tom Sawyer, but that ain't no matter. That book was made by Mr. Mark Twain, and he told the truth, mainly" (3). By writing in this dialect, Twain succeeds in making us understand Huck's ideas and his point of view.

Similarly, J. D. Salinger took us into the mind of his main character, Holden Caulfield, in the novel The Catcher in the Rye. This book begins with Holden saying, "If you really want to hear about it, the first thing you'll probably want to know is where I was born, and what my lousy childhood was like, and how my parents were occupied and all before they had me, and all that David Copperfield kind of crap, but I don't feel like going into it, if you want to know the truth" (3). This language showed that the boy narrating the book was educated and knew how to write, but that he is using his casual, street speech.

A more extreme attempt to represent a spoken dialect in writing was the novel Sitting Pretty, by Al Young. This book opens with the main character, named Sitting Pretty, talking about his life: "Maybe it was on accounta it was a full moon. I don't know. It's a whole lotta things I used to be dead certain about—like, day follow night and night follow day—things I wouldnt even bet on no more" (3). The words, grammar, and lack of punctuation (apostrophes) showed that the author wanted readers to focus on the sounds of the characters' voices. All three writers, Twain, Salinger, and Young, break the conventions of written language to help readers hear their characters' thoughts.

SUBJECT-VERB AGREEMENT

In Academic Written English, the main verb of every sentence must "agree" with its subject. Grammatical *agreement* means that the form of the verb matches the "person" and the "number" of the subject of the sentence. *Person* is a grammatical term that refers to the speaker's or the writer's relation to the subject of his or her sentence. If you speak or write about yourself, you know that you must use a *first-person* subject, *I*. If you are discussing yourself as part of a group, then you use the first-person subject *we*.

> *I* offered to help, and *we* started working on the project together.

If you are speaking or writing *to someone or to something,* you must use the *second-person* subject, *you. You* is used to address a single person or a group.

> *You* are the recorder for the group. The rest of *you* must decide what the group should do.

If you are talking or writing *about someone or about something,* you use a *third-person* subject: *he, she,* or *it* (for a single person, thing, or idea) or *they* (for a group). If the subject of a sentence can be replaced by the words *he, she, it,* or *they,* then it is a third-person subject. For example, each italicized subject below is a third-person subject:

Many *psychologists* have written about crowd behavior. *Gustave Le Bon* noted that when *a person* joins a crowd, *he* or *she* often stops thinking like an individual. People's *personalities* seem to dissolve as *they* start behaving and feeling like the crowd.

The subject of a sentence also has *number.* A subject can be *singular*—one person or thing (*I, you, he, she, it,* or "one thing") or *plural*—more than one (*we, you, they,* "several things"). For most singular nouns, all you have to do to make them plural is to add an *-s* or an *-es* ending:

The pain lessened as the doctor took out the stitch.
The *pains* lessened as the *doctors* took out the *stitches.*

Some plurals are formed by a change in spelling:

My child did not know the woman over there.
My *children* did not know the *women* over there.

The problem that some writers have with subject-verb agreement concerns the *-s* ending on a present-tense verb that is used with a "third-person-singular" subject. If you look at the following verb chart, you can see that the only verb that needs an *-s* ending is the one that is used with a third-person-singular subject.

PRESENT-TENSE VERB CHART ———————————————

	Singular	**Plural**
First person	I sing	we sing
Second person	you sing	you sing
Third person	she/he sings it sings	they sing

This *-s* ending is a "leftover" form from an older version of English. In "Old English" (A.D. 100–1100), every form of every verb had a different ending (*-e, -est, -on,* and *-eth*). By Shakespeare's time, the only verb ending that was regularly used was the *-eth* ending on verbs with third-person-singular subjects: "He lead*eth* us." Toward the end of the period of Middle English (1100–1600), people were pronouncing and writing this *-eth* ending as *-s*: "He leads us." All languages change over time. In the future, English may drop this *-s* verb ending. In fact, several current spoken dialects of English have already dropped it: "He lead us." However, the *-s* ending on third-person-singular verbs is still required for Academic Written English.

> **REMINDER** _____
>
> In Academic Written English, a third-person-singular subject (anything that is a "he," a "she," or an "it") needs an -*s* ending on its verb in the present tense.

Remember that the present-tense forms of the verbs *to be, to do,* and *to have* are different from those of other verbs. You have to change their spelling to indicate different types of subjects, as is shown in the chart below.

Present-Tense Forms of *Be, Do,* and *Have*

I *am*	I do	I have
you are	you do	you have
she *is*	he *does*	it *has*
we are	we do	we have
they are	they do	they have

Past-Tense Forms of *Be*

I *was*
you were
she *was*
we were
they were

WRITING ACTIVITY 11

Write in the correct present-tense form of the verb under each blank space. The first one has been done as an example.

1. When a person *walks* , *sits* , or *stands* , these move-
        (to walk)   (to sit)   (to stand)

   ments _____ from the action of his or her muscles.
      (to result)

2. A person's muscles _____ his or her bones _____.
              (to make)   (to move)

3. Muscles that _____ attached to the skeleton _____ in
           (to be)   (to work)

   pairs.

4. To move a bone, one muscle in the pair _____, or
   (to contract)

   _____, and the other one _____.
   (to tighten)   *(to relax)*

5. Skeletal muscles _____ in size and shape.
   (to vary)

6. The large muscle that _____ your thigh _____ about ten
   (to move)   *(to be)*

   inches long and half an inch thick.

7. In contrast, the muscles in your ear _____ about the size and
   (to be)

   the thickness of a pin.

8. Each skeletal muscle _____ attached to a bone by a tendon,
   (to be)

   which _____ and _____ like a cord or rope.
   (to look)   *(to feel)*

9. The human body _____ voluntary and involuntary muscles.
   (to have)

10. A voluntary muscle _____ whatever you _____ it to do,
    (to do)   *(to want)*

    but the body's involuntary muscles _____ without your being
    (to move)

    aware of them.

WRITING ACTIVITY 12

Below is an excerpt from a book of predictions about the future by the researcher Faith Popcorn. In this excerpt, Popcorn presents two very different pictures of America in the year 2010.

It's 2010.

More and more systems are breaking down. The pileup of toxic waste has gotten worse. Every year there's another mid-sized city in America that has to be evacuated.

The air's so bad you're only allowed to drive your car three days a week—which is all you can afford to drive anyway, because filling the tank costs about eighty dollars. Different-colored license plates will tell you on which days it's your turn to drive.

Someone owns the air franchise. Air conditioning is now called air purifying. And it costs a fortune.

Another mogul has bought and regulates the water sources. A long, hot bath is a metered luxury.

Or:

Corporate America as we know it today is over.

All the smartest people have left the mega-companies to start socially and ecologically responsible businesses of their own. Given the choice, consumers are more than willing to buy "correctly."

No one has to drive much anyway. Life feels smaller in scale— we're working at home, involved in the world with networks of friends through the electronic systems that bring in and send out information day and night.

Living within our means and resources, we're slowly healing the planet.

Write an essay about your predictions for America in 2010. Like Faith Popcorn, you might want to focus on a single problem (such as natural resources, food, health care, education, employment, child rearing, and so forth). You can write one description of your vision of our nation's future, or you can write two opposing descriptions (as Popcorn did). Write this essay in the *present* tense, as if you were writing it in 2010. When you finish revising your essay, check every verb and make sure that you have used its present-tense form. Be particularly careful about -*s* endings on third-person-singular verb forms.

GROUP WORK 3

Form a group with two or three classmates, and together do the following. Fill in each blank space with the present-tense form of any verb that makes sense in the sentence.

The human body _____ four different types of tissues.

These tissues _____ classified by the different jobs that they

_____. Epithelial, or skin, tissue _____ the entire

body. It also _____ the linings of the body's organs. Muscle

tissue _____ the kind of tissue that _____ the body to

move. Muscles _____ attached to organs and bones. They

_____ by alternately contracting and relaxing. Tendons and

ligaments _____ composed of muscle tissue. The third type of

tissue _____ connective tissue. This type _____ organs

together and _____ in the spaces between organs and other

tissues. The fourth type _____ nerve tissue. It

_____ the nervous system, which _____ to changes

inside and outside the body. The brain _____ made of nerve

tissue. All four types of body tissues _____ together all the time.

SPECIAL PROBLEMS IN SUBJECT-VERB AGREEMENT

In order to make sure that your verbs are correct according to Academic Written English, you have to determine whether the subject of each verb is singular or plural. Here are some tricky subjects that may confuse you.

1. When the Subject Is Compound. A compound subject is made up of two or more nouns that are joined with the word *and*. Generally, compound subjects need a plural form of the verb.

> A *muscle works* to make bones move.
> A *muscle and its tendon work* together to move a bone.
> A skeletal *muscle, its tendon, and its ligament are* all attached to one another.

However, when two or more subjects in a sentence are joined with words such as *or, either, neither,* or *nor,* the verb form is usually determined by the subject that is closest to the verb.

> Neither the heart muscle nor the stomach *muscles are* voluntary.
> Neither the stomach muscles nor the heart *muscle is* voluntary.

> The doctor or *her assistants know* how to tape a damaged muscle.
> The doctors or *the assistant knows* how to tape a damaged muscle.

2. When Words Separate a Subject from Its Verb. Don't be confused by singular or plural words that appear between a sentence's subject and verb.

Words that come between a subject and its verb do *not* affect the number of the subject. (They do not function like the word *and* in a compound subject.)

> One *muscle* in your upper arm *is* called a bicep.
> Those *muscles* in your upper arm *are* called triceps.

Be particularly careful about subject-verb agreement when the words that separate a singular subject from its verb sound as if they are making the subject plural. Expressions such as ''in addition to,'' ''as well as,'' ''including,'' and ''together with'' do *not* make the subject plural even though they sound as if they do.

> An involuntary cardiac *muscle,* together with its tendons, *makes* your heart beat.
> An involuntary cardiac *muscle* and its tendons *make* your heart beat.

WRITING ACTIVITY 13

In the uncorrected paragraph below, (1) underline the subject of each sentence, (2) circle the main verb, (3) cross out every verb that does not agree with its subject, and (4) write the correct form of the verb above it. The first one has been done as an example.

has

The professional athlete (have) to keep his or her muscles in shape all year round. Professional athletes in any sport needs to stretch their muscles continuously, even when their "season" end. The problems that occurs when athletes stops working out ranges from pulled muscles to broken bones. Most professional athletes work with an athletic trainer every week. The typical athletic trainer in most sports keep track of the health of the players and supervise recovery programs for injured athletes. The trainer, along with the team doctors, decide what treatment are appropriate. They also determine whether physical therapy exercises or medical treatment are better for healing specific injuries. Thus, the professional athlete depend on the athletic trainer to travel with the team and attend the games. Many amateur athletes, in addition to the professional player, works with athletic trainers on a regular basis. All athletes on any type of team needs to take care of their muscles and their bodies.

---

3. When a Subject Comes After Its Verb. A verb agrees with its subject, whether the verb comes after the subject or before it.

> At one end of a nerve cell *is an axon.*
> All around the axon *are dendrites.*

If you begin a sentence with the "dummy" subjects *There* or *Here,* the actual subject of the sentence *follows* the verb (and determines the form of the verb).

> There *is* a small *nucleus* in each nerve axon.
> There *are* many *dendrites* around each nerve axon.

Note that the dummy subject *It* always requires a singular form of the verb, even if the subject that follows is plural.

> It *is* the *dendrites* and the *axon* that conduct nerve impulses.

4. When the Subject Is an Indefinite Pronoun. A *noun* is a word that names a person, a place, a thing, a quality, or an idea. A *pronoun* is a word that can replace a specific noun or that can be used instead of a noun. Ordinarily we use a pronoun to replace a previously stated noun, which is called its *antecedent.* However, several pronouns can be used without an antecedent noun. These are called *indefinite pronouns* because they do not refer back to a specific, or "definite," noun. Here is a brief list of indefinite pronouns.

each	*everybody*
either	*somebody*
neither	*nobody*
anyone	*anything*
everyone	*everything*
someone	*everybody*
one	*nothing*
anybody	

When you use any of these indefinite pronouns as a subject, the pronoun is always singular, and it requires the singular form of the verb.

> *Everybody has* nerve cells that carry nerve impulses.
> *Each* of these cells *is* composed of an axon and dendrites.

Five indefinite pronouns—*all, any, most, some,* and *none*—may take either a singular or a plural form of the verb, depending on their meaning in a particular sentence.

> *Some* of the nervous system *branches* into the brain.
> *Some* of the nerves *branch* into the brain.
> *Most* of the brain *is* composed of nerves.
> *Most* of the nerve cells in the brain *are* connected.

WRITING ACTIVITY 14

In the paragraph that follows, fill in each blank space with the correct Academic Written English form of any verb that makes sense in the sentence.

One of the most interesting body systems _____ the

nervous system. Each of the nervous system's cells _____

information in the form of electrical nerve impulses. There

_____ three kinds of nerve cells: sensory, motor, and

associational. Each _____ composed of a cell body that

_____ attached to a long tube called an axon. Extending from

the cell body _____ dendrites, which look like tiny branches

on a tree. The axons on nerve cells _____ chemicals that

_____ to the dendrites of the closest nerve cells.

It _____ this release of chemicals between nerve cells that

makes information move from one part of the body to another. Some of

the jobs of the nervous system _____ sensing and responding

to stimuli such as pain and regulating body functions.

5. When the Subject Is a Collective Noun or a Quantity. A *collective noun* is the name of a group that usually functions as a single unit. Some examples include *committee, team, family, class, audience,* and *group.* If you are writing about the group as a single unit, then the noun is a singular subject and requires the singular form of the verb. If you are referring to all the individual members of the group, then the noun is a plural subject and requires a plural verb.

> This *group* of neurologists *has* been studying sensory nerve cells.
> That *group* of scientists *have* been studying different types of cells.

Like collective nouns, words stating a quantity or an amount (of time, money, height, length, width, space, or weight) usually function as singular subjects and need singular verbs. However, they can function as plural subjects when they refer to individual items.

> *Three seconds is* the time it takes for a nervous impulse to get from the toes to the brain.
> *Two-thirds* of the body's nerve cells *are* sensory cells.

6. When the Subject Looks Plural but Is Singular in Meaning. Several subjects are plural in form (in other words, they are nouns that end in *-s*) but are singular in meaning. These words require a singular form of the verb. They include the names of some school subjects, the names of some diseases, titles, and miscellaneous words such as *politics, news,* and *mathematics.*

> *Physics is* the focus of the *news* that *is* on the neurology department bulletin board.
> *Nerve Cell Disorders is* an important journal for neurologists to read.

GROUP WORK 4

Form a group with two other students to select verbs for the sentences below. Choose one person to fill in each blank space with the correct Academic Written English form of any verb that makes sense in the sentence.

The medical journal *Neurological Studies* _____ a

fascinating essay about the human brain. The essay _____ that

the brain _____ the most complex organ in the body. Three-

quarters of the body's nerve cells _____ contained in the

brain. More than 100 million brain nerve cells _____ together

to enable a person to think and function. This group of nerve cells

_____ very delicate, small, and light. Indeed, two pounds

_____ the weight of the average adult brain. Yet a number of

different body functions _____ dependent on the brain.

These _____ breathing, digesting, moving, thinking, feeling,

and remembering. The essay _____ that a team of Harvard

scientists _____ studying brain activity and that they _____

how brain cells conduct electricity. The brain _____ truly

fascinating. It _____ like a giant computer that

_____ all the information that _____ from every cell

in the body.

Below is a chart of typical errors in Academic Written English grammar and usage. Each error is preceded by the correction symbol that your teachers may use when they mark your writing and it is followed by the number of the page in this chapter that discusses the error.

CHART OF COMMON ERRORS AND CORRECTION SYMBOLS

Symbol	Description
S-V agr	error in agreement of subject and verb (p. 488)
noun	error in noun form (p. 470)
vb	verb error (p. 472)

✔ POINTS TO REMEMBER ABOUT GRAMMAR AND USAGE
(NOUNS, SUBJECTS, AND VERBS)

1. Read each sentence, one at a time, to make sure that it has a subject and a verb.
2. Decide whether you have used the verb tense that indicates the time that you wanted to discuss. Edit your verbs so that they are all in the verb tense that you have selected.
3. Make sure that you have used Academic Written English past-tense forms and past participles. If you are unsure of the correct spelling of any verb, look it up in a dictionary.
4. Double-check *-ed* endings: Did you forget to add one to past-tense verbs, to past participles, and to past-participial adjectives?
5. Check to make sure that the verb of each sentence agrees with its subject in person and number.

18

GRAMMAR AND USAGE 2: PRONOUNS, PLURALS, AND POSSESSIVES

In Chapter 17, you learned that a noun is a word that names a person, a place, a thing, a quality, or an idea. A *pronoun* is a word that stands for or is used in place of an *antecedent noun*—a noun that was mentioned previously in the sentence or paragraph. As you learned in Chapter 3, pronouns make a paragraph coherent by linking ideas in a sentence (see pages 87–93). Here is an example:

> The most amazing thing about the spinal cord is that it relays messages from the brain to every other part of the body. It is also responsible for the body's reflex actions. These are automatic responses that do not involve the brain. When a part of the body moves in a reflex action, it is responding to nerve impulses from the spinal cord.

PRONOUN FORM AND CASE

The different forms of pronouns include the following:

- *Indefinite* pronouns, which are used to refer to an indefinite person or thing (e.g., "someone")
- *Demonstrative* pronouns (*this, that, these,* and *those*), which are used to point out a specific person or thing

- *Interrogative* pronouns (*who, what, which,* and *whose*), which are ordinarily used to begin questions
- *Personal* pronouns, which refer to one or more persons or things
- *Relative* pronouns, which are used to introduce adjectives and descriptive clauses
- *Reflexive* pronouns, which are used to refer back to or to intensify personal pronouns

Personal pronouns have different forms, called *cases,* which depend on how these pronouns are used in a sentence. English has three personal-pronoun cases: *nominative* or *subjective* (pronouns that act as subjects), *objective* (pronouns that receive the action of the verb or that show the results of the verb), and *possessive* (pronouns that indicate ownership or a relationship). The following chart illustrates these three cases.

FORMS OF PERSONAL PRONOUNS

	Nominative (Subject)	Objective (Receiver)	Possessive (Owner)
First person			
Singular	*I*	*me*	*mine, my*
Plural	*we*	*us*	*our, ours*
Second person			
Singular and plural	*you*	*you*	*your, yours*
Third person			
Singular	*he*	*him*	*his*
	she	*her*	*her, hers*
	it	*it*	*its*
Plural	*they*	*them*	*their, theirs*

Objective personal pronouns are ordinarily used after verbs and after prepositions (see page 446 in Chapter 16 for a description and a chart of prepositions).

1. Objective Pronoun After a Verb:

The doctor *showed* my mother and *me* the X ray of my injury. Then he *asked her* to consult a specialist.

2. Objective Pronoun After a Preposition:

> I was so concerned about spinal injuries that I read a book *about them*. My doctor had given this book *to me*.

If you use a noun *and* a personal pronoun (or two personal pronouns) after a verb or after a preposition, use the objective form of the pronoun. Test the pronoun alone to see if you have selected the correct form.

The doctor showed my mother and _____ the X ray.

The doctor showed ~~my mother and~~ *I* the X ray.
or
The doctor showed *she* and *I* the X ray.   [No. These pronouns do not sound right; they are the nominative, or subjective, forms.]

The doctor showed ~~my mother and~~ *me* the X ray.
or
The doctor showed *her* and *me* the X ray.   [Yes. These pronouns are the correct, objective form.]

Another type of pronoun is the *relative* pronoun, which you learned about in Chapters 15 and 16. Relative pronouns also have different case forms, as shown in the chart below.

FORMS OF RELATIVE PRONOUNS _____

	Subjective	Objective	Possessive
Human	who	whom	whose
Nonhuman	that	that	whose
	which	which	

REMINDER _____

In spoken English, the use of the objective relative pronoun *whom* is slowly dying out. However, it is still required in academic writing. Thus, the pronoun *who* is incorrect in the following sentence: "The neurologist *who* I wrote to called me today." The relative pronoun in this sentence is the object of the verb and preposition *wrote to,* so it must be in the objective form: "The neurologist *whom* I wrote to called me today."

An additional type of pronoun is the *reflexive* pronoun, which is used to refer back to a personal pronoun. The following chart illustrates the forms of reflexive pronouns.

FORMS OF REFLEXIVE PRONOUNS ————————————————

	Singular	**Plural**
First person	*myself*	*ourselves*
Second person	*yourself*	*yourselves*
Third person	*himself*	*themselves*
	herself	
	itself	

REMINDER ————————————————

The third-person-singular possessive pronoun—*its*—is never spelled with an apostrophe. *It's* requires an apostrophe only when it is the contraction of *it is*. Here is an example: ''*It's* time to see if the dog can find *its* bone.''

WRITING ACTIVITY 1

Choose the correct form of the pronoun and write it in the blank space above it. The first one has been done as an example.

1. My brother and sister are fraternal twins. _____*They*_____ are the
    (*them, they, their*)
    same age, but _____*he*_____ is much taller than
    (*him, he, his*)
    _____*she*_____ is.
    (*her, she, hers*)

2. Fraternal twins grow from two different eggs, so _____
    (*their, they, them*)
    are no more closely related than any other brother and sister.

3. My twin siblings think of _____ as two very
    (*theirselves, themselves*)

different people _____ have different appearances and
(that, who, whom)
personalities.

4. Each twin has _____ way of doing things.
(his, her, their, his or her)

5. However, I think of _____ as being quite similar,
(they, them, their)
especially in _____ personalities.
(they, them, their)

 GROUP WORK 1

Form a group with two other students, and choose a recorder to write the group's answers. Together fill in each blank with any pronoun that makes sense. The first one has been done as an example.

My brother and _____I_____ have had many viral diseases.

Between the two of _____, we had almost every virus,

including flu, measles, and chicken pox. In addition, I had

mononucleosis, and _____ had mumps, both of _____

are also caused by viruses. However, my brother is healthier than

_____ am. I get more colds than _____ does (and

colds are also viral infections). Our doctor, _____ we both use

and trust, told _____ that we are probably giving these viral

diseases back and forth to each other. That is why we get

_____ so often. For example, if my brother has a virus,

and _____ touches or coughs on me or _____ food,

the virus jumps from _____ to _____. Once

_____ gets inside my mouth or throat, I get sick too. We try

to take care of _____, but we still keep getting sick.

What the two of _____ cannot understand is why

_____ parents do not catch these viral diseases. Neither

of _____ has had any of the viruses that we had (except for

colds and the flu). When I had mononucleosis, _____ were

sure that my father would catch _____, but _____

didn't get it. This was probably because he has always taken excellent

care of _____, and he is almost immune to illnesses. My

brother and _____ wish that scientists would invent a vaccine

that could protect _____ from getting any more viral

infections.

PRONOUN REFERENCE

When you edit your writing, make sure that every pronoun refers clearly to
an antecedent noun stated earlier in the same sentence or stated in a preceding
sentence. A pronoun that doesn't seem to have an antecedent or an unclear
pronoun reference confuses readers. Here is an example of these problems:

> Larry and Mikhail were waiting to go into the examining room. During
> the doctor's examination, he noticed that the patient's muscles were weak.

To whom is the pronoun *he* in the second sentence referring? Who is the
patient? Is the *he* referring to *Larry* or to *Mikhail*? We can't tell. We may
think that the *he* is referring to *the doctor,* but it cannot be, because the writer
did not use the noun *doctor*—the writer used the possessive noun *doctor's.* A
subject pronoun (*he*) cannot be used to refer back to a possessive noun. Thus,
the pronoun reference in the second sentence above is confusing. Using a noun
instead of a pronoun clears up this confusion.

Larry and Mikhail were waiting to go into the examining room. During the examination, the doctor noticed that Larry's muscles were weak.

These two sentences let readers know that Larry is the patient whom the doctor examined. If a pronoun doesn't have an obvious antecedent or you think that your reader might be unsure about the pronoun's antecedent, replace the pronoun with a noun (even if this means that you have to repeat the noun a few times).

In the hospital, *they* made *you* fill out a dozen different forms, and I hated *it*.   [Who is *they*? Who is *you*? Did the writer hate the hospital? If not, what is the *it* referring to?]

In the hospital, the *nurses' assistants* made the *patients* fill out a dozen different forms, and I hated *filling out those forms*.

WRITING ACTIVITY 2

The sentences below contain unclear pronoun references. Rewrite each sentence so that it is no longer confusing. You may have to add, omit, or change words. The first one has been done as an example.

1. In my medical textbook, *it* said that skin is made up of two layers.

    My medical textbook stated that skin is made up of two layers.

2. The outer layer is the epidermis and the inner layer is the dermis. Underneath *it,* new cells are continuously formed and *this* moves out to the surface.

3. *They* say that the skin is a living, growing part of the body, but the surface of the skin is dead.

4. The top layers of the epidermis are made up of dead cells. *They* don't hurt when *they* are scraped or scratched off.

_____

_____

5. The inner layer of the skin contains nerve endings and blood; *that is* why a scrape has to be deep enough to cut the dermis for skin to hurt or bleed.

_____

6. Because surgery cuts the lowest layers, *it* needs stitches to close *it.*

_____

7. The skin protects the muscles from germs, and it controls body temperature. *It* is an important job.

_____

8. My sister is a dermatologist (a skin doctor), but I am not interested in *it.*

_____

_____

PRONOUN AGREEMENT

Just as verbs have to agree with their subjects, pronouns must agree with the nouns that they refer to or with the nouns that they replace. Every pronoun should match its antecedent noun in three ways. It should express the same *person* (first, second, or third), the same *number* (singular or plural), and the same *gender* (masculine, feminine, or neuter—*it*). In other words, if you are writing about the *skin,* and you want to refer back to this noun with a pronoun, the pronoun that "agrees" with the noun *skin* is *it.* The noun *skin* and the pronoun *it* are both singular, third-person, neuter word forms.

Here is a chart that illustrates pronoun-antecedent agreement.

PRONOUN-ANTECEDENT AGREEMENT CHART

	Singular	**Plural**
First person	*Prof. Greenberg = I/me*	*my family = we/us*
Second person	*my audience = you/you*	*my audience = you/you*
Third person	*man = he/him*	*men = they/them*
	woman = she/her	*women = they/them*
	cat = it/it	*cats = they/them*

When the antecedent noun is a ''person'' (without the gender specified), the pronoun form that agrees with it is *he or she* or *his or her*. (See pages 535–536 on avoiding sexist language.)

Each *student* must revise *his or her* essay until *he or she* is satisfied with it.   [Not *their* and *they*]

If you don't want to use *he or she* or *his or her,* then change the antecedent noun to a plural and use *they* or *them* to refer back to it.

All *students* must revise *their* essays.

Here are examples of correct pronoun-antecedent agreement:

The skin acts as a waterproof barrier for people because *it* keeps *their* bodies from drying out and prevents diseases from entering. In addition, *it* serves other functions. Skin helps a person sense *his or her* environment. The nerves in the skin send signals to the brain, and the brain interprets *them* as different sensations.

SPECIAL PROBLEMS IN PRONOUN-ANTECEDENT AGREEMENT

1. When the Antecedent Is an Indefinite Pronoun. People often use an indefinite pronoun when they do not know the name of the specific person or thing that they are discussing or when they want to discuss people in general. In speech, most people use the plural form of a pronoun to refer back to an indefinite pronoun:

Everyone at the beach seems to be proud of *their* bodies.

However, Academic Written English requires writers to use a singular pronoun to refer to the following indefinite pronouns:

each	anybody
either	somebody
neither	nobody
anyone	anything
someone	something
one	nothing

Thus, the correct version of the sample sentence above is as follows:

Everyone at the beach seems to be proud of *his or her* body.

Remember that you can avoid the awkwardness of using *his or her* and *he or she* by changing the indefinite pronoun to a plural noun. Then you can use a plural pronoun to refer back to this plural antecedent noun.

All the *people* at the beach seem to be proud of *their* bodies.

Note that when you change the singular subject *everyone* to the plural subject *people,* both the pronoun and the verb change forms: *seems* changes to *seem,* and *his or her* changes to *their.*

> **REMINDER**
> Using the pronoun *his* to refer to a group that includes women is sexist. Instead, use *his or her,* or change the indefinite pronoun to a plural noun (as in ''The *people* at the beach seem to be proud of *their* bodies'').

2. **When the Antecedent Is a Collective Noun.** A collective noun (such as *family, group, committee,* or *team*) requires a singular pronoun when the noun refers to the group as a single unit. If a collective noun refers to the individual members of the group, use a plural pronoun to refer to them.

The *Science Committee* has finished *its* entire report, but the *Software Committee* are still writing *their* separate sections.

3. **When Two or More Antecedents Are Joined by *Or* or *Nor*.** When two or more nouns are joined by *or* or *nor,* the pronoun should agree with the noun that is closest to it.

Neither the head *dermatologist* nor the dermatologic *interns* are seeing *their* patients today.
Neither the dermatologic *interns* nor the head *dermatologist* is seeing *her* patients today.

WRITING ACTIVITY 3

Circle the correct pronoun in each sentence below.

1. Three respiratory therapists work at Memorial Hospital, and each of them has (*their, his, her, its, his or her*) own unique job.
2. All the respiratory therapists use (*their, his, her, its, his or her*) equipment and medicines to help patients with breathing problems.
3. However, only one of them has (*their, his, her, its, his or her*) degree in teaching, so that particular therapist is responsible for teaching exercises to patients who need to increase their lung capacity.
4. Neither of the other two therapists has expressed (*their, his, her, its, his or her*) desire to teach these exercise classes.
5. The hospital's Respiratory Committee is finishing (*their, his, her, its, his or her*) report on respiratory therapy for people with asthma.
6. Either the Respiratory Committee or the respiratory therapists will decide how (*it, he, she, they*) will share the contents of the report with the other hospital staff members.

(handwritten annotations: "take out prop. phrase." / "prop. phrase?" / "deal ē Neither." / "prop. phrase." / "S →their.")

WRITING ACTIVITY 4

Below is a student essay about communicable diseases. On a separate piece of paper, rewrite this composition, changing every *underlined* plural noun (such as *diseases* and *pathogens*) to its singular form (*a disease* or *a pathogen*). Changing each noun to its singular form will require you to change each main verb to its singular form. You will also have to make corresponding changes in the pronouns that refer to these nouns, and you may have to change the wording of some sentences. The first sentence has been changed as an example.

A Communicable diseases *is an* ~~are~~ illnesses that spread from one person to another (or from one animal to another). These types of diseases are caused by pathogens. Pathogens are microorganisms, such as bacteria, viruses, and fungi, that can grow and reproduce in the body. Pathogens harm the body in several ways. Some kinds of pathogens injure or destroy specific cells in organs or in the blood. They do this by interfering with the cell's ability to reproduce itself and grow. Other pathogens produce toxins or poisonous substances. These harm the body by poisoning the bloodstream.

Communicable diseases result when pathogens are spread by direct or indirect contact. For example, if people kiss or shake hands with someone who has a cold, they will probably get the cold virus on their mouth or hand. If people with an infection cough or sneeze, everyone around them will inhale the infectious pathogens. In addition, contaminated foods spread bacteria or viruses, as do infected insects that bite or sting a person. Communicable diseases are difficult to avoid. The best ways to stay healthy are to stay away from sick people until they are no longer contagious and, if this isn't possible, avoid direct contact with them.

PRONOUN CONSISTENCY

When you edit a paragraph or an essay, check to make sure that your pronouns are consistent in person (first, second, or third) and in number (singular or plural). (See pages 501–502 for a review of the various forms of pronouns' person and number.) For example, if you are writing about a person, thing, place, or idea, use third-person-singular pronouns (*he, she,* or *it*). Don't shift into the plural (*they*) if you are writing about a singular subject. Here is an example of an illogical pronoun shift that the writer has identified and corrected:

As far as is known, a person with the AIDS virus eventually dies from his or her ~~their~~ AIDS-related illnesses. However, a person who has tested HIV-positive may not develop AIDS for a long time. By taking new drugs he or she ~~they~~ may stay healthy even longer.

Another pronoun problem to check for when you edit is the tendency to shift from a third-person pronoun (*he* or *they*) to the second-person pronoun (*you*) and/or to the first-person pronoun (*I*). Here is an example of these inconsistent shifts:

If people want to stay healthy, *they* should take precautions with people who have communicable diseases. *You* should stay away from people who have colds and other viruses. *You* should also avoid cups and utensils that infected people have used. Another way that *I* stay healthy is by washing *my* hands before eating, drinking, and touching *my* face.

The writer should have used third-person pronouns in every sentence:

If people want to stay healthy, *they* should take precautions with people who have communicable diseases. *They* should stay away from people who have colds and other viruses. *They* should also avoid cups and utensils that infected people have used. Another way that *they* can stay healthy is by washing *their* hands before eating, drinking, and touching *their* faces.

In general, don't directly address the reader with the pronoun *you* when you are writing Academic Written English paragraphs and essays (unless you are writing a memo or a set of directions and you actually do mean *you*—the intended reader). Using *you* makes your writing sound informal. (Note that I just used *you* and *your* in the two preceding sentences. I did that because I *am* addressing ''you''—my reader. I am not talking about a person or people in general; I am giving advice to you.)

Instead of using *you,* use the noun that your paragraph or essay is about. For example, if you are writing a paragraph about *students,* use that word (*students*) or the appropriate pronoun (*they*) instead of using *you*. What impression does the use of *you* give readers in the following sentence?

Students should follow good health practices to keep their bodies well. You should eat a nutritious diet, get enough sleep, exercise, and manage stress effectively. Doing these things will help you stay strong and healthy.

By using *you* here, the writer assumes that all her readers are students. If they are, then her use of *you* makes sense. However, if her readers are not students— if she is writing an essay for a teacher—then the *you* is inaccurate and inappropriate. In this case, the writer should have changed each *you* to *students* or to *they* or *them.*

Students should follow good health practices to keep their bodies well. *They* should eat a nutritious diet, get enough sleep, exercise, and manage stress effectively. Doing these things will help *them* stay strong and healthy.

GROUP WORK 2

Form a group with two other students and choose a recorder to write the group's answers. Together examine the paragraph below, which *should* have been written in the third-person-plural form throughout. Circle any pronoun that shifts to its singular form or to a different-person form, and write the correct third-person-plural form above it. The first one has been done as an example.

Teenagers can avoid contracting the AIDS virus if ~~you~~ *they* follow certain precautions. AIDS is a deadly pathogen that you can get only through contact with infected blood or some bodily fluids. If he or she wants to avoid getting AIDS, teenagers should refrain from having sex, because the only totally safe sex is no sex. If teenagers do have sex, you should use protection. If you use condoms with spermicides containing Nonoxynol 9, you can reduce the chances of contracting AIDS. In addition, teenagers should not use drugs, particularly those that are injected with hypodermics, because an infected needle can give you the AIDS virus if it sticks them. Finally, I don't kiss anyone whom I don't know extremely well. Although experts say that saliva doesn't have enough AIDS virus in it to infect you, teenagers should be careful about kissing someone whose gums or mouth is bleeding. If you have any questions or doubts about AIDS, teenagers should ask your doctor, because silence can be deadly.

PLURALS AND POSSESSIVES

When editing your writing, look for the three types of words that need -*s* endings: (1) present-tense verbs used with third-person-singular subjects, (2) plural nouns, and (3) possessives. You might want to review the guidelines for adding an -*s* ending to verbs, discussed on pages 488 and 490 in Chapter 17.

THREE TYPES OF -*s* ENDINGS _____

Edit your writing to make sure that you have included the correct -*s* endings on verbs, nouns, and possessives.

1. Present-tense verbs need an -*s* ending when they are used with a third-person-singular subject: "The AIDS virus *causes* the destruction of the immune system."
2. To make most singular nouns plural add an -*s* ending: "The *origins* of the AIDS virus are still a mystery." (See page 514 for additional information about plurals.)
3. To indicate that a noun "possesses" another noun, add an apostrophe and an -*s* ending to the first noun: "The *doctor's* study of the causes of AIDS is providing some important insights. (See pages 514–515 for additional information about possessives.)

As the chart above indicates, plural nouns generally end in -*s,* and they need the plural form of the verb, which usually does *not* end in -*s:*

Some communicable *diseases*   [= plural noun]
destroy [= plural verb] the immune system.

If the noun is singular, then it needs a verb that ends in -*s*.

One communicable *disease*   [= singular noun]
destroys [= singular verb] the immune system.

In other words, the -*s* ending is used for plural nouns and for singular verbs.

REMINDER _____

In general, if you are writing in the present tense, you should check to make sure that when a subject ends in -*s,* its verb does *not* end in -*s.* As you edit, remind yourself: Put an -*s* ending on the subject *or* on the verb, but *not on both* and *not off both.*

---

1. **Plurals.** You know how to form the plural of <u>most nouns</u>: Simply add -s to the end of the noun.

writer	*writers*
boy	*boys*
Smith	*Smiths*

2. To form the plural of a noun that ends in *-s, -x, -z, -ch,* or *-sh,* add an *-es* ending.

guess	*guesses*
ditch	*ditches*
box	*boxes*

agreement

3. To form the <u>plural</u> of a noun that ends in *y* preceded by a consonant, <u>change</u> <u>the *y* to *i* and add *-es*</u> (except for a <u>proper name</u> that ends with *y*).

story	*stories*
theory	*theories*
Kelly	*Kellys*

4. To form the plural of a number, a letter, or a symbol, add an apostrophe and an *-s*. If you write out the number, letter, or symbol, add only the *-s*.

A	*A's*
6	*6's*
ten	*tens*

5. To form the plural of compound nouns, add an *-s* ending to the main word.

mother-in-law	*mothers-in-law*
baby-sitter	*baby-sitters*

WRITING ACTIVITY 5

On a separate piece of paper, write the plural form of each of these words:

1. video	6. shelf	11. six-year-old
2. prefix	7. Kennedy	12. church
3. enemy	8. coach	13. tooth
4. turkey	9. belief	14. six
5. clue	10. spy	15. valley

Possessives. The *-s* ending on a plural noun means that the noun expresses "more than one." An <u>apostrophe-*s* ending indicates</u> a different meaning: It shows that the <u>noun that ends in -'s "owns"</u> or "is related to" the word or words that follow it in the sentence.

Ownership: Paulina's briefcase is here.

Relationship: Paulina's aunt is here.

To form the possessive of most nouns, simply add an apostrophe and an -s ending to the noun.

writer	*writer's*
Smith	*Smith's*

To form the possessive of singular nouns that end in -s, also add an apostrophe and an -s to the end of the noun.

dress	*dress's*
James	*James's*

To form the possessive of plural nouns, add *only* the apostrophe.

writers	*writers'*
Smiths	*Smiths'*

To form the possessive of compound nouns, add the -s ending to the last word.

mother-in-law	*mother-in-law's*
baby-sitter	*baby-sitter's*

Never add an apostrophe or an apostrophe and an -s to a possessive pronoun. For example, write *hers* (never *her's*), and remember that *it's* is the contraction of *it is,* not the possessive form of *it* (which is *its*).

REMINDER _____

Never use an apostrophe and an -s to form the plural of a word. For example, do not write, ''My two friend's are revising their essays.'' The correct version of this sentence is ''My two friends are revising their essays.''

WRITING ACTIVITY 6

On a separate piece of paper, write the possessive form of each of these words:

1. stereo
2. Dr. Seuss
3. dogs
4. city
5. women
6. secretary
7. princess
8. Ms. Torres
9. child
10. children
11. son-in-law
12. boys
13. nurse
14. sister
15. bus

WRITING ACTIVITY 7

Below is an excerpt from a student essay about vitamin C. On a separate piece of paper rewrite this excerpt, changing every *underlined* singular noun (such as *vitamin C* and *food*) to a plural form (*vitamins* and *foods*). This change from singular to plural will require you to change the form of each main verb. You will also have to make corresponding changes in the pronouns that refer to these nouns, and you may have to change the wording of some sentences. The first sentence has been changed as an example.

Vitamin C is a substance that the body needs to stay healthy. Vitamin C's job includes promoting the growth of bone tissue and helping in the formation of hormones. This vitamin also enables the body to dissolve food's components and to release its energy. In addition, it helps prevent damage to cell membranes. Vitamin C is found in a green vegetable and in a potato and a tomato. Another excellent source of vitamin C is a citrus fruit, like an orange or a lemon. A citrus fruit's juice supplies almost all of the vitamin C that a person needs in a day. Vitamin C is water soluble. It is dissolved and transported through the blood in water. Scientists have a theory about whether the body can store a water-soluble vitamin. It probably cannot, so a person needs to consume vitamin C every day.

WRITING ACTIVITY 8

In the uncorrected student paragraph on the next page, many verbs, plural nouns, possessives, and pronouns are missing -*s* endings or have unnecessary -*s* endings (according to Academic Written English conventions). Circle each word that needs an -*s* ending or that has an incorrect one. Write the correct form of the word above each error that you circled. The first one has been done as an example.

Recently, many journals reported new ⟨change⟩ in the ⟨kind⟩ of food that ⟨peoples⟩ should eat to get the amount of ⟨nutrient⟩ that their ⟨body's⟩ *bodies* need. For many years, medical researcher's asserted that the healthiest diet consist of "the four food group." They said that these group includes (1) dairy food, (2) vegetables and fruits, (3) breads and cereales, and (4) meat, chickens, and fishes. The daily number of serving's per group vary from two to four. No single food group or no foods are adequate for supplying all the nutrient that the body's need to grow. Everybody need to eat a variety of food from the four food group. This past year, however, the United State's Public Health Service changed its direction's for a balanced diet. It's doctors recommended that instead of organizing food into four group, the publics should imagine food as a pyramid. The dairy and meat product in the tiny top of the pyramid are the foods people should eats the least of. On the large bottom of the pyramid is the foods that are healthiest for peoples to eat frequently—fruits, vegetable, and breads. Eating a diets of foods that is high in fiber and starchs and low in fat can keeps people healthy.

Below is a chart of typical errors in Academic Written English grammar and usage. Note that each error is preceded by the correction symbol that your teachers may use when they mark your writing and is followed by the number of the page in this chapter that discusses the error.

CHART OF COMMON ERRORS AND CORRECTION SYMBOLS

| *pron* | pronoun case or form error (pp. 499–501) |
| *pron ref* | pronoun reference error (pp. 504–506) |

(Continued)

pron agr   pronoun agreement error (pp. 506–508)

pl   error in a plural noun or ending (p. 514)

poss   error in a possessive pronoun or ending (pp. 514–515)

✔ POINTS TO REMEMBER ABOUT GRAMMAR AND USAGE (PRONOUNS, PLURALS, AND POSSESSIVES)

1. Read each sentence, one at a time, to make sure that it has a subject and a main verb.
2. Make sure that you used correct Academic Written English pronouns.
3. Check to see that each pronoun agrees with its antecedent noun in number and person.
4. Take your reader's perspective and check to make sure that he or she will understand all your pronoun references. Rewrite each sentence containing potentially confusing pronoun references.
5. Double-check -*s* endings. Did you forget to add an -*s* ending to noun plurals, to present-tense third-person-singular verbs, or to possessives?

19

VOCABULARY AND DICTION

Do you ever think that you know what you want to write, but that you don't have the right words to communicate your ideas? If you do, you should build your vocabulary. Most people's "reading vocabulary"—the words they understand—is much larger than their "writing vocabulary"—the words they use. One of the goals of this chapter is to help you tap your reading vocabulary and use more of these words in your writing. Another goal is to improve your *diction*—your choice of words and the way you use them. Vocabulary and diction are interrelated: Writers cannot choose words that they don't know or understand. This chapter will give you many opportunities to learn new words in general, to increase your academic vocabulary, and to choose words that say precisely what you mean.

IMPROVING VOCABULARY AND DICTION

In Chapter 1, you learned about the value of keeping an *Idea Bank.* Another type of "savings bank" you should consider is a *Word Bank,* a notebook in which you write every new word you read or hear, along with its definition. You might also want to write down the sentence in which you found the word, since a word's *context* (the words surrounding it and the circumstances in which it is used) can help you understand and remember the word's meaning. Here is a sample entry from a student's Word Bank:

evanescent ("Aruna's happiness was evanescent.")—
ephemeral, short-lived, fleeting, fading from sight:
The light from the shooting star was
evanescent.

WRITING ACTIVITY 1

Start keeping a Word Bank today. Record words that you see or hear that you do not know. Next to each word, write the sentence in which the word was used. Look up the word in a dictionary, and make sure that you have spelled the word correctly. Then copy the word's pronunciation and definitions and write a sentence using the word. Try to add at least five words to your Word Bank every day.

USING THE RIGHT WORD

In Lewis Carroll's book *Through the Looking-Glass,* Humpty Dumpty and Alice have the following exchange:

> "When *I* use a word," Humpty Dumpty said, in rather a scornful tone, "it means just what I choose it to mean—neither more nor less."
> "The question is," said Alice, "whether you *can* make the words mean so many different things."
> "The question is," said Humpty Dumpty, "which is to be master— that's all."

If you want to be a "master" of words, then you need to know that the meaning of almost every word varies depending on who is using it and where and why it is being used. You cannot write like Humpty Dumpty, assuming that your words mean exactly what you decide they should mean.

Choose words deliberately, since your diction reveals your thoughts and attitudes as clearly as your behavior does. For instance, if you describe one friend as "assertive" and another as "bossy," your label indicates a difference in your attitude toward these friends. These two adjectives are similar in meaning, but *assertive* suggests that the person is positive and confident, whereas *bossy* implies that the person is overbearing or a bully.

Denotations and Connotations. Most words can have several meanings, or layers of meanings, depending on their context. Words that share the same general meaning but have slightly different meanings are called *synonyms.* For example, the words *look* and *stare* have the same general meaning, but they differ in intensity: *stare* means "to look steadily and intently."

Dictionaries give a word's *denotations*—objective, literal definitions of the word at the particular time that the dictionary was written. Two words can have the same denotation but suggest very different feelings. For example, the words *stare* and *glare* have the same definition—"to look at intently"—but they have different *connotations*—different emotional associations. *Stare* is neutral; *glare* has a negative connotation (for example, the person doing the "glaring" is angry or annoyed).

Connotations can have strong effects on readers, so you need to consider them carefully. For example, the words *family values* can have many different connotations, depending on the readers' age, sex, ethnic background, religion, political beliefs, and marital status. What do "family values" mean to you? Write your answer in the space below.

_____

_____

_____

_____

_____

Can you think of different meanings that the words *family values* might have for other people? Here is an excerpt from an essay by William Safire about the meanings of the expression *family values* in the fall of 1992:

"Integrity, courage, strength"—those were the *family values* as defined by Barbara Bush at the Republican convention in Houston. She added "sharing, love of God and pride in being an American." Not much controversy in that definition.

But on "family values night," as Marilyn Quayle described the session dominated by Republican women, the values took on an accusatory edge: after recalling that many in the baby boom had not "joined the counterculture" or "dodged the draft," the Vice President's wife made clear to cheering conservatives what she felt was at the center of family values: "Commitment, marriage and fidelity are not just arbitrary arrangements."

Pat Robertson, the religious broadcaster who sought the Presidential nomination four years ago, eschewed such innuendo and slammed home the political point: "When Bill and Hillary Clinton talk about family values, they are not talking about either families or values. They are talking about a radical plan to destroy the traditional family."

We have here the G.O.P.'s political attack phrase of the 1992 campaign. When Mario Cuomo stressed the words *family* and *values* in his speech to the 1984 Democratic convention, he used them in a warmly positive sense. But this year, packaged in a single phrase, the terms are an assertion of moral traditionalism that carries an implicit charge: the other side seeks to undermine the institution of the family by taking a permissive line on (a) abortion rights, (b) homosexual rights and (c) the "character issue," code words for marital infidelity.

If you used the words *family values* in an essay, you would have to elaborate on them to make sure that they communicated the emotional shades of meanings that you intended them to convey.

Connotation is important to your search for the "right" words. For example, here are two descriptions of the same person. The words in both paragraphs have similar denotations, but they paint very different pictures of this person:

My next-door neighbor is a thin, proud woman who is shy and solitary. She is a choosy person, and her house and garden are very tidy. She is also a thrifty, economical spender. She is curious about my problems, but she is a discreet neighbor.

My next-door neighbor is a scrawny, snobbish woman who is an introvert without any friends. She is a picky person, and her house and garden are very fussy. She is also a stingy, cheap spender. She is nosy about my problems, and she is a sneaky neighbor.

Words with strong emotional connotations—like *cheap* and *nosy*—are *loaded words*—words intended to provoke strong feelings. Be careful when you use loaded words, since they can give the impression that you are prejudiced, or biased.

WRITING ACTIVITY 2

Below is a list of words that may have positive, negative, or no emotional connotations for you. In the space next to each word, describe the feelings that the word elicits from you. The first one has been done as an example.

1. guzzle *Negative - drink like a greedy animal*

2. aggressive _____

_____

3. dentist _____

_____

4. police _____

_____

5. shrewd _____

_____

6. duty _____

_____

7. nude _____

_____

8. beady _____

_____

GROUP WORK 1

Form a group with three or four classmates. Compare your responses to
the words in the preceding Writing Activity to your classmates' connotations. Together answer the following questions.

1. Which words had similar connotations for everyone in the
   group?
2. Which words elicited different responses from the group members?
3. Why did these words elicit different responses?

WRITING ACTIVITY 3

For each set of words listed below, write an explanation of the meaning that the words have in common and an explanation of how their connotations differ. (Write your answers on separate paper.)

1. thin, skinny, slender
2. curious, inquisitive, nosy
3. determined, stubborn, obstinate
4. beg, implore, solicit

Dictionaries and Thesauruses. You are probably familiar with a dictionary of English definitions, but did you know that there are several other types of dictionaries? There are bilingual dictionaries, synonym and antonym (words with opposite meanings) dictionaries, computer dictionaries, crossword puzzle dictionaries, rhyming dictionaries, and gazetteers (geographical dictionaries). Dictionaries are valuable learning tools. In addition to providing the spelling, the meaning, and the pronunciation of words, a dictionary also presents information about the history of each word, about its modern usage, and about its synonyms and their connotations. If you do not already own a dictionary, get a good one—an unabridged or a college dictionary. These include *The American Heritage Dictionary of the English Language, The Random House Webster's College Dictionary,* and *Webster's New World Dictionary,* college edition.

Here is an entry for the word *incriminate* from the college edition of *Webster's:*

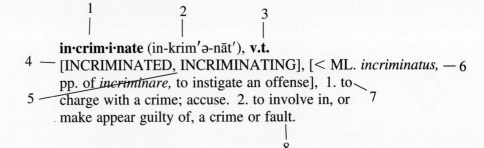

1   Correct spelling of the word, with dots indicating the separate syllables
2   Pronunciation, with markers to indicate the syllable that gets the primary stress (′) and the one that gets the secondary stress (′)
3   Part of speech (v.t. = "transitive verb," or a verb that needs an object)

4   Correct spelling of the past-tense form of the verb (which for this verb is the same as the past-participle ending)
5   Correct spelling of the *-ing* ending for this verb
6   History of the word's meaning (ML. = Medieval Latin)
7   First definition of the word
8   Second definition of the word

Different dictionaries offer different information because each dictionary represents the judgments of the group of people who wrote it, and these judgments mirror the constantly changing nature of language itself.

Most American dictionaries arrange their words in alphabetical order, and they begin with an introduction that explains what the book contains and how the entries for each word are arranged. Read the introductory material in your dictionary so that you know how to use it and know what the abbreviations stand for. Then carry it with you and *use it.*

WRITING ACTIVITY 4

Get a college dictionary and follow the directions below. First look up the word *conjugate.*

1. How do you spell each of the syllables that make up this word?
2. What are the different ways of pronouncing this word?
3. What language did *conjugate* come from, and what did it mean in that language?
4. What three parts of speech can this word be used as?
5. List every definition of *conjugate* in its form as a transitive verb (v.t.).
6. Write a sentence using this word as a transitive verb.

GROUP WORK 2

Form a group with two other students and choose one person to record the answers to the following questions (on separate paper).

1. What two languages did the word *offend* come from, and what did it mean in those languages?
2. What are the definitions of this verb?
3. What synonyms does the dictionary give for *offend*?

4. Look up each of these synonyms. How does the connotation of each one differ slightly from the connotation of *offend*?

5. Write a sentence using the first definition of the word *offend*. Then write a sentence for each of the synonyms for this verb.

A *thesaurus* is a dictionary of synonyms. You can use it to find synonyms for words that you repeat too often in your writing. You can also use a thesaurus to find more formal or more academic synonyms for informal or slang words and expressions. Here is an entry for the noun *accusation* from the 1965 St. Martin's Press edition of *Roget's Thesaurus of English Words and Phrases:*

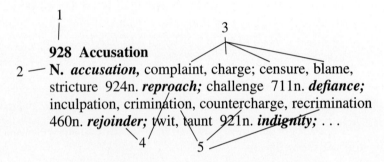

1   The number under which the "head" word ("accusation") is indexed
2   This word's part of speech (N. = noun)
3   Synonyms for the head word
4   "Keyword" synonym (synonym that is described elsewhere in the thesaurus) and its number and part of speech (n. = noun)
5   Synonyms for each key word

> **REMINDER** ————————————————————
>
> Many thesauruses do not list words alphabetically. Instead, they group synonyms according to subject categories (or head words), and you have to use the index to find the synonyms for the word that you are looking up. Buy a thesaurus that is alphabetically arranged so that you can look up words easily.

WRITING ACTIVITY 5

Use a thesaurus to look up synonyms for the four words in this activity. Write down the first three synonyms for each word. Then use your dictionary to look up the meaning of each synonym. Write a sentence using each synonym.

1. *impromptu*

   1st Synonym _____

   Definition _____

   Sentence _____

   _____

   2nd Synonym _____

   Definition _____

   Sentence _____

   _____

   3rd Synonym _____

   Definition _____

   Sentence _____

   _____

2. *authority*

   1st Synonym _____

   Definition _____

   Sentence _____

   _____

   2nd Synonym _____

   Definition _____

Sentence _____

_____

3rd Synonym _____

Definition _____

Sentence _____

_____

3. *happy*

1st Synonym _____

Definition _____

Sentence _____

_____

2nd Synonym _____

Definition _____

Sentence _____

_____

3rd Synonym _____

Definition _____

Sentence _____

_____

4. *probity*

1st Synonym _____

Definition _____

Sentence _____

_____

2nd Synonym _____

Definition _____

Sentence _____

_____

3rd Synonym _____

Definition _____

Sentence _____

_____

UNDERSTANDING LEVELS OF USAGE

Choosing the ''right'' word or expression depends on the situation in which you are using the word. The choices that you make in different contexts are called *levels of usage*. Levels of usage in writing vary from the most formal (for written reports and school essays) to the most informal (for notes to yourself or your family). For example, if you were writing a letter to a friend, you might use informal usage that sounds conversational:

> Boy, have I been having some lousy things happen. I'm totally stressed out, and it's killing my body and my mind. Daily life has been a grand pain (too many bills, traffic jams, and broken pipes), and now I've got to cope with my parents getting sick and possibly dying.

If you wanted to write an academic paragraph about this topic, you would probably choose more formal words to express your ideas:

> Many experiences can be extremely stressful, harming people's bodies and their psyches. In addition to the ordinary aggravations of daily life (such as paying bills, sitting in traffic jams, and fixing malfunctioning plumbing), most people have to cope with their relatives' illnesses and possible death.

Spelling out the contractions (*I've/I have*) and switching from the first person (*I*) to the third person (*people/they*) make the paragraph sound more formal and less chatty. In addition, using abstract words (*stressful, psyches, malfunctioning plumbing*) instead of concrete words makes the writing sound more formal and distant, as if the writer were outside the experience, analyzing it.

Remember that formal usage is not always "better" than informal usage. For instance, if you wrote the second paragraph to your best friend, he or she might think you were being very unfriendly! Different language is appropriate for different situations. Choose words and craft sentences that are appropriate for your audience and your purpose.

Slang. *Slang* words and expressions are very informal usages that are almost always inappropriate for academic paragraphs and essays. Some slang words and expressions are very colorful and metaphoric: *coffin nails* (cigarettes), *grossed out* (disgusted), *chill out* (calm down), *bummer* (unpleasant experience), *pump it up* (get louder or more excited), *lighten up* (relax). However, most slang words and expressions are vague and unclear, and they go out of date or style quickly.

WRITING ACTIVITY 6

Rewrite the following sentences so that they are more "academic" and formal. Remember to replace all slang words with formal substitutes.

1. Meditation is an awesome way to deal with daily garbage.

   _____

   _____

2. When you meditate, you chill out and focus your entire attention on an object or a word.

   _____

   _____

3. People who are stressed out can learn to lighten up by meditating because it cools anxieties.

   _____

   _____

4. When dudes meditate, their minds stop thinking and they don't give a damn about problems or distractions.

_____

_____

5. Meditation relaxes people, making them feel calmer and less hassled.

_____

_____

6. It produces a peaceful state of mind, but the meditator is awake, not sacked out.

_____

_____

7. Studies have shown that meditation is really a turn on because it enables people to relax and find inner peace.

_____

_____

8. Meditation is a super-easy kind of therapy that people don't have to shell out big bucks for.

_____

_____

 GROUP WORK 3

Choose a revision that you wrote for one of the assignments in this book or for your teacher. Exchange papers with a classmate. After you read your partner's paper, write answers to the questions on the next page. Do *not* discuss each other's papers until you are both finished writing your comments (on separate paper).

1. What do you think the writer was trying to show or prove in this paper?
2. Did any words confuse you or seem unclear? If so, which words?
3. Which words suggest connotations that the writer might not have intended them to suggest?
4. Where do you think the writer's language is too informal or inappropriate for his or her purpose and reader?

When you are finished answering these questions, return the essay to your partner and discuss it. Suggest alternate words for any of the words that you noted in your comments.

REVISING VAGUE WORDS AND EXPRESSIONS

If an instructor tells you that you are having a test soon, do you know when the test will be given? When is "soon"? Can you tell when "soon" is in the paragraphs below? In his book *Jazz Country,* writer Nat Hentoff tells what happens when a teenager who loves jazz meets his musical idol, Moses Godfrey, and Godfrey's friend, Bill Hitchcock:

> I had to find something to say. "Are you going to have a new album out soon?"
>
> "When is soon?" Godfrey said. His voice surprised me. It was soft and high. I'd expected he'd sound like a bear. "Soon." He said it again slowly. "If I told you," he said to Hitchcock, "your arm would fall off next year, would that be soon?"
>
> Hitchcock smiled. "Too soon. Much too soon."
>
> "But if I told you there'd be no money this week. Maybe soon, but not this week. Would that be soon enough?"
>
> Hitchcock laughed. "Soon enough to bring you up before the union."
>
> "You see?" Godfrey looked at me. "You didn't make yourself clear. What is soon to you might not be soon to me."

As this excerpt reveals, words that are clear to you might not be clear to your readers. Most readers get annoyed at having to guess at a writer's meaning. For instance, if you were reading a review of a new film that you were considering seeing, what would your reaction be to a review that stated the movie was "great"? What does "great" mean to you? Does this evaluation tell you anything about the movie? *Great* is an "all-purpose" word that doesn't communicate much.

Here are some other "all-purpose" words that can ruin the precision of your writing.

VAGUE, "ALL-PURPOSE" WORDS _____

Find precise replacements for the following "tired" words and expressions:

great	*terrific*	*incredible*	*wonderful*	
good	*fine*	*nice*	*okay*	*all right*
terrible	*awful*	*bad*	*strange*	*interesting*
a lot	*lots*	*many*	*plenty*	
thing	*aspect*	*factor*	*stuff*	

Vague words are a shorthand language that writers should avoid. Another form of shorthand that you should eliminate from your final revisions is *clichés* (pronounced "klee-shays"). A cliché is a phrase that has been used so often that it no longer means much. Readers don't pay much attention to clichés. For example, expressions such as "in today's world," "in this day and age," "dog-eat-dog world," and "the more, the merrier" give the impression that the writer is too lazy to think of an interesting way to say something. Clichés come to mind easily, so you will probably find them sprinkled among your discovery drafts. Cross them out, and substitute more precise language.

WRITING ACTIVITY 7

Rewrite the following sentences by substituting more precise language for each cliché. The first one has been done as an example.

1. Most young people think that adults over the age of fifty are over the hill.

   Many young people think that adults over the age of fifty are not able to function as well as they used to.

2. However, in today's world, old age is an individual matter, influenced by a person's health, strength, and attitudes.

   _____

   _____

3. People such as poet Marianne Moore and artist Georgia O'Keefe stayed fit as a fiddle in their eighties, and the cellist Pablo Casals was sharp as a tack well into his nineties.

_____

_____

_____

4. Older people who retire can find ways to keep up their spirits and can do things that they missed out on in their youth or middle age.

_____

_____

5. Many seventy- and eighty-year-olds stay busy as bees, doing volunteer work, pursuing leisure activities, and traveling with friends.

_____

_____

6. Of course, as people age, their physical organs deteriorate, and, slowly but surely, their arteries harden.

_____

_____

7. Last but not least, the brain produces less electricity as people age, so they may become less alert or more forgetful.

_____

_____

8. Thus, to make a long story short, the major job of growing old is maintaining one's self-esteem and energy in the face of increasing physical losses.

_____

_____

_____

AVOIDING SEXIST LANGUAGE

Traditionally, the pronouns people use to refer to ''a person'' and indefinite pronouns (such as *anyone*) are masculine:

> As one grows older, *he* has to think about changes in *his* body and *his* mind. When *he* retires, *he* may worry that *his* family and friends will lose respect for *him*. However, this negative thinking is a mistake, and everyone should learn from *his* mistakes.

Word choice and usage depend on context, and many speakers and writers see nothing wrong with the sentences above. However, many others are offended by the use of masculine pronouns and nouns to refer to people of both genders. They call this usage *sexist*.

In addition to being offensive to some people, sexist language is often inaccurate. For example, can you find the inaccuracies in the sentences below?

> The typical American seventy-year-old becomes more accepting of his disappointments in life. As he ages, he becomes more objective, and he can weigh his successes and failures in the perspective of time.

All the masculine pronouns are inaccurate because the ''typical American seventy-year-old'' is female. (Women live approximately 10 percent longer than do men—whose average lifespan is sixty-eight years.)

Sexist inaccuracies are just as incorrect as are other types of errors. The pronoun agreement errors in the following sentences are no different from or worse than the errors in the sentences above:

> The typical American seventy-year-old becomes more accepting of their disappointments in life. As one ages, they become more objective, and they can weigh their successes and failures in the perspective of time.

The ''typical American seventy-year-old'' refers to a single person, so writers cannot use a plural pronoun (*their, they*) to refer back to this person. You can use *his or her* (and *he or she*), or you can change all the nouns and pronouns to their plural forms.

> Typical American seventy-year-old*s* become more accepting of their disappointments in life. As *people* age, they become more objective, and they can weigh their successes and failures in the perspective of time.

Here are some guidelines to follow so that you don't offend anyone with sexist language in your writing.

GUIDELINES FOR NONSEXIST DICTION _____

1. Use *he or she, his or her,* and *him or her* to refer to indefinite pronouns:

   Someone over the age of seventy must come to terms with *his or her* impending death.

2. Use plural nouns and pronouns instead of singular ones:

   Most elderly *people* make adjustments to the losses in *their* lives.

3. Omit unnecessary pronouns wherever you can:

   Each person who retires must continue to try new things in life.   [Instead of "in his life" or "in his or her life"]

4. Use *Ms.* instead of *Mrs.* or *Miss* (unless you are writing a letter to a woman who has a professional title—such as *Dr.*—or who has requested that you use *Mrs.* or *Miss*:

   Ms. Vargas was accepted into law school on her sixty-first birthday.

WRITING ACTIVITY 8

Reread an essay that you wrote for an assignment in this book or for your teacher. Circle every instance of sexist language, and write a nonsexist substitute for it. Revise the entire essay so that it no longer has sexist language in it.

REVISING WORDINESS

Wordiness is the use of several words instead of a single word. It results when writers strain to make their diction sound academic or overly formal. Unnecessary words can make sentences confusing or boring. For example, what is your reaction to the following wordy sentence?

At this point in time, many people think and believe that Americans tend to conform too much, since many varied groups of people feel that if numerous numbers of people in American society are doing or getting something, then that thing must have great positive value.

This sentence would be easier to understand if the writer had eliminated all its "deadwood"—meaningless or repetitive words:

~~At this point in time,~~ ^Many people think ~~and believe~~ that Americans ~~tend~~
to conform too much, since ~~many varied groups of people,~~ feel that if ~~nu-~~
~~merous numbers of people in American society are~~ doing or getting
something, then that thing must ~~have great positive value.~~

Americans *often*
everyone is
be valuable.

As writing teacher William Zinsser noted, "Clutter is the disease of American writing. We are a society strangling in unnecessary words, circular constructions, pompous frills, and meaningless jargon." Heed the advice of writer George Orwell: "If it is possible to cut a word out, always cut it out."

Here is a list of common wordy phrases that may be cluttering your writing. Eliminate them as you revise your writing.

WORDY PHRASES AND POSSIBLE REPLACEMENTS

Wordy Phrase	Replacement
1. "at" phrases	
at the present time	currently
at this point in time	now
at a later date	later
2. "the fact that" phrases	
regardless of the fact that	although
in view of the fact that	since
in light of the fact that	because
aware of the fact that	know
in spite of the fact that	despite
3. "that" phrases	
for the reason that	for
it is important that	should
in the event that	if
on the condition that	if
4. "of" phrases	
on the subject of	about
pertaining to the subject of	about
in lieu of	instead

> **REMINDER** ━━━━━━━━━━━━━━━━━━━━━━━━━━━━━━━━━━
> As you revise your drafts, delete wordy phrases such as "In my opinion,"
> "I believe that," "I think that," and "It seems to me that." Since you
> are writing the paragraph or essay, readers know that you are expressing
> your beliefs and thoughts.

WRITING ACTIVITY 9

Take out an essay that you wrote for an assignment in this book or for
your teacher. Underline every "wordy" phrase that you find and substitute a single-word alternative for it.

UNDERSTANDING COMMONLY CONFUSED WORDS

English has several sets of words that writers frequently confuse because these
words resemble each other. When you edit your revisions, find and correct
every word that you have confused with another word. For example, do you
ever confuse *a* and *an*? Do you know that *an* is used before a word that begins
with a vowel sound (*a, e, i, o,* and *u*), and *a* is used before words that start
with a consonant sound (any other letter)?

Here are some other commonly confused words and their meanings:

accept to receive: We *accept* your gracious invitation.

except excluding or leaving out: All of us *except* our teacher will be attending
the concert.

affect to influence or change: The weather will not *affect* our plans to attend
the concert.

effect [verb] to cause: Music can *effect* an improvement in my mood.

effect [noun] the result or consequence: Music has a calming *effect* on my
behavior.

all ready all set or prepared: The orchestra members were *all ready* to play
after the intermission.

already previously or by this time: They had *already* tuned their instruments
twice.

amount refers to masses of things that cannot be counted: The auditorium
has a large *amount* of space.

number refers to things that can be counted: I saw a *number* of friends in the
orchestra.

beside by the side of: I sat *beside* my wife at the concert.
besides in addition to: Did anyone *besides* us see the conductor wave good-bye?

fewer refers to things that can be counted: Today, *fewer* teenagers attend classical concerts than teenagers used to attend a decade ago.
less refers to quantity of noncountable things or to degree: Today's teenagers seem to have *less* interest in classical music than did the previous generation of teenagers.

good describes nouns and pronouns: The conductor is a *good* musician.
well describes verbs: She works *well* with the other members of the orchestra.

moral [adjective] good or having good values: The conductor is also a *moral* person.
moral [noun] a lesson: She told us a story with an interesting *moral* about the consequences of lying.
morale spirit or mental condition: She always lifts up the musicians' *morale* when they feel tired or sad.

passed [verb] past-tense form of *to pass:* The conductor *passed* the musical score out to the musicians.
past [noun] a previous time or the history of a person or thing: The conductor told us stories about her *past* when she played with different orchestras.
past [preposition] by or farther on than: We drove *past* the auditorium where the concert would take place.

principal the most important or the head of a school: Ms. Zhang, the *principal* of our high school, is the *principal* leader of the supervisory committee.
principle a law, fact, or rule of conduct: Our entire school abides by Ms. Zhang's moral *principles.*

quiet silence, silent, or still: At home, the conductor likes a *quiet* atmosphere because she needs complete *quiet* to relax.
quite rather, very, or exactly. She is *quite* sure that an apartment house is not *quite* the right kind of home for her needs.

than [conjunction] used to compare people or things: The conductor is a better musician *than* I am.
then [adverb] used to refer to a specific time: I asked the conductor where she was living *then. Then* I asked her why she moved.

their [pronoun] the possessive form of the pronoun *they:* The musicians left the park after *their* concert.
there [adverb] in that place: We haven't gone *there* in a long time.
they're contraction of *they are: They're* going to play at the park again next Saturday afternoon.

GROUP WORK 4

Form a group with three or four classmates and work on this activity together. Choose the correct word in each set in the parentheses.

1. If our state government contributed more money to public education, we would have (*fewer, less*) students dropping out of school and (*less, fewer*) violence on our streets.
2. The governor must (*accept, except*) the fact that more resources are needed to help students stay in school and to (*affect, effect*) improved learning outcomes.
3. Unfortunately, for many students an increased allocation of assistance will (*already, all ready*) be too late.
4. These students—who are planning to drop out—need more (*then, than*) additional funding to raise their (*moral, morale*) and to help them stay in school.
5. Potential dropouts need special incentives to increase (*there, they're, their*) ability and desire to stay in school.
6. The teachers and the (*principal, principle*) can do (*an amount, a number*) of things to help these students.
7. It is (*quite, quiet*) important for teachers to collaborate with the community to develop comprehensive programs that meet students' needs and that have positive (*effects, affects*) on (*there, they're, their*) families.
8. (*Beside, Besides*) these efforts, teachers and guidance counselors must identify potential dropouts, attend to (*their, there, they're*) social and personal needs, and model mature and (*moral, morale*) behavior.
9. Counselors who have proven in the (*past, passed*) that they can work (*well, good*) with parents should talk with parents about each child's progress and problems.
10. If our state wants to enable more students to graduate from high school, it will provide adequate resources and assistance so that students see the positive (*affects, effects*) of staying in school and remain active participants in their own learning.

WRITING ACTIVITY 10

Correct every error in word usage in the following paragraph. The first one has been done as an example.

principal

Leadership is vital to a public school, and a strong (principle) must be a good manager and must collaborate good with faculty and staff. The affect of a strong principal can be felt by every member of the school, including students. Besides clarifying the educational and curricular principals of the school, the principle has to have well values and morales because he is a more important role model then the other adults in the school. Principles who supervise they're schools effectively usually make sure that teachers and students are already to work every morning. They distribute the large amount of supplies that each teacher needs, and they provide teachers with the number of money they need to purchase additional pedagogical materials. They except and encourage the participation of parents and community leaders in the life of the school. Strong principals can affect great improvements in the performance of both teachers and students.

In Chapter 17, you practiced using modifiers—adjectives and adverbs—to describe people, places, things, ideas, and actions. Most English adjectives and adverbs require different forms when you use them to compare *two* people or things and when you use them to compare *three or more* people or things. For example, look at the different forms of the adjective *lovely* and of the adverb *loud* in the following sentences:

> This concerto is *lovelier* than the one that the orchestra played last week. In fact, I think it is the *loveliest* concerto that I have ever heard. The audience clapped *louder* tonight than they did last week; indeed, this is the *loudest* I have ever heard an audience clap.

The form of a modifier (an adjective or adverb) that you use to compare two people or things is called its *comparative* form; it is usually created by adding *-er* to the modifier or by using the word *more* before it (*louder, more beautifully*). The form that you use to compare three or more people or things— the *superlative* form—is usually created by adding *-est* to the modifier or by using the word *most* before it (*loudest, most beautifully*). Here are some other examples:

Modifier	Comparative Form	Superlative Form
smart	*smarter*	*smartest*
slow	*slower*	*slowest*
happy	*happier*	*happiest*
easily	*more easily*	*most easily*
exquisite	*more exquisite*	*most exquisite*
rapidly	*more rapidly*	*most rapidly*

Here are some general guidelines for writing the comparative and superlative forms of modifiers.

COMPARATIVE AND SUPERLATIVE FORMS ———————

1. With a modifier that is one syllable, use the *-er* or *-est* form:
   safe/safer/safest   loud/louder/loudest
2. With an adjective that is two syllables, use the *-er* or *-est* form:
   silly/sillier/silliest   pretty/prettier/prettiest
3. With an adverb that is two or more syllables, use *more* or *most*:
   slowly/more slowly/most slowly   carefully/more carefully/most carefully

---

Some modifiers do not follow the guidelines above; they have *irregular* comparative and superlative forms that you will have to memorize:

Modifier	Comparative Form	Superlative Form
bad	*worse*	*worst*
badly	*worse*	*worst*
good	*better*	*best*
little	*less*	*least*
many	*more*	*most*
much	*more*	*most*
well	*better*	*best*

WRITING ACTIVITY 11

Identify all the incorrect comparative and superlative forms in the following paragraph. Cross out each incorrect form and write the correct form above it. (Some of the forms may be correct.)

The most best meal I ever ate was at Mulcahy's Manor in Miller Place. It is the most new restaurant in the area, and it is more prettier than any other that I've been in. It is also much more bigger than other restaurants because it consists of a series of magnificent dining rooms. Since the food at Mulcahy's is the goodest around and the prices are the cheapest, it is always crowded. The chef makes the bestest corned beef and cabbage dinner I have ever eaten (although the chef could use littler salt). She cooks everything more well (except for the carrots, which were the baddest and mushiest cooked vegetables that I've eaten in ages). Mulcahy's is a wonderful place to relax and get good food. Thus, it is more popularer than the other restaurants in town, and it is the most busy.

WRITING ACTIVITY 12

Write a paragraph comparing three restaurants, cafeterias, or fast-food places in which you have eaten lunch or dinner this past year. Which place is better than the others? Which is the best? Why? Use the correct comparative and superlative forms of modifiers to describe these places.

Below is a chart of typical errors in Academic Written English diction and vocabulary and the correction symbols that are usually used to identify these errors.

**CHART OF COMMON ERRORS
AND CORRECTION SYMBOLS**

cl	cliché (p. 533)
conn	inappropriate connotation (p. 521)
sl	slang (p. 530)

(Continued)

wc	error in word choice (p. 520)
w	wordy (p. 536)
ww	wrong word (p. 524)

✔ POINTS TO REMEMBER ABOUT VOCABULARY AND DICTION

1. If you are not sure of the denotation or the connotation of any of the words that you have used, look up each word in a college or an unabridged dictionary.
2. Use a thesaurus that is alphabetically arranged to look up synonyms for words that you have used too often or words with inappropriate connotations.
3. Examine the usage level of your diction and make sure that it is appropriate for your purpose, your topic, and your readers.
4. Find more appropriate and precise substitutes for overly informal words, for slang, and for vague, "all-purpose" words.
5. Reword any nouns and pronouns that readers might consider sexist.
6. Check words that you frequently confuse to make sure that you have used the word that you meant to use.
7. Eliminate unnecessary words and phrases from overly wordy sentences.
8. Examine every comparative and superlative modifier and make sure that you have used the correct form.

SPELLING AND CAPITALIZATION

Even talented and experienced writers often have difficulty with spelling. The spelling system of the English language is based on meaning rather than on sound. For example, the words *photograph* and *photographer* are not pronounced similarly, but they are spelled similarly because they share a related meaning (''producing an image with light'') and history (both are derived from the Greek word for ''light''). Similarly, the silent *g* in the word *sign* shows that it is related in meaning to words in which this *g* is pronounced: *signature* and *signal.*

You have already learned two ways to improve your spelling: (1) Keep a college dictionary with you and look up any word whose spelling you are unsure of, and (2) practice spelling new words (and words that you commonly misspell) in your Word Bank. This chapter will show you other strategies for learning how to spell words correctly.

IDENTIFYING THE CAUSES OF YOUR SPELLING ERRORS

All writers have particular spelling errors that they repeat over and over. As you edit your writing, look for repeated spelling errors and try to figure out why you are making them. Here are five possible causes of many spelling errors.

FIVE CAUSES OF SPELLING ERRORS ─────────────

1. *Addition*—You add a letter, usually because you pronounce the word with this letter:

    hunde̲reds (hundreds)   *athe̲letes (athletes)*

2. *Deletion*—You don't write a letter, usually because you don't pronounce it:

    Febuary (February)   *tempe̲rmental (temperamental)*

3. *Transposition*—You transpose (switch) a letter with the letter next to it:

    jewle̲ry (jewelry)   *recie̲pt (receipt)*

4. *Substitution*—You substitute a letter that has a similar sound:

    absense̲ (absence)   *excellant̲ (excellent)*

5. *Homonym*—You confuse a word with another word that it sounds like (See "Commonly Confused Words" on pages 538–539 of Chapter 19):

    principle/principal   *sight/cite/site*

Here is a student paragraph with several spelling errors. Examine each error. Can you figure out which two types of errors are causing this student's spelling problems?

Throughout most of humankind's presense on the earth, all societies suvived by hunting anamals and gathering wild froots and vegtables. Primative civilazations were all "hunter-gathers," and they had a relitively simple existance. They suceeded in feeding their famlies by moving around frequently in serch of food. Hunting-gathring groups had a davision of labor based on gender: men and women did diffrent things. Mostly, men hunted and women gatherd. This proved benaficial for the hole sosiety.

This writer clearly has a pattern of "substitution" and "deletion" errors (for example, he writes *presense* instead of *presence* and *suvived* for *survived*).

His spelling errors represent the exact way that he pronounces the words. These errors indicate confusion over the spelling of sounds that can be spelled several different ways. The writer isn't even aware that he has spelled these words incorrectly. The only way that this writer could correct these spelling errors is to ask someone else to help identify them.

Many writing textbooks include lists of "spelling demons" or "frequently misspelled words," but these seem pointless because each writer has his or her own set of troublesome words to look for and correct every time he or she edits a paragraph or an essay. Experienced writers proofread for their typical errors, examining tricky words to see if these "look right," and they use a dictionary to check the spelling of words that are difficult for them to spell.

WRITING ACTIVITY 1

Here is the preceding student paragraph. Find every spelling error and circle it. Then write the correct spelling of the word above it. The first misspelled word has been corrected as an example.

Throughout most of humankind's (presense) *presence* on the earth, all societies suvived by hunting anamals and gathering wild froots and vegtables. Primative civilazations were all "hunter-gathers," and they had a relitively simple existance. They suceeded in feeding their famlies by moving around frequently in serch of food. Hunting-gathring groups had a davision of labor based on gender: men and women did diffrent things. Mostly, men hunted and women gatherd. This proved benaficial for the hole sosiety.

GROUP WORK 1

Work with a partner or two on this activity. Together identify and circle every misspelled word in the following paragraph. List the misspelled words on a separate piece of paper and write the correct spelling—in capital letters—next to each word. Examine the list and decide why this writer is making spelling errors. Which *two* of the five causes (listed on page 546) seem to be causing most of the errors?

The most obvios funtion of a college education is to provide students with the knoledge and skills necesary to suceed in sosiety. A college dagree enhanses a person's oppotunities for soshal mobility. College gradauates usualy become independant adults because they have learned how to make important dacisions about their lives. For example, while they were in school, they had to make their own scheduels and decide weather they could get to class on time. In addition, they had to chose witch coarses to take and when to take them (exept for required mathmatics, writing, and litrature courses). Finally, they had to select a major and a miner. Getting a college degree has substanshal effects on people's future achievments.

WRITING ACTIVITY 2

Examine the words in your Word Bank and the words that you have misspelled in recent writing assignments. Can you identify the causes of your common spelling errors? Can you find particular patterns of errors: Do you often add, delete, transpose, or substitute letters? Do you misspell homonyms or commonly confused words? Identify the causes of your spelling errors so that you can look for typical spelling errors whenever you edit your writing.

Spelling and History. Spellings that may seem strange to you are products of a time in English when every letter was pronounced. For example, between 1300 and 1500, *knight* was pronounced as "kenicht" and *sword* was pronounced "sewerd." The *k* and the *w* in these words have remained even though we no longer pronounce them. In addition, the *ough* in words such as *rough* and *fought* used to be pronounced similarly, as *ugh*. Now, however, the *ough* spelling is pronounced differently in different words (*through, bough, fought, dough, tough,* and *hiccough*), so you have to memorize the spelling of these words. Finally, the silent *e* at the end of many words was introduced in the 1400s to indicate that the syllable preceding this *e* had a "long" vowel (as in *hope, pine,* and *rate*).

Inconsistencies between the pronunciation and the spelling of many English words make English a very difficult language to spell, especially for people who are learning it as a second language. Here is a poem by an unknown author that sums up the problems caused by irregularly spelled words:

I take it you already know
Of tough and bough and cough and dough?
Others may stumble, but not you
on hiccough, thorough, slough, and through?
Well done! And now you wish, perhaps,
To learn of less familiar traps?
Beware of heard, a dreadful word
That looks like beard and sounds like bird.
And dead, it's said like bed, not bead;
For goodness sake, don't call it deed!
Watch out for meat and great and threat
(They rhyme with suite and straight and debt).
A moth is not a moth in mother.
Nor both in bother, broth in brother.

 ## GROUP WORK 2

Form a group with two or three classmates and proofread the following paragraph together. Circle every spelling error, and write the correct spelling above each.

Many of the Crusaders who fought to regain the Middle East for Cristianity in the eleventh century were nights. Nights were military servants to the kings and the popes. The Crusaders wre nights who fote for Pope Urban II. They wore armor to protect their bodies from the sorrds of other nights. Usually, they rode horses and carried metal napsacks in which they kept their food. Armies of nights woud ride thu villages, killing people and burning the towns. When the villagers ran away in frite from the huge horses and their nashing teeth, the nights would scream with laufter. The Ninth Crusade ended in 1272, and there is no dout that by that time, the Crusaders had massackered tens of

thousands of innosent people.

STRATEGIES FOR IMPROVING SPELLING

Usually, it is pointless to "sound out" the spelling of a word because a particular sound in it may be represented by several different combinations of letters. For instance, the long *e* sound can be spelled *ten* different ways in English: *e* (*she*), *ee* (*bee*), *ea* (*neat*), *ie* (*believe*), *eo* (*people*), *ae* (*Caesar*), *y* (*happy*), *ey* (*key*), *i* (*machine*), and *oe* (*amoeba*)! Use your dictionary to look up words that you do not know how to spell.

Here are six additional strategies for identifying spelling problems and for improving spelling ability.

1. Don't worry about spelling while you are writing or revising a piece of writing. Concentrate on developing your ideas, on adding details, and on crafting precise sentences. Wait until you have finished revising your writing before you check the spelling. If you start checking spelling before you get all your ideas on paper or on screen, you may forget what you wanted to write.

2. List every word that you misspell in your Word Bank (see pages 519–520 in Chapter 19). If you write down every misspelled word and its correct spelling, you will accomplish two important things: You will see the correct spelling of a word that usually confuses you, and you will begin to understand your typical patterns of spelling errors.

3. Write your assignments and the entries in your Word Bank *neatly.* Sloppy handwriting often produces a confused image of words and uncertainty about how they are spelled.

4. Use a college dictionary to look up the spelling and the pronunciation of words when you are editing. If you don't know the first few letters of a word (which you must know in order to look it up), ask a classmate, a teacher, or a friend for help.

5. Develop a set of hints for remembering words that give you problems. For example, if you confuse the different spellings of *there,* remember "*They're* home in *their* house over *there.*" Other memory tricks (called *mnemonics*) include "The princi*pal* is my pal," "There's a dance in atten*dance,*" "There's a rage in t*rage*dy," "There's a lie in be*lie*ve," and "I've *seen* that *scene* before."

6. Do crossword puzzles and other word games that require you to match meaning and spelling. Do *not* do "word search" or "word

hunt'' puzzles since these don't include any information about the words' meanings and they only stress letter shapes.

> **REMINDER** ━━━━━━━━━━━━━━━━━━━━━━━━
> Study the words in your Word Bank daily. This will help you learn how to spell them correctly and remember their meanings.

SPELLING RULES

Most spelling rules are overly complicated or have so many exceptions that they are useless. Only three rules are worth memorizing.

Rule 1: Doubling a Final Consonant. If you want to add a suffix (an ending) to a word that ends in a single consonant, double this final consonant if it meets these three conditions:

1. The suffix begins with a vowel (**a, e, i, o, u**).
2. The word consists of only one syllable *or* is accented on the final syllable.
3. The last two letters of the word are a vowel followed by a consonant.

Doubled	**Not Doubled**
fit—fitted	*bigot—bigoted*
hop—hopping	*hope—hoping*
forbid—forbidden	*mistake—mistaken*
propel—propeller	*forget—forgetful*

The exception to this rule is any word that ends in an *x: tax—taxed.*

Rule 2: Silent e. If you want to add a suffix to a word that ends in a silent *e* (that is, an *e* you don't pronounce), drop the *e* if the suffix begins with a vowel, but keep the *e* if the suffix begins with a consonant.

care—caring	*care—careful*
rare—rarity	*rare—rarely*

Some exceptions to this rule are the following words:

true—truly	*mile—mileage*
argue—argument	*agree—agreeable*

Other exceptions are any word that ends in an *e* that is preceded by a *g*, a *c*, an *o*, or a *y:*

cage—cagey	*hoe—hoeing*

An exception is the word *judge,* which becomes judgment (without the *e*).

Rule 3: Changing *y* to *i*. If you want to add a suffix to a word that ends in a *y*, change this *y* to an *i* if the suffix begins with any letter except *i*. (Keep the final *y* if the suffix begins with *i*.)

marry—marriage   marry—marrying
carry—carried   carry—carrying

Four words are exceptions to this rule:

day + ly = daily   lay + ed = laid
pay + ed = paid   say + ed = said

WRITING ACTIVITY 3

Check your understanding of these spelling rules by combining the following words and endings. The first one has been done as an example.

1. *study*   + ous   = _____*studious*_____ (Rule 3)

2. *arrive* + ing   = _____ (Rule 2)

3. *courage* + ous   = _____ (Rule 2)

4. *prefer* + ed   = _____ (Rule 1)

5. *omit*   + ing   = _____ (Rule 1)

6. *true*   + ly   = _____ (Rule 2)

7. *drop*   + ed   = _____ (Rule 1)

8. *lazy*   + ness = _____ (Rule 3)

9. *nine*   + ty   = _____ (Rule 2)

10. *plenty* + ful   = _____ (Rule 3)

11. *regret* + ed   = _____ (Rule 1)

12. *love*   + able = _____ (Rule 2)

13. *happy* + est   = _____ (Rule 3)

14. *argue* + ment = _____ (Rule 2)

15. *pay*   + *ed*   = _____ (Rule 3)

16. *begin*   + *er*   = _____ (Rule 1)

17. *imply*   + *ing*   = _____ (Rule 3)

18. *write*   + *ing*   = _____ (Rule 2)

19. *eat*   + *ing*   = _____ (Rule 1)

20. *messy*   + *ness* = _____ (Rule 3)

Problems with *ei* and *ie*. Do you confuse *ei* and *ie* when you spell words containing these pairs? The general rule for spelling words with these letters is stated in the elementary school jingle:

> Write *i* before *e* except after *c* or when sounded like *ay* as in *neighbor* and *weigh*.

This jingle may be helpful, but it doesn't mention all the exceptions, such as *either, seize, financier, weird, foreign,* and *height.* If *e/i* or *i/e* transpositions are a spelling problem for you, you may have to look up the correct spelling of every word that includes these letters.

WRITING ACTIVITY 4

Circle every spelling error in the following paragraph and write the correct spelling above each error. The first misspelling has been corrected as an example.

The death of a relative or a ~~freind~~ *friend* is often a sorce of great greif. Often we try to decieve ourselves and the dying person that he or she is not really dieing. We tell ourselves and the person that we beleif he or she will get well. However, this deception robs the dying person of the ability to come to terms with his or her impending death. By lying to a dying person, we stop him or her from acheiving acceptance; he or she forfiets the chance to greive for himself or

herself. It is far more compassionate and efficeient to be honest with
a dying person and provide him or her with as much releif from his
or her physical and mental pain as you can provide.

Numbers. Some guidelines for spelling out numbers in papers for most
courses are included in the following chart.

WHEN TO SPELL OUT NUMBERS ━━━━━━━━━━━━━━━

1. Use numerals for addresses, dates, time, and money:

   > We have an appointment at the Acme Company (*216 East 10th Street*) on *May 10th* at *8:30 A.M.* to ask for a raise of *$5.00* an hour in our salaries.

2. When you begin a sentence with a number, always spell out the number:

   > *One hundred fifteen* women became managers at the Acme Company this past year.

3. When you use a number within a sentence, spell it out if it can be written as one or two words. Numbers from twenty-one through ninety-nine require a hyphen when they are spelled out:

   > Of these women, *ninety-three* had worked for Acme for more than five years.

4. When you use more than one number in a sentence, if any of the numbers is more than two words, use numerals for the all the numbers:

   > Of the *115* female managers, *27* were promoted to vice presidents.

WRITING ACTIVITY 5

Circle every number in the following paragraph that is written incorrectly according to the guidelines above and write in the correction above the mistake. The first one has been done as an example.

seventy-nine

Last month, my 79-year-old mother had the flu for 2 weeks, so I took her to see the doctor. Our appointment was for 2 o'clock on March second, but the nurse called me on March 1st to switch the appointment to March fourth. We got to the doctor's office late because we couldn't find his apartment on East Fifteenth Street. (We accidentally went to 89 East Sixteenth Street.) Our appointment was for two o'clock, but the doctor was busy. 1 hour passed by, and he still did not call in my mother. We waited 25 more minutes, and then I told the nurse that if the doctor didn't see my mother in five minutes, we were leaving. Finally, the doctor saw us. The doctor took my mother's temperature (which was ninety-nine degrees), and he took 2 tubes of her blood. 15 minutes later, the exam was over. My mother was fine. However, I got sick when the doctor told me that his fee was one hundred twenty-five dollars for the exam, and this fee did not include the lab bill of $95.

GROUP WORK 3

Form a group with two or three classmates, and together proofread the following paragraphs. Identify every spelling error and number written incorrectly. Then choose one person to rewrite the paragraph with all the words spelled correctly and the numbers in their correct form.

I have an ecxiting and livly job as a policewoman in Metro City. Being a policewoman is truely a wonderful expereince; it has enabled me to acheive grate personal satisfaction. Altho police work is occassionaly dangerus and my hours are often unmanagable, I have never regreted becomeing a police officer.

Only 12 of the hundred and thirteen police officers in our city are female. In the begining, when women were permited to become Metro City police officers, there were actualy many arguements about a woman's ability to perform the job. The admition of women was raelly a very contravserisal issue in our town. When women were finally admited to the force, 8 male police officers resigned in protest and defyance, and two other policemen were releived of their dayly dutys because they made sexcist remarks to the women.

I myself have expereienced some embarassment from sexcist comments made by policemen and by the public. However, I ignore their remarcks (unless they are really outragous). I am secure in the knowlege that I am doing an excellant job as a police officer, and I am proud of my proffession.

EDITING CAPITALIZATION

Just as readers expect to see correct spelling in academic and professional writing, they also expect correct capitalization. Errors in capitalization distract readers, so memorize the rules governing the conventions of capitalization in Academic Written English. Here are the five most important rules.

1. Capitalize the first word of every sentence and of every sentence within a sentence or a quotation:

   My professor said, "Study for the makeup test."

   Do *not* capitalize quoted words that are not a complete sentence:

   My professor explained "cognitive dissonance."

   See pages 575–579 for additional information about using capital letters in quotations.

2. Capitalize the names of specific people, places, groups, businesses, and events:

On April 1, Prof. Greenberg, of Hunter College's English Department, will discuss literature written during the Reformation. This lecture will take place in the Kaye Auditorium from 1:00 to 3:00 p.m.

3. Capitalize people's titles and their abbreviations:

My teacher's name is Prof. Karen Greenberg, Ph.D.

4. Capitalize the names of specific courses, religions, languages, and organizations:

This semester, I studied political parties in my Political Science 200 course, and I learned about the Koran in my Arabic course.

5. Always capitalize the first word in a title (and the first word after a colon in a title). Capitalize all the other words except for *a, an, the,* coordinating conjunctions (such as *and* and *for*), and prepositions (such as *of* and *by*):

Star Trek IV: The Lost Country   [movie title]
"The Problems of the Middle Class"   [essay title]
"Ebony and Ivory"   [song title]
Sports Illustrated   [magazine title]
Christmas   [holiday title]

REMINDER _____

Do *not* capitalize titles used without names (for example, "the president," "the professor"), institutions or organizations without names ("college," "political party"), and school courses that are not languages or are used without a number ("mathematics," "law").

WRITING ACTIVITY 6

For each noun listed below, think of an example that is a person's name or a title. Use the noun and the name or title together in a sentence. The first one has been done as an example.

1. hockey player *My favorite hockey player, Mario Lemieux, is winning his battle against cancer.*

2. film _____

_____

3. city _____

_____

4. album or CD _____

_____

5. book _____

_____

6. musical group _____

_____

7. college course _____

_____

8. team _____

_____

_____

 WRITING ACTIVITY 7

Compose a sentence that uses each of the following words (exactly the way that they are capitalized). The first two have been done as an example.

1. heart *My father had a heart attack when he was only twenty years old.*

2. Heart *He survived, and he got a Purple*

Heart medal for his bravery in the Vietnam War.

3. coach _____

_____

4. Coach _____

_____

5. high school _____

_____

6. High School _____

_____

7. psychology _____

_____

8. Psychology _____

_____

9. doctor _____

_____

10. Doctor _____

_____

11. south _____

_____

12. South _____

_____

_____

_____

GROUP WORK 4

Work on this activity with a classmate. Together identify every word with an error in capitalization and write in the correction above the error.

During the past few decades, latin America produced some of the finest Writers of our time. For example, four latin American Writers have won the nobel prize for Literature. These include gabriela mistral (chile), miguel angel asturias (guatemala), pablo neruda (Chile), and gabriel garcía márquez (colombia). The two most famous of these nobel prize winners are mistral and garcía márquez. mistral was the first latin american to receive the nobel prize. She was a Teacher and a Poet who lived in Rural Chile and wrote about the way Mothers love their Children. Gabriel garcía márquez is a wonderful Novelist, whose book *love in the time of cholera* describes a dying tropical port at the turn of the Century. these writers are not the only Internationally Respected latin american writers. Several other writers with Worldwide Reputations are jorges luis borges (argentina), carlos fuentes (mexico), and isabel allende (chile). These writers have brought latin america great Cultural Prestige.

WRITING ACTIVITY 8

Write a brief guidebook for a tour of your neighborhood, village, town, or city. Imagine that a relative or friend is coming to stay with you for the first time and that this person wants to tour your town (on foot or by car). List the exact name of each object that the visitor will pass by (each store, building, farm, river, plaza, mall, and so forth) and the street name where this object can be found. Here is an example:

As you walk down my block, Rugby Lane, you will see a large mocha brown sign with faded black letters announcing the presence of Rugby Farm. If you look to your left after you pass this sign, you can see the south side of Rugby Farm—a working dairy farm.

Describe each sight briefly. When you finish writing and revising your guidebook, edit it for correct spelling and capitalization.

REMINDER ───────────────────────────────────
If you use a computerized word-processing program to write, make sure that the program has a spell-checker to edit your spelling and capitalization, and use it!

Below is a chart of typical errors in Academic Written English spelling and capitalization and the correction symbols that are commonly used to identify these errors.

CHART OF COMMON ERRORS
AND CORRECTION SYMBOLS ─────────────────────
Cap   capitalization error (pp. 556–557)
lc   use a lowercase letter (do *not* capitalize) (p. 557)
sp   spelling error (pp. 551–552)

✔ POINTS TO REMEMBER ABOUT SPELLING
AND CAPITALIZATION

1. Do not worry about spelling or capitalization while you are writing or revising a piece of writing.
2. Keep a Word Bank and list every word that you misspell in this book.
3. Try to identify the cause or causes of your common spelling errors. (Do you often add, delete, transpose, or substitute letters? Do you misspell homonyms or commonly confused words?)

4. Use a college dictionary to look up the spelling and the pronunciation of words when you are editing.
5. Develop a set of hints for remembering words that give you problems.
6. Proofread for *ie/ei* transpositions.
7. Proofread for numbers and make sure that you have spelled each correctly or written the numeral form of each if it is required.
8. Proofread for correct capitalization.

CHAPTER

21

PUNCTUATION AND
PAPER FORMAT

Punctuation is important because it tells readers where you want them to stop, to pause, or to notice your emphasis. Punctuation also signals the relations among your ideas and between the parts of your sentences. Thus, your paper is not finished until you have edited it for appropriate punctuation.

Your last job in preparing a paper for a teacher, another student, or an employer is to edit it so that it follows the conventions of manuscript format that the reader expects to see. A neat, correct paper lets your reader know that you value what you have written.

EDITING PUNCTUATION

When you speak, you have many vocal and visual options for ''punctuating'' your meaning, including your tone of voice, pitch, pauses, and facial expressions. When you write, you have only punctuation marks to communicate your stops, pausing, and emphasis. Punctuation can shape the meaning of your sentences. If you leave out punctuation or insert unnecessary punctuation, you can change the meaning of a sentence and confuse readers. Here are two pairs of sentences that illustrate this problem. How does the punctuation change the meaning of each pair?

A. Our English professor quit failing all his students.
B. Our English professor quit, failing all his students.

C. Not long after the professor gave a public speech.
D. Not long after, the professor gave a public speech.

Sentence *A* states that the teacher stopped failing his students; sentence *B* says that the teacher resigned and failed his students. Which do you think the writer intended in the first pair?

The comma also controls the meaning of the second pair of sentences (*C* and *D*). If the writer of the second pair intended to write sentence *D* but accidentally omitted the comma, then she created sentence *C,* which is a fragment.

Punctuation serves six basic functions in writing:

1. Punctuation ends sentences.
2. Punctuation combines sentences.
3. Punctuation separates items in a series within a sentence.
4. Punctuation separates words or phrases that modify a sentence.
5. Punctuation separates quoted words or phrases from the rest of a sentence.
6. Punctuation indicates the possessive case of nouns.

1. Punctuation Marks Are Used to End Sentences. The period, the question mark, and the exclamation mark are called *end punctuation* because they are used at the ends of sentences:

I always remember my first bungee jump with a tingle of fear. One of the bungee cords broke! Was I going to smash to the earth and die? Thank God, the other cord held, and I was saved.

Here are some guidelines for using end punctuation.

The Period

Use a period to end a sentence that makes a statement or a command. Also use a period after an abbreviation.

Prof. Hildago told the students to hand in their essays.
''Bring them in on Wednesday at two o'clock,'' he said.

REMINDER
Most abbreviations (that end in periods) are alphabetized according to their spelling. In other words, the abbreviation *Mr.* is alphabetized before words beginning with *mu* rather than with words beginning with *mis.*

The Question Mark

Use a question mark to end a sentence that asks a question.

On which Wednesday are we supposed to hand in our research essay? My teacher heard me, and he asked, ''Didn't you hear my directions?''

Some sentences, called *indirect questions,* report a question but do not directly ask it. These sentences end in a period, *not* a question mark.

> DIRECT QUESTION: The teacher asked the students, ''Why don't you write down my directions in your books?''

> INDIRECT QUESTION: The teacher wondered why the students don't write his directions in their books.

Note that you put the question mark inside the final quotation mark when the quotation is a question. The question mark goes outside the quotation mark when the quoted material is not a question, but the rest of the sentence is a question.

When the quotation is a question:

> The teacher asked the students, ''Why don't you write down my directions in your books''?

When the sentence is a question but the quotation is not:

> Did the teacher actually say, ''Write down all my directions in your books''?

The Exclamation Mark

Use an exclamation mark to end a sentence that expresses strong emotion, surprise, or emphasis.

> I couldn't believe what that teacher just said!

WRITING ACTIVITY 1

Below is an uncorrected student paragraph that is missing all end punctuation. Use a caret (∧) to insert the appropriate punctuation mark, and capitalize the letter that follows it. The first one has been done as an example.

Spike Lee's 1992 film, *Malcolm X,* celebrated the struggle of one of black America's great heroes. When the film came out, everyone I know started wearing X clothes to commemorate the movie and its hero all my friends, African American and white, sported X hats, X shirts, X jackets, and even X backpacks every time I saw someone wearing an X, I would ask him or her, ''Do you know what that X stands for" some friends knew that it was part of the name given to Malcolm by the Nation of Islam others thought that the X stood for the number 10 none of my friends knew that Malcolm dropped the X in the last year of his life in fact, not one person knew that Malcolm renounced the X when he broke away from the Nation of Islam in order to show that he was a true Muslim, Malcolm made a pilgrimage (a "Hajj") to Mecca and took the name El-Hajj Malik El-Shabazz this was the name he wanted and the name he gave his family indeed, his wife and his daughters still use the name Shabazz if Malcolm chose to become Malik El-Shabazz, why did everybody make such a big deal about his X

---

2. Punctuation Marks Combine Sentences. You can combine sentences with a semicolon, a colon, or a comma with a coordinator. (See Chapter 16 for additional information on coordination.)

The Semicolon

Use a semicolon to join two sentences when (1) the idea in the second sentence is a continuation of the one in the first *and* (2) a period could be used to separate the two sentences. A semicolon expresses a pause that is greater than a comma's but not as great as the pause indicated by a period or a colon.

> All the other students in my class handed in their papers on time; I was the only exception.

You can use a semicolon to join two sentences with a transitional word or phrase. (See pages 87–88 in Chapter 3 for a list of transitional words and phrases, also known as *conjunctive adverbs*.)

> All the other students in my class handed in their papers on time; *however,* I was unable to do so.

Do *not* use a coordinator if you are using a semicolon.

> All the other students in my class handed in their papers on time; I was unable to do so.

The Colon

Use a colon to connect a sentence with a phrase or another sentence if the phrase or the second sentence contains an illustration of the first.

Professor Chiang has three class requirements: perfect attendance, carefully revised essays, and passing grades on all of the tests. Students believe that her attendance requirement is too rigid: No one can come to every single class on time.

Also use a colon before a list of people or items, particularly after expressions such as "the following" or "are as follows."

In Prof. Chiang's Evolution 101 course, students will learn three skills: dating fossils, developing a geologic time scale, and demonstrating how evolution occurs. Students are required to purchase the following lab materials: modeling clay, plaster of Paris, forceps, petroleum jelly, and a ruler.

A colon is also used after the opening in a formal letter and between the hour and the minute when you write time in its numeral form.

Dear Prof. Chiang:

Please excuse my lateness this morning. I could not get to biology lab until 8:30 a.m. because my daughter's baby-sitter arrived late. Thank you.

Sincerely,
Alex Garvano

The Comma Followed by a Coordinator

Use a comma and a coordinator to link two related sentences.

Professor Chiang accepted Mr. Garvano's late note, *and* she asked him to try to come to class on time in the future.

GROUP WORK 1

Form a group with two or three classmates, and edit the following student letter. This uncorrected letter has many run-ons. (If you are not sure how to identify and correct run-ons, see pages 424–428 in Chapter 15.) Together decide where each sentence ends and the next one begins. Use a caret (∧) to insert a *colon,* a *semicolon,* or a *comma and a coordinator* at each sentence boundary.

Editor

Journal of Nursing Collegians

3612 South Roxbury Road

Durham, NC 27704

Dear Sir or Madam

I am a student at Duke University I am planning a career in nursing. My career adviser recommended that I write to you he said that your journal often publishes essays in response to student requests. I would appreciate it if you could publish articles about career opportunities in nursing, particularly the following specialties pediatric nursing, geriatric nursing, and hospice nursing.

I would also like to see you publish essays about getting internships or part-time jobs in nursing this information would help students get valuable experience. Most college students do some kind of voluntary nursing. This does not offer any payment. College students need money to survive thus, information about nursing internships is critical.

Since I am male, I am particularly interested in employers who do not discriminate against men. I have been subjected to many sexist comments because I want to be a nurse most people believe nurses should be female. Many nurses are women however I believe that men can provide expert nursing care and maintain their dignity.

I look forward to reading your response I hope to see articles on nursing in future issues of your journal.

Sincerely,

Harris Coleman

THE COLON (:) A REVIEW ————————————————

1. Use a colon to connect a sentence to a phrase or another sentence if the phrase or second sentence contains an illustration of the first sentence.
2. Use a colon after the opening in a formal letter.
3. Use a colon to introduce a list of items.

---

3. Punctuation Marks—Commas or Semicolons—Separate Three or More Items in a Series. Use a comma to separate items (a series, or list, of three or more words, phrases, or sentences).

Words in a series:

Most employers interview prospective employees to learn about their *personalities, capabilities,* and *experiences.*

Phrases in a series:

Students can prepare for an interview by *polishing their communication skills, finding out about the company,* and *being interviewed by a friend.*

Sentences in a series:

For the interview, *students should dress appropriately, they should bring a notepad and pen,* and *they should arrive on time.*

Use a comma after each item in the series, including the second-to-the-last item (unless your teacher tells you that this comma is not necessary).

During an interview, people should do the following: relax, maintain eye contact with the interviewer, listen and observe carefully, and speak clearly.

A semicolon—rather than a comma—should be used to separate items in a series if any of the items contains a comma.

Most employers interview prospective employees to learn about their personalities; *their capabilities, including any unique talents;* and their work-related experiences. Students can prepare for an interview by polishing their communication skills; finding out about *the company, the position, and the interviewer;* and being interviewed by a friend. For the interview, students should dress appropriately; *they should have clean skin, hair, and nails;* and they should have a neat appearance.

WRITING ACTIVITY 2

Decide which sentences below need commas, semicolons, or commas and semicolons. Use a caret (∧) to insert each comma and semicolon. The first one has been done as an example.

1. Most employers prefer to hire students who have had work-related experiences such as summer jobs, volunteer work, and internships.
2. Many hiring managers say that they do not have the time or the money to explain the differences between school and work to train new employees or to explain schedules and deadlines.
3. Students who work after school during the summer and during vacations learn to adjust to the culture of the business world.
4. Working provides students with experience with money for tuition books and clothes and with a chance to work with professional colleagues.
5. To get summer jobs, students should contact businesses near their homes ask professors about contacts and ask relatives about the companies shops and factories where they work.
6. Students should also consider writing to potential employers calling them and setting up appointments to talk with them.
7. If the manager invites students to visit, they should find out as much as they can about the company the job and the manager they should take notes on what they find out and they should prepare for the visit.
8. If a student gets the job that he or she wants, he or she will learn how the company works how to make goals and plans and how to work collaboratively with other employees.

THE SEMICOLON (;) A REVIEW

1. Use a semicolon to combine two sentences whose ideas are closely related.
2. Use a semicolon instead of a comma to separate items in a series if any of the items contains a comma.

---

4. Punctuation Marks (Commas) Separate Modifiers from the Rest of the Sentence. In Chapter 16, you practiced adding descriptive words and phrases to sentences to make them more interesting and informative. These descriptive modifiers include adjectives, adverbs, prepositional phrases, appositive phrases, and participial phrases—phrases that begin with an *-ing/-ed/ -en* verb. (See Chapter 16 for additional information about these descriptive words and phrases.) Descriptive modifiers can be placed at the beginning, the middle, or the end of a sentence.

Beginning:
In most cases, college graduates get the jobs that they want.
By preparing carefully, college graduates can get the jobs that they want.

Middle:

College graduates, *in most cases,* get the jobs that they want.

College graduates, *by preparing carefully,* can get the jobs that they want.

End:

College graduates get the jobs that they want *in most cases.*

College graduates can get the jobs that they want *by preparing carefully.*

Writers have options for using commas to punctuate modifiers at the beginning or in the middle of a sentence. Here are some guidelines for punctuating modifiers that introduce or interrupt a sentence.

Descriptive Words and Phrases That Introduce a Sentence

Use a comma to separate an introductory word or phrase from the main sentence.

ADVERB: *Surprisingly,* many students do not see the value of summer employment.

PREPOSITIONAL PHRASE: *For this reason,* students should get a summer job in their potential profession.

APPOSITIVE PHRASE: *A good source of information,* the college adviser may have valuable industry contacts.

PARTICIPIAL PHRASE: *Working closely with corporate managers,* advisers often know about internships and other job openings.

WRITING ACTIVITY 3

Decide which sentences below need a comma to separate the modifying words or phrases from the rest of the sentence, and use a caret (∧) to insert each comma. The first one has been done as an example.

1. As computer science majors know,∧the basic qualification for a job as a computer operator is training ∧or experience in data processing.
2. However most employers prefer their candidates to have a bachelor's degree in computer science.
3. In fact a degree is a necessity for advancement in the computer industry.
4. To get a good salary a computer operator has to have extensive knowledge about hardware and software.
5. As with most computer jobs operators have to be able to work independently and to follow directions carefully.

6. Ranging from $20,000 to $30,000 the salaries for computer operators are some of the highest earned by new college graduates.
7. Consequently the number of computer science majors in four-year
   and two-year colleges is increasing.
8. For this reason computer science majors supplement their academic learning with experience in a computer-related job.
9. To get ahead computer science majors should constantly upgrade
   their skills and learn new systems.
10. With the right skills and attitude a computer operator can advance
    to become the manager of computer operations.

Descriptive Words and Phrases That Interrupt a Sentence

Use a comma before *and* after descriptive words or phrases that interrupt the
flow of a sentence *if* these descriptive modifiers are *not* necessary for identifying the subject of the sentence.

> Many students, *surprisingly,* do not know how to plan for a career or job
> search. Unprepared students, *lacking an awareness of what they need to
> do,* often do not know about the many sources of job information that
> are available to them.   [The pair of commas in each of these sentences
> indicates that the information they enclose could be left out without
> confusing readers about the subject of the sentence.]

Here is an example of how setting off a modifier with commas can change
the meaning of a sentence.

> A. My sister, Maxine, got a job as a computer programmer a month after
>   she graduated from college.
> B. My sister Maxine got a job as a computer programmer a month after
>   she graduated from college.

Sentence *A* indicates that the writer has only one sister. The modifier *Maxine*
is not necessary to identify the subject (*my sister*). In sentence *B,* however,
the writer has more than one sister. In sentence *B,* the modifier *Maxine* is
necessary to tell readers which sister the writer is referring to. This information
is essential for readers to identify the subject, so it is *not* set off by commas.

In Chapter 16, you learned about *nonrestrictive clauses*—relative clauses
that add information that is not necessary for identifying the subject (see pages
462–463). Sometimes called *nonessential clauses,* nonrestrictive clauses are
surrounded by commas because the information in them is not essential for
the reader to understand the main idea of the sentence.

> The Job Assistance Selection Service, *which was developed in 1992,* is
> a computerized database that lists vital information on job vacancies of

more than 1,000 employers.   [If the writer omitted the information in the relative clause (''which was developed in 1992''), the reader would still understand the subject and main idea of this sentence.]

However, do *not* use commas to set off interrupting modifiers that are essential to the meaning of the sentence.

Students *preparing for a job interview* should do mock interviews with friends and advisers.   [In this sentence, the participial phrase ''preparing for a job interview'' is necessary to let readers know exactly which students the writer is referring to.]

Similarly, do *not* use commas before and after a relative clause that is necessary for the reader to identify the subject that the clause is describing. If the information in the clause is essential to the sentence's meaning, the clause is a *restrictive* (or *essential*) *clause,* and it is *not* set off by commas.

Graduates *who impress an employer with their communication skills* often receive job offers.   [In this sentence, the clause ''who impress an employer with their communication skills'' is necessary to let the reader know exactly which graduates the writer is discussing. If the writer omitted this clause, the reader would not know the specific subject of the sentence; that is, ''Graduates often receive job offers.'']

GROUP WORK 2

Work with another student on this activity. Together decide which sentences below need commas to set off the modifying words, phrases, or clauses from the rest of the sentence. Use a caret (∧) to insert each comma wherever you and your partner think it is needed. The first one has been done as an example.

1. Students who are admitted to graduate school,either public or private,can get financial aid from various sources.
2. Graduate schools are usually expensive and unlike undergraduate schools do not offer income-based financial aid.
3. Graduate students for example are not eligible for Pell grants or other federal grants.
4. They can however get loans from the school itself or from sources outside the school.
5. For example tuition scholarships which are very common at private universities enable graduate students to go to school for free.
6. Some schools will even waive tuition and provide a stipend for students who excel academically.

7. Economically disadvantaged students unable to afford tuition can apply to become graduate teaching assistants.
8. Teaching assistants known as TAs help professors prepare materials for undergraduate courses and mark students' papers and tests.
9. Some TAs particularly those who have excellent communication skills are even asked to teach a course or two.
10. Students who work as TAs are part-time employees of the university and they get a monthly salary.

USING THE COMMA (,) TO SEPARATE A WORD OR A PHRASE FROM THE REST OF THE SENTENCE: A REVIEW

1. Use a comma to set off an introductory word or phrase from the rest of the sentence.
2. Use a comma before *and* after descriptive words or phrases that interrupt a sentence *if* these words are *not* necessary for identifying the subject of the sentence.
3. Use a comma before *and* after a nonrestrictive (nonessential) clause that interrupts a sentence because the information in this clause is not necessary for identifying the subject of the sentence.

Enclosing or Emphasizing Interrupting Material

Two other punctuation marks that writers use to interrupt a sentence to add information are *dashes* and *parentheses*. Use dashes when you want to make the interrupting words stand out; use parentheses to deemphasize the interrupting material. Here is an example of each.

Dashes:
Only about 9% of the managing editors at newspapers, radio programs, and television programs are people of color—including Hispanics and Asians—and this number must be increased.

Parentheses:
Only about 9% of the managing editors at newspapers, radio programs, and television programs are people of color (including Hispanics and Asians), and this number must be increased.

The dashes make the information that they surround sound more important than do the parentheses, by stressing the sudden break in the main idea of the sentence.

WRITING ACTIVITY 4

Each of the following sentences has a blank space for you to add "interrupting" information that makes sense. After you add this information, decide whether to enclose it in a pair of commas, a pair of parentheses, or a pair of dashes, and write in these punctuation marks. The first one has been done as an example.

1. The number of students interested in careers in the media *(in radio, television, or journalism)* is increasing every year.

2. Most students _____ fantasize about being famous journalists or anchors.

3. However, these positions _____ are almost impossible to achieve.

4. Moreover, the real power in the media _____ rests with the executive producers and managing editors.

5. Executive producers and managing editors oversee all of the

    paper's or program's resources _____ and determine how money should be spent.

6. Producers and editors _____ are the reporters whose words the public never hears or sees but who make all the major decisions.

DASHES (—) OR PARENTHESES (( )): A REVIEW _____

1. Use dashes before and after information that interrupts a sentence if you want to emphasize this information and make it stand out from the rest of the sentence.
2. Use parentheses before and after information that interrupts a sentence if you want to deemphasize this information.

5. Punctuation Marks Separate Quoted Material from the Rest of the Sentence. Use a pair of quotation marks to set off the exact words that someone has spoken or written. Quotations of three or more words are usually preceded by a comma.

Television news anchor Sheila Stainback recently said, "We need more African Americans in journalism."

When you begin a sentence with a quotation, put the comma inside the closing quotation mark.

"We need more African Americans in journalism," said television news anchor Sheila Stainback recently.

DIRECT AND INDIRECT QUOTATIONS

Use quotation marks to set off a *direct* quotation—a quotation consisting of the exact words that someone has spoken or written.

Sheila Stainback noted, "All the media need more African Americans as decision makers."

Do *not* use quotation marks to set off an *indirect* quotation—a quotation that summarizes what was spoken or written (and is usually preceded by the word *that*).

Sheila Stainback noted that all the media need more African Americans as decision makers.

Use a pair of quotation marks to set off the titles of stories, poems, magazine articles, newspaper articles, and chapters in books.

Ms. Stainback's comments were reported in an essay titled "Careers in Journalism" in the journal *The Black Collegian*. In this essay Ms. Stainback cited statistics from the "Journalism Careers/Jobs" section of *The Occupational Outlook Handbook, 1992–1993*.

Always put commas and periods *inside* the closing quotation mark.

Sheila Stainback noted, "All the media need more African Americans as decision makers."

However, put colons and semicolons *outside* the quotation mark.

Sheila Stainback noted, "All the media need more African Americans as decision makers"; however, she also added, "The real power is in being a managing editor."

Put question marks, exclamation points, and dashes *inside* the closing quotation mark when they are part of the quoted material.

A student asked, "What does a managing editor do?"   [The question mark is part of the direct question being quoted.]

However, question marks, exclamation marks, and dashes go *outside* the closing quotation mark when they are part of the larger sentence in which the quotation is enclosed.

What did the student mean by "a managing editor"?   [The question mark ends the question in which the quoted words "a managing editor" are enclosed.]

WRITING ACTIVITY 5

Decide which sentences are composed of (or include) direct quotations. Insert the quotation marks *and* the appropriate punctuation marks with carets. Proofread to see if any lowercase letters need to be capitalized after you have added a quotation mark. The first one has been done as an example.

According to a recent *New York Times* article, the best entry-level job in journalism is copy editing. The American Society of Newspaper Editors echoed that assertion in a recent comment, which stated that every newspaper and newsmagazine needs copy editors. As Linda Walker, an executive at the Dow Jones Newspaper Fund, stated even while newspapers have been closing down and calling for freezes on newspaper reporting positions, there are still requests for copy editors. Big city newspapers have few openings she says but their suburban editions often do.

What do copy editors do? In Tony Chapelle's words copy editors examine and make final changes to the stories written by print reporters or newswriters. Mr. Chapelle, a producer in the Cable Network News Bureau in New York City, added that copy editors often assist in the writing of minor stories.

Other opportunities for entry-level copy-editing jobs include regional cable news channels, which always need people to edit the stories that are aired twenty-four hours a day. Moreover, as Sheila Stainback has said cable news channels are a godsend for people of color; she added that they want multicultural newsrooms, and they're hiring more people reflective of all of society.

QUOTATION MARKS (" "): A REVIEW

1. Use quotation marks before and after a direct quotation—the actual words that someone spoke or wrote.

(Continued)

> 2. Use quotation marks before and after the titles of stories, poems, magazine articles, newspaper articles, and chapters in books.

Other Uses of Commas. Three other conventional uses of commas are as follows:

1. Use a comma to separate items in dates, numbers, and addresses.

   My family moved to San Diego, California, on May 10, 1993. I went to a high school there that had more than 1,100 students enrolled in it.

2. Use a comma before and after a title or an abbreviation if it comes after a person's name.

   The principal of the high school was Juanita Fernandez, Ph.D., a woman who knew every student's name. The assistant principal, Jack Edwards, Jr., also knew all the students.

3. Use a comma after the salutation of a friendly letter and after the words before the signature.

   Dear Karen,

   I miss you, and I hope I see you soon. Our children are fine. Take care and write back.

   Sincerely,
   Kenny

If you are writing a formal letter, use a colon after the salutation ("Dear Dr. Fernandez:").

THE COMMA (,): A REVIEW _____

1. Use a comma and a coordinator to link two related sentences.
2. Use commas to separate items in a series (three or more words, phrases, or sentences), unless one of the items includes a comma. If it does, use a semicolon to separate the items in the series.
3. Use a comma to separate an introductory word or phrase from the main sentence.
4. Use commas before *and* after descriptive words, phrases, or clauses that interrupt the flow of a sentence *if* these words,

phrases, or clauses are *not* necessary for identifying the subject of the sentence.
5. Use a comma before quotations of three or more words.
6. When you begin a sentence with a quotation, put the comma inside the closing quotation mark.
7. Use a comma to separate items in dates, numbers, and addresses.
8. Use a comma before and after a title or an abbreviation if it comes after a person's name.
9. Use a comma after the salutation of a friendly letter and after the words before the signature.

Problems with Commas. When we speak, we signal "chunks" of meaning by pausing briefly after meaningful word groups and by stressing specific words. When we write, we use punctuation marks to represent these pauses and stresses. Commas are important tools for signaling "chunks" of meaning in written sentences and paragraphs. However, unnecessary commas are distracting to readers; indeed, adding unnecessary commas is as confusing as leaving out commas where they are needed. Here is an example of how omitted and unnecessary commas can confuse readers.

> To succeed, in America today we Hispanic Americans must educate ourselves about, our history about, our families and about, current social and political issues issues that will determine our, future as a people. We must realize and make, others understand that if we don't, help each, other we will not, make progress.

Did you understand the writer's meaning in the two sentences above? Here is how these sentences would be "chunked" if you spoke them aloud:

> To succeed in America today/ we Hispanic Americans must educate ourselves/ about our history/ about our families/ and about current social and political issues/ issues that will determine our future as a people. We must realize/ and make others understand/ that if we don't help each other/ we will not make progress.

It is difficult to grasp the meaning of a piece of writing that is missing commas, but sentences with unnecessary commas are even more difficult to read. The commas keep forcing the reader to stop in the middle of a chunk of meaning, and this is extremely annoying. Some writers can read their writing aloud and hear the pauses where the various punctuation marks belong. For example, read aloud the correctly punctuated paragraph below, and consider whether you pause very briefly at the commas.

> To succeed in America today, we Hispanic Americans must educate

ourselves about our history, about our families, and about current social and political issues, issues that will determine our future as a people. We must realize, and make others understand, that if we don't help each other, we will not make progress.

If you did not hear the pauses at the commas, you will have to follow the rules in this chapter to use commas correctly.

Here are some reminders about when you should not use commas.

PLACES WHERE YOU SHOULD *NOT* USE COMMAS

Many students sprinkle commas throughout their writing as if these punctuation marks were spices that could enliven their sentences. However, there are two places where commas are definitely not needed.

1. Do *not* use a comma to separate a subject and its verb. For example, the comma in the following sentence is *not* needed:

   Students of all ethnic backgrounds, are obligated to help improve our society.

2. Do not use a comma before a coordinator if the words that follow the coordinator do not include a subject. For example, the comma in this sentence is wrong:

   Students can prepare themselves to be leaders by setting good examples, and developing their talents.

   The phrase ''developing their talents'' does not have a subject, so the sentence does not need a comma before the coordinator *and*. However, if a subject is added to the phrase, then the sentence needs a comma:

   Students can prepare themselves to be leaders by setting good examples, and *they* should develop their talents.

WRITING ACTIVITY 6

Proofread the following paragraphs for comma errors. Insert commas where they have been omitted, and cross out commas that are not necessary.

Many college graduates especially, those who have never been employed hold, unrealistic expectations about their first jobs. Many expect, to get the exact job that they want, and assume they will be paid a great deal of money. While it is true that a college degree helps, people to enter, and to advance in most professions it is also a fact that, most entry-level jobs do not match people's expectations.

Professional employment agencies, and corporate recruiters give similar advice to students: ''Work hard in school plan, your time carefully and try to get experience, in your prospective field.'' Students who follow this advice usually excel, academically, and thus are prepared to work hard, in their first jobs after graduation. However hard work, is not enough; students must also be prepared to solve problems to work independently and, to do whatever it takes to get the job done.

One of the realities of the corporate world is, that employees are expected to take responsibility. Unlike school where teachers tell students what to do, and when to do it professional jobs, require people to be self-starting. In addition most jobs require, people to work collaboratively, in teams and this type of interdependence is often difficult, for students who have spent four years, competing for individual grades.

In conclusion graduates, who accept the fact that work like life in general, is not always fair will be able to adjust, to the unpredictability of employment. Graduates who have, a positive attitude who are willing to work hard and, who learn quickly will succeed in their chosen careers.

---

6. Punctuation (the Apostrophe) Indicates the Possessive Case of Nouns. Add an apostrophe and an *s* to form the possessive of nouns that do not end in *s*.

Students should study their *family's* history in order to understand their sociocultural roots.

Add only the apostrophe to form the possessive of nouns that already end in *s*.

Students should study their *parents*' history in order to understand their sociocultural roots.

REMINDER ────────────────────────────────────

Do *not* add an apostrophe to a possessive pronoun (for example, *his*, *hers*, *yours*, *ours*, and *its*.

GROUP WORK 3

Form a group with two classmates and work together on this activity. Below are two paragraphs without any punctuation. Insert punctuation marks (periods, question marks, semicolons, colons, commas, quotation marks, and apostrophes) wherever they are needed. Make sure that you capitalize the first letter of every new sentence that you create. The first one has been done as an example.

Writing fluently and correctly is a critical skill in most professional and corporate careers. Graduates who work hard who are very intelligent and who have positive attitudes will not get the job they want if they are ill-prepared in standard written English by the time students reach their senior year in college they should know how to write revise and edit the following kinds of papers essays research reports lab reports critical analyses and business letters

Some managers are so concerned about employees writing abilities that they give them writing tests and make them take writing courses if they fail these tests other employers make workers pay for written mistakes for example the publisher and editor-in-chief of *Success* magazine wrote staffers a memo in which he warned them if you misuse the commas around a restrictive or nonrestrictive clause I'll charge you a mere $25 for the first few times he then added if you mispell the name of the main person in the story I'll clobber you for the $500 minimum the ironic thing about his memo is that he made an error in it he misspelled the word *misspell* I wonder whether he charged himself a fine for his error

WRITING ACTIVITY 7

Below is a paragraph excerpted from an essay by the writer E. B. White. Each of White's punctuation marks has been replaced by a blank line. In each blank, write in the punctuation mark that seems most appropriate to signal the intended meaning (a period, semicolon, dash, parentheses, or comma). If you put in a period, capitalize the first letter of the following word.

There are roughly three New Yorks ___ there is ___ first ___ the New York of the man or woman who was born there ___ who takes the city for granted and accepts its size and its turbulence as natural and inevitable ___ second ___ there is the New York of the commuter ___ the city that is devoured by locusts each day and spat out each night ___ third ___ there is the New York of the person who was born somewhere else and came to New York in quest of something ___ of these three trembling cities the greatest is the last ___ the city of final destination ___ the city that is a goal ___ it is this third city that accounts for New York's high-strung disposition ___ its poetical deportment ___ its dedication to the arts and its incomparable achievements ___ commuters give the city its tidal restlessness ___ natives give it solidity and continuity ___ but the settlers give it passion.

When you finish this activity, turn to page 588 to see the author's punctuation marks.

PLANNING THE PAPER'S FORMAT

When you finish proofreading and editing your revisions, you need to prepare the final copy according to academic manuscript format. Each subject area in college may have different requirements for the format of paragraphs, essays, and reports. If your teachers do not specify the format for papers in their disciplines, you might want to ask them about their format requirements. Here are general guidelines for the format of college writing assignments.

Typed Papers. Use $8\frac{1}{2}$-by-11-inch, unruled, white standard typing paper (*not* onionskin or erasable paper, both of which smudge). Leave $1\frac{1}{4}$-inch margins on all *four* sides of the paper. Type or print on only one side of each sheet of paper, and use only a black typewriter or printer ribbon. *Double-space each line.* Leave two spaces after a period (before the next word); leave one space after all other punctuation marks. If you need to make insertions or corrections, handwrite them in carefully and neatly.

Handwritten Papers. Use 8½-by-11-inch ruled, white, paper. Leave one inch margins on all *four* sides. Write on only one side of each sheet of paper and skip lines. Use dark blue or black ink (*not* a pencil). Make sure that your capital letters are clearly distinct from your lowercase letters. Write all punctuation marks firmly and clearly. If you need to make insertions or corrections, write them in carefully and neatly.

Word-Processed Papers. Make sure that your computer and printer are working correctly and that your software is operating correctly. Check to see that your disk is formatted correctly. Proofread your writing on the monitor and use your spell-checker (and grammar-checker, if you have one) before you print the essay or report. *Save* your work; do not print until you have created a backup file of your essay or report. Never use coated or erasable bond paper in a computer printer because the ink and the type smudge on these kinds of paper. Also, don't use printer paper that is thinner than ''20-weight,'' or it will tear too easily.

Corrections. Use correction paper or fluid to correct small errors. If your teacher permits it, add missing letters, words, or punctuation marks with a caret (∧). However, do not correct strikeovers, misspelled words, and other obvious mistakes; instead, retype or reprint the entire page.

First Page. Ask your teacher where to put your name, the course name and number, and the date. Some teachers prefer this information on a cover page; others want it typed at the top of the first page. In addition, some teachers prefer the title of the paper to appear only on the cover, whereas others tell students to put it on the cover and on the top of the first page. Follow your teacher's instructions.

Center the title of the composition or report on the first line of the first page. Do *not* underline this title; do *not* put quotation marks around it. Capitalize the major words in the title, including the first word. Skip two lines between the title and the first line of the text. Indent the first line of every paragraph in about half an inch (five spaces) from the left margin.

General Layout. Number all pages except the cover page and the first page. Although you should not number the first page, think of it as page 1, so the second page should be numbered page 2. Use numerals (''2'') to number the pages, but do *not* precede these numerals with any words or letters (e.g., do *not* write ''page 2'' or ''p. 2''). Write or type the number in the upper-right-hand corner or center it on the top of each page.

Here is a sample of the first three pages of an essay that follows these guidelines for paper format.

Stephen Hawking's Legacy

by

Ishmael Kundu

Science 102

Section 004

Professor Erica Martinez

December 9, 1993

Stephen Hawking's Legacy

Stephen Hawking is an astrophysicist who is the most famous scientist alive today. His colleagues in the world of physics call Hawking "Einstein's heir" (Green 44). By the time he was thirty-seven years old, Hawking had already accomplished more than Isaac Newton and Albert Einstein: He won hundreds of awards and prizes (including the prestigious Albert Einstein Award for the most important research in physics), and he was the youngest person ever appointed Lucasian Professor of Physics at Cambridge University, a position held by both Newton and Einstein (White and Gribbin 188).

Even more impressive is that Hawking accomplished all of these things while he was confined to a wheelchair, wasting away from a motor neuron disease (called amyotrophic lateral sclerosis) that he developed at the age of twenty-one. This disease does not affect a person's brain, but it destroys every muscle in the body. Thus, at thirty, Hawking became completely paralyzed, "speechless and unable even to lift his head should it fall forward" (White and Gribbin 3). Hawking cannot move his mouth to utter a word. He communicates with the only muscles that still work: two fingers on his left hand, which he uses to tap letters on a computer that is built into his wheelchair.

2

Hawking uses these two fingers to write dozens of scientific papers. He taps out the words, one key at a time, and sometimes it takes him ten minutes to write a paragraph. Although the process is very slow, the results are brilliant. His explanations of the origin of the universe have changed our understanding of the relations between time, space, and matter. Hawking's 1988 book, <u>A Brief History of Time</u>, became an international best-seller among scientists and among the general public.

Hawking's book is the greatest legacy to science. In <u>A Brief History of Time</u>, Hawking explores the ways in which relativity and quantum mechanics interacted at the beginning of time.

POINTS TO REMEMBER ABOUT PUNCTUATION AND PAPER FORMAT

1. Do not worry about punctuation or paper format while you are writing or revising a piece of writing. However, remember to check both when you are finished revising.
2. Try to identify the punctuation errors that you make frequently. Proofread for these errors in all your papers.
3. Remember the six functions of punctuation marks:
   a. Use a period, a question mark, or an exclamation point to end each sentence.

   b. Use a semicolon, a colon, or a comma—followed by a coordinator—to combine sentences.
   c. Use a comma or a semicolon to separate items in a series within a sentence.
   d. Use a comma, a dash, or parentheses to separate words or phrases that modify a sentence.
   e. Use quotation marks to set off quoted words or phrases from the rest of a sentence.
   f. Use an apostrophe to indicate the possessive case of nouns.
4. Proofread for correct paper format.
5. If you have typed your paper, proofread it for ''typos.''
6. If you have word-processed your paper, use the SEARCH command to search for troublesome punctuation marks, and make sure that you have used each one correctly.

Here is the punctuation that E. B. White used in his paragraph about New York. Compare these punctuation marks to the ones that you inserted on page 583.

> There are roughly three New Yorks. There is, first, the New York of the man or woman who was born there, who takes the city for granted and accepts its size and its turbulence as natural and inevitable. Second, there is the New York of the commuter—the city that is devoured by locusts each day and spat out each night. Third, there is the New York of the person who was born somewhere else and came to New York in quest of something. Of these three trembling cities the greatest is the last—the city of final destination, the city that is a goal. It is this third city that accounts for New York's high-strung disposition, its poetical deportment, its dedication to the arts and its incomparable achievements. Commuters give the city its tidal restlessness; natives give it solidity and continuity; but the settlers give it passion.

Note that White's use of semicolons in the final sentence of his paragraph does not follow the guidelines for separating items in a series. Technically, the sentence should be punctuated as follows:

> Commuters give the city its tidal restlessness, natives give it solidity and continuity, but the settlers give it passion.

White's use of semicolons instead of commas was probably a stylistic choice. He might have wanted readers to pause between each chunk of meaning in the sentence (and a semicolon indicates a longer pause than does a comma). Writers have some flexibility in the use of punctuation marks—as long as their punctuation does not confuse their readers.

APPENDIX
Progress Logs

I. Writing-Editing Log

II. Teacher Conference Log

The following logs will be useful in keeping track of your writing progress and problems.

WRITING-EDITING LOG

Each time your instructor returns a piece of your writing—in your writing course *and* in every other course—make notes about the piece in this log. You will be able to chart progress and to identify those areas that need further improvement.

Date _____ Course _____

Title of Paper _____

Strengths:

Problems and Errors:

If you need more Writing Progress Log pages, make copies of this page.

Date _____ Course _____

Title of Paper _____

Strengths:

Problems and Errors:

TEACHER CONFERENCE LOG

Each time you have a conference with your writing teacher, summarize his or her comments in the space below. Use these notes to help you remember your teacher's comments and suggestions for future papers.

Date of Conference _____

Material Discussed _____

Teacher's Comments, Suggestions, and Assignments:

If you need more Conference Log pages, make copies of this page.

Date of Conference _____

Material Discussed _____

Teacher's Comments, Suggestions, and Assignments:

Dear Reader:

Please let me know your opinion of this textbook and of its strengths and weaknesses. When you finish the book, write me a letter about what you liked and disliked about it. (Send the letter to me at the address below.) If you don't have the time to write me a letter, please fill out the form that follows and return it to the address below.

> Karen L. Greenberg
> c/o Basic Skills Editor
> HarperCollins College Publishers
> 10 East 53rd Street
> New York, NY 10022-5299

Please be honest and be very specific so that I can make the next edition of the book better. If you include your name and address, I will write you a letter back.

If you are writing a letter to me, use a separate piece of paper. If you are filling out the following form, please do so in the spaces provided below.

1. How does this textbook compare to other writing texts or English texts that

you have used? _____

_____

_____

_____

_____

2. Which chapters were most helpful to you? Why? _____

_____

_____

_____

_____

_____

3. Which chapters were least helpful? Why? _____

_____

_____

_____

_____

_____

4. What materials or exercises in this book did you *dis*like? Why? _____

_____

_____

_____

_____

_____

5. What materials, exercises, readings, or writing tasks would you like to see in the next edition of this textbook?

_____

_____

_____

_____

_____

CREDITS

Chapter 6

Chapter 7

Chapter 8

Chapter 9

Chapter 10

From HOW IT FEELS TO LIVE WITH A PHYSICAL DISABILITY by Jill Krementz. Copyright © 1992 by Jill Krementz. Reprinted by permission of Simon & Schuster, Inc.

"Homes Don't Have to Pretend," by Jonathan Van Meter, November 28, 1991, Op-Ed page, *The New York Times.* Copyright © 1991 by The New York Times Company. Reprinted by permission.

Chapter 11

"Mother's Gifts Aren't Just for Girls" by Paul Vitello, NEWSDAY, April 27, 1993, p. 8. Reprinted by permission of the Los Angeles Times Syndicate.

Rachel Finzi, "My Daughter/Myself." Used by permission.

Chapter 12

Quote from an interview with Anna Quindlen reprinted with permission of Anna Quindlen.

A. Jerome Jewler, John N. Gardner, and Mary-Jane McCarthy. *Your College Experience: Strategies for Success.* Belmont, CA: Wadsworth, 1993, p. 227.

The article is reprinted courtesy of SPORTS ILLUSTRATED from the April 12, 1993 issue. Copyright © 1993, Time Inc. "No Skirting This Issue" by Phil Taylor. All Rights Reserved.

Chapter 13

"Send Your Children to the Libraries" by Arthur Ashe, February 6, 1977, *The New York Times*, Sport Section. Copyright © 1977 by The New York Times Company. Reprinted by permission.

Chapter 14

Excerpts from LIVING OUT LOUD by Anna Quindlen. Copyright © 1987 by Anna Quindlen. Reprinted by permission of Random House, Inc.

Form WS of the City University of New York Writing Assessment Test. Reprinted by permission of the City University of New York.

Chapter 15

Excerpt from "Letter from a Birmingham Jail" by Martin Luther King, Jr. Copyright © 1963 by Martin Luther King, Jr., copyright renewed 1991 by Coretta Scott King. Reprinted by arrangement with the Heirs of the Estate of Martin Luther King, Jr., c/o Joan Daves Agency as agent for the proprietor.

Chapter 16

From "Bradley on Race: One From the Heart," NEWSWEEK, July 29, 1991. © 1991 NEWSWEEK, INC. All rights reserved. Reprinted by permission.

Chapter 17

From "The Disappearing -ed," by William Safire, July 19, 1992, NEW YORK TIMES MAGAZINE. Copyright © 1992 by The New York Times Company. Reprinted by permission.

Faith Popcorn, THE POPCORN REPORT. New York: Doubleday, 1991, p. 18.

Chapter 19

From "On Language: Family Values" by William Safire, September 6, 1992, NEW YORK TIMES MAGAZINE. Copyright

© 1992 by The New York Times Company. Reprinted by permission.

Lewis Carroll, ALICE IN WONDERLAND, Macmillan, 1865.

Nat Hentoff, JAZZ COUNTRY, Harper & Row, 1965.

PHOTO CREDITS

Page 51 FOR BETTER OR FOR WORSE copyright 1992 Lynn Johnston Prod., Inc. Reprinted with permission of UNIVERSAL PRESS SYNDICATE. All rights reserved.

Page 175 Bill Ballenberg

Page 159 Wide World Photos

Page 330 Army materials provided courtesy of the U.S. Government, as represented by the secretary of the Army

Page 338 Doctors Ambrose, McKenzie and Arrindell, by D. Michael Cheers, from the book *Songs of My People*; copyright 1992 by New African Visions, Incorporated

INDEX